"Thankfully, millions of believers have learned the urgency of understanding and affirming the distinctively Christian worldview. Sadly, many of those same believers have little depth in their understanding of the Christian worldview and how it relates to everyday life and discipleship, as well as to the great issues of the day. *Christians in Culture* now arrives on the scene as an incredibly helpful guide and resource. I highly commend it to Christians today. Read every chapter and put it into many hands."

—R. ALBERT MOHLER, JR., President,
Centennial Professor of Christian Theology,
The Southern Baptist Theological Seminary and Boyce College

"The late Ted Ward often quipped, 'The problem with Christian education is that too often it is neither.' I applaud this book not only because its subject matter is essential to ensuring that education is authentically Christian but also because of the Christian educational vision it models—rigorous faculty collaboration in the work of intellectual discipleship that forms students as they become biblically grounded, hopeful, restorative missional inhabitants of every dimension of a world created, ordered, and redemptively pursued by the living God."

—RALPH E. ENLOW, JR., Retired President,
Association for Biblical Higher Education

"It is a privilege to commend *Christians in Culture* for multiple reasons, but I will mention only two. First is the value of this volume as an excellent resource in the affirmation of and assistance to the focused endeavor of Christian education, which is to provide followers of Christ with a God-glorifying, Christ-centered, and Spirit-filled biblical worldview to engage the culture with a mind for Christ and the mind of Christ, to 'take every thought captive to obey Christ.' Second, this book is also a marker for the continued trajectory of Welch College in producing a rigorous academic initiative under the leadership of my friend Dr. Matthew Pinson and his team to produce students who are able to engage the culture in general and people in particular with a gospel-saturated mind for Christ and heart for Christ, being compelled by the love of Christ. Well done!"

—HARRY L. REEDER, III, Senior Pastor,
Briarwood Presbyterian Church

"Today Christians are asking what faithfulness looks like in twenty-first-century America with its increasing religious diversity, cultural confusion, and the digital age. Drawing from the robust Free Will Baptist tradition and the resources of the larger Great Tradition from church history, this book offers a compelling, courageous, Christ-centered guide for the church's mission. This book will spark important conversations, help pastors to equip their people, and stir in the heart of the reader a greater affection for Christ."

—DANIEL DARLING, Director of the Land Center for Cultural Engagement, Southwestern Baptist Theological Seminary

"A worldview tells us what matters, sets our priorities for us, and defines the good life for us. In this way, a worldview works much like the infrastructure of a building—unseen but determining the form of everything that is seen. *Christians in Culture* explains what a Christian worldview is—one that has Jesus Christ at the center and views all things through the lens of His lordship."

—KENNETH KEATHLEY, Director of the L. Russ Bush Center for Faith and Culture, Southeastern Baptist Theological Seminary

"I am happy to endorse *Christians in Culture*. This book is a wonderful resource from the Welch College faculty. It is my hope Christians everywhere will embrace this material and choose to go into the culture with the desire to point it toward Jesus Christ. May we see an army of Daniels, Hananiahs, Mishaels, and Azariahs go into the culture."

—EDWARD E. MOODY, JR., Executive Secretary, National Association of Free Will Baptists

"*Christians in Culture* is an aptly named book. It is an excellent work, equally as an intellectual exercise and a compelling example of how to think Christianly throughout life. Where too many titles try to swerve their readers into simplistic 'us vs. them' dichotomies or 'ten easy steps' to overcome the complexities of life, this book evades such vanities. Instead, this assembly of writers has given readers a rich study that offers a survey of the key issues surrounding a Christian worldview and provides a clear demonstration for how they might continue to learn and to live, taking the important doctrines of Sunday morning into the glorious mundaneness of their weekday afternoons. Even in those places where readers differ from a particular contributor on this or that point, they will recognize that these contributors have done their work in such a way as to leave everyone the better off for the discussion."

—TIMOTHY D. PADGETT, Resident Theologian, The Colson Center, Breakpoint Contributor

"Many Christians give lip service to the importance of 'Christian worldview,' but few take the time needed both to lay a firm foundation and to build a structure upon it. The authors in this volume do the hard work of constructive thinking, demonstrating how Christians have had and can continue to have a positive, Christ-centered influence on culture."

—JACOB SHATZER, Associate Professor of Theological Studies,
Associate Provost, and Dean of Instruction,
Union University

"Francis Schaeffer sometimes spoke of the purpose of apologetics as promoting Christian living under the lordship of Christ in the whole spectrum of life. This collection of essays by ten Welch College professors, exploring a Christian way of life and encouraging faithful participation in today's culture and subcultures, is an heir to Schaeffer's positive vision for commending the faith. By way of informative chapters touching essential disciplines such as history, the arts and entertainment, popular culture, literature, labor and vocation, technology, science, the state and public life, economics, and sports and recreation, and by persistently advocating for believers to engage rather than withdraw from these domains, *Christians in Culture* invites the reader to live lives of orthodoxy and orthopraxy and to display the lordship of Christ in tangible, attractive ways. This book will serve undergraduate students wanting to integrate their Christian faith with various fields of study, and it will aid all readers in better discerning a God-glorifying approach to cultural life."

—MARK P. RYAN, Director of the Francis A. Schaeffer Institute
and Adjunct Professor of Religion and Culture,
Covenant Theological Seminary

"Unapologetically theologically situated, *Christians in Culture* presents a well-modulated treatment of a wide range of critical cultural issues facing Christians in the West. It is not a book of conclusions but of information crucial to advancing meaningful discussions regarding the church and culture. A great resource for group discussions among the serious-minded."

—BRUCE A. LITTLE, Emeritus Professor of Philosophy,
Director of the Francis A. Schaeffer Collection,
Southeastern Baptist Theological Seminary

"As Francis Schaeffer once said, 'Each generation of the church in each setting has the responsibility of communicating the gospel in understandable terms, considering the language and thought-forms of that setting.' Likewise, the Bible refers to leaders who understood the signs of the times and knew the best course for Israel to take (1 Chronicles 12:32). *Christians in Culture* is the kind of book for helping you communicate the gospel and understand the signs of the times. It is sure to be a helpful resource for any thinking Christian."

—DANIEL DEWITT, Senior Fellow and Executive Director of the Center for Worldview and Culture, Southwest Baptist University

CHRISTIANS
in CULTURE

CHRISTIANS in CULTURE

CULTIVATING A CHRISTIAN
WORLDVIEW FOR ALL OF LIFE

Edited by Matthew Steven Bracey
and Christopher Talbot

WELCH COLLEGE
PRESS

Christians in Culture: Cultivating a Christian Worldview for All of Life

Copyright © 2023 by Matthew Steven Bracey and Christopher Talbot

Published by Welch College Press
1045 Bison Trail, Gallatin, TN 37066
www.welch.edu/welchpress

Printed in the United States of America
August 2023
First Edition

All rights reserved. No part of this publication may be reproduced, stored in a retrieval system, or transmitted in any form by any means—electronic, mechanical, photocopy, recording, or otherwise—without the prior written permission of the publisher, Welch College Press, except for brief quotations, and except as provided by US copyright law.

Cover design: Studio Gearbox
Cover image: Pieter Brueghel the Younger, The Four Seasons, Spring, which is public domain.
Interior design and typeset: Katherine Lloyd, The DESK

Unless otherwise noted, all Scripture quotations are taken from The English Standard Version® (ESV), copyright © 2001 by Crossway Bibles, a publishing ministry of Good News Publishers. Used by permission. All rights reserved.

Because of the dynamic nature of the Internet, any web address or links contained in this publication may have changed since publication and may no longer be valid.

Library of Congress Control Number: 2023902577
ISBN-13: 978-0-9976087-5-5

Contents

Foreword
David Dockery xi

Acknowledgments xiii

About the Editors xv

About the Contributors xvi

Introduction
Matthew Steven Bracey 1

PART I: ESTABLISHING THE CHRISTIAN WORLDVIEW

CHAPTER ONE
Reflections on Christian Cultural Engagement
J. Matthew Pinson 7

CHAPTER TWO
The Influence of Ideas
Christopher Talbot 19

CHAPTER THREE
The Classical Conservative Tradition
Matthew Steven Bracey 33

CHAPTER FOUR
Creation, Sin, and Renewal
Matthew McAffee 61

PART II: APPLYING THE CHRISTIAN WORLDVIEW

CHAPTER FIVE
Tradition and History
Phillip T. Morgan 81

CHAPTER SIX
The Principles of the Christian Critical Tradition
E. Darrell Holley 97

CHAPTER SEVEN
The Arts and Entertainment
Matthew Steven Bracey 113

CHAPTER EIGHT
THE CHRISTIAN AND POPULAR CULTURE
J. Matthew Pinson 135

CHAPTER NINE
LANGUAGE AND LITERATURE
Montgomery F. Thornsbury 159

CHAPTER TEN
LABOR AND VOCATION
Matthew Steven Bracey 177

CHAPTER ELEVEN
TECHNOLOGY AND INNOVATION
Christopher Talbot 197

CHAPTER TWELVE
CHRISTIANITY AND SCIENCE
Ian Hawkins 209

CHAPTER THIRTEEN
THE STATE AND PUBLIC LIFE
Montgomery F. Thornsbury 231

CHAPTER FOURTEEN
ECONOMICS, WEALTH, AND POVERTY
Phillip T. Morgan 251

CHAPTER FIFTEEN
SPORTS AND RECREATION
Greg Ketteman and Gregory Fawbush 271

CONCLUSION
Christopher Talbot 285

NOTES 287

SCRIPTURE INDEX 319

NAME INDEX 323

SUBJECT AND TITLE INDEX 327

Foreword

A Chinese proverb says, "If you want to know what water is, don't ask the fish." Water is the sum and substance of the world in which the fish is immersed. The fish may not reflect on its own environment until suddenly it is thrust onto dry land, where it struggles for life. Then it realizes that water provided its sustenance.

Immersed in our culture, many Christians have failed to take seriously the ramifications of a secular worldview. The influential sociologist Daniel Yankelovich (1924–2017) defined culture as an effort to provide a coherent set of answers to the existential situations that confront human beings in the passage of their lives. A genuine cultural shift is one that makes a decisive break with the shared meaning of the past. The break particularly affects those meanings that relate to the deepest questions of the purpose and nature of human life. What is at stake is how we understand the world in which we live and how we engage and answer the ultimate questions of life, which are worldview issues.

Christians everywhere recognize that there is a great spiritual battle raging for the hearts and minds of men and women around the globe. We now find ourselves in a cosmic struggle between a morally indifferent culture and Christian truth. Thus we need to shape a Christian worldview that helps us learn to think Christianly and to live out the practical realities of the Christian faith before a watching world.

Recognizing these realities, Matthew Steven Bracey and Christopher Talbot have assembled a talented group of colleagues from Welch College to address these very issues. Enabled by thoughtful reflections on Christian cultural engagement by Matthew Pinson, the various contributors to this wonderful resource that you hold in your hands have helped readers to think carefully and Christianly about establishing and applying a Christian worldview. With well researched and readable overviews of major areas such as philosophy, history, the arts, popular culture, literature, technology, science, economics, recreation, and other topics, this book provides an exemplary model for readers to learn how to engage major ideas and contemporary issues. Talbot's hopeful and challenging final chapter serves as an apt and fitting conclusion for this outstanding book, which will serve students and church leaders well for years to come.

A Christian worldview becomes a shaping force for life, providing for us a sense of God's plan and purpose for this world. Our identity is shaped by this worldview. A Christian worldview is not escapism but an energizing motivation for godly and faithful thinking and living in the here-and-now. It offers confidence for Christ followers for the future. Amid life's challenges and struggles, a Christian worldview helps us to stabilize life, serving as an anchor to link us to God's faithfulness and steadfastness.

Developing a Christian worldview is an ever-advancing process for us in which Christian convictions more and more shape our participation in culture. This disciplined, vigorous, and ongoing process will shape how we assess culture and our place in it. Otherwise, culture will shape us and our thinking.

This volume, *Christians in Culture,* provides a framework for Christians to think coherently about their calling to be salt and light in a fallen world. Contrary to the meaninglessness and purposelessness so prevalent in our confused, secular, and nihilistic culture, a Christian worldview offers meaning and purpose for all aspects of life, providing a different way of thinking, seeing, and doing, based on a new way of being. I heartily commend this volume as one that will enable readers to think and live in an informed way, grounded in the redemptive work of Christ and the grandeur of our majestic and gracious God.

—David S. Dockery
President, Southwestern Baptist Theological Seminary, and
President, International Alliance for Christian Education

Acknowledgments

Matthew Steven Bracey and Christopher Talbot

We the editors of *Christians in Culture* wish to express our sincerest thanks to the many people without whom the book would not exist. We owe an enormous debt of gratitude to the scholars, thinkers, and mentors who have influenced our intellectual development, especially with respect to the topic of culture, including many of the concepts and paradigms considered throughout this book: people like Francis Schaeffer, F. Leroy Forlines, Kenneth A. Myers, J. Matthew Pinson, E. Darrell Holley, and Abraham Kuyper. Additionally, Matt is thankful for the way in which the writings of Edmund Burke and Rod Dreher have impacted his thinking, and Chris is thankful for the writings and ideas of C. S. Lewis and Bruce A. Little.

We deeply appreciate the authors who have contributed to this volume, graciously giving their time and expertise. Likewise, we are so thankful to the many students at Welch College who have asked good questions in our Christianity, Culture, and Worldview courses, inspiring and shaping the form and content of this material.

We are also grateful for the proofreading work of Emily Vickery, Christa Thornsbury, Phillip T. Morgan, and Josh Hunter, and for the indexing work of Christa Thornsbury and Ellie Simpson. We also want to express our gratitude to J. Matthew Pinson, Welch College Press's Editor-in-Chief, who not only supported the publication of this book but also contributed several chapters and gave editorial assistance to it.

Many thanks to those who have shaped the look and feel of the book, including the cover design of Christopher Gilbert and David Carlson at Studio Gearbox and the layout of Katherine Lloyd at The DESK. We are thankful to the people at Versa Press, especially Jackie Miller and Michael Packard, who have helped with the printing process. We also appreciate the endorsers of this book.

We give many thanks to our families who, more than anyone else, support us in our work, including that of writing and editing this book. I, Matt, am thankful to my wife, Sarah, for her love and support of my endeavors resulting from God's calling on my life. I, Chris, want to thank my wife, Rebekah, for her enduring love and encouragement, as well as the encouragement and joy from my three sons.

Finally, we thank you, the reader, for reading this volume. We hope and pray that its material blesses you and helps you to cultivate a Christian worldview for all of life, whatever spheres of culture you inhabit, according to the wisdom and glory of the great God of heaven and earth.

About the Editors

MATTHEW STEVEN BRACEY serves as Vice Provost for Academic Administration and Assistant Professor of Theology and Culture at Welch College. He holds degrees from Cumberland School of Law (J.D.), Beeson Divinity School (M.T.S.), and Welch College (B.A.) and is ABD for his Ph.D. in Christian Ethics and Public Policy from the Southern Baptist Theological Seminary. He is presently writing his dissertation on Edmund Burke and the moral imagination. He is an editor and contributor to several books, including *The Promise of Arminian Theology* (Randall House Academic, 2016), *Sexuality, Gender, and the Church* (Welch College Press, 2016), and *Secularism and the American Republic* (Welch College Press, 2022).

In addition, Matt has written numerous peer-reviewed articles and book reviews in publications including *Biblical Higher Education Journal*, *Criswell Theological Review*, *D6 Family Ministry Journal*, *Evangelical Quarterly*, *Integrity*, and *The Southern Baptist Journal of Theology*, as well as popular articles in publications like *Books at a Glance*, *Christian Academia Magazine*, *FUSION*, *ONE Magazine*, and *The Brink Magazine*. He is a co-founder and Senior Editor of the Helwys Society Forum (thehsf.com). He and his wife Sarah have been married for eleven years.

CHRISTOPHER TALBOT serves as the Youth and Family Ministry Program Coordinator and Campus Pastor at Welch College where he also teaches courses in biblical and theological studies. He holds degrees from Welch College (B.S.) and Grace College (M.A.) and is currently pursuing a Ph.D. at Southeastern Baptist Theological Seminary in Apologetics and Culture. He has written numerous articles on Francis Schaeffer, who is the focus of his dissertation. He is also a Senior Contributor to the Helwys Society Forum.

Chris volunteers as Pastor of Youth and Families at Sylvan Park Free Will Baptist Church in Nashville, Tennessee. He is the Assistant Managing Editor for the *D6 Family Ministry Journal*. He has published articles in the *Journal of Youth and Theology*, *Theofilos*, *Eikon*, *D6 Family Ministry Journal*, and the *Journal of the International Society of Christian Apologetics*. Chris has also contributed chapters to edited volumes and written articles for popular publications, including *First Things*. He is the author of *Remodeling Youth Ministry: A Biblical Blueprint for Ministering to Students* (Welch College Press, 2017). Chris and his wife, Rebekah, live in Gallatin, Tennessee, with their three sons: William, James Elliot, and Samuel.

About the Contributors

GREGORY FAWBUSH serves as the Exercise Science Program Coordinator, Athletic Director, and Men's Basketball Coach at Welch College. He is also the Regional Coordinator for the Midwest NCCAA. He previously served as both youth and senior pastor of New Hope Free Will Baptist Church in Dover, Florida, where he concurrently served as a high school teacher, director of athletics, and basketball coach at Sefner Christian Academy for over twenty years. He holds B.S. and M.A. degrees from Welch College and has taken graduate courses in Exercise Science from Emporia State University. He currently serves as Pastor at Cane Ridge Free Will Baptist Church in Nashville, Tennessee. Greg and his wife, Angela, live in Greenbrier, Tennessee, with their two children.

IAN HAWKINS serves as the Dean of the School of Arts and Sciences and the Science Program Coordinator at Welch College where he also teaches courses in biology and chemistry. He has bachelor's degrees in both chemistry and biochemistry from East Carolina University, a master's degree from Vanderbilt University in Molecular Biology, and a doctoral degree from Middle Tennessee State University in Chemistry Education. Ian has been teaching for over sixteen years at Welch College. He has co-authored a chapter for a Royal Society in Chemistry book entitled *Problem Solving in Chemistry Education* and has also been published in several scientific journals regarding work on RNA splicing. He has written several articles for *ONE Magazine* and has presented at the National Association of Free Will Baptists on numerous occasions regarding science and theology. He has been married to his wife, Katie, for twelve years, and they have two sons: Joseph and Luke.

E. DARRELL HOLLEY is an instructor of English at Welch College. He holds a B.S. in Secondary Education from Pensacola Christian College (1979) and an M.A. and Ph.D. in English from Florida State University (1984, 1998). He taught high school for thirteen years and came to teach at Welch College in 1994. He is the author of *Churchill's Literary Allusions* (McFarland, 1984), *Fundamentals of English Grammar* (Randall House, 2008), and *Traditional English Grammar* (Randall House, 2012). His article in this volume first appeared in *Integrity*, the journal of the Commission on Theological Integrity of the National Association of Free Will Baptists. He is a member of Immanuel Free Will Baptist Church and lives in Gallatin, Tennessee.

ABOUT THE CONTRIBUTORS

Greg Ketteman serves as Vice President for Strategic Initiatives, Graduate Dean, and Professor of Education at Welch College. He earned a B.S. in Bible and Education at Welch College, an M.Ed. in Educational Administration at Middle Tennessee State University, and an Ed.D. in Administration at Tennessee State University. Before coming to Welch College as Provost in 2006, Greg served as a teacher, coach, and principal in the Metro Nashville Public Schools for thirty years. He is a member of Cross Timbers Free Will Baptist Church in Bellevue, Tennessee, where he serves as deacon. He has written monographs, articles, professional papers, and professional presentations. Greg and his wife, Jill, have just moved from their Nashville home of twenty-eight years to Gallatin, Tennessee. They have two grown children and six grandchildren.

Matthew McAffee serves as Provost and Professor of Old Testament at Welch College. He also serves as Dean of Welch Divinity School. His M.A. and Ph.D. are from the University of Chicago in Northwest Semitic Philology. He is also a graduate of the Southern Baptist Theological Seminary (M.Div.) and Welch College (B.A.). He has published articles and book reviews in such journals as *Journal of the American Oriental Society*, *Journal for the Study of the Old Testament*, *Journal of Biblical Literature*, *Journal of the Evangelical Theological Society*, *Bulletin for Biblical Research*, and others. He is author of *Life and Mortality in Ugaritic: A Lexical and Literary Study* (Pennsylvania State University Press, 2019) and co-author of *Going Deeper with Biblical Hebrew: An Intermediate Study of the Grammar and Syntax of the Old Testament* (B&H Academic, 2023). He has ministered in Free Will Baptist churches in Virginia, Tennessee, Illinois, and Canada. He is married to Anna, with whom he has five children: Abigail, Lydia, Samuel, Marianne, and Jonathan Isaac.

Phillip T. Morgan serves as the program coordinator for the History Program, as well as the Humanities and Arts Degree Program, at Welch College where he teaches. A former small businessman, he is currently pursuing Ph.D. studies in history at Kansas State University, where he is ABD, and holds degrees from Middle Tennessee State University (M.A., History) and Welch College (B.S., Music Performance, Biblical Studies). He has co-authored two books: *Light and Truth: A Seventy-five Year Pictorial History of Welch College* (Welch College Press, 2018) with J. Matthew Pinson and *The Cumberland Association: Celebrating 175 Years of Leadership, Ministry and Service* (RHM, 2018) with Roy W. Harris. He also contributed a chapter in *The Promise of Arminian Theology* (Randall House Academic, 2016) and has written many popular articles in *ONE Magazine* as well as for the Helwys Society Forum (thehsf.com). He and his wife, Megan, have been married for thirteen years and have five children: Isaiah, Julia, Deborah, Hadassah, and Maria.

J. MATTHEW PINSON has been president of Welch College in Gallatin, Tennessee, for more than twenty years and previously served as a pastor of churches in Alabama, Connecticut, and Georgia. He holds a B.A. and M.A. from the University of West Florida as well as a master's degree from Yale University and a doctorate from Vanderbilt University and is the author or editor of ten books, including *Forty Questions About Arminianism* (Kregel, 2002), *Four Views on Eternal Security* (Zondervan, 2002), *Perspectives on Christian Worship* (B&H, 2009), and *A Free Will Baptist Handbook* (Randall House, 1998). He has served on several nonprofit boards and is currently chairman of the Commission for Theological Integrity of the National Association of Free Will Baptists. He and his wife, Melinda, live in Gallatin and have two grown children: Anna and Matthew.

MONTGOMERY F. THORNSBURY is the English Program coordinator at Welch College. He holds a B.A. degree in history from Welch College and an M.A. degree in English from Valparaiso University. He is currently in the process of completing his Ph.D. in English at Middle Tennessee State University, where his studies have focused on early and nineteenth-century American literature. Frank has also been involved in local politics in his home state of Kentucky. He currently resides in Gallatin, Tennessee, with his wife, Christa, and their daughters: Elinor and Charlotte.

Introduction

Matthew Steven Bracey

The authors of *Christians in Culture* believe that the Christian worldview helps us evaluate every aspect of life. It is not focused only on sermons and evangelism but also on the stuff of culture: the arts, the humanities, the sciences, vocation, politics, sports, and so on. All kinds of Christians from different geographical locations and stations of life have held this view:

> Dutch Prime Minister Abraham Kuyper (1837–1920): "There is not a square inch in the whole domain of our human existence over which Christ, who is Sovereign over all, does not cry, Mine!"[1]

> American theologian H. Richard Niebuhr (1894–1962): "There is no phase of human culture over which Christ does not rule, and no human work which is not subject to his transforming power over self-will."[2]

> English novelist C. S. Lewis (1898–1963): "There is no neutral ground in the universe. Every square inch, every split second is claimed by God, and counterclaimed by Satan."[3]

Christians in Culture proposes to explain these basic beliefs.

The gospel of Jesus Christ is all-encompassing. Nothing is beyond the reach of its redemptive, transformative power. Consequently, we may engage in and even enjoy different spheres of culture, but, in so doing, we must "take every thought captive to obey Christ" and do "all to the glory of God" (2 Corinthians 10:5; 1 Corinthians 10:31). Even topics like economics, leisure, and technology are subject to the sanctifying work of God. Alluding to Revelation 21:5, Bruce Ashford writes that God will make "all things new" rather than making "all new things."[4] Indeed, God is mending a fragmented world through the redemptive work of Jesus Christ.

God does not save Christians within the world only then to remove them from the world. No, He has a purpose for us here and now. Jesus prayed in His high priestly prayer: "I do not ask that you take them out of the world, but that you keep them from the evil one. . . . As you sent me into the world, so I have sent them into the world" (John 17:15, 18). Jesus expects that believers will participate in culture, and He prays that the Father will "keep them from the evil one" and "sanctify them in the truth" (17:15b, 17). God desires that His children shine forth as bright lights in a dark world (Matthew 5:14–16).

Christians in Culture is written with Jesus' prayer in mind. In fact, chapter one will examine the passage in John 17 at some length. As we participate in culture, we must guard ourselves from unwittingly forming our cultural sensibilities according to the ever-changing whims of this present evil age (Galatians 1:4). Instead, we must allow God to sanctify us wholly, which will include our engagement with and enjoyment of culture according to His eternal truth. This book thus aims to explore how a Christian view of life and the world impacts our participation in today's cultures.

This book also serves as an introductory text to worldview thinking for Christians trying to make sense of the cultures in which they live. In a multi-author book like this one, not every author will agree on every jot and tittle. However, we all agree about the big picture. We all agree that all Christians should resolve to place all disciplines and subjects under the lordship of Jesus. We hope this book will benefit all Christians everywhere as they seek to connect their Christian confessions to their everyday lives.

Christians in Culture comprises two sections. Part one, "Establishing the Christian Worldview," begins with a chapter by J. Matthew Pinson, who gives the biblical basis for cultural engagement. In chapter two, Christopher Talbot surveys the periods of premodernism, modernism, and postmodernism and how they help explain the make-up of today's cultures. Next, I review the classical conservative worldview, which emerges from the Hebrew-Christian tradition and offers an important foundation for present cultural engagement. Finally, Matthew McAffee analyzes the biblical foundation for the formation of all culture, as well as discussing the implications for creation care.

Having established the principles undergirding the Christian worldview in part one, we begin applying them to specific spheres of cultural experience in part two. In chapter five, Phillip T. Morgan argues for the central importance of tradition and history in the Christian worldview. Chapters six through nine address the sphere of the arts. In chapter six, E. Darrell Holley presents the Christian critical tradition by evaluating principles from Philippians 4:8 for interpreting the arts. Next, I suggest a theological and practical approach to thinking through and interacting with the arts and the seemingly all-consuming world of entertainment. Then, Pinson analyzes the phenomenon of popular culture, after which Montgomery F. Thornsbury considers the roles of literature and narrative in our analysis of the arts.

Next, I review a Christian vision for labor and vocation, noting its worth and nobility. In chapter eleven, Talbot explores the opportunities and limits of innovation and technology. Then, Ian Hawkins considers the topics of science and origins, showing that Christianity and science are not enemies but friends. In chapter thirteen, Thornsbury discusses the importance of the state and public life, showing their relevance for all Christians. Morgan then reviews issues related to wealth and poverty, addressing topics such as the free market and socialism. Finally, Greg Ketteman and Gregory Fawbush co-author a discussion on sports and recreation, casting a vision for approaching these topics responsibly. Talbot then concludes the volume by considering how we should respond to the principles promoted throughout the book.

We cannot escape the fact of culture. It is in the air we breathe because it results inevitably from men and women living in the world. But we can escape succumbing to its sinful manifestations or living a life of spiritual and intellectual apathy. We hope instead to live lives informed by the Bible that are both winsome and wise. The Fall of man has perverted everything, including culture; mercifully, the grace of God is reforming everything, including culture. The question is not *whether* we will interact with culture but *how* we will interact with it. *Christians in Culture* invites you to think, feel, and act toward culture in a manner that is holistic, prudent, and transformative.

Part I

ESTABLISHING THE CHRISTIAN WORLDVIEW

CHAPTER ONE

Reflections on Christian Cultural Engagement

J. Matthew Pinson

What is culture that we are mindful of it?[1] This book seeks to answer that question. It is about the interaction of the church and culture. Before we can begin talking about *how* Christians in the church should engage their culture, we need to clarify *why*, according to the Bible, we should engage it in the first place. Jesus gives us reasons in John 17:14–19, a passage I will refer to throughout this chapter, which is adapted from a sermon series first preached in chapel at Welch College. John 17 is part of Jesus' high-priestly prayer to the Father on behalf of His followers. Jesus calls believers out of the world unto Himself so that He can send them on His mission into the world. Through most of this chapter, we will work our way through these verses before concluding with a few remarks on Christ and culture.

Called out of the World

If we are going to engage culture effectively, we must first understand that Christ has called those whom the Father has given Him out of the world: "I have manifested your name to the people whom you gave me out of the world" (John 17:6). Thus we as Christians are not *of* the world. As He told the disciples in John 15:19b, "You are not of the world, but I chose you out of the world."

Jesus' kingdom is not of this world. In calling us into His kingdom, He has called us out of the kingdom of this world. As a result, our day-to-day values, priorities, and sensibilities are shaped not by the kingdom of this present world but by His kingdom. The great Puritan preacher Matthew Henry wrote about this passage, saying, "Their most pleasing converse is, and should be, with another world, and their prevailing concern about the business of that world, not of this."[2] Jesus' teaching on the church and the world is rooted in His gospel of the kingdom. It is rooted in what it means to live a life of kingdom values in this present age.

Jesus talked frequently about a clash of kingdoms: the kingdom of God and the kingdom of this world. And that clash of kingdoms entails a clash of values. Jesus was trying to get His followers to live their lives by the values of His kingdom and not by the values of this present age. The kingdom that Jesus teaches about is both *already* and *not yet*. Yes, the kingdom is future. Thus the apostle Peter says that we are pilgrims in a strange land (1 Peter 2:11). We reside here, but our values and priorities are alien to this world.

Yet, in addition to being *not yet*, the kingdom is *already*. Jesus has already inaugurated it. It is breaking in on this present evil age and on our lives in the here and now and changing them, transforming them. As the Holy Spirit transforms our lives, He also transforms the lives of those around us. Thus Jesus teaches us to come out from the world because its values do not shape us. Instead, the values of an alien kingdom shape our whole view of the world and life.[3]

John repeats this teaching about coming out from the world in several places in his first epistle. In chapter two, he tells his readers not to love the world or the things in it because, if they do, the Father's love will not be in them. Allowing the world to shape our values and priorities is foolish, John says, because "the world is passing away along with its desires, but whoever does the will of God abides forever" (1 John 2:17).

John's teaching concurs with the New Testament teaching that Christian sensibilities are shaped by the powers of the age to come (Hebrews 6:5), not by those of this present evil age (Galatians 1:4), which is fading. In chapter four, John tells us that we will overcome the world because "greater is He who is in you than he who is in the world" (1 John 4:4)—the one Jesus had referred to as the prince of this world (John 12:31; 14:30). The reason we will overcome the world is because we are "from God" and not of the world, which lies in "the power of the evil one" (1 John 5:19).

Paul also reflects this idea in his teaching about Christians' not being unequally yoked with unbelievers, where, quoting Isaiah 52:11, he says: "Therefore go out from their midst, and be separate from them, says the Lord, and touch no unclean thing; then I will welcome you, and I will be a father to you, and you shall be sons and daughters to me, says the Lord Almighty" (2 Corinthians 6:17–18).

For this same reason, Paul admonishes the Romans not to be conformed to the world but to be transformed by the renewing of their minds. He taught that conformity to the spirit of the age would keep them from embodying God's desires for them as living sacrifices (12:1–2). Similarly, James explains that the essence of pure and undefiled religion includes keeping ourselves "unstained from the world" (1:27). Friendship with the world makes us God's enemies (4:4).

The early Christians took this apostolic teaching very seriously. They simply did not become like the culture to reach the culture. Rather, they were totally distinct from the culture. The early church was fond of the phrase *contra mundum* ("against the world"). The church fathers believed that the only way Christians could reach the world was through the church's being a countercultural outpost of the kingdom here on earth. Our residency is here, they taught, but our attitudes and values and behavior are shaped by another world, Christ's kingdom, which is breaking in on this present evil age and transforming it.

Those early Christians present an instructive historical-cultural parallel to the culture in which we find ourselves. Think, for example, about Clement of Alexandria in the early 200s.[4] He lived in a multi-cultural, multi-religious, pluralistic, relativistic, highly sexualized, image-driven, entertainment-saturated culture. Christians were a tiny minority in the culture, but they completely set their lives, culture, spirituality, and worship apart from those of the world. Yet, as sociologist Rodney Stark has shown, this period was precisely the time when Christianity grew like wildfire.[5]

These early churches were much more conservative than we are. Their worship services were simple, reverent, unadorned, and singularly *un*-multi-sensory in a time when, on their way to church, they might walk past all manner of multi-sensory entertainment, visual arts, games, fights, dramas, pantomimes, dancing, and raucous music. Even still, the churches were very much *unlike* the surrounding culture. By using the ordinary means of grace as revealed in Scripture—those cherished means that God has revealed for calling out a people for His name and fitting those people for His eternal kingdom—they prospered.

The early Christians believed that we, like Paul in Acts 17, must *engage* our culture and its people, using words they understand, making references to things they have read and viewed. Yet they believed that, in doing this, we need to challenge the culture. We need to point out the problems with its worldview and way of life. We need to show the ways in which it is inconsistent with Christian belief and practice.

Even while seeking to understand and communicate to their culture, these early Christians believed that a stark contrast emerges between the church and the world. In short, they believed and practiced Jesus' teaching that we must come out from the world. But they did not believe that that referred to physical separation or not engaging the culture. They thought it meant being intentionally *in* the world but also intentionally *not of* the world.

Thus Jesus, His apostles, and their earliest followers emphasized that the Lord has called His people out from the world and that their values and priorities and worldview and lifestyle are not shaped by the values of this world—this present evil age that is passing away. Instead, they believed that the church and its people should be shaped by the powers of the age to come, the kingdom that is breaking in and transforming this world according to its values.

Hated by the World

Because Christ has called us out of the world, we must not be surprised if the world hates us (1 John 3:13). The world is hostile to the church because the values and priorities of the kingdom of this world are utterly different from those of the kingdom of Christ. Jesus warns His followers of the cost of their discipleship: "If the world hates you, know that it has hated me before it hated you. If you were of the world, the world would love you as its own; but because you are not of the world, but I chose you out of the world, therefore the world hates you" (John 15:19). Jesus draws His disciples into His own life, but He warns them that, as they are drawn into His life and mission, they can be sure that the world will hate them.

When we choose Christ and His kingdom, we exchange the worldview and sensibilities we have absorbed from this present evil age for the worldview and sensibilities that are shaped by the age to come, which we learn from His Word. However, the world will hate us just like it hated Him. The more we are like Jesus—the more we think like Him, share in His affections, and act like Him—the more the world will hate us and show its hostility to us. The less we are like Him—the less we think like Him, share in His affections, and act like Him—the more the world will like us and embrace us and think we are cool after all. If the world says of the church, "They're not as bad as I thought. They're actually kinda cool," then the church is likely not Christlike enough. "Do not be surprised, brothers, that the world hates you" (1 John 3:13).

This hostility of the world results from a clash of kingdoms: the kingdom of God with the kingdom of this world. In these verses from the Gospel of John, Jesus explains that authentic kingdom living—authentic Christian discipleship—will put us at odds with this present evil age and its desires and powers. It will result in conflict, even persecution. People do not like having their ways of life challenged. So, when you come to them with kingdom values and priorities, no matter how loving and compassionate you are about it, Jesus warns you that they will persecute you. Yet, amid the suffering we will endure when we follow Him, Jesus holds up the consummation of the coming kingdom and its reward to bring us joy.

We do not need to worry about the world hating and persecuting us because Jesus will make our joy complete: "But now I am coming to you, and these things I speak in the world, that they may have my joy fulfilled in themselves" (John 17:13). If our suffering fulfills Christ's joy, then it does not matter if the world is hostile! The nineteenth-century Bible expositor J. C. Ryle is instructive in what being hated by the world does *not* mean: "We are not to court the world's enmity. A narrow, morose, uncourteous, and exclusive spirit, is downright wrong. But we are never to be the least surprised by the world's enmity if we meet with it; and the more holy we are, the more we shall meet with it. Christ was perfect in holiness; but the world hated Him."[6]

So far, we have seen that Christ calls us out of the world. We are not of the world, and our values and priorities are not those of this present evil age, which is fading, but those of the ever-enduring age to come. We have also seen that the world will not like us and will even hate us for our identification with the values of the age to come. But some Christians are too quick to stop at this point, and they fail to embrace the equally important teaching that Christ calls us to go into the world.

SENT INTO THE WORLD

Jesus clearly teaches His disciples that, while He has called them out of the world, He is also sending them into the world. While they are not of the world, they are nonetheless in the world: "I am no longer in the world, but they are in the world. . . . I do not ask that you take them out of the world, but that you keep them from the evil one" (John 17:11, 15). Jesus calls us into the world to be His representatives. Ryle was right when he said that removal from the world "would be bad for [the disciples], and bad for the world."[7] First, it would be bad for the world because we would not serve as God's instruments of grace to the world. God chose to keep us here to be instruments of His saving grace to bring salvation to the world, to help the world better reflect His truth that He manifests through His common grace, and to make it more conducive for His saving grace.

Yet Ryle gives a second reason why Jesus left us here, and it is rooted in 2 Timothy 2:11: "If we have died with him, we will also live with him." Jesus left us here, says Ryle, to be "duly trained for heaven, and taught to value the blood and intercession and patience of [our] Redeemer."[8] Jesus wants us here in the world. "Nothing, we may be sure, glorifies grace so much as to live like Daniel in Babylon, and the saints in Nero's household,—in the world and yet not of the world—tempted on every side and yet conquerors of temptation, not taken out of the reach of evil and yet kept and preserved from its power."[9]

Jesus' teaching goes against the teaching of monasticism, which says that the surest way to holiness is retreat from the world and desertion of our public role in the world, going instead into monasteries and convents. This mentality is the error of the Amish as much as it is of the Roman Catholic Church. In the Gospels, Jesus admonished His disciples on how they should live out kingdom lives in a pagan world, and it was not retreat but rather witness. Jesus used two poignant images for this lifestyle in the Sermon on the Mount: salt and light (Matthew 5:13). If we are going to bear witness to Him and His kingdom rule over our lives, if we are going extend that kingdom rule as far as we can in our world, then we must realize that we are salt and light. By being salt and light in this fallen world, we will extend His kingdom rule and glorify Him.

REDEMPTION FOR THE WORLD

From Jesus' teaching on salt and light, we can learn much about how to live out kingdom lives as disciples of Christ in a pagan culture. First, our being salt and light affects all of our relationships. It affects the way we relate to God, to ourselves (our self-concept), to other people (interpersonal relationships), and to creation.[10] Creation does not refer just to natural creation but also to what human beings create: culture and its products (including society, the state, and all the arenas of culture discussed in this book). Being salt and light affects the secular things as well as the religious things, the small things as well as the big things, Monday through Saturday as well as Sunday. In short, it applies to everything. As Abraham Kuyper said, "There is not a square inch in the whole domain of our human existence over which Christ, who is Sovereign over all, does not cry, Mine!"[11]

Several recent books discuss the ways that Christianity has transformed the world even when many individuals in a given society did not consciously submit to the lordship of Jesus Christ.[12] Christianity has affected world civilization artistically and scientifically and culturally and educationally and politically, as well as in terms of healthcare and the environment and the alleviation of poverty. The list could go on and on. Christianity influences and changes culture, which then becomes more conducive to the gospel.

We see this pattern throughout church history. We see it in William Carey's role in the transformation of India, where people received Christ, made Him Lord of their lives, and then transformed their cultures. We see it in John and Charles Wesley's revivals, with huge numbers of people converting to the life-changing gospel of Christ. In fact, this awakening prevented England's own version of a revolution like the bloody French Revolution.

We need to get away from the notion that there is a dichotomy between soul-saving and cultural renewal. They go hand in hand. Being salt in our culture—being that preservative agent and that cleansing agent in a decadent world—means that the gospel is going to change people's hearts and minds. It means that when their hearts and minds are changed, they are going to begin to repent, and God will begin to change their lives. Then they are going to start changing everything around them: in their personal and familial and cultural lives. And that is a cycle: the more Christianity transforms the culture around it, the more conducive that culture is for evangelism.

George Barna and other researchers say that too many of the churches in our country are filled with people who do not have a Christian worldview and whose lives are not being changed, even though they are attending church and even though they have said the sinner's prayer.[13] Our attempts to make our faith as much like the surrounding culture as we can have backfired on us. We are not changing the culture because we are instead trying to mimic the culture. And many churches are not even changing their own people because they are not offering them anything other than entertainment, self-help preaching, and six steps to a better you.

Christ has sent us into the world to restore the world. The mission of the church is to make disciples of Christ by the power of His gospel and to help transform their lives by His truth, teaching them to observe all His commandments in every area of their lives. And that transformation will lead to the transformation of their lives, families, and churches. This transformation cannot help but to affect the cultural practices and institutions around them. The main reason we as Christians are losing the cultural battle is that we are losing the spiritual battle.

This concept of the transforming power of redemption applies to *all* things that we seek to submit to the redemption of God in Christ. Part of what it means for the kingdom to break in is to renew culture, to renew society. This renewal, however, is always transformative. Often we hear people talk about redeeming pop culture and so forth. Yet on second glance, it looks as if they have not really done anything to change the actual cultural product that they say they are attempting to redeem. They are simply "baptizing" a secular form with Christian content, but they believe they have redeemed that secular form.[14] The problem with this interpretation is that redeeming something means radically transforming it. Because redemption alters and transforms things, those things in our lives we set about to redeem will necessarily undergo transformation.

The great church father Augustine talked about the Christian use of Greek and Roman learning. He spoke of this practice as the "plundering of the Egyptians" (Exodus 3:22; 12:36). He was referring to the fact that the Israelites took Egyptian gold and then redeemed it for a sacred use. Notice, however, what he says the Israelites did with the gold. They did not keep it in the forms of the Egyptians and simply imbue it with new sacred meaning or content. Instead, they melted it and used it to make the tabernacle furnishings as God had commanded. They used the gold of Egypt but only after they completely transformed it, setting it apart for God's purposes.[15]

The example of the Israelites illustrates what we should do as we seek to renew culture. The cultures and subcultures and family structures and emotional baggage that we bring with us when we come to faith undergo transformation just as our souls do. Redemption is not just for the soul or the spirit. It is for our whole selves, for all our relationships.

So, as Christ redeems us, our views on the things of this world will undergo radical transformation. The way we think will change. The way we talk will change. The things we read and watch will change. Our parenting practices will change. The sort of art and music with which we surround ourselves will change. Our tastes will change. Our political views will change. Our views on how we use our time and how much time we fritter away on the things of this passing evil age—those will change too. As redemption works its work in us, things that used to be important to us will become unimportant or problematic for us. The chapters in this book explore these different spheres (as well as others) in greater detail and delve into the ways that Christ's redemption transforms them.

In this work of cultural transformation, we must resist the temptation of our consumeristic culture to be time wasters, to be passive consumers of culture. We need to be culture makers, as Andy Crouch says.[16] We need to make good culture rather than simply mimicking shallow, thin, disposable pop culture. We need to be creators of literature and art and architecture and music and science and gardening and technology and cinema and cuisine and politics—all in a manner that reflects kingdom values. We need to be creators of cultural products that embody the wisdom and virtue of the Bible and the Great Christian Tradition.

This concept has implications for those of us who are involved in cross-cultural mission work—and all of us are to some extent, even if we do not go overseas. As Jeff Turnbough reminds us, we must beware of a cultural relativism that sees all cultures and cultural products as relative and not subject to redemption. Turnbough rightly states that, first, much of our philosophy of how to bring people from other cultures and subcultures to Christ has been corrupted by a secular cultural relativism. Second, he avers, we must be aware that many things within cultures have been darkened to the light of the gospel and will have to undergo radical changes to be transformed by the redemption of God in Christ.[17]

Mission to the World

As we have considered, Christ calls us out of the world, and it hates us for it. Yet He has left us in the world as His representatives of the message of a transformative redemption—a message that applies to everything. In so doing, He sets us apart for truth and for mission. Speaking of truth, Jesus prays, "Sanctify them in the truth; your word is truth. . . . And for their sake I consecrate myself, that they also may be sanctified in truth" (John 17:17, 19). Speaking of mission, He says, "As you sent me into the world, so I have sent them into the world" (17:18). Jesus explains that God, by His truth, is sanctifying the disciples *for the purpose of* fulfilling the mission He is sending them on. This purpose statement is so ironic. It seems out of place in our contemporary setting to say it. But Jesus is saying that it is precisely this holiness—this otherness, this set-apartness, this representing of an alien kingdom and its values—that God uses to win the world.

No one has said it better than Frédéric Godet: Jesus separated the disciples "from the world for the precise purpose of preparing them to fulfill a mission to the world."[18] What Jesus is saying here is, "Father, just as you have set Me apart from the world for My saving mission to the world, so I am asking You to call My followers out of the world and to set them apart from the world for the precise purpose of sending them on a mission to the world."

Godet's point is exactly what Jesus was talking about in John 10:36 when He said that the Father had sanctified Him and sent Him into the world. In other words, Jesus was consecrated—set apart and separated from the world so that He might be on mission from God. And now He is setting His disciples apart, calling them out of the world and separating them from the world so that they might be on mission from Christ to the world.

These truths mean that the way for us to reach the world is to set ourselves apart from it in our values, priorities, and sensibilities. This message is so counterintuitive to the way so many Christians think today about reaching the world. However, as Jesus said in the Sermon on the Mount, the way to let your light shine before men is to be that city on a hill that draws people to Christ. It is to be holy. It is to let your light so shine before men that they may see your good works and, seeing your holiness and your sanctification, glorify the Father (Matthew 5:16).

God's glory is simply the bright-shining manifestation of His holy character or His complete perfection. Jesus teaches us that, if we want people to glorify God—to allow His holy character to manifest itself in their lives—then we will consecrate ourselves, set ourselves apart for God's holy use, and order our lives according to God's holy character. This ordering seems to go against the grain of some modern-day thinking about how to win the world by being as much like the world as we can be. But the best way to get people in the world to glorify God, to extol His perfect character and greatness, is to live lives that are set apart from the world unto God.

Jesus' model for cultural engagement presents the wonderful paradox that the church and the world need so desperately today. The church is called out of the world by God to be a royal priesthood, a holy nation, set apart to God for good works (1 Peter 2:9), that reflects His holy character and the values and priorities of His cosmic kingdom.

This set-apartness is what Jesus says is absolutely necessary if we are to let our light shine. This set-apartness should shape our views on the relevance of the gospel message. Too often we are so worried that we have to add things to the gospel and to God's ordinary means of grace to make the gospel and the Bible relevant, as if they do not have their own intrinsic Spirit-given relevance.

If we want to be a light to the world, we will put a high priority on good works, on lives that reflect the values and priorities of Christ and His kingdom. This ethic will include living pure and holy lives set apart for God's holy use, as well as lives of service and compassion for poor and hurting people.

In addition, our good works will be countercultural; they will run counter to the mindset of the world. Remember what I said earlier about William Carey's role in the transformation of India and John and Charles Wesley's work in revival that brought cultural change to England? These great movements of the Holy Spirit, one a great mission movement and the other an evangelistic awakening, bore a singular mark: the most notable thing about these movements is that their leaders strongly taught and practiced and modeled nonconformity to the world, the importance of separation from the world, the necessity of holiness and set-apart living in the world, the need for the church to be different from the world, and the necessity to go beyond the minimum we have to do to be converted to live lives of excellence for Christ. Yet these movements brought about some of the most astounding evangelistic and church growth results in world history. They also brought about some of the most amazing transformations of their civilizations that the world has ever known.

Do you want to be a part of something like that? Do you want to be on mission like Carey and the Wesleys, to bring people to Christ and to affect the lives and families and cultures of the people around you? If you want to be this kind of world changer, then I exhort you to allow God to set you apart from the world for His special, holy use. Pray and study and ask the Lord to imbue your life with the worldview and values and priorities of His kingdom that are not of this world. And immerse yourself in the structures of this world, letting the kingdom break in, even now, to this present evil age and transform it for the glory of Christ, the evangelization of the world, and the extension of His rule over all of life.

Engaging the Culture of the World

The question remains as to what cultural engagement looks like for the countercultural Christian. The modern evangelical model of cultural engagement is much different from the early church's model of Christ and culture, to use Richard Niebuhr's phrase.[19] Some conservative evangelicals tend to be "Christ against culture" (not of the world and not in the world). Liberals and progressives (including, sadly, many modern evangelicals) have tended to be "the Christ of culture" (in the world and of the world).

Yet the biblical ideal is to be "Christ transforming culture" (*in* the world yet *not of* the world). This ideal involves, of course, starting off with "Christ against culture" (*contra mundum*) because if one is not against the values, attitudes, habits, and choices of the surrounding culture, then he will have no reason to transform them. However, some conservative evangelicals just stay with the "against" part and never get to the "transforming" part. Much modern evangelicalism does not see any need to seek the transformation of the actual culture and its products, attitudes, and values. Therefore, in many cases it does not have enough "against" to become "transforming."

We need to study how the apostles and the early church related to the culture around them, which is much like our own, rather than naively to assume that the church must be *like* the world to reach the world. That approach does not characterize what Jesus and John and Paul taught. Early Christianity had a transformational effect on the cultures it engaged, yet it had to engage those cultures to transform them. It did not cocoon itself off in a Christian enclave. Instead, it confronted pagan cultures with a gospel that had a transformative effect on those cultures.

Cultural critic and *Mars Hill Audio* producer Ken Myers says that many evangelicals fit another model: of the world but not in the world. The trend in some evangelicalism is to withdraw from the larger culture and not attempt to transform it with Christian cultural sensibilities. These Christians set up their own version of pop culture that simply mimics the styles of pop culture and then puts Christian content to it. Thus evangelicals have created their own religious subculture that is a mirror of popular culture, "complete with Christian rock bands and night clubs, Christian soap operas and talk shows, Christian spy and romance novels, and Christian exercise videos. They have thus succeeded in being of the world, but not in the world."[20]

In an article in *Fusion* magazine, Russell Moore referred to such evangelicals as "off-brand evangelicals."[21] He writes elsewhere that this mentality has resulted in a cultural approach that is somewhat like cologne machines in truck stops: if you like Polo, you'll like . . . and then it gives the imitation cologne's name.[22] People sometimes say that if you like Post Malone, you'll like . . . (fill in the blank with a Christian artist). If you like P!NK, you'll like . . . (fill in the blank with a Christian artist) . . . and so on. (If these artists seem outdated, that illustrates the very problem I am addressing.)

This book is designed to help its readers grapple with what it means to be in the world but not of it—what it means for the church to be in the world without the world's being in the church. This question is crucial for Christians of our day. The need of our day is for Christians to build truly countercultural communities of faith. The key to fulfilling this need is for Christians to figure out how to be truly in the world, profoundly engaging the culture, while not being of the world, instead being truly countercultural to win the world. This is the challenge for the church in our time.

Before we launch into this book-length exploration of how Christ's redemption transforms culture, we need to understand one more thing: culture is both *what is* and *what ought to be*. Johann Gottfried Herder defined *Kultur* as "the life-blood of a people, the flow of moral energy that holds society intact." By contrast, he defined *Zivilisation* as "the veneer of manners, law, and technical know-how." Some thinkers have defined culture like Herder, while others, like Wilhelm von Humboldt and T. S. Eliot, have seen it in more classical terms, as *cultivation*.[23]

So, in one sense, we can view culture as what *is*: a description of the state of things in a given society, like a patch of ground untended and uncultivated. But in another sense, we can view it as what *ought to be*: like a beautiful, fruitful garden, carefully tended and cultivated.[24] This book uses the term *culture* in both ways.

We are living our lives in the midst of a culture, in the midst of a set of beliefs and attitudes and behaviors and products (things produced or created). However, since we as Christians believe that our faith has a transformative effect on the culture in which we live, we subscribe to the latter understanding of culture. We see ourselves as cultivating the culture around us, as a gardener would painstakingly cultivate a garden. In fact, we see this cultivation as part of our being created in the image of God (Genesis 1:26–27). We see it as part of God's mandate for us to exercise dominion over the earth (1:28). We believe that God has created us to be creators.[25]

So, whatever sphere of culture we engage, whether family or church, art or science, farming or politics, industry or cooking, making music or helping people, being a neighbor or sewing, reading or writing—all topics that are covered in this book—we want to cultivate it according to the values and attitudes of King Jesus and His kingdom priorities and the rule He is extending over our lives. Thus the way that this book's authors use the word *culture* sometimes reflects the first understanding and sometimes the second one. Sometimes it speaks of the way things are, "the culture we're living in," and at other times it refers to our shaping of the culture according to the virtues and values of a greater culture, that of the kingdom of Christ, whose gospel truth is transforming our own lives and cultures.

The editors of this book have prepared these chapters to present a broad range of angles from which the church's engagement with contemporary culture can be viewed, including creation, history, the arts and entertainment, popular culture, literature, labor and vocation, innovation and technology, science, the state and public life, economics, and sports and recreation. Each of these chapters presuppose that the church should engage the culture, not withdraw from it, and that, in engaging the culture, the church should challenge the culture to a more profound sense of what it means to be a human being created in God's image for God's purposes.

These chapters work on the assumption that God has an "end" or goal in mind for people—what theologians and philosophers call *telos*. And when we seek to transform every area of our lives according to the attitudes and values of the kingdom of God, then we will engage our world. Yet our values and attitudes, which Christians receive not from this world, not from this present age, but from the age to come, bring change and transformation to our world, to our culture. The remainder of this book will explore what this change, what this transformation, looks like, first by establishing the principles of the Christian worldview and, second, by applying them to the areas that most fill our lives.

CHAPTER TWO

THE INFLUENCE OF IDEAS

Christopher Talbot

Understanding our cultural moment is a difficult task. If we are not careful, we can naively assume we are born into a culture that is a *tabula rasa* (or blank slate), as if it is somehow detached from the history preceding it. We can also assume that we maintain complete objectivity about the world around us. We might even assume that our generation has somehow jettisoned the apparent shackles of our forebears and instead has begun anew with pristine clarity about the world and knowledge.[1]

Yet history course after history course has shown that this accounting is simply not the truth. At any given moment, we are at once receiving age-old ideas and navigating the unknown future. We are the stewards of that which others have passed down to us: thoughts, art, philosophies, and more. God has called us to steward these things well.

However, we are not to dwell exclusively on the past; we are called also to interact with the ideas of the here and now and seek to know how to move forward into the future. While I disagree with much of what he said, the philosopher Søren Kierkegaard (1813–1855) keenly noted, "It is perfectly true, as the philosophers say, that life must be understood backwards. But they forget the other proposition, that it must be lived forwards."[2] To borrow a colloquialism, we must know where we have been to know where we are going.

When we engage the culture through our Christian worldview, we participate in the world as a "bridge-builder." God exhorts us to understand the history of ideas so that we might thoughtfully—and graciously—interact with the world of today. We live between two worlds, seeking to build a bridge between the past and the present. As Alister McGrath says, "Every generation believes it stands at a critical point in history."[3] Undoubtedly, every generation *does* stand at a critical point in history and is given a responsibility and ability to affect its culture, and ultimately history itself, in one way or another.[4] We must receive this responsibility with the utmost care and thoughtfulness.

Concerning our current state, philosophers generally agree that Western culture has found itself in a particularly difficult—and one could say, interesting—cultural moment. "No longer is there any single story, a metanarrative (in our terms a worldview), that holds Western culture together," writes James Sire. "It is not just that there have long been many stories, each of which gives its binding power to the social group that takes it as its own. The naturalists have their story, the pantheists theirs, the Christians theirs, ad infinitum. With postmodernism no story can have any more credibility than any other. All stories are equally valid, being so validated by the community that lives by them."[5] Sire is right; we now live in a day and age in which Christianity is no longer the guiding metanarrative.[6]

Not only is Christianity any longer society's guiding narrative, but any metanarrative seeking to explain reality has also been largely rejected. For this reason, and others, we must understand the ideas that have shaped our world and culture. Of course, when trying to comprehend the grand flow of thought through the ages, we must remember that we cannot help but to paint with broad strokes to capture the overall ethos of the age.

The following overviews of cultural thought will not necessarily describe the thought of everyone who inhabited those times, whether philosopher or pastor, painter or plumber. The same is true today. Although we live in a distinctly postmodern context (a topic we will cover later), we are not all inherently characterized or defined by postmodernism. Nevertheless, since we live within a postmodern ecosystem, we should be literate in the ideas and language of the culture around us. Often, the only way to abstain from the *zeitgeist* (or spirit of the age) is to be familiar with the *zeitgeist* itself.

To appreciate how we have gotten to where we are, we will begin by retracing our cultural steps. We will first define two major ideologies: modernism and postmodernism. In so doing, we will see how society has slowly moved to where it is today by considering the effects of these movements on philosophy, art, theology, and other cultural artifacts.[7] We will note key figures and ideas but will not highlight all influences that have affected our current milieu.

Defining Modernism

Before Modernism

To understand modernism and postmodernism, and specifically our own cultural moment fully, we must first consider "premodernism," the cultural thought prior to the rise of modernism. While a diversity of thought existed during this period, people generally abided by a set of commonly held beliefs. Premodernists believed in the supernatural, though this belief did not necessarily amount to belief in the Judeo-Christian God. Yet premodernists overwhelmingly believed in a transcendent being(s) because they believed in the reality of the supernatural.

Premodern societies and cultures held this basic presupposition of the transcendent, and premodernists viewed institutions such as the state, family, and church as authoritative. These institutions generally operated as arbiters of truth for members of society and, as a result, people looked to them for an understanding of what is true and right. Gene Veith states, "Life in this world owed its existence and meaning to a spiritual realm beyond the senses."[8] Spiritual reality was threaded through premodernists' comprehension of the cosmos, and external authorities of truth validated a belief in spiritual truth.

Although various worldviews were not in complete agreement with one another in the premodern era (e.g., Greek paganism and Christianity), they were not opposed to each other in *every* detail. Veith writes, "They agreed that there was a transcendent reality beyond this world, to which this world owed its meaning."[9] Because of this basic presupposition, these other worldviews shared a major touchstone with Christianity, unlike the modernism and postmodernism of today. Again, while these various worldviews in the premodern era were easily at odds with one another in some distinctive ways, they all nonetheless affirmed a supernatural reality (a metaphysical realism). This common emphasis on the transcendent, however, permitted a greater degree of synthesis across worldviews and created several problems moving forward in history.

For more than a thousand years, biblical truth, classical rationalism, and pagan mythologies often intermingled to the detriment of the Christian worldview. At times the Christian worldview was compromised, while at other times it emerged untarnished.[10] One significant figure from this period that sought to synthesize all truth, and to marry faith and reason, is Thomas Aquinas (1225–1274). However, because he emphasized Aristotelian philosophy in his understanding of the knowledge of God and human reasoning, he articulated a view about basic reality and knowledge that differed in key ways from the Augustinian synthesis that preceded him or from the Reformed tradition that would follow him.[11] While subsequent figures would rip asunder what he attempted to put together, Thomas helped to plant the seeds for modernity.

William of Ockham (1285–1347) would divorce the marriage of faith and reason with the philosophy of nominalism, which precipitated philosophical disaster for the end of the premodern period.[12] Nominalism rejects the existence of universals and holds, therefore, that things do not have a nature: "According to nominalism, there is no such thing as human nature, or the nature of man, or man in general. . . . There is no such thing in reality as justice or injustice, only acts that we see as resembling each other in some way."[13]

Nominalism results in a universality that exists only in words, not in reality. Therefore, according to nominalism, particulars and universals are not connected. Additionally, men and women can know only particulars; they can reason only inductively and hence by probability. Nominalism leads to skepticism since probability is not certainty.[14] Thus William, in the late premodern period, contributed significantly to the eventual rise of modernity, the effects of which still impact us in the present day.

This analysis does not mean that Christianity should identify totally with premodernism, which had its own problems. Yet one vital truth characterizes the period: "Most people assumed that God is real and must be taken into account."[15] Therefore, overall, premodern people did not reject belief in God, revelation, and objective truth.

We might ask ourselves, "What went wrong? How did Western culture move away from this overall embrace of the supernatural?" To some extent, we can find the roots of modern rationalism and empiricism millennia ago in pagan Greek culture. As Michael Goheen and Craig Bartholomew explain, "The development of modernity is a long history of interaction between the Christian and the classical humanist worldviews. . . . . Thus began the long relationship and interaction of two all-embracing, and often opposing, visions of life."[16] Nonetheless, a catalytic change occurred with the Enlightenment. Classical humanism and Christianity had coexisted for centuries, but the rise of the Enlightenment introduced a great divide between these two dominant worldviews.

The Enlightenment

The Enlightenment refers, generally, to a movement in the eighteenth century that emphasized individualism and rationality in place of tradition. Those wanting to specify the beginning of modernism will often point to René Descartes (1596–1650), a French philosopher, scientist, and mathematician who lived during the seventeenth century. While you may not know his name, you are probably aware of his oft-quoted maxim: "*cogito, ergo sum*," meaning, "I think, therefore I am." Though we would oversimplify the issue to think of Descartes as the first modernist philosopher, we can see in his thinking a helpful archetype for much modern thought.

Scholars often identify Descartes's work, especially his epistemic skepticism (skepticism about *knowledge*), as a major catalyst of the Enlightenment. Due in part to the changes in cosmological thinking of his time, Descartes began to employ a methodological doubt about what he thought he knew to the point that he doubted virtually everything, including himself. However, he became convinced that the fact of his doubting demonstrated that he really existed, hence "I think, therefore I am." He writes, "I rightly conclude that my essence consists solely in the fact that I am a thinking thing."[17] Following this line of thought, Descartes argued that an individual's own reasoning is sufficient for epistemic certainty.[18]

However, unlike Descartes, who was a devout Catholic, those who followed him in later modernist thought would "cast aside past authorities—such as the church, Scriptures, and tradition—in favor of individual logic and empirical observation. Humankind, the modernist would assert, had come of age and no longer needed authority figures to guide them in truth."[19] Man was king, the final authority, under modernism. Mankind had become the measure of all things (to use the language of the ancient Greek Protagoras). If human reason arbitrated truth, then it would subjugate God's revelation beneath itself. Thus Scripture would no longer hold the position of authority it once held in society.

This high view of human reason, and subsequently a high view of human autonomy, contributed to the rise of epistemological empiricism. Strict empiricism argues that we can verify the truth of something only if it is proved exclusively through our sensory experience. That is, if people can test a hypothesis with one of their senses, then they can verify whether the hypothesis is real and true. McGrath notes, "This outlook [of modernism] was shaped by a belief in a universal human reason, common to all people and times, capable of gaining access to the deeper structures of the world. Reason was the key that unlocked the mysteries of life, and argument was its tool of persuasion. Rational argument became the trusted tool of this cultural age."[20]

Yet as Christians, we believe, with D. A. Carson, that "God cannot be captured, measured, weighed, manipulated, or domesticated."[21] Thus the epistemology of modernism stands at odds with that of Christianity. On one hand, the modernist argues that rationalist and/or empiricist epistemologies can answer the deepest questions of life.[22] On the other hand, the Christian argues that only God can answer these questions, and He reveals the answers to them through His inspired, inerrant Word. In the words of Hans Rookmaaker, "The Enlightenment may have begun as a philosophical movement, but deep spiritual problems related to religious truth were also very much at stake. Its influence was not only on the minds but also on the hearts of men, it affected their sensitivity and emotions, it really changed their life in all its aspects."[23]

Another philosopher, who followed Descartes and influenced Western thinking, was Immanuel Kant (1724–1804). Kant was a key figure in the Enlightenment, pushing modernist theories toward their natural conclusion. In some ways, if Descartes was the beginning of the Enlightenment, then Kant was the end. Kant recognized that pure empiricism and pure rationalism cannot be the conclusion, that we cannot capture some realities solely through empirical and rationalistic means.

For this reason, Kant introduced a distinction between the *phenomenal* world, which we can know in part, and the *noumenal* world, which we cannot know. The phenomenal world is the world as we perceive it. The noumenal world is the world as it truly exists. In his epistemology Kant distinguished between the true (noumenal) and our perception of the true (phenomenal). From the noumenal Kant built ethics (e.g., categorical imperative) and aesthetics. He wanted to synthesize empiricism, rationalism, and individualism.[24] However, a Kantian divide between the noumenal and phenomenal emerged.

Referring to the rise of the Enlightenment, Kant argued that humanity had occupied a self-imposed immaturity for too long: "*Immaturity* is the inability to use one's own understanding without the guidance of another. This immaturity is *self-incurred* if its cause is not lack of understanding, but lack of resolution and courage to use it without the guidance of another. The motto of enlightenment is therefore *Sapere Aude!* [Dare to be wise!] Have courage to use your *own* understanding!"[25] Here again, we see how modernism was quick to jettison any external authority outside of man. To appreciate fully the comprehensive force of modernism, we should look at how this philosophy has affected every area of thought.

In seeking to understand the far-reaching effects of Enlightenment thought, we should examine the thought of the "five bad boys of modernism."[26] These five men, in their respective fields, brought about the full rise and end of modernism: Charles Darwin, Karl Marx, Julius Wellhausen, Friedrich Nietzsche, and Sigmund Freud. These men all lived during the nineteenth century and thus inherited nearly 150 years of thought from the time of Descartes. Each figure operated within the assumptions of modernism as they sought to articulate its implications for their own respective fields. In addition, each sought to land fatal blows against Christianity as an authoritative worldview.

First, Charles Darwin (1809–1882) was a geologist and biologist, known most for articulating a theory of evolution, which he presented in his 1859 book *On the Origin of Species*. Based on research he conducted while traveling on the HMS *Beagle*, Darwin argued that all living organisms have a single source and have diversified over time because of natural selection and mutation. Darwin argued that this process was accomplished through what Herbert Spencer called the "survival of the fittest." In doing so he rejected the scriptural account of the origin of species (and ultimately the origin of everything). Also, he articulated that man is no more than an intelligent animal.

Second, Karl Marx (1818–1883) was a philosopher and political theorist known for the political scheme that bears his name. Marxism influenced many areas, including politics. Marx, being a child of modernism, famously stated, "Religion is the opiate of the masses."[27] He believed that religion pacifies people and that it is ultimately unnecessary.

Marxism itself argues for a political system in which everyone receives an equal share of a society's wealth. In its ideal form, Marxism creates a government-run utopia, and man, in himself, is sufficient to rule. The underlying assumption to this governmental theory is that man is fundamentally good and, where he is not, right motivators and structures can make him good. Marxism thus stands in stark contrast to the orthodox doctrine of mankind's total depravity.

Third, Julius Wellhausen (1844–1918) was a German biblical scholar, known for propagating a composite theory of the Pentateuch called the Documentary Hypothesis. While Wellhausen was not the originator of the theory, scholars often credit him with being the popularizer of it. The Documentary Hypothesis holds that Moses did not write the first five books of the Bible (contrary to what Scripture itself states). Instead, the Torah comprises *at least* four different sources, identified as JEDP (Jehovist/Yahwist, Elohist, Deuteronomy, Priestly), which a later redactor (compiler) synthesized. By propagating this theory, Wellhausen laid an axe to the root of belief in traditional authorship of the beginning of the Bible, thereby effectively rejecting the doctrines of the Bible's inerrancy and inspiration. By rejecting this long-held view of Scripture, Wellhausen paved a way for others also to reject the authority of the Bible.

Fourth, Friedrich Nietzsche (1844–1900), a German philosopher, infamously wrote, "God is dead. God remains dead. And we have killed him."[28] While we would argue with much of what Nietzsche proposed, we would agree on one foundational truth: he believed that a rejection of God would lead to a rejection of a universal understanding of the world. Though he did not care for the institutional church, Nietzsche nonetheless wrestled with the person of Jesus, who, he thought, was unique and somewhat akin to his *Übermensch*, or "Overman/Superman."

Nietzsche's concept of the *Übermensch* was based on the concept of a psychologically superior human being. Therefore, Nietzsche was more concerned with how Jesus epitomized the best of humanity, not with Jesus as God incarnate. This point further demonstrates Nietzsche's (and modernism's) push to put man in the place of God. Nietzsche himself did not believe in an objective reality but rather in perspectivism (knowledge is inescapably limited to one's perspective). Consequently, he fully rejected Christianity. He stated, "I call Christianity the one great curse, the one great intrinsic depravity, the one great instinct for revenge for which no expedient is sufficiently poisonous, secret, subterranean, petty—I call it the one immortal blemish of mankind."[29]

Finally, Sigmund Freud (1856–1939) was a neurologist and the founder of psychoanalysis. Freud contended that belief in God, psychologically speaking, is necessary only in more primitive civilizations to quell violence and to promote peace. Although he considered himself Jewish, he believed that God is an illusion. Freud argued that belief in God is a manifestation of man's need for a strong father figure. He also articulated three parts of the human psyche: the id, the ego, and the superego. Freud often described these as external forces, not as personal attributes with inherent moral guilt as the Scriptures teach.

Ultimately, what we see in these five thinkers is a complete rejection of the premodern era's supernaturalism and is instead a radical focus and elevation of the autonomy of the person. In science Darwin rejected the scriptural account of our origin. In politics Marx rejected the need for religion in society. In biblical studies Wellhausen rejected the inerrancy and dependability of Scripture. In philosophy Nietzsche rejected the notion of God and universal truth, thus rejecting objective reality. Lastly, in psychology Freud rejected God, postulating Him as nothing more than a supreme imaginary friend, used to make us behave. These men (and many more) effectively "sold the farm" on the supernatural and, unbeknownst to them, laid the groundwork for postmodernism.

The Effects of Modernism

At its inception, the philosophy of modernism was incredibly optimistic. After all, the term *Enlightenment* would likely not be used in despondency. After fixing man as the center of life, thus contributing to the rise of secular humanism, modernists believe that progress and human innovation may lead to utopia.

Modernists aim to integrate self-evident truths and the autonomous self to make mankind the center of understanding. Unfortunately, that approach leaves no room for transcendent truths, specifically those transcendent truths that call us to die to self (Mark 8:35; Luke 9:23; 1 Corinthians 15:31; Galatians 2:20) and to proclaim Christ as King (Isaiah 9:6; Daniel 2:44; Matthew 2:6; Revelation 11:15).

To be sure, modernism has significant philosophical problems. In fact, it began its trajectory on a faulty foundation. Leroy Forlines writes,

> Modernism is forced to believe that matter is eternal. Some may speak of energy rather than matter, but that is only a matter of terminology. From the viewpoint of naturalism either matter is eternal, or "nothing" created matter out of nothing. The latter is unthinkable. There can be no proof that matter is eternal, but in modernism it is a logical necessity. The next problem is that either life must have been eternal, or it must have originated from life-less matter. It is quite a burden to be borne by the intellect, but the usual belief of modernism is that life originated from lifeless matter. This is considered to be an easier burden on the mind than believing that life has been eternal. Modernism is in effect giving many of the attributes and activities usually ascribed to deity to matter. Matter is eternal. Matter is the Creator. Does matter seem to be capable of all this? Modernism fails the test of causal adequacy.[30]

Modernism and its implications were not quarantined to philosophy courses and textbooks. Like all ideas, modernism has had consequences, which are evident in art, music, culture, and theology.[31] Furthermore, those who sought to synthesize modernism and Christianity did not realize that these philosophies could not coexist. In the words of E. J. Carnell, "Not all men immediately saw that one cannot have his cake and his penny, too; one cannot succumb to the scientific method as the only way of knowing reality, and still cling to Christian supernaturalism."[32]

The attempt to synthesize modernism and Christianity led to the rise of theological liberals who embraced biblical criticism, rejected supernaturalism, and overthrew the gospel. Carnell explains that "liberalism has reduced Christianity to an ephemeral, normless, this-worldly, tentative religion. In its abortive zeal to harmonize Christianity and the empirical sciences, it has given the conciliatory olive-branch to the latter. It has made Christianity empirical and scientific, rather than science Christian—the difference is vast!"[33] In other words, modernists have consistently overemphasized a view of epistemology that stands at odds with the Christian worldview.

Defining Postmodernism

The Decline of Modernism

The problem with modernism (which is the problem with any worldview other than Christianity) is that it does not deliver on its promises, nor does it satisfy our deepest needs. Modernism promised a secular humanist utopia, but then the world erupted into war not once but twice. Modernism promoted autonomous, empirical "truth" but resulted in eugenics and genocide.

"We have for many years moved with a brash confidence that man achieved a position of independence which rendered the ancient restraints needless," wrote Richard Weaver, summarizing the modernist program. "Now, in the first half of the twentieth century, at the height of modern progress, we behold unprecedented outbreaks of hatred and violence; we have seen whole nations desolated by war and turned into penal camps by their conquerors; we find half of mankind looking upon the other as criminal."[34]

Modernism fell out of favor and was replaced by postmodernism. Francis Schaeffer argued that the move from modernism to postmodernism in society—what he calls falling below the "line of despair"—was not an automatic change but rather a slow one. This paradigmatic shift in culture did not relegate itself to one area of thought, though. Schaeffer argues that the move from modernism to postmodernism began with philosophy, then moved to art, music, general culture, and ultimately affected theology.[35]

The Rise of Postmodernism

As I stated previously, understanding our cultural context is not only helpful but also necessary because of a singular reality: truth. The tension at the heart of both modernism and postmodernism is one concerning truth. For these two worldviews, the issue "ultimately involve[s] . . . whether there is a source of truth higher than, and independent of, man; and the answer to the question is decisive for one's view of the nature and destiny of humankind," according to

Weaver.[36] Therefore, we must understand how these worldviews have defined truth.

Our failure to reckon with these philosophical developments of the past and present is wreaking havoc in our culture. Schaeffer explained, "The tragedy of our situation today is that man and woman are being fundamentally affected by the new way of looking at truth and yet they have never even analysed the drift which has taken place." Even those from Christian homes and in the Christian community are experiencing a dislocation. "Young people from Christian homes are brought up in the old framework of truth. In time they become confused because they do not understand the alternatives with which they are being presented. Confusion becomes bewilderment, and before long they are overwhelmed. This is true not only of young people, but of many pastors, Christian educators, evangelists and missionaries as well."[37] To borrow an illustration from my colleague Phillip T. Morgan, we find ourselves in a "cultural riptide of extreme magnitude."[38]

Understanding postmodernism can be challenging. In some ways, the moniker itself is unhelpful, with many thinkers referring to it as rather elusive and vague.[39] The movement we call postmodernism is not entirely a rejection of modernist ideas; it might be better understood as the natural progression of modernism. Thinkers like E. Darrell Holley have thus referred to it as transmodernism. Others, like Charles Taylor, have referred to this period as late modernism.[40] Thomas Oden called it ultramodernism or hypermodernism.[41] Whatever we call this movement, scholars generally agree that something momentous has happened within Western culture recently and that we should take note of what that "something" is.

Many argue that postmodernism in the United States exhibited itself in the 1960s and is often tied closely to the sexual revolution of that decade. While the exact beginning is difficult to pinpoint, the United States unquestionably demonstrated what David Wells refers to as "the heart of the postmodern rebellion" during that time. He continues, explaining that postmodernists "turned away from meaning that is fixed and universal and turned toward meaning that is private and subjective. It shifted away from absolute moral norms to those that are simply private."[42] Forlines has also made observations about this shift, explaining, "Modernism presupposed that nature was rational and moral, but it had no foundation to support this presupposition."[43] Thus postmodernism arose from the ashes of modernism, and, because modernism was too optimistic, postmodernism has emerged as equally pessimistic.[44]

McGrath notes that postmodernism also rejects what he calls "uniformitarianism," which he defines as "the insistence that there is only one right way of thinking and only one right way of behaving."[45] Ironically, though postmodernists argue that any form of "uniformitarianism" is too exclusive, postmodernism itself exhibits its own form of uniformitarianism in pushing for the "universality" of relative truth among people and groups. Because postmodernism denies the existence or knowability of universals, culture has lost all sense of harmony.

To understand our cultural dilemma better, Carnell encourages us to think of a student in the throes of postmodernism in the public university: "Having so departmentalized our fields of learning that they completely lack a coordinating principle of harmonization . . . the modern student [must] wander from classroom to classroom, armed with no metaphysical principle to unite the disciplines he studies."[46] Additionally, this context relegates traditional Christian teachings, such as believing that the Bible is a true and sufficient guide for life and for practice, to the dustbins of history. Such people believe that these teachings are antiquated and myopic. "The denial of universals carries with it the denial of everything transcending experience," writes Weaver. "The denial of everything transcending experience means inevitably—though ways are found to hedge on this—the denial of truth."[47]

The Effects of Postmodernism

Postmodernism has also severely affected the church. It has created the challenge of correctly responding to this new cultural orientation while simultaneously remaining faithful to historical orthodoxy. An institution, such as the church, that holds to the vital facts of history, transcendent absolute truth, and a holistic metanarrative stands at odds with the ethos of postmodernism. For these reasons, Christians must understand the effects postmodernism may have on them and those around them.

First, postmodernism rejects any knowable, transcendent, universal norm and metanarrative. According to postmodernism, if we enlist a universal metanarrative, then we oppress everyone under that absolute (totalitarian) metanarrative. Forlines explains, "The rejection of a metanarrative by postmodernism means that they reject the idea of a worldview that explains the whole of reality."[48] Postmodernism often denies the existence of objective truth or else the possibility of knowing truth; in either case, it cannot explain why things are the way they are.

Second, by rejecting truth, the only "transcendent" norm in postmodernism is the community or the self. Remember that premodernism gladly affirmed external transcendent truth. Then modernism moved away from the supernatural but still held to absolutes, which were proven empirically and not through any kind of *a priori* knowledge (knowledge resulting from theoretical reasoning without necessary reference to observation and experience). However, because empiricism proved an insufficient method for explaining the complexities of the world around us, the search for transcendence moved only further inward. As a result, postmodernism exchanged an objective conception of universal truth for a subjective one, which is often demonstrated in expressive individualism (consider the expressions "my truth" and "your truth" in place of "the truth").

Expressive individualism refers, in the words of Taylor, to a "kind of self-orientation," which "seems to have become a mass phenomenon."[49] Yuval Levin defines it similarly as "not only a desire to pursue one's own path but also a yearning for fulfillment through the definition and articulation of one's own identity. It is a drive both to be more like whatever you already are and also to live in society by fully asserting who you are." Expressive individualism is hyper-subjective self-determination. Levin then links expressive individualism to the concept of liberty, saying, "The capacity of individuals to define the terms of their own existence by defining their personal identities is increasingly equated with liberty and with the meaning of some of our basic rights, and it is given pride of place in our self-understanding."[50] However, expressive individualism positively signifies a misappropriation of liberty.

Finally, therefore, postmodernism completely rejects any authority greater than self or community. Although previous cultural ideologies planted the seeds for this rejection, it has fully bloomed within our current culture. Each of the "five bad boys of modernism" cast off the authorities of their past, as did Wellhausen with long-held beliefs about Scripture and Darwin with belief in biblical creation. Postmodernism represents a disposition whereby its adherents fully commit to the position of modernism. Thus postmodernism does not assert any ultimate authorities, any real arbiters of truth, except the self or the community.

Postmodernity has affected our culture in some wide-reaching ways. It shows itself in the avant-garde forms of art that hang in studios and galleries and in the random-chance music of men like John Cage. It shows itself in the everyday life of ordinary men and women who quip to one another: "That may be true for you, but it isn't true for me." And it shows itself in our theology and churches, whether in the neo-orthodoxy (what Schaeffer referred to as "neo-liberalism") of mainline denominations, or simply in the relativized and individualized orientation of American evangelical Christianity.

Thinking about the significant effects of postmodernism can give any Christian pause and cause plenty of concern. It has prompted a swath of believers to panic and to cast off their long-held beliefs for a more culturally relevant form of Christianity. Yet we must remember that we are a people who are founded upon *the* Truth, even if, throughout history, we have wrestled with what truth is and how to ascertain it.

David Wells speaks to this foundation in *The Courage to Be Protestant*, saying, "Christianity ... spread with astonishing speed through the apostles' declaration of the gospel and the simple witness of those who had come to know Christ. This proclamation was not simply a telling of their private experience, nor just their own personal opinion. It was not what had become truth for *them*." He continues, "It was a proclamation about truth for *all*. The gospel, which is the same gospel for all people, in all ages, and at all times, is 'the word of truth.' . . . Christianity, in short, is from first to last all about *truth!* It is about he who is the Way, the *Truth*, and the Life."[51]

As believers, whether we are fighting against the ideas of modernism, postmodernism, or something else, we have one thing that the world does not have. We have the truth, manifested in Christ, and revealed to us in the Holy Scriptures. To borrow from Wells, we should not be scared. Instead, we should have courage.

Conclusion

As we look back over this short survey of history and the various influences of ideas, we should remember that Christianity itself embraces the long arc of history. Christianity is not afraid of the history of ideas but instead *is* the history. As Greg Forster writes,

> Christianity is preeminently the historical religion. Other religions offer escapes from time and history. . . . Among the world's religions, only Christianity really gives us history. The indispensable key that unlocks all the secrets of human existence is not some set of timeless philosophical truths, nor some body of eternally recurring ritual and unchanging institutions. It is a series of events unfolding in history: creation, fall, redemption, glorification. The Christian message is good news. Good news is not just good, it's also news. "News" is just another word for a report of history.[52]

Therefore, as we think about how these various worldviews impact the world around us, we should also realize that Christians are messengers of the greatest news in the universe. No matter the cultural moment, the gospel holds joy, hope, and life for all those who will believe. And that will always be relevant.

CHAPTER THREE

The Classical Conservative Tradition

Matthew Steven Bracey

Thus far *Christians in Culture* has invited readers to reflect on God's call that Christians engage the culture (chapter one), and it has surveyed a history of ideas that has impacted contemporary Western cultures (chapter two). This chapter turns to specific principles that will help us think through how to engage the myriad cultures and subcultures in which we find ourselves. These principles, or canons, come from the inherited wisdom of the classical conservative tradition, which itself is a distillation of the beliefs emerging from a premodern Christian ethic.

Conservatism does not refer simply, or even primarily, to a political disposition. Instead, it describes someone's broader worldview, including what he or she believes about culture, history, knowledge, ethics, aesthetics, the state, and more. In the words of Roger Scruton, conservatism is "about our whole way of being."[1] The Christian conservative is one who seeks to conserve that which accords with the good, the true, and the beautiful, which God has revealed in space and time (i.e., history), including, significantly, in the Hebrew-Christian Scriptures.

The modern conservative tradition emerged during a period when Western intellectuals began disregarding a Hebrew-Christian view of life and the world. Thus it came from a consensus that takes seriously the principles of true, revealed religion. Many credit Russell Kirk (1918–1994) with reviving conservatism during the heyday of liberalism.[2] He was a prolific author of more than three dozen works, including non-fiction, novels, short stories, and letters.

At a time when critics believed that conservatism was in its twilight, Kirk illuminated its still shining light. For this reason, Rod Dreher identifies Kirk as "one of the key figures in the renascence of twentieth-century American conservatism."[3] Kirk emphasized key leaders of conservatism throughout his writings, many of whom this chapter will consider, including Edmund Burke (1729–1797), a foundational figure for conservatism.

Over the course of his career, Kirk studied the underlying principles of conservatism throughout the centuries. In *The Politics of Prudence*, he outlined ten canons of conservatism, which we will reflect upon.[4] This chapter will present conservatism and discuss aspects of liberalism and progressivism. To some extent, these descriptions are broad, general overviews of each category that do not touch on exceptions and nuances. Nonetheless, each description paints a picture of conservatism, liberalism, or progressivism that is generally true. What follows are brief summaries of each category that will be expanded upon throughout the chapter.

Conservatives, liberals, and progressives each seek the *common good* yet differ in how they define it according to their distinctive theological-philosophical commitments. In addition, conservatives, liberals, and progressives differ in their dispositions toward the past and toward change. More specifically, a conservative seeks to *conserve* the wisdom of the past yet also recognizes the need for sensible change amid new circumstances and injustices.

A liberal emphasizes *liberty* (individual and/or social) to the disregard of prudent limitations on what a person or society should or should not do. (People sometimes use the term *classical liberal* to distinguish this position from "progressive liberals." However, I will designate these positions by *liberal* and *progressive* through the duration of this chapter.) The conservative also values liberty but believes that it is subject to the limitations of truth and morality, which the tradition bequeaths to its children.[5] Consequently, the conservative views liberty as a means for human flourishing, whereas the liberal views it as an end itself, which can lead to sinful license as well as personal and societal disaster.[6]

Modern-day usage of the terms *conservatism* and *liberalism* often confuses their technical definitions for popular meanings. For example, people may define a conservative as someone who upholds traditional morality and believes in small government and probably votes Republican, whereas they may see a liberal as someone who is open-minded about morality and affirms a bigger role for government and probably votes Democrat. Or people may popularly associate conservatism with right-wing politics and liberalism with left-wing politics. However, the historic meanings of *conservatism* and *liberalism* defy popular characterizations, in addition to the broader point that these movements refer to broad systems of thought about culture generally rather than referring to politics exclusively.

Finally, a progressive elevates *progress* to the point of detriment to tradition; in popular usage, people may use the word *liberal* when they properly mean *progressive*. The conservative also advocates for progress but views it as the progress *of* history, as opposed to progress (away) *from* history. Thus the conservative respects tradition yet also seeks its prudent reformation when it exhibits injustice. On the contrary, the progressive (and the liberal to some extent) often pursues violent revolution to overthrow tradition. In sum, the conservative values true liberty and true progress without falling prey to errors of the liberal and the progressive. We now turn to Kirk's ten canons of conservatism and a fuller presentation of these ideas.

Canon One: Belief in an Enduring Transcendent Moral Order

First, conservatism affirms belief in an enduring, transcendent moral order.[7] Morality is not left simply to the changing whims of individuals or groups of people but is rooted in an objective, supernatural reality. Hence conservatives affirm that divinity has revealed the moral order through divine revelation and natural law.[8] The moral order teaches men and women how to live as individuals within society. Conservatives seek first to order themselves—reason, emotion, and will—according to the moral law.

Contrary to the liberal individualism of people like John Locke and John Stuart Mill, conservatism teaches that it is not good for man to be alone (Genesis 2:18). William Ernest Henley's lines illustrate liberal individualism well: "I am the master of my fate: I am the captain of my soul."[9] By contrast, conservatism teaches that people should order their souls not according to their own ingenuity but rather within a community of like-minded people. In other words, conservatives extol true religious instruction. Numerous thinkers illustrate this point.

In the words of Burke, writing in the context of eighteenth-century Europe, "Nothing is more certain, than that our manners, our civilization, and all the good things which are connected with manners, and with civilization, have in this European world of ours, depended for ages upon . . . the spirit of religion."[10] He described religion as "one of the great bonds of human Society; and its *Object* the supreme good, the ultimate end and *Object*, of man himself."[11] Similarly, John Crowe Ransom, a scholar of the American South, included "the pulpit," an image representative of *religion*, among the "social arts."[12] Thus conservatives affirm that religion (the pulpit) plays a significant role in peoples' socialization.

From well-ordered souls come well-ordered societies and political orders. However, the more society and state are filled with people who have not ordered their souls, the more disorder that society and state will experience. Hence conservatives observe an important relationship between the "inner order of the soul" and the "outer order of the commonwealth."[13] Kirk wrote, "True politics is the art of apprehending and applying the Justice which ought to prevail in the community of souls."[14]

Whereas conservatives and classical (Lockean) liberals alike hold that civil bodies ought to fashion laws in a manner that is consistent with the natural law, progressives often affirm a positive law (the law that a legislative body establishes) to the exclusion of natural law.[15] In other words, progressives would order society without reference to a transcendent moral order that a divine Being has embedded within the heart of man and the structure of the world (Romans 1:18–20; 2:14–16)—without adherence to true religion. Instead, they may establish laws on social consensus, which changes from generation to generation. By contrast, conservatives seek to order their personal and public lives according to what T. S. Eliot (1888–1965) called the "permanent things."[16]

Canon Two: Adherence to Custom, Convention, and Continuity

The second canon of conservatism is adherence to those customs and conventions of the tradition that reflect the transcendent moral order so that contemporary generations establish continuity with past generations. Conservatives value this principle for several reasons.

First, it pushes us to recognize that we stand on the shoulders of our predecessors.[17] "I know, of course, that in America especially there is the impulse among Christians to forget the work of the hands and hearts and minds of those who have preceded us in the faith and, with New Testament in hand, to think and act as if the church began here this morning," observes Nicholas Wolterstorff. "To me this seems profoundly dishonoring to our forebears in the faith."[18] Instead, conservatives uphold what the Hebrew-Christian tradition calls honor of father and mother (Exodus 20:12; Deuteronomy 5:16)—what G. K. Chesterton called the "democracy of the dead" and Jaroslav Pelikan referred to as "the living faith of the dead."[19] Conservatives invite their ancestors to speak into their lives. They avoid what C. S. Lewis called chronological snobbery, the belief that their age is superior to that of their forebears.[20]

By contrast, non-conservatives display "contempt for tradition."[21] As Roger Scruton put it, they demonstrate "oikophobia," or "the repudiation of inheritance and home."[22] However, Burke offers a sobering warning about that way of thinking:

> When ancient opinions and rules of life are taken away, the loss cannot possibly be estimated. From that moment we have no compass to govern us; nor can we know distinctly to what port to steer.... We are afraid to put men to live and trade each on his own private stock of reason; because we suspect that this stock in each man is small, and that the individuals would do better to avail themselves of the general bank and capital of nations, and of ages.[23]

Without custom, convention, and continuity, the individual loses an important foundation and flounders.

In the eyes of conservatives, though, tradition embodies the collective wisdom of the past. To forsake it is to forsake the tried and the true. Time has not tested the morals of the present as it has the morals of the past. Thus this canon serves as a check "both upon man's anarchic impulse and upon the innovator's lust for power."[24] It humbles humanity's prideful tendencies.

A second reason conservatives defend customs and conventions that reflect the transcendent moral order is that these form the glue that holds together families and communities and societies.[25] Groups of people necessarily find collective identity according to the habits, histories, morals, and stories they share. An individual's identity is formed within a particular cultural and historical context. Custom and convention contain the content of one's cultural heritage, one's cultural memory.

Cultural memory plays an important role in the conservative sensibility. Rudyard Kipling illustrated this theme beautifully in *The Jungle Books*. The brown bear, Baloo, is teaching Mowgli, the Man-cub, about the ways of the Jungle and, speaking about the *Bander-log* (the Monkey-Folk) states, "They have no law. . . . Their way is not our way. They are without leaders. They have no *remembrance*. They boast and chatter and pretend that they are a great people about to do great affairs in the Jungle, but the falling of a nut turns their minds to laughter and all is forgotten."[26] Conservatives' adherence to customs and conventions is adherence to the law of a people. Non-conservatives do not have the law of the past because they have forgotten it; they do not remember it.

Dreher, who writes as a Christian conservative, connects these various dots of history, culture, and memory: "Without collective memory, you have no culture, and without a culture, you have no identity. . . . History is in the stories we tell ourselves about who we were and who we are. . . . History is culture—and so is Christianity. To be indifferent or even hostile to tradition is to surrender to those in power who want to legitimate a new social and political order."[27] But notice that these progressive totalitarians succeed only insofar as they sever the link between collective memory and a new social and political order. For such reasons, conservatives remember the past.

Yet conservatism does not uphold the past indiscriminately. Conservatives affirm only those customs and conventions that accord with the transcendent moral order. Where the morals of the past have disordered men and women and their societies, conservatives support change. But the manner of change is important. Conservatism has historically supported evolutionary change (slow) over revolutionary change (sudden).[28] Societal change is not like a quick and (relatively) simple inpatient surgery; rather, it is like an outpatient surgery requiring great care and patience.

Kirk compared civilization to a complex system of roots. The innovator who chops abruptly at the tree of convention "never knows how near the taproot of the tree he is hacking" so that the "destroyers of custom demolish more than they know or desire."[29] Consequently, the irresponsible hewing off of tradition may amount to more than a felled tree; it may result in the death of a civilization. In such cases, the cure proves worse than the disease. In Kirk's words, "It is perilous to weigh every passing issue on the basis of private judgments and private rationality."[30] Conservatives also seek to cure civilization from its diseases. But rather than swinging and slashing, they aim carefully to prune the ecosystem of civilization so that the disease is removed, and the life is preserved.

Canon Three: The Principle of Prescription

The principle of prescription is the third canon of conservatism. Prescription is simply the application of those customs and conventions of our forebears.[31] Conservatives recognize that we not only inherit a particular tradition but also apply its truths to present-day problems.

Kirk explained, "Conservatives sense that modern men and women are dwarfs on the shoulders of giants, able to see farther than their ancestors only because of the great stature of those who have preceded us in time."[32] Civilizations truly progress not by tearing down the past but rather by building on the truth that the past would bequeath. Because conservatism is a disposition about life generally, this principle applies to issues of morality, culture, religion, community, and even the created order, in addition to economics and politics.[33]

Burkean conservatism has tended to speak about the principle of prescription in terms of "prejudice." To modern ears, the affirmation of prejudice may sound offensive because of its association with racism, sexism, and the like. However, Burke lived in the eighteenth century when people distinguished between just prejudices and unjust prejudices. At its etymological root, prejudice refers simply to "pre-judgment," or a judgment that has been made beforehand. Prejudices are good and righteous insofar as they reflect truth and cultivate virtue within people but are bad insofar as they do not.

For example, Burke pointed to the folly of liberal rationalists who would "cast away the coat of prejudice" and "leave nothing but the naked reason." He argues that prejudice offers "ready application in the emergency; it previously engages the mind in a steady course of wisdom and virtue, and does not leave the man hesitating in the moment of decision, sceptical, puzzled, and unresolved."[34] In other words, good prejudices teach men and women how to act and react virtuously in the circumstances of life almost as a matter of instinct.

Significantly, Burke held that men and women learn good prejudices from religious instruction. Man is "by his constitution a religious animal," and the "church establishment," which teaches us "profound and extensive wisdom," is "the first of our prejudices."[35] The "sacred temple" of the "religious system" is "purged from all impurities of fraud, and violence, and injustice, and tyranny."[36] Further, Burke described "the Christian religion" as "our boast and comfort, and one great source of civilization among us."[37] In short, Burke contended for the prejudice of Christian religion because it forms people according to justice and virtue.

No one has the resources or time to reason out *everything* for himself (to say nothing of the faults of human reason). Thus everyone will accept *some* things on the authority of those they trust.[38] This proposition means that all people have prejudices because they necessarily inherit what Kirk described as the "half-intuitive knowledge that enables [them] to meet the problems of life without logic-chopping."[39]

For example, a father may rightfully have a prejudice toward a dog that is foaming at the mouth and thus prescribe that his three-year-old son should not go near the dog. However, the father may also judge it best not to talk to his toddler about the finer details of rabies at that moment so that the child may accept his father's prejudice on authority and without "logic-chopping."

Contemporary expressions of conservatism often (understandably) drop the language of *prejudice* owing to its regrettable association with various injustices. Perhaps that is prudent. However, the broader point of conservatism is that we should look back before we look forward and bring the past to bear on the present to the extent it reflects the transcendent moral order.

By contrast, liberalism often tends toward a "consuming individualism" that disregards the prescriptions of the broader community of humankind, whether past or present.[40] Progressivism may emphasize community more than liberalism but tends to treat the prescriptions of the past in a disrespectful and smug manner. Conservatism guards against these liberal and progressive tendencies by honoring the age-old wisdom of the past. In the words of Burke, "The individual is foolish . . . but the species is wise."[41]

Canon Four: The Principle of Prudence

Wisdom, fittingly, is the subject of canon four. Consonant with belief in transcendence (canon one), conservatism confronts the challenges of life from the perspective of the divine and not simply from the perspective of the self. The Hebrew-Christian tradition teaches that the "fear of the Lord" is the beginning of wisdom (Proverbs 1:2a, 7). Significantly, Solomon, author of the Proverb, identifies the "father's instruction" and "mother's teaching" (1:8) as the means through which we learn true wisdom—the experience of *tradition*.

Kirk characterized this principle this way: "Providence has taught humanity, through thousands of years' experience and meditation, a collective wisdom: tradition, tempered by expedience. A man should be governed in his necessary decisions by a decent respect for the customs of mankind; and he should apply that custom or principle to his circumstances by a cautious expedience."[42] By so saying, Kirk demonstrated that wisdom is a synthesis of the first three canons of conservatism—providence (canon one), custom (canon two), and application of custom (canon three).

Hence conservatives do not approach life's difficulties in an impetuous or rash manner but rather a careful and patient one. "The march of providence is slow," said John Randolph of Roanoke; "it is the devil who always hurries."[43] When addressing injustices within families, cultures, and societies, conservatives weigh the long-term consequences of a given course of action or policy choice against its short-term gains—is the price worth the cost? Thus conservatism is reflective, not reactionary. In addition, conservatives do not adopt a solution to a problem merely because it is convenient or popular. In fact, the path of wisdom may be difficult and trying.

By contrast, non-conservatism, by definition, does not conserve the "collective wisdom" that Providence has revealed through the ages. In fact, it distorts it. As Thomas Sowell has rightly observed, propaganda about the past has replaced education about the past, resulting in "twisting our history for ideological purposes."[44] Both liberalism and progressivism may characterize tradition as oppressive and enslaving when it impedes their pursuit of individual and/or social license. Or, as Jean-Jacques Rousseau put it, "Man is born free, and everywhere he is in chains."[45] Rousseau centers freedom in man rather than in an inherited tradition that reflects divine truth.

Non-conservatism tends to focus on short-term gains over long-term costs, such that it can come to demonstrate the very meaning of "unintended consequences." The clarion call of "progress" does not make much room for patience, whether patience with the past or patience for the future.

Canon Five: The Principle of Variety

Conservatism and non-conservatism differ not only about morality, tradition, and virtue but also on their views of the human species and human systems, whether cultural, social, or political. Conservatism holds that human existence is full of "proliferating variety." This principle means that humankind comprises distinct men and women who are different from one another, in contrast to the "narrowing uniformity, egalitarianism, and utilitarian aims of most radical systems."[46] A Christian conservative maintains that these differences result from the purposeful design of the Creator.

Conservatives readily acknowledge that man's mental capacities are limited; they do not have a God's eye view of the world. Such limitations extend to man's knowledge of the human species and human systems. Hence the principle of variety guards men and women from the dangers of pride, the vice of the Enlightenment presumption of liberalism and progressivism. In addition, this principle reinforces the virtue of humility because it preserves the mystery and wonder of existence.

On Natural Distinction

Many people have pointed to the principle of natural distinction within the human species. Such thinkers include (in order of birth) Edmund Burke, John Adams, Pope Leo XIII, Abraham Kuyper, C. S. Lewis, Friedrich Hayek, Pope John Paul II, Russell Kirk, Michael Novak, Thomas Nagel, Roger Scruton, Thomas Sowell, and others. Among the natural distinctions that they mention are differences in ability, capacity, complexion, energy, figure, grace, health, height, intelligence, muscles, nerves, skill, strength, talent, and will.[47] In short, we are all unique.

"There is no equality of persons," wrote the Dutch statesman and theologian Abraham Kuyper. "Everywhere one man is more powerful than the other, by his personality, by his talent and by circumstances.... There is no life without differentiation, and no differentiation without inequality."[48] By so stating, Kuyper was not arguing that some people have greater dignity or inherent worth than others; in reality, that position is characteristic of liberal and progressive movements that have supported policies of eugenics and abortion.

Instead, Kuyper was acknowledging the inequalities that all people have *by nature* (a position I further explore below from the Scriptures); human beings are not uniform but distinct. Because God has uniquely created all people, we differ in terms of our characteristics, personalities, abilities, interests, and gifts.

On Social Order

As this chapter has demonstrated, conservatism is not, first, a political program. It is, first, a worldview that affirms certain beliefs concerning divinity, morality, tradition, virtue, and so forth. Thus conservatism, as Burke articulated it in eighteenth-century England, was not a new thing but rather a rebuttal to the rising tide of liberalism. Nonetheless, conservatism (including Christian conservatism) has cultural and social and political implications, as all full-orbed worldviews do. This fifth canon teases out some of those implications.

Kirk explained that the conservative affection for variety and mystery demonstrates that "civilized society requires orders and classes, as against the notion of a 'classless society.' With reason, conservatives have been called 'the party of order.'" Orders and classes emerge because men and women make different choices concerning their native abilities.

Consequently, conservatives stand against attempts at unnatural "political leveling" whereby "order and privilege are condemned" because such leveling stands against a law of nature that no amount of progressive engineering can undo.[49] This reality does not mean that all such orders and privileges are good (some are, while others are not), only that an order of some kind will necessarily exist by nature according to how people apply themselves—whether they are sluggardly or hardworking, for instance (Proverbs 6:6–11). This reality also does not mean that all such orders and privileges are fixed, as if people cannot elevate their station (a point we will consider at greater length below).

The ancients readily recognized the conservative sensibility of ordered societies. For example, Plato envisioned a society of artisans, craftsmen, and leaders.[50] The apostle Paul also imagined an ordered society but used an anatomical example: just as the ear, the mouth, and the toe play different roles within the body, so also different people play different roles within a given community (1 Corinthians 12:12–31). Lewis, commenting on this imagery, states, "In the Church we strip off this disguise [of artificial equality], we recover our real inequalities, and are thereby refreshed and quickened. . . . The Christian life defends the single personality from the collective, not by isolating him but by giving him the status of an organ in the mystical Body."[51] Hence human beings necessarily manifest functional inequalities (differences) within a society because they fulfill distinct roles resulting from their natural variabilities. Even so, all human beings have ontological equality as divine image-bearers (Genesis 1:26–27).

On Justice as Equality of Ontological Condition

Conservatism's recognition that all human beings are different in certain respects has great implications for its vision of justice. That is, conservatives do not conflate equality with justice or inequality with injustice. Sometimes justice and equality overlap, but other times they do not. "Justice and equality are not the same," explained Ronald Nash. "There are inequalities that are just and equalities that are unjust."[52] The opposite also holds true: some inequalities are unjust, while some equalities are just.

To illustrate, Kuyper and Kirk explained that inequalities resulting from the disparate treatment of people before God, the church, or the law constitutes injustice.[53] However, distinctions in biological sex, ethnicity, nationality, socioeconomic status, status of birth, and the like do not, in any way, remove people's ontological equality as human persons. All men and women are equal in terms of human dignity and moral worth. Consequently, all human beings have equal standing before God in Christ (Galatians 3:26–28), deserve impartiality before the church (James 2:1–13), and warrant the due process of habeas corpus before the law (the right to appear before a judge or court).[54]

On the other hand, inequalities resulting from nature are not unjust per se. Natural differences in height, talent, and so forth are not unjust. However, if we could somehow make everyone the same height or give everyone the same talent, we would render a condition of natural equality that is unjust because God has chosen to make people dissimilar. In addition, "equality of condition," said Kirk, "means equality in servitude and boredom."[55] The multitudinous variety that God has given people is exciting and interesting.

Inequalities resulting from the consequences of free choices are also not unjust per se. That one student earns a grade of A but another a grade of F is also not unjust. However, the effect of giving every student an A, thereby rendering a condition of consequential equality, would be unjust because the law of nature gives people what they merit.

Conservatism seeks to *conserve* the classical view of justice found in the Hebrew-Christian and Greco-Roman traditions. For example, King David, the prophet Jeremiah, the apostle Paul, and even Jesus Himself acknowledge that different people will bear different fruit and receive different rewards according to their free choices (Psalm 1:1–6; Jeremiah 17:5–8; Luke 6:39–45; 2 Corinthians 5:10). Similarly, everything from Aristotle's *Nicomachean Ethics* to the Roman *Institutes of Justinian* associate justice with rendering to people their due. The early church figure Augustine of Hippo brings these two traditions together in the *City of God*, arguing that people receive their just deserts according to the fruit they bear or the crop they harvest.

Nevertheless, progressivism criticizes this conception of justice, arguing that it results in social injustice. Thus progressives argue for what Sowell calls a "social justice" that would eliminate those inequalities resulting from nature and free choice. The progressive vision of justice, says Sowell, "seeks to correct the happenstances of fate, the gods or the cosmos, and could more fittingly be called cosmic justice instead of social justice."[56] However, man is not God; man is neither transcendent nor omniscient.

Sowell continues, saying that "a cosmic injustice is not a social injustice, and proceeding as if society has both the omniscience and the omnipotence to 'solve' the 'problem' risks anti-social justice, in which others are jeopardized or sacrificed."[57] In short, Sowell criticizes the progressive vision of justice that plays the character of God, a role for which he is unfit. Even the liberal Walter Lippmann observed, "Man is no Aristotelian god contemplating all existence at one glance," and for man to presume that he is results in more harm than good.[58]

In sum, conservatism upholds the principle of variety, which explains the natural distinctions and social orders that exist among humankind. Justice is not violated by inequalities resulting from nature and free choice. Rather, justice is honored when societies treat people as having equal dignity and moral worth before God, the church, and the state.

On Justice as Equality of Socioeconomic Condition

In contrast to the conservative vision of justice, the progressive vision promotes socioeconomic egalitarianism. For example, in the early-nineteenth century, Rousseau posited that humankind could eliminate material inequalities and societal injustices by returning to a hypothetical pre-society that existed in the state of nature without orders, divisions, and classes. He pointed to the ideal of the "noble savage," the belief that man is naturally good and that civilization has made him bad.

However, Rousseau's anthropology was faulty on several fronts. Social order is an inescapable fact of life because people differ in ability and interest. Leaders will emerge in any group, even in Rousseau's hypothetical pre-society. And where leadership exists, distinction exists. Order itself is not an injustice; rather, immoral order is an injustice. When bad leaders emerge, conservatism works toward the reformation of right order and good leadership, whereas progressivism aims to eradicate bad leaders via revolution.

William Golding effectively illustrated the foolishness of Rousseauian thinking in *The Lord of the Flies*. In this novel, adolescent boys find themselves alone on an island in the state of nature. The state of nature brings not blessing but disaster as things go from bad to worse to deadly as Jack and his compatriots rule the island. "If natural distinctions are effaced among men, oligarchs fill the vacuum," Kirk explained.[59] That is exactly what we see in *The Lord of the Flies*, as destruction, mayhem, and murder ensue.

The so-called noble savage is, in fact, the ignoble savage. The state of nature cannot escape the establishment of society and order; therefore, the problem is not order but the immorality of people within that order. Rousseau failed to account not only for man's natural inequalities but also for his natural bent toward wicked behavior rather than virtuous behavior, an observation that leads to canon six.

Canon Six: The Principle of Imperfectability

Like canon five, canon six concerns anthropology. Just as humankind is subject to "proliferating variety," he is also subject to imperfectability, at least in this life. "Sin," explained Kirk, is "the greatest force that agitates society."[60] This principle, like the prior canons, reflects the Hebrew-Christian tradition (Psalm 14:3; 53:3; Jeremiah 17:9; Matthew 15:9; Romans 5:12; 1 Corinthians 15:22).

Because sin disorders the soul, it disorders the community; and because it disorders the community, it disorders the soul. While conservatives believe that the soul and community can be reformed, they do not affirm the notion of a progressive-socialist utopia.[61] The bigger the institution, the greater the probability exists within it for corruption and wickedness, whether in Big Business, Big Government, or Big Tech.

Liberalism and progressivism also observe wrongdoing in the world but misdiagnose the root problem: they "deny that humanity has a natural proclivity toward violence and sin."[62] Rather than building on the foundations laid by Paul or Augustine, liberals and progressives build on those laid by Pelagius, Locke, and Rousseau.[63] Rather than following the doctrine of original sin, they follow the teaching of *tabula rasa* (blank slate), denying that humankind is born into sin with innate knowledge. They believe that, if man has learned sin, he can unlearn it; in addition, they exculpate man from moral blame because he is the victim of a bad hand or a crummy circumstance.

Because liberalism and progressivism reject the doctrine of original sin, these systems also advance wrongheaded proposals to solve the problems that wreak havoc in our lives and societies. Concerning poverty, for example, liberals often tell people, "Pull yourself up by your bootstraps," whereas progressives say, "Let the experts handle it," and point to governmental programs. However, J. D. Vance, who grew up in Appalachian poverty, criticizes each of these answers, arguing that neither of them worked in the case of his family or in the case of many other Appalachian (and, more broadly, American) families.[64]

Progressivism particularly, because it fails to temper its ambitions with the sheer mystery of human existence, presumes that "education, positive legislation, and alteration of environment can produce men like gods."[65] However, man is not a programmable machine. Man-made macro-proposals cannot account sufficiently for the multitudinous differences existing between individuals. Nor can they solve the underlying issue that has given rise to these difficulties in the first place, namely sin; external solutions cannot fix internal problems. As James Fitzjames Stephen notes, man has a "fearful disease," and God alone has the antidote for man's spiritual sickness.[66]

These observations demonstrate why progressive, big-government schemes of socialism cannot finally succeed. Undoubtedly, not all philosophers and economists define socialism precisely the same way but make different judgments and nuances about its essence—to say nothing of its myriad forms (e.g., democratic socialism versus revolutionary socialism). However, Nash offers a helpful working definition, explaining that it is "an economic system that replaces the market as the means of providing for consumption, production, and distribution with central planning. Physical capital under socialism is either owned or controlled by the state."[67]

According to Paul Elmer More, socialism affirms that leaders of the state are basically good and benevolent, doing what is best for society, and that members of the state will work for a wage to produce that which is not theirs but rather the government's to use and redistribute as its leaders see fit.[68] However, critics of socialism point to several problems with this way of thinking.

For one, state leaders lack sufficient integrity to steward others' earnings. Governmental actors are susceptible to and guilty of the very problems they are presuming to correct. In addition, their wrongdoing is more dangerous than that of an individual because of the position of power they hold. A man who poorly manages his own property succeeds in ruining but one life; a man or woman (or group of people) who poorly manages the property of a nation succeeds in ruining the lives of multitudes.

Second, critics of socialism argue that a society based on the premise that man will work for that which he will not see is bound to fail, resulting in greater problems than those that can follow non-socialist proposals. To do good work, man requires incentive, such as that of reaping the fruit of his harvest or receiving the wages of his work. And without some incentive, men and women will not work hard, seeking innovation and excellence, but will take the path of least resistance. In time, without some incentive for its citizens or subjects to work, society will default, for, in the words of Edwin Lawrence Godkin, "Who will pay the bills of socialism?"[69]

Third, critics of socialism have observed that it gives wrong answers not only about the nature of man but also about the existence of God. In his masterpiece *The Brothers Karamazov*, Fyodor Dostoyevsky traced the religious conversion of the character Alyosha, who serves to counterbalance his atheistic brother Ivan. In the passage below, Dostoyevsky, who interacted with various forms of socialism throughout his lifetime, tied the question of religion and socialism together:

> As soon as he [Alyosha] reflected seriously he was convinced of the existence of God and immortality, and at once he instinctively said to himself: "I want to live for immortality, and I will accept no compromise." In the same way, if he had decided that God and immortality did not exist, he would at once have become an atheist and a socialist. For socialism is not merely the labor question, it is before all things the atheistic question, the question of the form taken by atheism to-day, the question of the tower of Babel built without God, not to mount to Heaven from earth but to set up Heaven on earth.[70]

Thus, according to Dostoyevsky and these various critics, socialism represents not simply a particular system of government and economics but more fundamentally a particular view of man and of God, a view that (as this overview has demonstrated) conflicts with the basic tenets of conservatism.

Conservatism recognizes that man cannot build heaven on earth. "All that we reasonably can expect," said Kirk, "is a tolerably ordered, just, and free society, in which some evils, maladjustments, and suffering will continue to lurk."[71] Conservatives take seriously the imperfectability of man and reflect that truth in their economic-political vision of society, which is the subject of canon seven.

Canon Seven: Belief in the Close Link between Freedom and Property

With canon seven, the creeds of conservatism become more explicitly political even if not exclusively so. Conservatives believe in a close link between freedom and property, each reinforcing the other.

Freedom and Property

Conservatism upholds a view of freedom that understands it as a means of human flourishing, not an end itself that may lead to sinful license. Again, this latter view of freedom characterizes liberalism. Conservatives' view of freedom demonstrates an additional reason for their preference for smaller governments over larger ones. Virtuous people within society and state may more easily address corruptions within localized sovereignties than they can within national ones.

Corrupt governments are like angry cats: if you have an angry house cat by the tail, you may get some scratches, but at least you will escape with your life; if you have an angry lion by the tail, the prospect of survival (much less flourishing) is much more tenuous. Similarly, small corruptions are easier to manage than big ones.

Conservatives recognize that men and women apply their freedoms to all kinds of goals, a key goal being the pursuit of property. Property may refer to land and buildings and such (sometimes called *real property*, see 1 Kings 21), as well as to clothing and computers and vehicles and other movable properties (sometimes called *personal property*, see Exodus 22). All working-aged people pursue property. Property refers, at root, to the fruit of one's labor, a concept introduced in canon six, which we use in the exchange of goods and services. In the words of Burke, people "have a right to the fruits of their industry; and to the means of making their industry fruitful."[72]

Through the centuries, numerous thinkers have pointed to reasons for the superiority of private property rights over alternative arrangements. For example, Thomas Aquinas provided several practical insights. First, private property encourages greater personal responsibility and stewardship: "Every man is more careful to procure what is for himself alone than that which is common to many or to all: since each one would shirk the labor and leave to another that which concerns the community." People generally care for their homes better than they do for public spaces.

Second, private property encourages greater order in society: "Human affairs are conducted in more orderly fashion if each man is charged with taking care of some particular thing himself, whereas there would be confusion if everyone had to look after any one thing indeterminately."

Third, private property stimulates greater peace in the state: "A more peaceful state is ensured to man if each one is contented with his own. Hence it is to be observed that quarrels arise more frequently where there is no division of the things possessed."[73] This last point especially flows from an accurate view of man's imperfect nature (canon six).

Thomas's observations reflect the broader Christian tradition. For example, the Eighth Commandment, "You shall not steal" (Exodus 20:15; Deuteronomy 5:19), has no meaning unless individuals have a right to private property against illegitimate takings, including that which occurs under the guise of governmental sanction.[74] On this latter point, John Calvin wrote that one form of theft occurs by a "concealed craftiness" whereby "a man's goods are snatched from him by seemingly legal means."[75]

Chad Brand extends this principle explicitly to the government's confiscation and redistribution of its citizens' property, which he characterizes as "sin" and "legalized theft" representative of the policies of socialists and social democrats.[76] Similarly, Carl F. H. Henry observed rightly that "forced redistribution" and "welfare statism" does not accord with true justice (as previously observed in canon five) partly because it does not rightly honor freedom and property.[77]

The prospect of owning property, conjoined with the exercise of true freedom toward that goal, results in human flourishing. As introduced in our discussion of canon six, conservatives recognize that human beings naturally respond to the incentives before them. The possibility for earnings creates incentives for men and women to work. These earnings afford people the opportunity not only to purchase, consume, and reinvest but also to do good, practice charity, and exercise hospitality. Kirk wrote elegantly on these points:

> For the institution of several property—that is, private property—has been a powerful instrument for teaching men and women responsibility, for providing motives to integrity, for supporting general culture, for raising mankind above the level of mere drudgery, for affording leisure to think and freedom to act. To be able to retain the fruits of one's labor; to be able to see one's work made permanent; to be able to bequeath one's property to one's posterity; to be able to rise from the natural condition of grinding poverty to the security of enduring accomplishment; to have something that is really one's own—these are advantages difficult to deny. The conservative acknowledges that the possession of property fixes certain duties upon the possessor; he accepts those moral and legal obligations cheerfully.[78]

Socialism

Like conservatism, liberalism has tended to support private property rights. However, progressivism has more frequently denounced such doctrines in favor of collectivist and socialist schemes. "The ancient rights of property, especially property in land, are suspect to almost all radicals; and collectivistic reformers hack at the institution of private property root and branch."[79]

Sadly, some people, including some Christians, are attracted to the vision of socialism as a type of charity. For example, some have pointed to Acts 2:44, in which Christian believers share "all things in common" as support for socialism. However, this passage is an argument against socialism, not for it, for two reasons: (1) the sharing occurred precisely because the believers maintained an ownership interest in their property; and (2) the sharing was voluntary rather than coerced. In addition, a responsible hermeneutic will conflate neither description with prescription, nor an ecclesial practice with a political one.

Advocates for socialism may also commend it in the name of peace, equality, and justice. However, that vision of socialism is a false vision that does not accord with reality. Revolutionary forms of socialism (which have, at times, manifested in communism) have resulted in the deaths of millions upon millions of people in countries like China, Russia, North Korea, and Cambodia, as well as others, to say nothing about the ways that day-to-day human flourishing has diminished in these places.[80] Kirk explains, "The ideologues who," in the name of socialism, "promise the perfection of man and society have converted a great part of the twentieth-century world into a terrestrial hell."[81]

Even democratic socialism, for which we see support among some in the United States, exchanges a material right for a natural one. However, state-enforced socioeconomic outcomes do not demonstrate justice but rather injustice because they disregard the differences of each person's nature and efforts. "Since talent, ability, energy—indeed the sheer attachment to life—are unequally distributed," writes Scruton, "so too therefore will be property."[82]

To revisit an illustration given above, the student who earns a grade of F does not deserve an A, and the student who earns a grade of A does not deserve an F. To give both the same result, say a grade of C, irrespective of their natural abilities or personal study habits, would be unjust. In the words of Burke, "All men have equal rights; but not to equal things."[83] Thus unequal outcomes, whether with respect to grades or property, are not *prima facie* unjust.

In addition to differences in peoples' ability and application, Sowell argues that socialistic policies have served to decrease, not increase, human flourishing, such as in Burma, Ghana, the Ivory Coast, and Thailand. These are nations that were once prosperous but adopted socialistic policies and now struggle with poverty. Sowell's study of these issues leads him to conclude, sarcasm full in tow: "Socialism in general has a record of failure so blatant that only an intellectual could ignore or evade it."[84]

A key problem with socialism is that it does not sufficiently account for the imperfectability of man (canon six): men and women are sinful, including those in leadership. And where national leaders manage the entire country's means of production, as is the case with socialism, rather than thousands upon thousands of what Alexis de Tocqueville described as little governments (towns, counties, states), the potential for utter catastrophe is high.[85]

Man, whether he is a leader or not, is not naturally noble but self-serving. Men and women require accountability, without which corruption will ensue. Perhaps they unjustly benefit themselves based on "insider" knowledge, or perhaps they inconsistently apply market rules. Just consider the wealth the leaders of corrupt socialist states (or governments) can have and then compare that to the poverty of the populace at large.

Finally, the system of socialism leads to the spoiling of freedom. Because it destroys private property rights, it destroys the freedom even to steward what God has given us as the fruit of our labor. According to socialist dogma, any property an individual has is "his" only because the government has given it to him. But that makes the state into a god that giveth and taketh away. For such reasons, Dostoyevsky discussed the religious dimensions of socialism, which he associated with atheism; and, for such reasons, Kirk warned, "Separate property from private possession, and Leviathan [the state] becomes master of all."[86]

Free Market

Contemporary conservatives view the free market as the superior economic-political system. The free market incentivizes work, innovation, and excellence. It preserves freedom and property. It provides greater goods and services for lower costs to everyone in society. It can produce that which is good and useful even from what others have intended for bad. For example, the butcher who works because he is greedy still benefits the person who purchases meat from him to feed his family.

However, socialism cannot generate good results from bad intentions; often, it cannot even generate good results from good intentions. To be sure, the free market is not perfect and requires maintenance when wicked men and women use it to ill effect. Still, it is a superior system to socialism because it does not concentrate its power in the hands of a few. Concentrated power, Jay Richards and Thomas Sowell argue, generates even greater poverty than power that is divided among the myriad participants of a market.[87]

Undoubtedly, Christian conservatives acknowledge the imperative to care for the poor (James 1:27), but they contend that the free market provides a more humane and virtuous solution to poverty than socialism does. Markets operate on the idea that anyone, including those in poverty, can generate wealth through the application of ingenuity, hard work, and tenacity. John Bolt contends that the poor, who should be treated with dignity because they bear God's image, should receive opportunities to create wealth but do not have a right to the fruit of another's labor; yet also argues that all people, including the wealthy, have an obligation of charity.[88] Wealth is not a limited commodity where those with less have less because those with more have more. Richards identifies that error as the "materialist myth," which is based on a false view of wealth as being limited when, in fact, it is not.[89]

Michael Novak observed that a person with less property in a free society with unequal outcomes is still better off than he or she would be in a coercive society with equal outcomes: "While the free society will never be able to guarantee the outcomes desired by those who speak of 'social justice,' it does bring more rewards to all, on all reward levels, than any known system. It cannot and will not produce equal rewards for all, only higher rewards for all."[90] Hence the free market has the capacity to give everyone more wealth and does not seek to take or steal from one to give to another.

Invariably, the topic of wealth disparity follows discussions of wealth and poverty (which is covered at greater length in chapter fourteen of *Christians in Culture*). Wealth disparity usually results from differences in how people receive their wealth, which encompasses income, gifts, inheritance, and the like, as well as in how people spend their wealth. Whereas progressives often assert that such disparities are intrinsically unjust, conservatives (and liberals) generally hold that wealth disparities may be just or unjust, depending on the underlying reasons for the disparity in question.

For example, an income gap between two people is likely unjust if it results merely from differences in ethnicity, gender, or other such designations that relate to man's nature or ontology because the conservative concept of justice recognizes that all people bear equal dignity and moral worth. However, an income gap resulting from differences in workers' respective roles and responsibilities, or from differences in their work ethic, does not constitute injustice. To demonstrate, the CEO of a company who works more hours, assumes more risk, and bears more responsibility may rightly receive greater compensation than the entry-level employee. Likewise, the hardworking employee may rightly receive greater compensation than the lazy one. Again, the conservative view of justice recognizes that people receive what they earn. Hence income gaps are unjust when they reveal an underlying injustice but not otherwise.

Wealth disparity arises from differences not only in how people receive wealth but also in how they spend it. For example, a given society will value certain goods and services differently than other goods and services. Consequently, a greater percentage of people will spend money on popular or useful products, thereby creating wealth disparity between the creators of those products and the people creating less helpful products. However, in this scenario, no one has committed injustice. And, insofar as the better product advances human flourishing, justice has been honored, and everyone has benefitted, including the poor, who can use such products to advance their stations.

Robert Nozick proposed a thought-experiment in the 1960s involving the basketball player Wilt Chamberlain to illustrate these points:

> Now suppose that Wilt Chamberlain is greatly in demand by basketball teams, being a great gate attraction. . . . He signs the following sort of contract with a team: In each home game, twenty-five cents from the price of each ticket of admission goes to him. . . . The season starts, and

people cheerfully attend his team's games; they buy their tickets, each time dropping a separate twenty-five cents of their admission price into a special box with Chamberlain's name on it. They are excited about seeing him play; it is worth the total admission price to them. Let us suppose that in one season one million persons attend his home games, and Wilt Chamberlain winds up with $250,000, a much larger sum than the average income and larger even than anyone else has. Is he entitled to this income? . . . If so, why?[91]

In this example, we see a massive income gap, and hence massive wealth disparity, between Chamberlain and the typical ticket holder, and yet no injustice has occurred. In fact, everyone has made free choices and received benefits: Chamberlain gets paid doing what he enjoys (playing basketball), and fans pay a relatively small fee (25¢) to do what they enjoy (watching Chamberlain play basketball). Other people choose not to pay the fee to watch Chamberlain shoot ball and, instead, save their money. Even they unwittingly contribute to a financial disparity because they have an additional 25¢ compared to those who chose to pay the fee; and still no injustice has occurred.[92]

Further complicating the scenario is the question of whether the fans who chose to purchase tickets to see Chamberlain act wisely or foolishly in spending their money. Imagine that one fan's financial circumstances are such that she cannot responsibly afford to purchase a ticket but does so anyway; her foolish decision generates wealth disparity but not injustice. This extended thought-experiment demonstrates that wealth disparities may exist where justice is honored because people receive and spend money with different goals and within specific cultural contexts.

In sum, the reason for unequal outcomes in a free society is that a free society allows its citizens to receive and spend wealth according to their own ingenuity, hard work, and tenacity. The condition of freedom within a free market provides the ability for all people, regardless of socioeconomic status, to apply themselves to worthy ends and to associate with people who can help them realize their goals.

The Christian conservative's prayer is not that everyone would have the same socioeconomic status, for God makes some rich and others poor according to His designs (2 Samuel 2:7). It is rather that the rich and poor would recognize their common bond before their Maker (Proverbs 22:2), that the wealthy would practice generosity toward the poor (Proverbs 19:17; 22:9; 28:27), that the rich and poor alike would serve the Lord with their wealth (Luke 21:1–4), and that men and women would learn contentment in whatever circumstance they find themselves, be it prosperity or poverty (Philippians 4:10–14; see James 1:9–11).

Canon Eight: Belief in Voluntary, Local Communities

Voluntary and Local

Whereas canon seven extends the value of freedom to property, canon eight extends it to community. Specific people choose freely to associate with certain groups, but perhaps not with others, according to their unique desires, hobbies, interests, and so forth. Conservatism thus defends the right of free association, which gives rise to local community, in contrast to "involuntary collectivism."[93]

Conservatism gives preference to the ideal of voluntary, local community over that of the national or global community because local communities generally protect the interests and rights of their members better than these others do. Hence Kirk wrote, "In a genuine community, the decisions most directly affecting the lives of citizens are made locally and voluntarily."[94] Progressivism tends to point to national solutions for society's problems.

However, local communities generally occupy a better position to address such challenges because they are invested in their members in a way that national communities, by their nature, are not: that is, we care about the people in our local communities differently than we do the people in other communities. Finally, voluntary, local communities teach people true virtue better than national and global communities do. "It is the performance of our duties in community that teaches us prudence and efficiency and charity."[95] Usually, people learn wisdom and love in the ordinary flow of communal life.

Big and Centralized

In contrast to the conservative ideal of voluntary, local community, progressivism idealizes big, centralized governments. However, such systems are woefully inefficient or, as Novak explained, "impersonal, inefficient, and expensive far beyond their original forecasts," as well as "too blind, too out-of-touch with the millions of individual wills at play in society, too domineering, too preachy."[96] Centralized governments, because they are so big, normally deal in generalities, thereby not addressing particularities and exceptions as effectively as non-centralized governments do, and, consequently, centralized governments become impersonal.

Centralized governments also pose a genuine threat to justice and human flourishing. "A central administration, or a corps of select managers and civil servants, however well intentioned and well trained, cannot confer justice and prosperity and tranquility upon a mass of men and women deprived of their old responsibilities," Kirk writes. "That experiment has been made before; and it has been disastrous."[97] For such reasons, conservatives support voluntary, local governments over improperly coercive, centralized ones. This principle does not mean that the conservative never supports national powers; sometimes national powers are better positioned and equipped to carry out certain tasks (e.g., border disputes). The point is that these instances are few and far between compared to localized powers (the exception rather than the rule).

The United States was originally founded with this conservative ideal in mind. The Constitution enumerates eighteen explicit powers to Congress.[98] The Tenth Amendment then states, "The powers not delegated to the United States by the Constitution, nor prohibited by it to the States, are reserved to the States respectively, or to the people."[99] The grammatical presumption of this amendment favors smaller communities over larger ones: first, toward the people ("reserved to," a positive construction); second, toward the states ("nor prohibited," a negative construction); and third, toward the federal government ("not delegated," a still stronger negative construction).

However, the current state of affairs in the United States has reversed this presumption through an imbalanced federalism with the presumption going to the federal government, then to state governments, and then finally to smaller communities. Rather than operating from the bottom up, the United States increasingly works from the top down, but, by so doing, it violates the sanctity of the local community. Bruce Ashford and Chris Pappalardo refer to this arrangement as "statism," which "occurs when the state oversteps its boundaries by inappropriately interfering with the healthy development of the other spheres."[100] Local communities cannot flourish with respect to the arts, technology, vocation, leisure, sport, and so forth (the subjects of this book) with authoritarian regulation.

Issuing from its support for big, centralized governments, progressivism also promotes the redistribution of property, wealth, and income (as mentioned in our discussion of canons six and seven), which is characteristic of socialist and totalitarian systems. According to this view, experts of government occupy a better position than property owners to manage what individuals have earned or received by their or their families' work. Individual rights of private ownership take a back seat to the presumption of state actors who redistribute peoples' property according to whim. However, conservatism observes that such schemes undermine the goal of human flourishing rather than enhancing it.

In summary, conservatism upholds the ideal of voluntary, local community because it better protects peoples' interests, it better preserves justice, and it better promotes human flourishing and virtue. The promotion of freedom serves good ends. However, freedom is not its own end but requires righteous restraints, leading to the ninth canon.

Canon Nine: The Principle of Restraint on Power and Passion

Canon nine makes explicit what is implicit in canon eight: the principle of prudent restraint on power and passion (fervor or lust).[101] Additionally, this canon follows naturally from the principle of imperfectability (canon six).

Conservatism seeks to restrain the power and passion of men and women because it recognizes that they can do great harm to the self and to society when they fail to practice restraint. Conservatives hold that no individual, or group of individuals, should have absolute power in any sphere. Christian conservatives specifically support the principle of restraint because they recognize that God alone is sovereign and holy. By contrast, humankind is finite and fallen.

For such reasons conservatives support certain economic and political systems over others—free markets over socialism, localism over statism and cosmopolitanism—because these systems better restrain the powers and passions of participants than others. The localism of conservatism avoids the disorder that can result from two extremes: on one hand, it avoids atomism (or individualism), which characterizes liberalism; and on the other hand, it avoids collectivism, which characterizes progressivism.

Whereas conservatives seek to restrain power and passion because they maintain that men and women are not the proper objects of great power, non-conservatives tend to give too much power to the individual (liberalism) or to the collective (progressivism). Historically, liberalism gives way to anarchy and then to tyranny. "When every person claims to be a power unto himself," explained Kirk, "then society falls into anarchy. Anarchy never lasts long, being intolerable for everyone.... To anarchy there succeeds tyranny or oligarchy, in which power is monopolized by a very few."[102] Governments assume too much power because people assume too much power.

The history of the United States demonstrates that basic pattern. Most of America's founders recognized the truth of this canon of restraint, which is evident in three ways. First, they did not concentrate power in one branch of government but spread it across three: the legislative, executive, and judicial. Second, they did not concentrate power in one sovereign but across numerous sovereignties: a federal government and myriad state and local governments, with the presumption going to smaller governments and communities (as detailed above in the discussion on canon eight). Finally, the founders did not address the country's first president with the kingly designation of "his majesty" but with the humbler yet respectful title of "his excellency."

Regrettably, the march of American history has been one against this conservative principle of restraint as its liberal and progressive presidents have slowly but surely thrown off the prudence of conservatism and embraced the imprudence of radical individualism and collectivism. We have seen the rising tide of liberalism with the emergence of the so-called right of privacy, which has become a pretext for all manner of immoral license; and we have seen the rise of progressivism with the concentration of greater and greater power in the federal government and especially in the executive branch at the expense of civil societies, smaller governments, and other governmental branches. In the case of progressive presidents, they all, in the moment, make the case that they wield power for good. Whether they do is debatable. But even assuming they do, ignobility follows nobility; corruption follows concern.

Historical and literary reflection demonstrates that short-term gains are often not worth the long-term costs. As the story of Jacob and Esau teaches us, a mess of pottage is not worth one's birthright (Genesis 25:29–34). Or, as J. R. R. Tolkien's *The Lord of the Rings* reminds us, whoever wields the one ring of power, whether the individual or the collective, does so unto destruction because the human heart is corrupt. Kirk's warning is poignant: "In every age . . . men and women are tempted to overthrow the limitations upon power, for the sake of some fancied temporary advantage. It is characteristic of the radical that he thinks of power as a force for good—so long as the power falls into his hands."[103] Stated another way, everyone supports theocracy, so long as they play the part of "Theo."[104]

Conservatism strikes the right balance between the poles of individualism and collectivism, and the licentiousness and authoritarianism that can result from them. The failure to curb man's lust for radical autonomy (liberalism) and for radical authority (progressivism) ends in human suffering rather than in human flourishing. "Constitutional restrictions, political checks and balances, adequate enforcement of the laws, the old intricate web of restraints upon will and appetite—these the conservative approves as instruments of freedom and order."[105]

Hence conservatism protects the interests of the community (e.g., historical and local) and the individual so that the individual does not supersede the community (liberalism), nor the community swallow the individual (progressivism). The way to avoid both abuses is the way of wisdom (canon four), which we learn from obedience to transcendence (canon one) and from respect for tradition (canons two–three).

Canon Ten: The Balance of Permanence and Change

Finally, conservatism balances permanence and change in life and society. The unreflective man alone accuses conservatives of being stuck in the past; the thinking person understands that conservatives value the past because it informs the present both positively and negatively.

Positively, the past informs the present by offering it permeance through custom, convention, and prescription. Such practices establish continuity with those parts of the past that accord with the right ordering of things. Conservatives submit themselves to its true teachings, which reveal the way of true progress. Hence Burke denounced those who work toward "the subversion of that order of things, under which our part of the world has so long flourished, and indeed, been in a *progressive* state of improvement."[106] That is, true progress does not reject the past but rather brings its revelation of order and flourishing into the present.

While not rejecting true progress, conservatism nonetheless rejects progressivism, or "the cult of Progress, whose votaries believe that everything new necessarily is superior to everything old."[107] Progressives emphasize change without the appropriate counterbalance of permanence, which "gives us stability and continuity; without that Permanence, the fountains of the great deep are broken up, society slipping into anarchy."[108] The past provides a positive foundation for the present and future without which the structure of civilization, culture, society, and the like falls.

However, the past also provides warnings and is valuable in teaching us which mistakes to avoid. C. S. Lewis wrote winsomely on this point:

> The only palliative is to keep the clean sea breeze of the centuries blowing through our minds, and this can be done only by reading old books. Not, of course, that there is any magic about the past. People were no cleverer then than they are now; they made as many mistakes as we. But not the same mistakes. They will not flatter us in the errors we are already committing; and their own errors, being now open and palpable, will not endanger us. Two heads are better than one, not because either is infallible, but because they are unlikely to go wrong in the same direction.[109]

This negative function of history—reminding us of the mistakes of the past—illuminates the role change plays within the conservative sensibility. Conservatism values the past (permanence) but is not stuck there (change). Burke wrote, "A state without the means of some change is without the means of its conservation."[110] Likewise, Kirk explained, "Change is essential to the body social, the conservative reasons, just as it is essential to the human body."[111] Hence conservatives aim to establish discontinuity with those parts of the past that do not accord with the right ordering of things.

However, the manner of change is important. Conservatism values contemplation over innovation. Burke remarked, "A spirit of innovation is generally the result of a selfish temper and confined views." The innovator disregards not only the past but also the future. "People will not look forward to posterity, who never look backward to their ancestors."[112] However, the failure to consider the future can have disastrous consequences for future generations. For this reason, conservatives warn against "hasty innovation" because it lacks care and reflection.[113] Nonetheless, conservatives do support "prudent reform and improvement" and "reasoned and temperate progress."[114] Slow and steady wins the race.

The Fifth Article of the Constitution of the United States illustrates this conservative sensibility. It explains the process by which the Constitution may be amended: first, an amendment must be proposed, and second, it must be ratified. An amendment may be proposed in two ways: either the Congress may propose an amendment after two-thirds of both houses (the House of Representatives and the Senate) shall "deem it necessary," or a convention of states, which is "two thirds of the several States," may propose an amendment. Once an amendment has been proposed, it must be voted on. An amendment may be ratified in two ways: either the legislatures or the ratifying conventions "of three fourths of the several States" may ratify a proposed amendment.[115] This process balances permanence and change well because it guards against hasty innovation, especially hasty innovation that does not reflect the people and their representatives. Conservatism *conserves* what is worth conserving (permanence). Yet it seeks to *liberate* individuals and societies from injustices so that men and women might *progress* to greater flourishing (change).

Conclusion

The conservative ethic is a principled one that emerges from a Christian outlook. It respects divinity, as well as the dead. Conservatives look to transcendence and to tradition to give them wisdom as they confront the challenges of life, whether in family, society, or politics. In addition, they follow a realistic anthropology, one that recognizes that human beings are mysterious and distinct yet also imperfect and sinful and that a well-functioning society arises from a right view of man. Consequently, a good society values freedom, property, and voluntary community; it places prudent restraints on the worst aspects of man's nature; and it accepts the dual roles of permanence and change.

Coda: Crunchy Cons

In 2006, Rod Dreher published *Crunchy Cons*, in which he included a statement that is inspired by the classical conservatism of thinkers like Burke and Kirk. It serves as a helpful companion to Kirk's ten canons:

1. We are conservatives who stand outside the contemporary conservative mainstream. We like it here; the view is better, for we can see things that matter more clearly.
2. We believe that modern conservatism has become too focused on material conditions, and insufficiently concerned with the character of

society. The point of life is not to become a more satisfied shopper.
3. We affirm the superiority of the free market as an economic organizing principle, but believe the economy must be made to serve humanity's best interests, not the other way around. Big business deserves as much skepticism as big government.
4. We believe that culture is more important than politics, and that neither America's wealth nor our liberties will long survive a culture that no longer lives by what Russell Kirk identified as "the Permanent Things"—those eternal moral norms necessary to civilized life, and which are taught by all the world's great wisdom traditions.
5. A conservatism that does not recognize the need for restraint, for limits, and for humility is neither helpful to individuals and society nor, ultimately, conservative. This is particularly true with respect to the natural world.
6. A good rule of thumb: Small and Local and Old and Particular are to be preferred over Big and Global and New and Abstract.
7. Appreciation of aesthetic quality—that is, beauty—is not a luxury, but key to the good life.
8. The cacophony of contemporary popular culture makes it hard to discern the call of truth and wisdom. There is no area in which practicing asceticism is more important.
9. We share Kirk's conviction that "the best way to rear up a new generation of friends of the Permanent Things is to beget children, and read to them o' evenings, and teach them what is worthy of praise: the wise parent is the conservator of ancient truths. . . . The institution most essential to conserve is the family."
10. Politics and economics will not save us. If we are to be saved at all, it will be through living faithfully by the Permanent Things, preserving these ancient truths in the choices we make in everyday life. In this sense, to conserve is create anew.[116]

CHAPTER FOUR

Creation, Sin, and Renewal

Matthew McAffee

Why should Christians care about creation? Does the Bible not teach us that the world will be burned up and done away with someday? After all, are we not all going to heaven when we die? Why does it matter what happens to this earth? Why does it matter what happens to our bodies since they will decay and return to dust? Why do we have to work? Is that not a result of the Fall?

These questions and others like them can easily betray an unbiblical view of reality. One might even say that such questions arise from premises altogether foreign to the overall trajectory of the Scriptures. They begin in the wrong place.

Because so much confusion exists on this topic, the task of this chapter is to probe the nature of our relationship to creation. We may be tempted to think that the advocates of environmentalism are foisting these questions on us. Nevertheless, the basic question—what is our relationship to creation?—is central to the overarching story of Scripture. The roots of this question run deep within the lines of the creation story of Genesis 1–2.

Furthermore, our responsibility to creation concerns more than our stewardship of the environment, which is commendable. Rather, it is much broader in scope than that. In fact, our relationship to creation serves as one of the opening scenes in God's story of redemption and therefore has central importance in the Scriptures.

This chapter will begin with a survey of the creation story: who are we, and what is our relationship to creation? A proper theology of creation is essential for a sound biblical theology, as well as for an understanding of our role in culture. Also important in this task is establishing what was lost when Adam and Eve sinned: what is sin, and how has it affected creation? How has sin impacted our role with regard to creation? What is God doing to renew creation, and what is our role as human beings in that renewal?

In many ways this chapter lays the groundwork for the subsequent chapters of this book. Though it discusses our role in creation, the framework extends to all our cultural work. The message of Scripture is one of hope and restoration. Once we properly understand this truth, we will begin to be transformed in the way we think about the world, including the various subjects covered in part two of this book. Hence this renewal of the mind will affect our understanding of tradition and history, the arts and entertainment, literature and labor, technology and science, politics and economics, sports and recreation, and more.

THE INHABITANTS OF AN INHABITABLE WORLD

Principles

The creation account offers a picture of the ideal world that God created before sin marred and distorted it. In many ways it gives us an idea of where we are heading in God's future restoration. Within this portrayal of God's creation, we find a place of habitation that God designed appropriately for its inhabitants.

Genesis 1 offers a lofty view of God's creative activity. The text places emphasis on the spoken word of Elohim. By the word of His mouth, created things come into being: "Let there be light . . . and it was so."[1] The movement of each creation day builds in anticipation of the sixth day, the creation of humankind.

The first few scenes of creation depict the formation of the cosmos. At the very beginning of everything, God created the heavens and the earth by the sheer power of His word. But as Genesis 1:2 reminds us, the first act of creation produced the formless and void substance of the world that God used to order and fashion something beautiful and lovely. "The earth was formless and void; darkness was upon the face of the deep and the Spirit of God was hovering over the face of the waters."

The activity of the Spirit in this instance designates contemplative preparation as God carefully designs the world He is about to create.[2] This portrayal reminds us of the depiction of Lady Wisdom in Proverbs 8, who declares that she was with God at the very beginning of His creative ways.[3] The creation story is interested not only in the origin of matter (i.e., the stuff of creation) but also about the proper ordering of that matter into a place that is conducive for habitation.[4]

The creation days can be arranged into two corresponding groups: habitations and inhabitants. During the first three days, God turns this unformed substance into suitable living spaces with established divisions of time. God then creates the inhabitants of these inhabitable spheres during the fourth through sixth days. The following arrangement of the creation days demonstrates this correspondence:[5]

	HABITATIONS			INHABITANTS
Day 1	Light and the division between day and night		Day 4	Light-bearing entities and the division of day and night, seasons, and years
Day 2	Heavens and the division between waters below and waters above the firmament		Day 5	Sea creatures and birds
Day 3	Division between land and sea		Day 6	Land animals and humans

Light is established on the first day, overcoming the darkness on the face of the deeps. It provides the means of dividing day from night. On the fourth day, God creates the light-bearing entities to inhabit the universe, further ordering reality into days, seasons, and years. The firmament of the heavens separates the waters below the sky from the atmospheric waters above. These watery habitations—sky and sea—are filled with all kinds of birds and sea creatures. On the third day, God separates the waters under the sky from the dry ground, establishing a suitable habitation for land animals and humans created on the sixth day.

The narrative offers a qualitative judgment of what God has made. Five times throughout the story, we read that God saw that what He had made was good: day three (vv. 10, 12), day four (v. 18), day five (v. 21), and day six (v. 25). Each one of these qualitative statements highlights important aspects of creation:

(1) the distinction of dry land from the sea;
(2) vegetation on the land;
(3) light-bearing entities that govern day and night;
(4) creatures to fill sky and sea; and
(5) beasts to fill the land.

The climax of God's evaluative judgment comes at the end of the sixth day after the creation of humankind. Once God creates humans to steward the earth, He sees all that He has made as very good (v. 31).

Implications

Why is the story of creation important? For one, God has designed the world to be a place of habitation. Inhabitants include inanimate things like the stars of the heavens and animate entities like the swarming sea creatures and the roving beasts of the earth. God's world is a home for all kinds of life. The heavens provide a home for the celestial beings while the earth offers a home for plants, animal life, and human beings. But God established humanity as the *pinnacle* of His creative activity to steward the rest of earth's inhabitants.

Another important observation is that the world is orderly. God has made things with a certain rhyme and reason. Genesis is unlike other creation stories from the ancient world because it does not begin with the chaotic struggle of deities out of which the world was made. In the beginning, God creates the unformed substance of the world and then shapes it into an orderly whole—no divine struggle, no preexisting primordial soup. God stands at the beginning as the Designer and Creator of all things.

The biblical worldview is also distinct from the modern, evolutionary worldview. Darwinism views the world as having evolved over time from random chaos toward a progressive development of order and greater complexity. We cannot reconcile that notion with Genesis 1–2 (see chapter twelve of this book). The world began in the mind of God, coming into being by the word of His power at a particular point in time. In the beginning, God created.

A further implication is that the stuff of creation is pronounced "good"—even "very good." The physical world and its material cultures are not evil but, instead, have intrinsic value. This value derives from the fact that God made it. As Francis Schaeffer once wrote, "The value of the things is not in themselves autonomously, but that God made them, and thus they deserve to be treated with high respect."[6] It is also confirmed by the repeated divine affirmation that it is good.

Scripture stands in judgment against the idea that the material world is fundamentally evil and therefore expendable. The Greek philosophy called Platonism (named after Plato) would come to hold a dualistic understanding of the world. Some expressions of dualism would even teach that the material-physical world is innately evil while the immaterial world is innately good. These would also teach that man can attain the good, the true, and the beautiful only by limiting and ultimately eliminating the physical. The result of this idea is the downplaying of the importance of the physical world, viewing it as a hindrance to the greater realm of the so-called spiritual.

Certain strands of Christianity have been affected by this way of thinking as well. It is all too common to hear people talk about heaven as an escape from the material world. In this way of thinking, death means the destruction of the physical, evil body in exchange for one's spiritual existence in heaven. Creation becomes an evil that must be overcome in order to achieve true spiritual healing. But this perspective is irreconcilable with Genesis 1–2.

Undoubtedly, the entrance of sin into the world in Genesis 3 has devastatingly damaged God's good creation. It does not, however, mean that the creation is now innately evil never to be restored again. The story of redemption and creation renewal tells us otherwise. Besides, we know from Scripture that there are good spiritual beings (angels) and bad spiritual beings (devils and demons). *Spiritual* is therefore not necessarily a synonym for good (or even simply for the immaterial), and neither is *physical* necessarily a synonym for bad.

As we will see, the notion that God made and declared the world to be good has significant ramifications for how we care for it. Identifying what these ramifications are first requires that we give attention to our status as vice regents of the earth.

Vice Regents of the Earth

The Creation Mandate

Two important passages describe the creation of humanity: Genesis 1:26–29 and 2:7–8, 15–25. The first passage describes the latter part of the sixth day of creation. According to Genesis 1:26–28, mankind was created in the image of God:

> God said, "Let us make man in our image, according to our likeness, that they might rule over the fish of the sea, over the birds of the heavens, over the beast, and over all the earth, and over every creeping thing that creeps upon the earth." God created man in his own likeness; in his likeness he created him; male and female he created them. And God blessed them and God said to them: "Be fruitful, multiply, fill the earth and subdue it, that you might rule over the fish of the sea, the birds of the heavens, and over everything that creeps upon the earth."

Human beings serve as representatives of God on the earth. They mirror Him in both their constitution and function. God constitutionally "makes" mankind in His likeness. Just as God has designed the earth as an inhabitable space for humanity, so too has He carefully crafted mankind for the unique purpose of imaging Him within that habitation. The purpose of this image is found in the clause "that they might rule over the fish of the sea, over the birds of the heavens, over the beast, over all the earth, and over every creeping thing that creeps upon the earth" (v. 26b).

That statement describing our responsibility as divinely commissioned stewards of creation is central to the subject of this chapter. Theologians often call this passage God's "creation mandate," which encompasses several imperatives that each build on the one before it, including being fruitful, multiplying, filling the earth, subduing it, and ruling over its animals. Each of these commands are grounded in the *imago Dei* (image of God). Additionally, because man's *subduing*, or cultivating (Genesis 2:5, 15), the earth and ruling over its animals necessarily results in the phenomenon of culture, some theologians have even called this command the "cultural mandate."[7] The cultural mandate is the foundation that has led to the establishment of all the fields discussed throughout this book: the arts, vocation, technology, the state, economics, sports, and so forth.

Significantly, this mandate is something received. God has given it; therefore, humanity has no right to take it over for himself so that he usurps God's rightful authority over His created order. Instead, he is to exercise God's dominion for God's glory. The psalmist explains it this way: "The heavens are the heavens of Yahweh, but the earth He has given to the sons of man" (Psalm 115:16).

The concept of imageness is likewise seen in the ancient Near Eastern notion of kingship. We can find a notable example in the Aramean inscription of King Hadad-yisʻi. Hadad-yisʻi set up an image of himself in the Syrian city of Guzan to stand before his god Hadad. This image (*demut*) constituted a concrete representation of the royal personage invested with divine purpose and significance.[8] I draw attention to this comparative material simply to stress the royal aspect of the concept of image. It is already present in the biblical account's use of the verb *yarad* "to rule" as the *telos,* or purpose, of God's image in humanity.

Coupled with man's royal status is his priestly function, especially emphasized in Genesis 2. God places Adam in a garden (*gan*), which in Hebrew refers to an enclosed space where God has taken up residence on earth. The caretakers of this temple enclosure serve (*'abad*) as royal priests.

A strong relationship also exists between multiplying and filling and between subduing and ruling. God has invested man with the divine gift of life—procreation—for the purpose of filling the earth, which is the means by which he subdues it. Presumably, as the image of God in man increases in the earth, it is filled with the divine rule of God.

Human beings are caretakers of the world, yes, but God has invested them with a mandate to exercise His rule over it. Furthermore, this purpose is carried out within the confines of our intimate fellowship with the Creator as His temple servants. God takes man and places him in the Garden of Eden so that he might "work/serve it and guard it" (Genesis 2:15). We are both workers within the garden and caretakers who are to protect and preserve it.

The Covenant with Creation

In addition, we should understand the royal and priestly functions of humanity from within the confines of covenant. Many interpreters refer to God's covenant with creation. The first explicit mention of this covenant occurs in Genesis 9 after the flood. God declares to Noah, "I myself am raising my covenant with you" (v. 9). The expression "raise a covenant" implies the ratification of a previously established covenant.[9]

That observation corresponds with what we already know from Genesis 1–2. God had stipulated the obligations of the covenant to Adam and Eve when He told them that they were not to eat of the tree of knowledge of good and evil (Genesis 2:17a). The curse of the covenant is clearly stated as well: "On the day you eat of it you will surely die" (v. 17b). As Augustine explained, all of Adam's children "are breakers of God's covenant made with Adam in paradise."[10] The covenantal context of creation tells us that God created human beings with certain expectations and that, when those expectations were not met, the consequences of covenant unfaithfulness ensued.

A covenant with creation establishes a covenantal framework by which God administers His rule over the cosmos. He did not simply create the world and leave it alone. Rather, God made it and instituted a means of governance. Within that governance, humanity functions as His chief steward. Man should steward the sphere God has given him under His lordship. As Schaeffer perceptively observed, God's covenant with creation during the time of the flood was between God and the earth, not simply between God and man.[11]

Within God's economy (Greek *oíkonomía*), we also must give attention to the various relationships that bear upon our God-given responsibilities as human beings. F. Leroy Forlines describes four basic relationships that we must maintain: our relation to God, self, others, and the created order.[12] The two greatest commandments relate specifically to the basic relationships: (1) you shall love the LORD your God with all your heart, soul, and strength (Deuteronomy 6:5); and (2) you shall love your neighbor as yourself (Leviticus 19:18). Jesus would later refer to each of these commandments. The second of these assumes our relationship to self. We relate to others based on a proper ordering of our internal psyche. What Christians often neglect (or even forget), however, is their relation to creation. But even the Decalogue reminds us that this relationship, too, composes a part of God's expectations for His people. We are to observe the Sabbath, since God created the world in six days and rested on the seventh (Exodus 20:11).

Genesis 2 likewise highlights man's relationship with creation by drawing a close tie between humanity and the ground from which he is made. Verse 7 complements the creation of man as depicted in 1:26, in which man's creation is lofty, emphasizing the divine work of speaking man into existence as the divine image. On the other hand, Genesis 2:7 shows the intimacy of Yahweh, the covenant Lord of Israel, stooping down and forming man from the dust of the ground. Verse 7 reads, "Yahweh God fashioned man (*adam*) of the dust (*'apar*) from the ground (*'adama*), breathed into his nose the breath of life, and man became a living soul (*nepesh hayya*)." Humanity, the image-bearer of God, has been given the life-breath of God. It is what makes him human. He is not simply dust from the ground but is invested with life that can come only from God.

Even so, we must not downplay the fact that man is uniquely connected to the dust of the ground. The words *human* (*'adam*, masculine) and *ground* (*'adama*, feminine) are from the same root, solidifying this connection linguistically. The word *'apar* is also important. Throughout the Old Testament, it is often associated with one's mortality.[13] We are made from dust; and to dust we will return. We should note that this concept could develop only in a post-Fall world. We are to care for the earth, which reminds us of our God-given place within it. We may have a uniquely given divine responsibility, but we fulfill it as fellow creatures, made from the very soil we cultivate.

Schaeffer articulates humanity's position in the created world as both "upward" and "downward." The upward aspect of man's position regards his relationship with the personal Creator. The downward side concerns his relationship with the other created things God has made. "Man's relationship is not basically downward but upward. Man is separated, as personal, from nature because he is made in the image of God," Schaeffer explains. "That is, he has personality and as such he is unique in the creation, but he *is* united to all other creatures as being *created*. Man is separated from everything else, but that does not mean that there is not also a proper relationship downward on the side of man's being created and finite."[14]

We are closely related to the animal kingdom as well. This truth is often downplayed in effort to avoid the error of Darwinian evolution. However, the creatures are created on the same day as humans: day six. They are also described in a similar manner: human beings become a living soul in Genesis 2:7, but animals are also called living souls in 1:30. However, that connection does not mean that humans are more fully developed animals. Humans distinctly bear the divine image, and God has given them the responsibility to care for the earth. Nonetheless, this language demonstrates a strong tie between humans and animals.

As Schaeffer reminds us, man's relationships to the ground and to the animals are rooted in a theology of creation that values creatures and other created things because God has made them. He explains it this way: "As a Christian I say, 'Who am I?' Am I only the hydrogen atom, the energy particle extended? No, I am made in the image of God. I know who I am. Yet, on the other hand, when I turn around and I face nature, I face something that is like myself. I, too, am created, just as the animal and the plant and the atom are created."[15] It also makes sense of the fact that God established a covenant with creation, of which we are a part.

Our divine stewardship to care for the earth constitutes the God-given vocation of humanity. It invariably involves work, and that work is good. We find this aspect in Genesis 2: God placed humanity in Eden to work. An obvious principle from this passage is that work did not come from the Fall (see chapter ten of this book). Everything presented in Genesis 1–2 represents the good world as God meant it to be. By design, our work is intended ultimately to bring honor to the Creator, but it also yields joy and fulfillment for us as creatures. It is not done under compulsion or duress but is a meaningful function of human nature.

We are less than human when we do not work. Not working brings psychological and emotional harm. Disregard for our divinely given vocation likewise contributes to the demise of creation and culture. Vocation is central to our fulfillment of the cultural mandate. As Forlines helpfully summarizes, "The Cultural Mandate sanctifies and elevates to the level of divine service the work of farmers, housekeepers, skilled workers, helpers, scientists, engineers, artists, etc. . . . When done for the glory of God, all that we do is a divine service."[16]

Cursed Be the Ground

The Effect of Sin on Man
The picture presented above is one that emphasizes the way things ought to be, or the way that God intended things to be. However, the presence of sin has undermined the order, propriety, and beauty of the world. Sin has marred the

good creation that God made. When we think about sin, we must distinguish between its guilt and its effects.

We are probably more familiar with the guilt of sin. The creation story tells us that, once Adam and Eve partook of the forbidden fruit, they immediately felt guilt and shame. Suddenly, they were aware of their nakedness (Genesis 3:7a). In their shame they sewed fig leaves as coverings and hid from God (v. 3b). This attempted covering was inadequate, as we can see from the fact that God provided a more appropriate covering made of animal skins. While man could not cover his shame, God could cover his shame, but it required He kill an animal to get those skins.

The first couple likewise incurred the penalty of death, as Genesis 2 had warned: "In the day you eat of it, you shall surely die" (v. 17). Death represents the sentence of personal guilt. It is the reason that all men die, from Adam until now. It is the reason why we need a second Adam—Christ Jesus—who did what the first Adam could not (1 Corinthians 15:22). As the author of Hebrews explains, Christ also partook of our flesh so that "he might render powerless him who had the power of death, that is the devil" (Hebrews 2:14). Our sin incurred guilt, and the sentence of our guilt is death. It is a sentence that none of us could pay short of eternal punishment in hell. Christ is the seed of the woman who would bring ultimate victory over the cursed serpent's seed, as that first statement of redemptive hope expresses in Genesis 3:15.

The reality of our individual guilt is one we cannot escape. The story of God's covenants of promise with Noah, Abraham, Moses, and David is the story of God's creation renewal. God purposed before the foundation of the world to redeem humanity from sin and death. But redemption has another aspect that we cannot forget: God is also concerned about the effects of sin in the world. Those sins certainly affect us individually, but they affect the created order as well. How does this idea contribute to a proper theology of creation and creation renewal?

We begin answering that question by considering how the effects of sin impact us personally. Living under the effects of sin brings impurity and defilement. The Old Testament often refers to that concept as ritual impurity. The instructions from the book of Leviticus, for instance, attempted to deal with the impurities produced by sin's effects. The sin offering in Leviticus 4 illustrates this principle well. This type of offering (sometimes called "purification offering") was a means of dealing with ritual defilement. Childbirth (Leviticus 12), skin diseases (Leviticus 13), mold (Leviticus 14), and bodily discharges (Leviticus 16) all produced impurities and required purification.

Such purifications did not mean that God necessarily viewed these circumstances as somehow sinful. Rather, they represented certain components of the fallen world that can contaminate us through sin's effects. One commentator distinguishes the difference between these two aspects of sin this way: sin requires forgiveness while its effects need cleansing.[17] Allen P. Ross remarks, "Living in this sinful world, one has to deal with contamination, corruption, diseases, and death."[18] We bear the marks of sin in our bodies in various ways, but God's redemption through Christ will eventually restore our bodies through creation renewal, ultimately guaranteed in the final resurrection.

The Effect of Sin on the Natural World

The effects of sin not only impact humanity but also affect the natural world. Have you ever wondered why chaos and disorder exist in the world? Why do animals kill one another? Why do the natural elements create storms? Why do certain natural processes seem so savage? The immediate answers to these questions take us back to Genesis 3, where God curses the ground on account of man's sin: "Cursed be the ground because of you" (v. 17), and then again, "Thorns and thistles it will sprout for you" (v. 18). This curse is profound. Work is difficult for humanity, and the very ground that once yielded the lush produce of Eden will now bring forth thorns and thistles.

Sin's effects have thrown the natural world into chaos and calamity. Paul comments on this problem in Romans 8:19–22: "For the creation waits with eager longing for the revealing of the sons of God. For the creation was subjected to futility, not willingly, but because of him who subjected it, in hope that the creation itself will be set free from its bondage to corruption and obtain the freedom of the glory of the children of God. For we know that the whole creation has been groaning together in the pains of childbirth until now" (ESV). Creation itself awaits renewal when it will be freed from the tyranny of sin's effects. Creation groans in agony.

A robust theology of creation accounts for the turmoil on display in the world around us. The sinfulness of humanity is the only satisfying explanation for the violence at work in society. The human heart is deceitful and sick (Jeremiah 17:9). Moral evils like murder and sex trafficking are all the result of sin's effects on the human heart. And this raging in the heart of man is working to unravel the very fabric of society. Furthermore, this fire is fueled by demonic influence and activity, as people align themselves with the cursed seed of the serpent. The social order of the world is under attack. And it has been this way since Genesis 3.

The entire cosmos has been thrust unwillingly into the drama of human sin, reeling in pain like a mother in childbirth. Hurricanes, floods, violence in the animal kingdom, disease, and pain all attest to creation's groaning under sin's effects. Modernism helps us understand what is wrong with the world, but it cannot adequately account for why these problems exist. Sin's effects have plunged society and the natural world into a state of confusion and calamity.

Childbirth is now painful. The ground yields weeds, thorns, and thistles. Poisonous insects can bite and kill human beings. Humans and animals can become sick and even die.

Some animals, including bears, lions, canines, monkeys, and numerous rodents, even eat their own young. Researchers have even noted that, in some cases, this practice of cannibalism results from a mother that cannot reasonably provide for her sick offspring. In other settings, a male is known to kill the offspring of a competing male so that the mother will give birth to his own offspring.[19]

Researchers struggle to categorize such behavior. Is it pathological, as some have suggested? According to the Christian worldview, it is tangible evidence that something is wrong with the world in which we live. It furnishes evidence for the effects of sin at work in the world. Herman Melville beautifully describes the nature of the sea as an example of sin's effects in the following excerpt from *Moby Dick*:

> Consider the subtleness of the sea; how its most dreaded creatures glide under water, unapparent for the most part, and treacherously hidden beneath the loveliest tints of azure. Consider also the devilish brilliance and beauty of many of its most remorseless tribes, as the dainty embellished shape of many species of sharks. Consider, once more, the universal cannibalism of the sea; all whose creatures prey upon each other, carrying on eternal war since the world began.[20]

The effects of sin have radically permeated every facet of God's good earth. The economy of God's governance over creation has been undermined and supplanted by a multitude of "gods." The cultural mandate was a focal point of God's covenant with creation, which He entrusted to mankind to fulfill. Creation groans under the tyranny of human beings who have sought to become gods, supplanting the role for which they were created. No ground is neutral. Culture and society are infected by the rebellion. All of our basic relationships—with God, man, self, and creation—show signs of infection and decay. Each one needs radical transformation and re-creation.

After the passage quoted above, Melville shifts from exploring the violence of the sea to introducing the prospect of solace amid its storm:

> Consider all this; and then turn to the green, gentle, and most docile earth; consider them both, the sea and the land; and do you not find a strange analogy to something in yourself? For as this appalling ocean surrounds the verdant land, so in the soul of man there lies one insular Tahiti, full of peace and joy, but encompassed by all the horrors of the half-known life. God keep thee! Push not off from that isle, thou canst never return![21]

Amid the reality of sin, we have the hope for peace and joy. However, contrary to Melville's beliefs, man's salvation comes not from man but from God alone.

Creation Renewal

Hope

The dismal picture of the post-fallen world described above starkly contrasts with what was lost. The picture of paradise prior to the Fall depicted in John Milton's *Paradise Lost* highlights this disparity. In the following passage, Satan surveys its bliss just before his attack:

> Beneath him with new wonder now he views
>
> To all delight of human sense exposed
> In narrow room Nature's whole wealth, yea more,
> A Heav'n on earth, for blissful Paradise
> Of God the garden was, by Him in the east
> Of Eden planted; Eden stretched her line. . . .
>
> His far more pleasant garden God ordained;
> Out of this fertile ground he caused to grow
> All trees of noblest kind for sight, smell, taste.[22]

The blissful enjoyment of the garden has been lost, but hope is not. From eternity past, God has purposed to right the wrongs of sin in the world (Ephesians 1:4). The initial kernel of this redemptive plan is found in Genesis 3:15—what many theologians call the proto-*euangelion* or "first gospel": "I will put enmity between you and the woman, between your seed and her seed. He will bruise you on the head, but you will bruise him on the heel."

These words of hope appear amid God's cursing of the serpent. The curse is directed against the serpent, but its content is laced with hope for both Adam and Eve to hear. It highlights the violent struggle that will occur in the world, as the serpent's seed determines to supplant God's covenantal rule over creation. The struggle will be intense with many casualties along the way, but the woman's seed will be victorious, suffering a bruised heel but causing a mortal blow to the head! The curse represents more than "a prediction of constant strife between men and snakes," as one scholar put it.[23]

A thread of hope weaves through the pages of the Old Testament story. The flood story recounts God's judgment of the world since the intent of man's thoughts was evil continually (Genesis 6:5). Nonetheless, the flood likewise represented creation renewal. The language of creation appears in the midst of the flood account itself: "the fountains of the great deep broke open" (Genesis 7:11; see 1:2).

The restatement of divine blessing and the creation mandate to Noah in Genesis 9:1 is also instructive: God blessed Noah and his sons and said to them, "Be fruitful, multiply, and fill the earth." This verse tells us that the mandate to exercise God's rule in the world is still operative, despite the damaging effects of sin. The negative judgment of the flood—what Forlines calls a "negative divine intervention"—is also a statement of creation renewal.[24] It signals God's divine plan to recreate the world by restoring His covenant with creation. Within that economy of governance, the interconnected mandates to be fruitful, multiply, and fill the earth serve as the vehicle for redemptive restoration.

The Creation Mandate Renewed

The creation mandate, and its implications for culture, did not end with Noah and God's covenant with creation, however. It was carried on and applied to the special covenant of grace entrusted to Abraham and his seed. We see this point especially in God's promise to Jacob in Genesis 35:11–12: "God said to him, 'I am El Shaddai. Be fruitful and multiply. A nation and assembly of nations will come from you, and kings will come out from your loins. The land that I gave to Abraham and Isaac I am giving to you, and I will give the land to your seed after you.'" The restatement of the Abrahamic covenant to Jacob incorporates creation language, particularly the language of the creation mandate. What God is doing through Abraham's seed involves the renewal of creation.

The same emphasis occurs in the covenant with Moses and the Israelites at Sinai. The opening scene of the book of Exodus reads: "Now the sons of Israel were fruitful, and swarmed, and increased, and became exceedingly mighty, and the land was filled with them" (1:7). The words "were fruitful" and "multiplied" are taken directly from the creation mandate. The expression of "swarming" also comes from Genesis 1:21, where it described the sea creatures: "with which the sea swarms." But here in Exodus the idea of swarming or teeming in the sea is transferred to the multitude of Abraham's seed swarming in the land of Egypt.

Again, the tie between God's initial creation activity and His new-creation activity through His covenant people is explicit. God is making all things new (Revelation 21:5), and He is doing so through His covenant people. Christopher J. H. Wright summarizes it well: "Creation is *not* just the disposable backdrop to the lives of human creatures who were really intended to live somewhere else, and someday will do so. We are not redeemed *out of creation*, but as a *part of* the redeemed creation itself—a creation that will again be fully eternal for God's glory, for our joy and benefit, forever."[25]

Rest

God invites humanity to experience once again the blessings of divine rest. The rest that the created order once experienced with God on the seventh day was interrupted by man's sin. Nevertheless, God's work of creation renewal is an offer of rest renewed. Rest should not be limited to refrainment from physical exertion; it includes a spiritual component as well. In fact, rest is explicitly covenantal. Moses singles it out as one of the covenant stipulations listed in the Decalogue (Exodus 20:8–11):

> Remember the Sabbath by sanctifying it. Six days you shall work and do all your labor, but the seventh day is a Sabbath to Yahweh your God. You shall not do any work, you, your son, your daughter, your servant, your maidservant, your cattle, or your sojourner who is in your midst. For in six days Yahweh your God made the heavens, the earth, the sea and all that is in them, and he rested on the seventh day. Therefore, Yahweh blessed the seventh day and sanctified it.[26]

The Fourth Commandment formalizes the obligations of our relationship to creation. Adherence to Sabbath observance is meaningful only when it is done within the confines of the covenant, whereby God rightly orders the sin-fallen cosmos. The ramifications of our obligations to covenant are highlighted by the fact that the people of Israel were required to allow their animals to rest as well (see also Exodus 23:12). This principle is also broadened to include the land itself. For example, God instructed His people to leave the produce of the field uncultivated and its after-growth unharvested every seventh year (Leviticus 25:4). God wanted everyone to eat freely, including its owner, household servants, foreigners in the land, and even cattle and wild animals (vv. 5–7).

Telos

The climax or *telos* (end, goal) of creation renewal is realized in the death and resurrection of Christ. He is the embodiment of the Word of God and thus inaugurates the new-covenant reality, which is likewise a new-creation reality. Paul observes that Christ "rescued us from the domain of darkness" and brought us over to His own kingdom (Colossians 1:15). Christ is the answer to the sin of Adam and the distorted *imago Dei*: "the image of the invisible God, the firstborn of all creation" (v. 15). By *firstborn* Paul means to communicate that Christ is the new Adam who has fully established new creation reality. By taking on human flesh and defeating sin, Christ represents the first fruits of the new creation (1 Corinthians 15:20).

Paul continues in Colossians 1:16, 19–20: "For by him all things were created in the heavens and on earth, visible things and invisible things, whether thrones, dominions, rulers, or authorities. All things were created by him and for him. . . . For it was his pleasure that all the fullness should dwell in him, and in him to reconcile all things to him, making peace through the blood of his cross, through him, whether things on earth or in the heavens." Christ's work on the cross was a work of reconciliation whereby He reconciles all things to Himself.

This reconciliation includes the restoration of man and indeed of all created things over which he was given dominion; consequently, men and women can obey God's creation mandate, including the cultural mandate, in the way God intended, which has implications for the assorted topics addressed through the remainder of this book. The effectiveness of this obedience is guaranteed by Christ's resurrection. He is the firstborn from the dead (Colossians 1:18).

The new covenant reality inaugurated by Christ has transformed the Sabbath rest motif into an eschatological hope. The direction of its gaze shifts forward to the new heavens and the new earth. Jesus' disputes with the Pharisees over Sabbath rest move us in this direction. They were focused on God's creative activity in the past.

But Christ's resurrection unites His work of creation in the past with the eschatological hope of His new-creation work in the future. Christians have historically worshipped on the first day of the week rather than the seventh day because of the significance of Christ's resurrection. It signifies the inauguration of new creation and points to the eventual consummation of God's kingdom reign upon the earth. As the author of Hebrews describes it, "There remains a Sabbath rest for the people of God" (Hebrews 4:9).

So, What Now?
Implications for Creation Care and More

Having understood the effects of sin on the world and God's plan to renew creation, we as Christians can agree about the diagnoses we have established through this chapter for the problems within society and nature. Hence we support the efforts of creation care, which is just a way of describing man's stewardship of the created order.

We can agree that pollution in the atmosphere is a terrible thing—that it is bad for humanity and nature. We can also take a stand against animal cruelty, deforestation, or wanton hunting and fishing with no regard for conservation. It is a good thing for lumber companies to invest in planting trees, not just cutting them down. Pollution control is good for the flourishing of human society, so long as those efforts are balanced with an appropriate ordering of society, and we consider the dignity of human life.

We can also appreciate the beauty and order of the world if we understand that God made it. Our renewed dominion over the earth restores a proper acknowledgment of beauty. Francis Schaeffer calls this restoration one of the "first fruits" of creation's healing:

> The aesthetic values are not to be despised. God has made man with a sense of beauty, in a way no animal has: no animal has ever produced a work of art. Man as made in the image of God has an aesthetic quality, and as soon as he begins to deal with nature as he should—as having dominion but not exploiting nature as though it had no value in itself, and realizing it also as a creature of God as man is—beauty is preserved in nature.[27]

Schaeffer's acknowledgement of aesthetics within the proper order of things provides support for further reflection on the arts and entertainment, Christian analysis of the arts, popular culture, and literature and narratives (chapters six through nine of this book).

The healing of creation ought to renew in us an objective sense of beauty and excellence, one that is rooted in the standards of Scripture: "Whatever is true, whatever is honorable, whatever is right, whatever is pure, whatever is lovely, whatever is of good report" (Philippians 4:8). We are to rescue beauty and excellence from the tyrannical subjectivity of the postmodern individual who claims that beauty is found only in the eye of the beholder. We must allow the Scriptures to train our sensibilities to explore and discover the order of the universe that God has made, and our cultural products are a means of representing such order and design, whether through architecture, music, and poetry.

At the same time, however, the Christian recognizes his own limitations. We are fellow creatures created with divine purpose. We are vice regents, not despots determining the course of the universe. We cannot save the world by human willpower and ingenuity. As the hymn writer reminds us, "This is [our] Father's world."

In our dispositions toward the created order and culture, we must avoid one of two extremes. On the one hand, we must eschew all disregard for the dignity of creation, whether human or non-human, animate or inanimate. The things that God has made hold a certain dignity, even in their fallen and imperfect state. Image renewal in man involves a restoration of our stewardship over the world. Man's stewardship is one of the ways by which God sovereignly transforms the world around us.

"I who am made in the image of God can make a choice. I am able to do things to nature that I should not do. So I am to put a *self*-limitation on what is possible," Schaeffer helpfully reminds us. "The horror and ugliness of modern man in his technology and in his individual life is that he does everything he can do, without limitation. Everything he *can* do he *does*. He kills the world, he kills mankind, and he kills himself."[28]

We should carry out our efforts to transform the fallen world in the sobriety of our own creatureliness and in our submission to the Almighty Creator. This disposition involves necessary self-limitation—a limitation that is governed by God's mandate to rule over creation on His behalf. We must filter our creativity through the lens of Scripture and the principles it teaches us about the nature of creation and our accountability to God. For instance, our motivation for technological achievement is not, "Can it be done?" but rather, "Should it be done?" If the answer is yes to this latter question, then we ought to ask how such advancement will cultivate the image of God in others and in ourselves.

This mindset helps us to avoid the other extreme. To avoid trashing the good earth that God has made, we may be tempted to surrender the cause of creation care to leftist environmentalism. This solution is not a good one but rather swings the pendulum to the other side. It is another symptom of man's depravity and his inability to save the world. Our hope lies not in our human efforts to turn back the tide of sin's effects on the cosmos. Rather, we conduct our efforts humbly with confidence in the new-creation reality inaugurated by our resurrected Lord. His resurrection supernaturally enables us to work toward restoring our proper relation to creation in anticipation of His coming kingdom.

In addition to those of the environment, we will also attune ourselves to the needs of society. Hence this book addresses questions of tradition and history; the state and public life; and economics, wealth, and poverty (chapters five, thirteen, and fourteen). We must recognize that the effects of sin drive the dysfunction of society. It is not the result of lack of opportunity or of bad environment alone. Yes, bad environment and limited opportunity will inevitably contribute to problems in society. However, the root problem is sin and its effects on human relationships. We must apply the gospel of the cross to all of life, including to the ills of society.

We must unite as believers in God's work to transform structures of society in view of Christ's kingdom values. Furthermore, we must remember that the cries for "social justice" in the modern world are coming from a worldview that is ultimately unable to remedy the problem. Our agenda for social change must first and foremost arise organically from a proper theology of creation, one that recognizes the scriptural meta-narrative of creation, Fall, redemption, and new creation.

Conclusion

For Christians, the creation mandate and its implications for the making and renewing of culture are still valid. But we must renew culture through the gospel. Gospel transformation takes place in each of our four basic relationships: our relationships with God, others, self, and the creation. In one sense the subject of this book addresses the application of the gospel to all four relationships, but its focus inevitably is on creation. As I have intimated throughout this chapter, science, politics, language, literature, art, technology, leisure, and more all fall under the purview of creation renewal.

We must filter every aspect of the material world and the cultural products and institutions we create through the lens of special revelation. The Scriptures help us to evaluate what is wrong with the world we live in so that we might restore our divinely given responsibility to care for and order it in accord with the ethic of Christ's kingdom. The chapters that follow attempt to outline how we may work toward the restoration of important spheres of creation and culture.

Part II

APPLYING THE
CHRISTIAN WORLDVIEW

CHAPTER FIVE

Tradition and History

Phillip T. Morgan

In the mid-1990s, two professional historians, Roy Rozenzweig and David Thelen, set up an in-depth nation-wide survey to find out how the average person thought about and engaged with the subject of history. They expected to find few people who were interested in history and even fewer who took an active part in preserving or studying it. However, they were pleasantly surprised. For the people in their study, "the past was pervasive, a natural part of everyday life, central to any effort to live in the present."[1] In the end, they found that the average American was deeply invested in local and family history but did not enjoy the hard work of academic history.

After analyzing the results, Rozenzweig and Thelen cast the blame for the average person's dislike of history at the feet of academic historians because they focus on names and dates to the exclusion of narrative. Though academic history does demand the memorization of dates and names, Rozenzweig and Thelen were largely correct in their analysis of the problem. Most people's perception of the past has been shaped by a high school or college history course that failed to explain the subject's connection to the individual student's life. Perhaps you have had a similar experience. I know I have.

However, the past is not about the dry recitation of facts. Instead, God has designed us to live in the present with a view toward the future by holding firmly to the past through tradition and the study of history, as the chapter on the classical conservative tradition established. While most people and cultures prior to the nineteenth century were deeply invested in preserving their heritage, the West over the past one-hundred-and-fifty years has systematically and exhaustively tried to uproot connections to its past. As a result, our civilization teeters in the balance between order and chaos. But by reclaiming deep respect for the past through tradition and history, we help to mend the social fabric of our culture, and we obey God.

In this chapter, we will examine the concepts of tradition and history from a biblical perspective. Then we will consider how our contemporary culture has deviated from the biblical understanding of tradition and history before concluding with an appeal that we robustly engage these topics so that they can appropriately inform thought and life.

Tradition

Communities transfer their cultures informally through traditions that are passed along in the rhythms and grooves of daily life with family and friends. All cultures and communities, no matter how large or small, create and pass on tradition. Undoubtedly, we can all think of special traditions in our families or with our close friends that bind us together. They usually occur without forethought or reflective analyses; they are just enjoyed. Tradition instructs us in the ways of our community, pressing the fabric of our culture against our skin so that we feel the connections of our shared life viscerally.

At its best, tradition is formed by the accumulated results of trial and error over generations. Mistakes are painful but effective teachers. Much energy is required to think through what caused a particular failure. Thus we often respond to failure by altering the actions we most associate with causing the miscue, whether they are the actual culprits or not.

If these changes seem to forestall a similar incident in the future, they become embedded in our personalities as habits and customs. Russell Kirk (1918–1994) helpfully described tradition as the "treasured up experience of the species" and "the wisdom of unlettered men . . . [who] come from the sound ancient heart of humanity."[2] In short, responding to communal problems and mistakes causes cultures to adapt and grow.

Once formed, tradition acts as an intuitive guide for the members of a community. Like a habit, tradition is a reflexive action that allows us to respond quickly to situations. For this reason, as the eighteenth century British intellectual Edmund Burke (1729–1797) explained, tradition is most useful in an emergency because "it previously engages the mind in a steady course of wisdom and virtue, and does not leave the man hesitating in the moment of decision, skeptical, puzzled, and unresolved."[3] Quick decisions are some of the most difficult to make well. Without the requisite time or energy to assess every facet of a problem, we can easily make disastrous mistakes by relying on our own wisdom and ability, which are faulty guides even in the best of circumstances.

Of course, ideally, we should make all decisions only after long reflection on the presuppositions and unintended consequences of a particular action. However, the average person does not have the time, inclination, or gifting to spend long hours contemplating and studying the articulated reasons for the way he lives his life; neither do the circumstances of life usually afford him that luxury.

Thus, for most of mankind, tradition provides a surer guide to right action than half-reasons could ever hope to promise.[4] Even when skill and time allow, man's abstract speculation has a failure rate that would be hilarious if it were not so consistently treacherous—even murderous. Tradition is fallible, but, more often than not, it provides prudent guidance, even when it may seem erroneous.

Tradition is not stagnant or frozen but changes slowly to adjust to meet the specific challenges of the present (as the tenth canon of conservatism establishes). The principles that underlie tradition remain the same, but they responsively modulate to address new circumstances and situations. As the ancient Greek playwright Sophocles (c. 497–405 B.C.) explained, "These laws are not for now or for yesterday; they are alive forever."[5] Being alive, they are flexible. Still the changes are slow, even glacial, responses, often to unperceived needs rather than "some infatuation of the hour" that promises a quick fix with no pain.[6] The laws of tradition are "moored safe and steady" and, as Sophocles exhorts, life "is best spent maintaining" them.[7]

Throwing off tradition in favor of "mathematical precision or bluebook uniformity" almost never produces the desired results.[8] Rather, without tradition to give direction to the individual conscience, "society can be saved from destruction only by force and a master."[9] Thus cultures that attempt to jettison their tradition completely turn invariably to murderous dictators to maintain order (such as during the French Revolution and the Communist revolutions in China, Cuba, and Russia).

Cultures are most tempted to abandon their traditions when they have succumbed to *traditionalism*, which is distinct from tradition. When cultures and communities refuse to allow for adaptation, the shroud of traditionalism settles over the corpse of tradition. Traditionalism refuses any changes, impossibly and irresponsibly demanding that everything remain the same.

Church historian Jaroslav Pelikan (1923–2006) described the difference this way: "Tradition is the living faith of the dead. Traditionalism is the dead faith of the living."[10] Once traditionalism takes hold, cultures react by throwing off tradition altogether for fear they will suffocate. Thus tradition is always in danger. Because of its age, tradition is a delicate creature, "slow to rise, easy to injure, hardly possible to resuscitate."[11] We reject traditionalism, but we embrace tradition, which we receive from history.

History

Education formally instructs us about our culture. In most modern societies, centralized schools are tasked with officially articulating these cultural norms. However, even premodern societies engaged in formal education, usually through the family. Parents and grandparents bore a duty to instruct children rightly about the society that they had received from their ancestors and shared with the community. Note that our culture is received from those who preceded us.

For this reason, a complete education will explain the historical origins of our present moment regardless of whether a school or family member carries out the education. This kind of instruction requires forethought and intentional communication of the historic principles that bind a culture together.

Our culture, past and present, is presented to us for inspection as though it were a choice dish that we willingly eat and take on in our flesh.

Because it shows us the path that has brought us to the present, the study of history is a fundamental aspect of formal instruction. As we learn about our heritage, we gain identity, guidance, encouragement, and hope. Yet wisdom is required to ascertain which historical facts are relevant to our culture. This reality makes the process of studying history challenging and rewarding.

We all should value historical knowledge but, sadly, do not. Bradley Green helpfully associates the dangers of historical ignorance with Alzheimer's disease.[12] When people fall ill with dementia, they progressively lose their grasp on their personal history until they eventually no longer know who they are. Sometimes those who suffer also experience extreme personality changes, leading close family members to say things like, "This is not the person I have always known." If they live long enough, patients with dementia require full-time care from someone they trust completely because they are no longer mentally capable of caring for themselves.

Historical ignorance shares many of these disturbing and dreadful results. A people who have forgotten their past have lost their identity and become susceptible to manipulation. Demagogues use peoples' ignorance to build political support and make themselves wealthy, which results in societies becoming divided and tearing themselves apart. To avoid total chaos, communities riven with strife often accept a state or ruler with extreme power to protect themselves from the results of their own ignorance and ineptitude; such people come to accept their own slavery.

In contrast to historical ignorance, historical knowledge serves as the articulated companion to tradition in forming our identity. The events of the past (artistic, cultural, martial, philosophical, political, and social) are significant factors in making us who we are in the present. Knowing these influences helps us understand better our own motives and actions.[13]

Knowledge of history also explains the underlying philosophy and social circumstances of those around us, giving us insight into our relationships. This deeper understanding of ourselves and others is supplemented by knowledge of the results of past actions. Applying this knowledge to present circumstances allows us to "provide accountability to the present in light of the past."[14] Thus historical knowledge gives us wisdom for how to live well in the present.

Often we are fooled into focusing only on the present. The problems of each day stack up until they block out everything else. History helps us to place our challenges in perspective by allowing us to compare them to past struggles. According to the Roman poet Horace (65–08 B.C.), history encourages us when all seems dark and doubtful: "If all goes badly now, some day it will not be so."[15] Horace's contemporary Virgil (70–19 B.C.) argued that studying the acts of former heroes gives a sense of "future history's glories" that encourages us to live honorably in our moment.[16] Knowing that our actions are historically significant and realizing that right action can bring victory in difficult days provide much encouragement and hope to the soul.

Yet not all historical facts affect us equally. George Washington (1732–1799) crossed many rivers during his life, though we generally consider only his crossing of the Delaware River as significant because it led to a major defeat of the British. We all naturally make such evaluations about historical events. When someone asks about our past, we select certain details we think give the best sketch of our overall identity. Interestingly, we do not all agree about which events are important. A historian's worldview plays a significant role in his interpretation and selection of the endless historical facts at his disposal.

For this reason, we must always evaluate the philosophical, political, and religious positions of historical narrators. We will consider the worldview of historians in more detail below, but we must realize, for the moment, that different people can generate different historical narratives simply by reflecting their differing worldviews. Given history's powerful influence over the forming of our identities, the guiding of our present decisions, and the providing of hope for the future, we must recognize the importance of following the most accurate historical narrative. In fact, true historical narratives are worth fighting and dying for.

Tradition and history are both essential for healthy humans and societies. They offer us identity and a sense of belonging to something larger than ourselves. They are wise counselors because they draw from the wisdom of the human race accumulated throughout time. Their rich perspective helps to balance our immediate focus and promotes courage, faithfulness, hope, and patience.

A Biblical Basis for Valuing Tradition and History

Valuing tradition and history is also an act of Christian obedience. God speaks at length on these topics and calls us to give them careful attention. He warns us that ignoring them or casting them off will bring disastrous results. Thus we need to understand what God requires of us.

Tradition

God is deeply interested in tradition. Throughout Scripture, He commands us to honor tradition as a means of cultural memory as well as worship. As we participate in tradition, our focus will shift from the momentary to the timeless. Yet God's Word must still guide tradition. Therefore, our engagement with tradition must not be passive.

The Ten Commandments highlight the interesting nature of tradition and its importance to God. The first four commands deal directly with man's relationship with God. The last five commands concern man's relationship with other people. But the Fifth Commandment ties these types of relationships together: "Honor your father and your mother, as the Lord your God commanded you, that your days may be long, and that it may go well with you in the land that the Lord your God is giving you" (Deuteronomy 5:16).

The Fifth Commandment commends to us a deeper disposition toward the past. On the surface, God clearly expects us to respect—even to study carefully—the lives and words of our parents. However, just as we know that Jesus' commentary on the commands against murder and adultery in the Sermon on the Mount demonstrates that they refer not simply to physical realities but also to spiritual realities (Matthew 5:21–30), we must admit that the same is true with reference to honoring our parents. The Fifth Commandment has both physical and spiritual applications. God is commanding His people to consider, cherish, and conserve their heritage. Jesus held to this teaching, and Christians have affirmed it for two thousand years.

When the apostle Paul gave instructions for family relationships to the Ephesian Christians, he reminded them that honor of father and mother "is the first commandment with a promise" (6:2). God promises that "your days will be long" and that it will "go well with you in the land" when you honor your forebears. In practice, this commandment means that healthy engagement with tradition promotes strong and peaceful communities.

In Deuteronomy 5, Moses recapitulated the Ten Commandments for the Israelites just before they entered the Promised Land after having wandered in the wilderness for forty years. When he came to the Fifth Commandment, the Holy Spirit guided him to add a short phrase: "as the Lord your God commanded you." No other commandment received such a direct reminder of God's past communication. In this context, the reminder serves as a magnification of God's statute about honoring our forebears.

God uses the embedded traditions of our communities as a vehicle for cultural memory and common grace. In Exodus 13, God gave instructions for the annual celebration of the Feast of Unleavened Bread. In verse 14, He explained that this tradition should prompt families to remember His works on their behalf. "And when in time to come your son asks you, 'What does this mean?' you shall say to him, 'By a strong hand the Lord brought us out of Egypt, from the house of slavery.'" So, in this instance, tradition served as a prompt for formal historical and theological instruction.

God continually refers to Himself as the God of Israel's fathers, thereby emphasizing the importance of familial-traditional connections. In 2 Timothy 1:3, Paul mentions that he served God the way his ancestors had before exhorting Timothy a few verses later (2 Timothy 1:13) to continue serving God as his mother and grandmother had. Thus, as Kirk explains, tradition links us with "God in the infinity above and with [our] father[s] in the grave[s] at [our] feet."[17]

Nor is tradition limited to the biological family. When writing to the Christians in Thessalonica, Paul explained that their salvation was part of a long narrative of redemption extending back before the dawn of creation. Throughout the Old Testament, God had been working out this plan of salvation and progressively revealing Himself to humanity. Therefore, Paul exhorts the Thessalonians to "stand firm and hold on to the traditions" that they had been taught (2 Thessalonians 2:15). Similarly, in writing to Timothy, Paul instructed the young minister to pass down the teachings he had received and to instruct others to do likewise (2 Timothy 2:2). In short, tradition is an integral part of God's kingdom work and plan of salvation.

Despite its emphasis on the past, tradition does not disregard the present and future. Time and again, Scripture emphasizes that we should focus our attention on the eternal and lasting rather than on the transient. In 2 Corinthians 4, Paul explains that we must focus not on the transient things of life but on the eternal because we are being prepared for "an eternal weight of glory" (2 Corinthians 4:17). As theologian Leroy Forlines (1926–2020) has noted, sin's power over us is drawn, in part, from an emphasis on the present because all sin is a sacrifice of the eternal "on the altar of the immediate."[18] Attentiveness to tradition gives priority to lasting principles, institutions, and modes of living that serve as barriers against sin.

Yet tradition is not infallible. Jesus chastised the Pharisees and scribes roundly for having set aside the commands of God in favor of traditions that violated God's will (Matthew 15:1-9; Mark 7:1-13). Such traditions lead us into deep patterns of disobedience to God that are destructive to entire communities and societies. Likewise, the books of the Kings relate the history of Israel's descent into sin and covenant unfaithfulness that ended with exile from the land. Each king of Israel and Judah is introduced by referring to the tradition they follow. Israel's kings are wicked like Abijam who is described as "walk[ing] in all the sins that his father did before him" (2 Kings 15:3).

This wicked tradition of Israel is contrasted by the godlier line of Judah, most of whom are introduced similarly to Azariah who "did what was right in the eyes of the LORD, according to all that his father Amaziah had done" (1 Kings 15:3). We see here that not all traditions are equally good. God's Word informs and guides good traditions even when they are imperfect, while traditions that have rejected God's Word are wicked.

We should also note that God will hold us responsible for the traditions we follow. Under the leadership of Ahaz, Judah broke with their godly heritage and began walking "in the way of the kings of Israel" (2 Kings 16:3). For the next few generations, we can see the successive kings of Judah battling over which tradition to follow, but the general trend was not good. In the end, God sent Judah into exile for walking in wicked traditions.

More than two millennia later, the leaders of the Reformation faced a similar situation in the sixteenth century. They observed that the traditions of men from the medieval period had corrupted the pure doctrine and practice of the apostolic church. Roman Catholic leaders ignored, time and again, the appeals of Martin Luther (1483–1546) and others that divine Scripture takes precedence over conflicting human traditions in relation to ecclesiastical and doctrinal reform. This cry led to the Reformers' emphasis on *sola Scriptura* (Scripture alone but not excluding tradition) but not *nuda Scriptura* (bare Scripture without admitting any tradition). The Reformers rightly believed that traditions are important and valuable, but they are not the final standard of Christian belief and practice.

God is deeply interested in our engagement with tradition. He commands us to honor those who have preceded us and rewards us for following them in obeying His Word. Yet, as historian Robert Rea cautions, we must be discerning.[19] Ungodly traditions will lead us into wickedness and judgment. Studying history carefully can help us determine the nature of our traditions. This, too, is part of God's design.

History

Christianity is inherently concerned with history. Early twentieth-century historian Marc Bloch (1886–1994) went so far as to say, "Christianity is a religion of historians."[20] He could make this claim because, unlike other religions, Christianity does not derive its doctrines or rituals from mythology that is inherently outside of time. Rather, "for sacred books, the Christians have books of history."[21] The Bible is filled with history and provides humanity with a firm basis for studying the past.

Christians derive from Scripture a firm philosophical foundation for the discipline of history. First, the doctrine of creation demands that Christians take history seriously. As Matthew Steven Bracey has written, history reveals God's creative acts in time as He crafts the universe and directs the continuation of His creation.[22] Scripture is filled with commands to remember God's works in history so that we may avoid sin (e.g., Deuteronomy 4:9–10; 8:19–20). Paul explains that we become vain in our reasoning and darkened in our hearts when we ignore these works so that we turn to idolatry, from which God gives us up to the lusts of our hearts (Romans 1:20–25). History pushes us beyond this idolatry of self because it is the study of changes in ideas, political structures, societies, and cultures that are external to the self. Our faith in God's creative act provides an essential pillar in the foundation of our confidence that we can know this outside world.[23]

The person of Jesus Christ also brings value to history. Green notes that the "fundamentally *incarnational*" character of Christianity emphasizes the importance of history.[24] When God took on flesh, He entered time and space, bearing witness to His statement in the beginning that creation is good. As Francis Schaeffer (1912–1984) points out, this truth means the Judeo-Christian religion is "rooted in space-time history."[25]

As with the doctrine of creation, the doctrine of the incarnation also speaks to the possibility of historical knowledge. Both Luke and John argued that careful investigation of the material world supports the veracity of the incarnation. Luke investigated sources and compiled evidence (Luke 1:1–4), and John spoke of the physicality of Jesus that had been witnessed (1 John 1:1–3). Paul made clear in 1 Corinthians 15:14–17 that Jesus' historical, physical resurrection is foundational to our faith. These men plainly affirmed that we could understand the truth of historical events through careful investigation. As Earl E. Cairns (1910–2008) noted, these are the "essential elements of historical discipline."[26]

God's narrative plan of redemption speaks to history's linear nature (with a beginning, middle, and end) and gives an intellectual framework for interpreting the rest of human affairs. Throughout the Bible, God recalls past events and points toward future events, demanding a linear narrative. Paul explained that Jesus came in "the fullness of time" (Galatians 4:4; cf. Ephesians 1:3–10), which means that God was waiting for a particular moment in the development of human history to enter in. When this concept is coupled with Jesus' statement that the Father alone knows the timing of the final judgment (Matthew 24:36; Mark 13:32), we must conclude that history is linear and that God is deeply invested in its fulfillment.

Additionally, God's plan for history provides us with a polestar to guide us as we try to make sense of events in time. Gordon Clark (1902–1985) clarifies this point by explaining that, while the Bible presents history as linear, it is a "thin line."[27] God was very selective in what historical events He recorded in the Bible. Yet these events serve as the "norm and judge of all the rest."[28] Therefore, we can have confidence that all historical events receive their fullest meaning in relation to God's metanarrative of redemption, even if we do not now fully perceive how in every circumstance.[29]

Still, even though Scripture gives us confidence in the ability to know the facts of history and provides us with the metanarrative that gives all of history meaning, these two points do not give Christians an infallible understanding of history. Scripture does not fully reveal the entire redemptive narrative. God has chosen to keep secret many things about the past and the future. Therefore,

Christians cannot claim to hold an exhaustive understanding of history. Nor can we assume that our interpretation of historical events matches God's plan. We can hold this kind of confidence only when God reveals the interpretation of events in Scripture.

Augustine of Hippo (354–430) was the first Christian thinker to engage this biblical foundation for studying history. When Rome was sacked in A.D. 410, many Romans blamed Christianity and called for a return to the old pagan religions. To counter these accusations, Augustine spent over a dozen years penning *The City of God*. He argued that the world consists of two opposing cities: the city of God (founded and ruled by God) and the city of this world (ruled by humanity's sinful desires).[30] According to Clark, Augustine held that the "interaction, competition, and antagonism" of these two cities "produce history."[31]

Underlying Augustine's approach to history is his belief that the Bible is the "outstanding authority in which we put our trust concerning those things which we need to know for our good, and yet are incapable of discovering by ourselves."[32] According to Augustine, we grasp the truth through an understanding that is guided by faith.[33] This specifically applies to our methods and metanarrative, as well as to our understanding of the nature, source, limits, and reliability of knowledge (epistemology). Augustine's general historiographical framework was thoroughly biblical and theological. His ideas about history, among others, dominated the Western world for nearly fourteen centuries, even if individual historians brought their own developments and refinements to the subject.

The Christian worldview venerates tradition and history. God has used both to communicate to His creation. Both serve as reminders of God's powerful deeds for His people in time, most significantly in the historical person of Jesus Christ. They are meant to help us avoid sin and its ruinous affects. As Christians slowly transformed the society of the ancient world, their understanding of tradition and history came to dominate in Western society.

Tradition and History in our Current Context

It is very possible that the first part of this chapter has sounded unfamiliar. Modern Western culture has largely rejected the value of tradition and history, instead emphasizing the immediate, titillating, banal, commodified, and easy pleasures of popular culture. As J. Matthew Pinson has pointed out, this sensibility makes our era unique: "We are the first culture and time period in history that has no respect for our ancestors, and this is true not just of traditional Christianity but of every major world religion and culture in history."[34] Understanding how we should respond to these circumstances requires us to think about the developments that led our culture to this point.

The Abandonment of Tradition

The slow strangulation of Western tradition began in earnest during the Enlightenment, which culminated in the French Revolution. Enlightenment thinkers sought complete individual freedom from all authority except that of reason. With all the old verities (including God) cast aside, they "found themselves launched on a new quest—not for the divine, but the natural."[35] In the attempt to find the "authentic" and "natural" self, they abandoned every existing institution. Thus they argued that "every practice and custom should be questioned" and measured against the standard of their current and constantly changing understanding of the world, which was based on reason alone.[36]

Enlightenment thinkers revised or, more often, abandoned whatever practices and customs they determined did not measure up to their arbitrary and shifting standards. As a result, Westerners discarded the old traditional social framework of binding, intuitive obligations and loyalties. In its place, they adopted a modern social framework of provisional, self-centered social allegiances that they may break up if they deem the allegiance unprofitable (not just in the economic sense) for the individual.[37]

Over the nineteenth century, this incessant and all-consuming questioning of authority slowly strangled the life out of premodern culture steeped in tradition. In its place, the modern world birthed popular culture, much of which also questions and ridicules tradition. Rather than emphasizing the eternal and transcendent, much (though not all) pop culture idolizes the momentary and the limited. Too much pop culture often appeals to and enflames our base desires.

Consumerism has exacerbated the situation. It commodifies everything in our daily lives for consumption—food, music, clothing, sex, and even family (Did you know you can rent a grandma?).[38] In this context, we have a very difficult time even imagining what tradition is and how it could influence us. We merely assume that the worst of pop culture's emphases are normative, and we suffer from what Christopher Talbot has called the "narcissism of now."[39]

In fact, much pop culture offers us a different kind of tradition, standing against the true tradition. As Pinson has argued, when we think we are being "creative and new" by discarding tradition, we have "simply traded one tradition" (the tradition we inherited) for the "anti-tradition of pop culture."[40] Further, we are most prone to making this trade when we deny the fundamental existence of tradition. Unwittingly, though, we adopt the sensibilities and attitudes of some tradition. The question is, "Which tradition will [we] embrace?"[41]

The Neglect of History

Enlightenment faith in (false) objectivity also began to conflict with the Christian worldview of history during the nineteenth century. History as an academic discipline emerged during this time with a few paid university positions in Europe and America. In addition to teaching, these professors focused on researching and refining their discipline.

The German historian Leopold Van Ranke (1795–1886) was the most influential professional historian from this group. Drawing on the methodology of classical philology, Ranke taught his students to appraise sources critically and to marshal arguments through detailed analysis and documentation.[42] Though Ranke was indeed refining the historical method, his ideas on this matter had firm biblical support.

However, through Ranke's influence, historians also optimistically began to believe that, if they followed these methods, they could produce objective knowledge of the past that was not shaded by their subjective perspectives. This Enlightenment mindset made history rather than religion the arbiter and revealer of truth.

Karl Marx (1818–1883), drawing on the philosophy of Georg Friedrich Hegel (1770–1831), especially showed a fondness for Ranke's understanding of history.[43] He and other materialists like him began to suggest that history could not only provide objective knowledge of the past but also predict accurately the future. Marx's theory of historical development remains very influential and thus deserves some explanation.

Marx argued that nothing exists beyond the physical world. We call this idea *materialism*. According to this theory, the truth of history is confined to the bare material actions of humans engaging in economic relationships. Or as William Dennison has written, "humanity makes history," and "history replaces the illusions of religion, taking its place as the authentic revealer of truth."[44]

According to Marx's materialist presuppositions, history reveals the "truth" that all social and cultural change occurs through class conflict. Marx argued that each society consists of oppressive and oppressed economic classes that exist in tension. Eventually the tension grows too great, and the oppressed lower classes overthrow their oppressors and make the structure of the economy and society more amenable to their desires. According to Marx, this historical narrative would culminate in a communist utopia where no one owns personal property, where all economic oppression has ceased, where religion is absent, and where peace reigns.

Marx was not an academic historian. However, professional historians began developing professional historical organizations and journals that constructed and enforced a "consensus not only on how history should be written but on what history was about."[45] While historians disagreed about the specifics, most affirmed that history is knowable, linear, and headed to a definite destination. However, they rejected God's metanarrative and involvement with humanity.

By the end of the nineteenth century, most professional historians had adopted a secular version of the old Augustinian understanding of history.

However, this understanding of history becomes brittle and tenuous when separated from its biblical foundation. Thus the discipline of history, like the rest of the humanities, splintered under the power of socio-political ideologies in the twentieth century such as neo-Marxism (or what some people have referred to as cultural Marxism), as well as feminism (which is based on many of the same presuppositions).

After World War I (1914–1918), historians, like many in the West, lost their confidence in reason and progress. Historians and other Western intellectuals also faced an intellectual crisis when reports of mass murder and oppression began making their way slowly out of the Soviet Union and other Marxist governments (Marxist governments during the twentieth century murdered roughly 100 million of their own people).[46] Thus the pessimism of postmodernity began to seep into the cultural cracks left by worldwide conflict and the murderous totalitarianism of Marxism.

Historians began to doubt that objective knowledge or indeed any knowledge of the past is possible to attain. Some gamely tried to carry forward economic Marxism by writing social histories that focused on class conflict, but they no longer alluded to utopian socialist futures. Furthermore, Marxists, led by Antonio Gramsci (1891–1937), began to lose their faith in the proletariat (working class) who often proved stubbornly disinterested in violent revolution, even when an elite group of intellectuals led them. The disappointingly placid proletariat coupled with the terror of the actual practice of socialism and communism finally led most intellectuals to follow Gramsci in adopting a Marxist position that emphasizes the cultural oppression of minority groups rather than economic class warfare.[47]

These Marxists began reinterpreting history through the lens of power and oppression.[48] To them, the ideas and actions of historical figures are important only as tools of oppression against "marginalized" groups. Rather than treat people of the past and present as individuals who have both goodness and wickedness, they see them only as members of social groups based on gender, sexuality, and skin color. Under the influence of this ideology, most twenty first century historians interpret history as a long and ghastly tale of unmitigated oppression.[49]

Every important figure and institution of the past is now subjected to accusations of racism, bigotry, and hypocrisy for not holding the particular social and political positions of modern progressive intellectuals. To be clear, we stand against actual racism and injustice, but now those terms are too often defined by progressive ideology. Identity politics has consumed much, if not most, of modern historical discourse. Some even question the biblical and Western concept of linear time.[50] Intellectuals are pursuing this line of thinking because they want to change the structure of society fundamentally.[51] For this reason, most historians have concluded that any universal explanation of history is impossible.

In the American classroom, a Marxist analysis of history emphasizes the dry recitation of facts, analysis of systems of power and oppression, and vitriolic hatred of anyone in the past that they can identify as an oppressor because of their political power, religion, skin color, sexuality, or gender. This dry recitation of facts flows from a lack of cohesive narrative for the past. Without the Christian metanarrative, identity politics is all that is left. As a result, some teachers emphasize political abuses of the past, whether real, exaggerated, or imagined.

This change is most obvious when we consider how scholars of the past several decades have reinterpreted (misinterpreted) America's founders.[52] When we consider the American founders within the broader context of human history and cultures, we will find that most of them were prudent and careful leaders attempting to modify deep, complex, and ancient social structures in a careful manner to produce a more just society.

However, modern historians rip the founders from the past and place them within the context of twenty-first-century American standards, which distorts their image like a fun-house mirror exaggerating their least flattering qualities unnaturally and making them seem intentionally backward, bigoted, and uncaring. As a result, the founders are skewered too often in our culture for being in the past and for not knowing the future and changing their behavior accordingly.

The destruction and reinterpretation of tradition and history has sent our culture careening into an identity crisis that threatens to harm our society. To this point, Green argues that the past is "central to true knowledge" and warns that, when we ignore it, "we are, in one sense, becoming less than fully human."[53] Twentieth-century intellectual Richard Weaver (1910–1963) reached a similar conclusion, leading him to suggest that there is something "suicidal" about our culture's emphasis on the present and rejection of the past: "No man exists really except through the power of memory. . . . If he does not want identity, if he has actually come to hate himself, it is natural for him to try to get rid of memory's baggage. He will travel light."[54] Such self-loathing and past-loathing is "fundamentally anti-Christian" in its obsession with the immediate.[55]

The effects of our culture's suicidal sensibilities are plain for us to see on the nightly news and on social media. The social barriers to our moral and cultural decline seem to have been annihilated. Even the most extreme sexual perversion is accepted and celebrated by many intellectual and cultural leaders in universities, politics, and the media. Prudent financial investment and saving have been eschewed in favor of unadulterated deficit spending on self-gratification both in our homes and in the halls of government. In the absence of transcendent meaning provided by religion, tradition, and history, our society has splintered into tribal identity groups that are pitted against one another by intellectuals and politicians. The fruit of the modernist tree is bitter and poisonous, murderous and destructive.

Being Salt and Light: An Appeal for Robust Engagement with Tradition and History

Some thinkers, like Irving Babbitt (1865–1933), believe that the damage done to the tradition of Western civilization is irreversible and that we are headed for a final collapse with no remedy.[56] However, such a defeatist attitude can act as a self-fulfilling prophecy. Christians have even less reason for pessimism about the future, though many in the twentieth century have adopted various bleak interpretations of the end times.[57] Jesus clearly explained that no one except the Father knows the hour of His returning (Matthew 24:36). Therefore, we have a responsibility to live well in the time that He has given us, looking hopefully for His return today or three millennia in the future.

Christians of the past faced dark times as well. Augustine was prompted to write *The City of God* when he saw Rome, which was more than a millennium old, destroyed by barbarian invaders. Alfred the Great (849–899) experienced the invasion of the Vikings that left every church on the English isle in ashes. Yet through Alfred's faithfulness, the Vikings were first defeated and then converted to Christianity. We are fighting a spiritual battle against the prince of the power of the air, and "the weapons of our warfare are not of the flesh but have divine power to destroy strongholds. We destroy arguments and every lofty opinion raised against the knowledge of God, and take every thought captive to obey Christ" (2 Corinthians 10:4–5). Therefore, let us not grow weary in this time of crisis. We can all take some basic steps to slow the cultural decay around us and heal the social fabric of our communities.

First, actively and intentionally limit your engagement with popular culture. As we have noted, pop culture's sensibilities and practices tend to differ significantly from the Christian's. Because Jesus has sent us "into the world" (John 17:18), we should not remove ourselves completely from the world. But neither should we allow the "alienated and hostile" minds of the unbelieving world (Colossians 1:21) to influence our sensibilities. Perhaps the best balance is to saturate ourselves in Scripture, tradition, and history, while staying abreast of broad trends in pop culture and enjoying those pop culture products that are virtuous and ennobling (explored further in chapters seven and eight of this book).

Second, get to know your grandparents! If your grandparents are absent, find an older person or couple that is well respected in your community. Spend a significant amount of time with people who have the perspective and gathered wisdom of age. Listen carefully to their stories (even if they repeat themselves . . . a lot) and watch their practices with humility. Follow the example that is set before you with discernment, realizing that no one is perfect. "Let the wise hear and increase learning," realizing that "fools despise wisdom and instruction" (Proverbs 1:5a, 7b) and suffer from what C. S. Lewis called "chronological snobbery."[58]

Third, claim quality traditions of family and community as your own. Do not passively attend the social gatherings of family and friends. Become an active participant who embodies the best of your community and passes on an enthusiasm for its institutions and sensibilities through your infectious excitement and involvement. In some cases, you may want to develop new traditions for your community from historical examples that instantiate and encourage virtue and social health.

Fourth, actively engage in preserving your community's history. Likely, your family, church, and community have had many interesting interactions with broader historical events. The tales of your community help refine your identity, influencing your actions in the present. Take the time to help research and preserve your local history. Save important documents, photos, and heirlooms. Interview important members of your community and make a lasting record of their thoughts and actions.[59]

Fifth, become historically literate. Christianity is founded in historical facts and holds that we are currently amid a historical metanarrative that will conclude with the return of Christ. Theology offers all Christians reasons to take at least a passing interest in studying history. Further, history is important for repairing the social fabric of our communities and country.

Last, actively engage in passing down a great love for tradition and history. Your excitement and engagement with the past will be infectious to those around you. Do not be afraid to share your loves with the people in your sphere of influence. When you act as if the past is important and significant for the present, others will follow your lead.

History and tradition have been badly handled by our culture. Most of us have imbibed the spirit of the age and find it difficult even to conceive of how or why the past could be relevant to the present. I hope this chapter has suggested several reasons for Christians to invest deeply in tradition and history. With the past as our guide, we will live better in the present and build a better future. As the German poet Goethe put it, "What you have as heritage, take now as task; for thus you will make it your own!"

CHAPTER SIX

The Principles of the Christian Critical Tradition

E. Darrell Holley

When I was young, I learned a little song that went like this:

> Tell me why the stars do shine,
> Tell me why the ivy twines,
> Tell me why the sky's so blue,
> And I will tell you just why I love you.
> Because God made the stars to shine,
> Because God made the ivy twine,
> Because God made the sky so blue,
> Because God made you, that's why I love you.[1]

That, I believe, is the basis for the Judeo-Christian view of the arts. At the center is the belief in a single, personal Creator. It is the working out of that very basic belief that has formed the foundation of what might be called the Christian critical tradition. For two thousand years now, Christians have been trying to understand the arts from a uniquely Christian perspective and to express themselves in art that is in keeping with that perspective. An exploration of that tradition reveals certain ideas that have been the motivating principles behind both that criticism and that creativity.

A Defense of the Arts

The Russian Bolshevik Leon Trotsky, no lover of Christianity, once pointed out that "all the varieties of idealistic formalization, either openly or secretly, lead to a God, as the Cause of all causes.... A single personal Creator is already an element of order."[2] Trotsky, of course, disdained religion, particularly Christianity, but his statement represents a keen insight into the theistic, and particularly Christian, view of literature. Though he hated it, Trotsky clearly saw that the Christian belief in the personal Creator results in a unique literary criticism.

Because personal belief systems are intricately tied with art, Hegel, in his *Philosophy of Fine Art*, said:

> Fine art is not real art till it is . . . free, and only achieves its highest task when it has taken its place in the same sphere with religion and philosophy and has become simply a mode of revealing the consciousness and bringing to utterance the divine nature, the deepest interests of humanity, and the most comprehensive truths of the mind. It is in works of art that nations have deposited the profoundest intuitions and ideas of their hearts; and fine art is frequently the key—with many nations there is no other—to the understanding of their wisdom and of their religion. . . . [The] mind . . . generates out of itself the works of fine art as the first middle term of reconciliation between pure thought and what is external, sensuous, and transitory, between nature with its finite actuality and the infinite freedom of the reason that comprehends.[3]

By looking at the art a person creates, one can look into the person, into his mind, and find the ideas that dwell there. Marcel Proust said, "Through art we can know another's view of the universe."[4]

If Hegel is true that the Idea will manifest itself in the work of art, then the critic is quite justified in trying to get at that Idea, in trying to understand just what the artist is saying. Criticism, in the Christian tradition, has attempted to do just that. It has attempted to discover the "view of the universe" which the art expresses and to judge that view by Christian beliefs. The Christian critic looks upon the work of art as a complex statement of the artist's beliefs and thoughts. Again, Hegel said:

> The universal need for expression in art lies . . . in man's rational impulse to exalt the inner and outer world into a spiritual consciousness for himself, as an object in which he recognizes his own self. He satisfies the need of this spiritual freedom when he makes all that exists explicit for himself *within*, and in a corresponding way realises this his explicit self *without*, evoking, thereby, in this reduplication of himself, what is in him into vision and into knowledge for his own mind and for that of others. This is the free rationality of man, in which, as all action and knowledge, so also art has its ground and necessary origin.[5]

With this view of the "meaning" of art, it has been quite possible for Christians to view the arts incorrectly. Christians have "from time to time puritanically denounced the Arts as irreligious and mischievous, or tried to exploit the Arts as a means to the teaching of religion and morals."[6] There have been famous apologies and defenses of the arts, such as Sir Philip Sidney's *Defense of Poesy*, which defended the arts from the charge of impiety or immorality. Often these "defenses" attempted to show that art could be "used" for moral purposes. These defenses of the arts themselves, however, viewed the arts incorrectly. Hegel says:

> In this aspect of the matter, the fine arts being granted to be a *luxury*, it has been thought necessary in various ways to take up their defence with reference to their relation towards *practical* necessities, and more especially towards morality and piety, and, as it is impossible to demonstrate their harmlessness, at least to make it credible that the mental luxury in question afforded a larger sum of advantages than of disadvantages.[7]

The viewing of art as a luxury was often combated by viewing art as a tool, a means of getting to some desired end. But this also demeans art. It turns it into something not independent at all but something "servile."[8] It leads to a fierce didacticism, to the attaching of an Aesopian "the moral of this story is" to the end of every work.[9]

These mistaken views are not the Christian view of the arts, though they have often been mistaken for it. The Christian view of the arts is rooted, as Trotsky implied, in the Christian belief of the personal Creator. Art has value "because a work of art is a work of creativity, and creativity has value because God is the Creator"—this is the Christian view.[10] Francis Schaeffer said:

> An art work has value as a creation because man is made in the image of God, and therefore man not only can love and think and feel emotion, but also has the capacity to create. Being in the image of the Creator, we are called upon to have creativity. In fact, it is part of the image of God to be creative, or to have creativity. We never find an animal, non-man, making a work of art. On the other hand, we never find men anywhere in the world or in any culture in the world who do not produce art. Creativity is a part of the distinction between man and non-man.[11]

This is a much more balanced view of art and much more in keeping with the principles of the Christian critical tradition. The Christian critic sees the work of art not as a whimsical luxury nor even as a tract, but as a thing of meaning of itself. Now, this should not be confused with the idea of "art for art's sake." In the Christian view, the work does not have to maintain its value alone; it is an outgrowth of man's basic creativeness, an aspect of his God-given humanity, and therefore has value. A work of art has value as a work of creativity.[12]

Because art is a result of man's creativity, it is, as Hegel said, "of a spiritual nature." Man's mind "imbues all the products of its activity with thought."[13] The Christian critic therefore examines a work of art and hopes to ascertain the "thought" behind the work. Paul, in his Second Epistle to the Corinthians, speaks of "bringing into captivity every thought to the obedience of Christ" (10:5). The Christian critic, when he has interpreted a work (ascertained the "thought" behind it), then evaluates that work in light of Christian principles, principles ultimately revealed in the Scriptures.

An Introduction to the Basic Principles of Christian Criticism

In his Epistle to the Philippians, Paul writes: "Finally, brethren, whatsoever things are true, whatsoever things are honest, whatsoever things are just, whatsoever things are pure, whatsoever things are lovely, whatsoever things are of good report: if there be any virtue, and if there be any praise, think on these things" (4:8). In this passage Paul presents six basic principles that, throughout the history of Christian criticism, have served as criteria by which to evaluate art. Rookmaaker, the twentieth-century art critic, has called this passage "the mental attitude involved in being essentially human, expressing the true humanity which Christ came to restore."[14] John Calvin called it "general exhortations which relate to the whole of life."[15]

These principles express that works of art are the product of human thought and rationality and can therefore be examined in the light of that thought. Paul's Idealism which he expresses in this passage is at the very heart of the Christian concept of the arts.

Paul here understands all products of human artistry as products of the artist's beliefs and ideas. The work of art (or "external element," as Hegel would call it) does indeed partake of the nature of the artist.

> We assume something further behind [the external element], something inward, a significance, by which the external semblance has a soul breathed into it. It is this, its soul, that the external appearance indicates. [The work of art is not] exhausted in these mere particular lines, curves, surfaces, borrowing, reliefs in the stone, in these colours, tones, sounds, of words [sic], or whatever other medium is employed; but it should reveal life, feeling, soul, import, and mind, which is just what we mean by the significance of a work of art.[16]

Paul calls for the examination of art and not just the *examination* of art but the *evaluation* of it. C. S. Lewis says that the Christian will "take literature a little less seriously than the cultured Pagan" due to the transitoriness of life.[17] If this life is all that there is, if there is no immortality, then indeed the pagan is quite right to take this life very seriously, for it is all that there is. Man's salvation must then be found in this life alone. If this life must be everything to man (and it must, if there is no other), then he should indeed take it most seriously. Ultimately, he will find, however, that this life—which must be everything to him—will begin to seem valueless and insipid, for, in a strange paradox, if this life must be everything, it will begin to seem like nothing—for it must certainly fail to be everything. But to the Christian, this life is not everything. There is a life beyond the realm of space and time. This life therefore does not have to be everything; it can be merely the something that it is. The Christian can then enjoy the delights of this world as they are, not asking too much of them, not requiring that they be one's salvation, for "salvation cometh of the Lord."

This view of life is at the heart of what Paul talks about. For the Christian, art is not everything, but it can be the something that it is. Art can be enjoyed merely as the product of man's creativity, not as a means of salvation.

Some may criticize the construction of a "Christian criticism" as being a narrowing view of art. Some may contend that the application of these six principles will be stultifying on the arts, will result in the arts' being "frozen." Rookmaaker answers that objection:

> The norms of art are in fact basically not different from the norms for the whole of life. Art belongs to human life, is part of it, and obeys the same rules. The fact that the artist must keep in mind the specific structures of art is the same as anyone else in other human activities must do: the government has to work within the structures of the state, the motorist within the structures of the way the car works and of the rules of the road. But whether you are an artist, a politician or a motorist you must apply not only the specialized structures of your own field of operations but also the structure of the whole of life, the fact that, being human, man is designed to work in a particular way, and that only by being wholly true to humanity will each activity really fulfill its purpose.[18]

The Christian view of the arts, far from "freezing" the arts, sets them free to fulfill their purpose.

Paul's criteria for evaluating works of art are six: truth, seriousness, righteousness, purity, beauty, and technical excellence.

Truth

Dorothy Sayers, the mystery novelist and friend of C. S. Lewis's, said:

> In this matter, as in so many others, Christianity displays its usual propensity for making everything as awkward as possible. It outrages the tidy-minded by occupying a paradoxical position. On the one hand, it made modern science and the modern views of history possible by insisting that the pattern of events was not (as the Greek philosophers thought) static or cyclic, but a progression in time from a beginning to an end. On the other, it tiresomely maintains that at every point in the developing temporal process, the conditional truths are referable to an extra-temporal standard of absolute truth, before which all souls enjoy complete equality, no aristocratic privilege being attached to the accident of later birth.[19]

This is the first principle: the work of art must be true. In light of the modern theories of criticism, this is an amazing statement. The Greek word translated "true" might also be understood as "real, actual."[20] One lexicon defines it as "truth, but not merely truth as spoken; truth of idea, reality."[21] In other words, the work must be true to "what is," that is, what is real. The Christian critic demands that works of art be true.

How can a work of art be true? Surely this does not mean that there must be an exact copy of reality; such an interpretation would result in no art at all, for "art is never a copy of reality.... Art always gives an interpretation of reality."[22] What then does truth in art mean?

> Truth in art does not mean doing accurate copies. But that the artist's insight is rich and full, that he really has a good view of reality, that he does justice to the different elements of the aspect of reality he is representing. Truth has to do with the fullness of reality, its scope and meaning. It is artistic truth! Hamlet may never have lived—but Shakespeare's Hamlet is true insofar as Shakespeare has been able to make the figure he created true to reality, to human character and potential.... So too fairy tales can be true, if they show human action and behavior in keeping with human character—within the framework of fairy tale reality.[23]

The principle of truth in art certainly does not prohibit fiction or fantasy. Even when dealing with an unreal situation, such as fantasy or science fiction, the author is still obliged to present moral truth. As Sayers said, this is the standard to which Christianity brings everything. In an essay on the English critic Charles Williams, Sayers says that he ran "counter to the modern trend in criticism." She says that he, like all early critics, judged works of literature "as if they were contemporaries, bringing their opinions to the bar of absolute, rather than of relative, truth.... He was thus never content with knowing under what pressure of social conditions a poet came to say what he did: he felt that this did not exhaust the subject or explain the poem away. He always went on to ask: 'Did the poet speak truth? and if so, what ought we to do about it?'"[24] If she is right about Williams, then he measures up as an excellent Christian critic, at least on this point. He did exactly what Paul recommends; he examined works in regard to their truthfulness.

It is of just this aspect of good literature that the great Russian novelist Alexandr Solzhenitsyn spoke in his Nobel Lecture:

> We will be told: What can literature do against the pitiless onslaught of naked violence? Let us not forget that violence does not and cannot flourish by itself; it is inevitably intertwined with *lying*. Between them there is the closest, most profound and natural bond: nothing screens violence except lies, and the only way lies can hold out is by violence. Whoever has once announced violence as his *method* must inexorably choose lying as his *principle*. At birth, violence behaves openly and even proudly. But as soon as

it becomes stronger and firmly established, it senses the thinning of the air around it and cannot go on without befogging itself in lies, coating itself with lying's sugary oratory. It does not always or necessarily go straight for the gullet; usually it demands of its victims only allegiance to the lie, only complicity in the lie.

The simple act of an ordinary courageous man is not to take part, not to support lies! Let *that* come into the world and even reign over it, but not through me. Writers and artists can do more: they can *vanquish lies!* In the struggle against lies, art has always won and always will. Conspicuously, incontestably for everyone. Lies can stand up against much in the world, but not against art.... In Russian, proverbs about *truth* are favorites. They persistently express the considerable, bitter, grim experience of the people, often astonishingly: *One word of truth outweighs the world.* On such a seemingly fantastic violation of the laws of the conservation of mass and energy are based both my own activities and my appeal to the writers of the whole world.[25]

It is precisely on this principle of truthfulness that much of the debate over the literature of the Eastern civilizations has hinged. In 1835 Thomas Babington Macaulay wrote his famous "Minute on Indian Education." The debate in Parliament centered on what form the government-subsidized education in India would take. Would the students study Arabic and Sanscrit works, or would they study the curriculum of the average English school? It was in behalf of the principle of truthfulness that Lord Macaulay spoke in behalf of the so-called "Anglicist" position: "What we spend on the Arabic and Sanscrit colleges is not merely a dead loss to the cause of truth; it is bounty-money paid to raise up champions of error. It goes to form a nest . . . of bigots."[26] After describing his conversations with scholars distinguished in Arabic and Sanscrit, he says, "I have never found one among them who could deny that a single shelf of a good European library was worth the whole native literature of India and Arabia."[27] At first glance, it appears that Macaulay was one of those bigots whom he denounced as "champions of error." What caused him to speak this way? He gives a reason:

> The first instance to which I refer, is the great revival of letters among the Western nations at the close of the fifteenth and the beginning of the sixteenth century. At that time almost everything that was worth reading was contained in the writings of the ancient Greeks and Romans. Had our ancestors acted as the Committee of Public Instruction has hitherto acted; had they neglected the language of Cicero and Tacitus; had they confined their attention to the old dialects of our own island; had they printed nothing and taught nothing at the universities but Chronicles in Anglo-Saxon, and Romances in Norman-French, would England have been what she

now is? What the Greek and Latin were to the contemporaries of More and Ascham, our own tongue is to the people of India.[28]

Macaulay champions the liberal arts, which do not lie, but lead men into truth.

Some no doubt will raise the question as to whether the arts do indeed express propositional truth. Now, certainly, a poem will express truth differently from a sermon or scientific treatise; a drama will state truth indirectly. ("The thought of Shakespeare [is not] to be found in the utterance of any particular character," wrote Allan Bloom. "That thought is in none of the parts but is somehow in the whole, and the process of arriving at it is more subtle than that involved in reading a treatise."[29]) But speak the truth they must. "That a work of art is in the form of fantasy or epic or painting does not mean that there is not propositional content. Just as one can have propositional statements in prose, there can be propositional statements in poetry, in painting, in virtually any art form."[30]

Schaeffer tells the story of a liberal theologian at Princeton who commented that "he did not mind saying the creeds, providing that he could sing them." Schaeffer comments on this:

> What he meant was that so long as he could make them a work of art he didn't feel that he had to worry about the content. But this is both poor theology and poor aesthetics. A lyric can be as emphatically (and accurately) historic [sic] as a straight piece of prose. *Paradise Lost*, for example, contains many statements which while artistically expressed are almost straight theology. Just because something takes the form of a work of art does not mean that it cannot be factual.[31]

Paul certainly did not believe in the lack of propositional truth in art. In his instructions to the early Christians about their worship, he instructs them to sing "psalms and hymns and spiritual songs" and to sing in the spirit—but to sing "with the understanding also" (Ephesians 5:19; 1 Corinthians 14:15). Obviously he viewed art as being able to express truth.

This principle of truthfulness in art would appear to break down when confronted by an abstract work, that is, a work with no actual "subject." Bach's *Concerto for Two Violins in d Minor*, for instance—how can it be said to express truth? Even abstract works "say something." Can anyone doubt that the ghostly, elongated figures of Giacometti speak of the alienation and loneliness so felt in modern culture? Can anyone doubt that the "music" of John Cage reflects his belief in the lack of rationality in life, his belief that human existence is basically irrational and absurd? The question, Is it true? must be applied not just to the "content" but also to the form of the work. The form that a work of art takes may be evaluated just as the content may be.

The first principle of Christian criticism is the principle of truthfulness. The Christian critic looks for truth. The Christian critic agrees with Hegel that "art has the vocation of revealing the *truth* in the form of sensuous artistic shape."[32]

SERIOUSNESS

The second principle by which the work of art is to be evaluated is the principle of seriousness. *Seriousness* does not seem to be the very best word to describe this principle, but it does as well as *noble* and *honest*, two of the ways the word has been translated in this passage. The Greek word so translated is defined as "venerable, honorable," "revered, august," and "grave, worthy of respect" in various lexicons. Perhaps *serious* will do as well as these.

A "noble" style of art is one which takes the content and the form seriously, which treats them with respect. People often speak of a "serious work" or "serious literature" or "serious music." This does not imply that the work must be humorless, that it cannot be a comedy. It certainly may, but, however it treats the content and the form, it must take them seriously. T. S. Eliot uses the term *maturity* to refer to the author, his manners, and his language. This "maturity" is certainly part of the principle termed here "seriousness."

It is at this point that the question of content versus form must be raised. Throughout the history of criticism, this issue has divided critics. Where does the Christian critic stand? Is he interested in content? Yes, of course he is. Is he interested in form? The principle of truthfulness shows that he must be. Where does the Christian critic come down?—somewhere in the middle, or better yet, on both sides; the principle of seriousness requires this. Hegel said:

> It is [art's] true task to bring to consciousness the highest interests of the mind. Hence it follows at once with respect to the *content* that fine art cannot rove in the wildness of unfettered fancy, for these spiritual interests determine definite bases for its content, however manifold and inexhaustible its forms and shapes may be. The same holds true for the forms themselves. They, again, are not at the mercy of mere chance. Not every plastic shape is capable of being the expression and representation of those spiritual interests, of absorbing and of reproducing them; every definite content determines a form suitable to it.[33]

"Every definite content determines a form suitable to it." This point is nothing more than Paul's principle of seriousness: a work must unite the content with a form suitable to it. Good "content" alone is not sufficient, for the "form" is also part of the content. "We should realize that if something untrue or immoral is stated in great art it can be far more destructive and devastating than if it is expressed in poor art or prosaic statement."[34] Moral excellence presented in a technically un-excellent manner says that that morality is slight, unimportant, negligible, perhaps even untrue; moral excellence presented in a technically un-excellent fashion is satire; the style pokes fun at the words and changes the meaning. Technical excellence is very important, but it is not alone sufficient; a wrong presented beautifully becomes all the more wrong and wicked.

As a postscript to the discussion of this principle, it might be good to deal with a criticism that Francis Schaeffer makes in his work *Art and the Bible*. He says, "We must distinguish carefully between style and message. Let me say firmly that there is no such thing as a godly style or an ungodly style. The more one tries to make such a distinction, the more confusing it becomes."[35] Schaeffer and others have criticized some Christians for rejecting works of art which attempted to put sound content with an alien (what they often considered "non-Christian") style. Now certainly, there have been Christians who were uncultured people too ignorant to look very deeply into a work for its correct "message" or too obstinately conservative to accept any new art form or style, whatever its qualities. But sometimes this has not been the case. This principle of seriousness (often, like all of these principles, held in simple form by people who have a background in Christianity but not in the arts) is an explanation for why the average Christian (or even the average non-Christian who has accepted Christian values and culture) hates some "modern art" or "modern literature" or "modern music." The problem is that those "modern" styles are not appropriate, do not suit well the Christian philosophical message. Those forms when united with that "message" change it.

As an example from our popular culture, this explains why the young person reared in one set of standards may greatly enjoy modern music (and, if he professes Christianity, even use it to express his religious faith) and another person (perhaps older or from a more conservative home) who was reared in a decidedly Christian culture may find it puzzling and alien and ugly. The latter (though he may not realize it) is not familiar with the "modern" worldview, only with the "older world-view still flavored with the salt of Christian values—open, knowing of a God, of justice and absolutes."[36] He realizes that this modern music (to him it is alien music) is not at all in keeping with the traditional Christian worldview. This may not reflect a rational thought that is the result of actual education on his part, either in music or theology; it may be simply a vague feeling of alienation or puzzlement.

Before going on to the next principle, it may be appropriate at this point to clarify something that may be unclear. The terms "Christian philosophic message," "Christian content," and "Christian theme" should not be understood to be limited to distinctly "religious" or "biblical" themes. Shakespeare's play *The Tempest* is as "Christian" as Augustine's *Confessions*, though it is not "religious." Rembrandt's *The Slaughtered Ox* is certainly more Christian, in the sense of this essay, than Picasso's *Last Supper*.

No, what is Christian in art does not lie in the theme, but in the spirit of it, in its wisdom and the understanding of reality it reflects. Just as being a Christian does not mean going round singing hallelujah all day, but showing the renewal of one's life by Christ through true creativity, so a Christian painting is not one in which all the figures have haloes or (if we put our ears to the canvas) can be heard singing hallelujahs. Christian art is nothing special. It is sound, healthy, good art. It is art that is in line with the God-given structures of art, one which has a loving and free view on reality, one which is good and true. In a way there is no specifically Christian art. One can distinguish only good and bad art, art which is sound and good from art which is false or weird in its insight into reality. This is so whether it is painting or drama or music. Christians, however full of faith they may be, can still make bad art. They may be sinful and weak, or they might not have much talent. On the other hand a non-Christian can make a thing of beauty, a joy for ever—provided he remains within the scope of the norms for art, provided that he works out of the fullness of his humanity, and does not glory in the depraved or in iniquity or glorify the devil.[37]

Righteousness

The third principle of Christian criticism is the principle of righteousness. The word means "equal, even, proportional," or "fair, impartial," or "righteous, balanced, doing what is right or dutiful." In particular usage in Christian homiletics, it is used to mean "just in the eyes of God, righteous."[38] Some might accuse Paul of stretching the point to apply this word to art criticism. One must remember that this word acquired its modern meaning of "holy" or "morally good" from its usage in religious contexts. Prior to its use by Christian theologians, it was used non-religiously. If the word has too much of a religious connotation, it could very easily be understood as "right-ness" without doing any damage to the thought. This principle is that of rightness.

Just as the principle of truthfulness applies to both content and form, so does the principle of righteousness. As far as there is a "subject" or theme to a work, the subject must be treated "rightly." This point does not mean that all the characters of a novel, for instance, must be righteous people or that the morally "right" must be rewarded materially. But the right must be seen to be the right. The character who murders in a novel must be seen as wrong, not right, even if he goes unpunished. Righteousness must be seen as such, and unrighteousness must be seen as such.

What if there is no subject, as in Bach's violin concerto? Is the principle inoperative? Quite to the contrary; justice, or righteousness, simply means doing right—that is, giving a thing the attention which, by its own nature, it requires.

(The word *right* is commonly used in this way when it is said that a man "did right by his family.") This point implies proportion, balance, even-handedness. "To be righteous," said Rookmaaker, "means to be right to the situation, to give each element its due: to create a right balance, a harmonious whole.... So 'righteousness' can be expressed in details of colour, composition ... even in a modulation of music."[39] A work of art must be balanced, well proportioned. Augustine speaks of "ordinate loves": things must be given the love, the attention, the thought they require, no more and no less. Either excess or lack leads to imbalance and to a type of "unrightness" or unrighteousness. Rightness is considered very much a part of good writing; all students of composition are taught "to search for the right 'finishing touch,' the right tone, the right word in the right place."[40]

Purity

Uneducated or uncultured Christians are often severely criticized for being narrowly parochial in their view of art. They are often very quick (at least this has sometimes been the case) to discover any scene in a novel, any line in a play, any picture in a book which they understand to be "obscene" or "vulgar," by which they mean "impure in regards to sexual morals" or "unchaste." Sometimes they have indeed been guilty of prudishness, seeing as unchaste or immoral what is, in reality, very natural and holy and ordained by God. But often they are merely following a very old Christian traditional principle that demands purity in the arts. Paul instructs his readers to examine things in regard to their purity or chastity.

To see what the Jewish and early Christian authors of the Bible considered chaste and unchaste, one might look at several Scriptural examples: David's sin with Bathsheba in 2 Samuel 11 or the story of the Levite and his concubine in Judges 19. There are other instances of various sexual misdeeds. There is the attempted homosexual rape of Lot's guests by the men of the city of Sodom. There is the incest committed by Lot and his two daughters. There is the story of the fornication of Shechem and Dinah, the daughter of Jacob. In the New Testament, there is the teaching of Paul concerning the conjugal duties of husbands and wives.

Paul and other early Christians understood that these passages showed that sexuality is certainly a real part of human life. In this sense, as in all others, the Scriptures themselves are true; they are true to life. Human sexuality is often a needful topic for discussion for various reasons. These passages deal with sex straightforwardly and honestly but without needless graphic description. Incidents are described and commented upon without "corrupting" the reader. The reader is narrated to, instructed, but never titillated. The Christian critic does not demand that a work be silent in regards to sex; such a work might be very unreal, untrue to life. He does demand, however, that sexuality be dealt with properly.

Our Lord taught us that it is wrong for a man "to lust after" a woman (Matthew 5:28). Paul warns women to dress "in modest apparel" (1 Timothy 2:9). People are both to avoid lust themselves and to avoid enticing others to lust. The writer must often deal with the subject of sex but not in such a way that a reader is led to think "lustfully." If the Bible itself, viewed as a work of literature, is any example, then this is best done by avoiding graphic portrayal. The work can be "sexual" (dealing with sex), but it must not be "sexy" (sexually suggestive).

> It is for the sake of humanity that we stand against every pressure that would drag the woman [or for that matter, the man] down to the level of an object of lust. For that same reason we are against all kinds of manipulation, in advertising, in the mass communication media.... Humanity, involving manhood and womanhood, is something of too great a worth to be deprived of its value and meaning.[41]

BEAUTY

Paul insists that a work must not only exhibit truthfulness, seriousness, righteousness, and purity; it must also exhibit loveliness or beauty. The word *lovely* means "worthy to be loved." Why is something worthy to be loved? A man may say he loves his friend. It may be because he does good things for him. He is "lovely" in his actions. It is in this sense that David sang, "Saul and Jonathan were lovely and pleasant in their lives" (2 Samuel 1:23). They had done things that had endeared them to the hearts of their countrymen. But actions do not alone constitute "loveliness," for Christians are commanded to love their enemies. Obviously one's enemy does not do things that please one. How can one's enemy be "lovely"—that is, worthy of being loved? For the Christian, the fact that every human being is made in the image of God constitutes a reason for loving him. There are innately in every person certain qualities that are lovely, worthy of being loved: the ability to reason, the ability to make free choices, the ability to create, and so forth.

We often say of a colorful sunset, "It is lovely." What does the sunset *do*? It does only one thing: it pleases us, pleases our taste for color or balance or any of a great number of qualities. It is worthy of being loved. This is not to say that all men will love it. Some men are so crass or so insensitive or so uneducated that the words "It is lovely" about a sunset do not make sense to them. They have no appreciation of it. But their insensitivity or mere ignorance does not change the inherent value of the "lovely" sunset. It is worthy to be loved, whether any one ever actually loves it or not.

It is on this point that the person with the "modern" non-Christian worldview will have extreme difficulty. He will say that there is no such thing as inherent beauty. We call a sunset beautiful, he will say, because we have been educated in a tradition that perceives sunsets to be beautiful, not because they are inherently so to all people at all times. Beauty is in the eye of the beholder, he will say. To this objection, Christian critics must respond, or else we can have nothing to say to modern men. But we can respond. Of course there are those who do not see the sunset as being beautiful, and the moderns are right that this view is a result of a different education. And it is here that Christian critics may be so bold as to proclaim the cultural superiority of Christian culture. These principles of Christian criticism are not *a* way of looking at the arts, just one of many; they are *the* way of looking at the arts. Any other way is less completely human. We believe these principles to be found in God's written revelation and in nature created by God. The Christian critic looks at a work to find beauty. A work must be beautiful, having those properties that should please us as readers or viewers or listeners. This is not to say that every part of the work will be beautiful.

Technical Excellence

In his last principle of Christian criticism Paul states that which, generally, all literary critics look for: technical excellence. Paul says that a work must be "admirable" or, as the King James Version says, "of good report." The work must be spoken well of by those who are in a position to know. The art critic must find in the painting those examples of the artist's skill in the techniques of painting. The literary critic must find in the work that skill in the use of language that marks it as being technically excellent. This technical excellence in the use of words will vary of course from language to language; it is the stuff of which composition classes are made.

Conclusion

The Christian critical tradition is a long and glorious one, including the great critics of the last two thousand years. It is a wide and grand stream of literature and other art forms that have met these criteria. For these are not criteria that result in only a selected few works meeting the approval of self-appointed censors. These are standards by which the great works of art of Western civilization have been weighed—and not found wanting. These are the standards by which the necessary works for a liberal-arts education have been chosen. There are no "great books of the Western world" that do not meet this standard; no book that fails to meet this standard is a great book. These criteria do winnow literature and the arts; they do separate the good from the bad. The lying, the frivolous, the immoral, the ugly, the impure, the poorly done—these have something to fear from these principles of Christian criticism; but the truthful, the serious, the rightly done, the pure, the beautiful, the excellent—these will be commended and extolled. The principles of Christian criticism are the source of Western art and are the means by which the arts can be evaluated.

> "Every good gift and every perfect gift is from above,
> coming down from the Father of lights"
> (James 1:17).

At midnight I went topside to have a last look at the aurora, but found only a spotty glow on the horizon extended from north to northeast. I had been playing the victrola while I waited for the midnight hour. I was . . . playing one of the records of Beethoven's Fifth Symphony. The night was calm and clear. I left the door to my shack open and also my trapdoor. I stood there in the darkness to look around at some of my favorite constellations, which were as bright as I had ever seen them.

Presently I began to have the illusion that what I was seeing was also what I was hearing, so perfectly did the music seem to blend with what was happening in the sky. As the notes swelled, the dull aurora on the horizon pulsed and quickened and draped itself into arches and fanning beams which reached across the sky until at my zenith the display attained its crescendo. The music and the night became one; and I told myself that all beauty was akin and sprang from the same substance. I recalled a gallant, unselfish act that was of the same essence as the music and the aurora.[42]

CHAPTER SEVEN

The Arts and Entertainment

Matthew Steven Bracey

Going to the movie theater is a serious business. First things first: get there early. The hustle and bustle of trying to purchase your ticket, drink, and popcorn at the last minute is just no fun—to say nothing of the fact that you are worrying about whether the previews have started, whether you will end up on the dreaded front row (or else in the nosebleed section), or whether you will have to go to the restroom in the middle of the movie.

Rather, to ensure a good movie-going experience, get there with plenty of time to spare. Also, ensure that you get a center seat that is eye-level with the middle of the screen. As you make yourself comfortable in one of those theater recliners, a burning sensation in your throat from the Pepsi and butter all over your fingertips from the popcorn, people begin to fill the theater as you watch the pre-previews and then the actual previews. Finally, the lights dim, the crowd hushes, and the movie begins. Something about this experience can be indeed magical!

Movies, as well as television and music, are some of the most popular forms of art in the present day. They serve as vehicles for all kinds of culture, including high culture, folk culture, and pop culture.[1] However, the arts encompass more than these three forms. They also include architecture, cooking, dance, drama, fashion, painting, photography, poetry, prose, sculpture, and more. Their broad scope demonstrates that the arts do not concern only the artistically minded (as some might stereotypically conceive of them) but rather all human beings because we all engage with the arts in some fashion.

How then should we as Christians approach the arts? Should we simply receive them passively, or should we engage them actively, analyzing them according to the Christian worldview? How would the Christian worldview apply specifically to the topic of the arts and entertainment? I begin this chapter by discussing theological foundations for thinking through these questions, focusing specifically on the motifs of creation, Fall, redemption, and witness. Next, I turn to the subjects of form and content before considering a practical approach to engaging the arts.

However, before considering those subjects, I briefly explain how chapters six through nine form a unit concerning the arts, building upon and depending on one another. Although they fit together as hand-in-glove, they are distinct in focus. In the previous chapter, E. Darrell Holley outlined the important foundation of the Christian critical tradition, which the next three chapters utilize for various purposes. I present a theological framework for thinking through the arts in this chapter. Next, J. Matthew Pinson offers sustained reflection about the phenomenon of popular culture in contrast to folk and high cultures. Finally, Montgomery F. Thornsbury concludes this four-chapter unit on the arts by championing a traditional and biblical view of language and literature.

THEOLOGICAL FOUNDATIONS

Creation: The arts result from man's divine image-bearing.

In the beginning, God created human beings in His image, according to His likeness (Genesis 1:26–27), instructing them to be fruitful, multiply, fill the earth, subdue the earth, and rule over the animals (1:28). These commands represent God's creation mandate, which results in the phenomenon of culture and hence the arts. Man, being obedient to God's cultural mandate, takes the raw material that God has created and makes all kinds of stuff from it.

In the words of J. R. R. Tolkien, we are "sub-creators" reflecting the image of God the Creator.[2] We imagine and invent and fashion and construct because we are made in the image of the Creator. In a word, what we make is *culture* (for which reason some commentators have referred to these commands as God's *cultural mandate*), which includes everything from languages to beliefs to food to the arts to social institutions to technologies.[3] Culture follows from man's *cultivation* of the world (Genesis 2:5). As Andy Crouch puts it, God has given to man the creative calling of culture making.[4]

The arts come from man's obedience to God's command to subdue the earth. As such, they follow from God's ordering of the world, which He evaluated as "very good" (Genesis 1:31). Hence the arts do not emerge from the Fall but out of the creative nature of man, for which reason they are good and deserving of active pursuit, genuine enjoyment, and serious reflection. However, sin has distorted what God made good.

Fall: Because of sin, man pursues and produces the arts in a fallen manner. Even so, the arts can convey God's grace, as well as His goodness, truth, and beauty.

Owing to the Fall of Adam and Eve, man's first parents, who succumbed to the serpent's beguiling (Genesis 3), sin now contaminates everything, including man's capacity to steward the God-given function of culture making as God intended. Even so, not all is lost. The doctrine of total depravity does not mean that things are as bad as they could be.[5] Sin is strong, yet God is stronger. His common grace still shines through the dark cloud of man's depravity. One way that this occurs is through God's giftings: He creates different people with different artistic abilities, talents, and interests.

Tim Keller describes these endowments as "gifts of wisdom, talent, beauty, and skill according to his grace," which God casts "across the human race like seed, in order to enrich, brighten, and preserve the world."[6] Just as the parent is pleased when his or her child finds pleasure in doing good things unto right ends, so God is pleased when His children find pleasure in good things, giving Him the glory for them and not making them into idols. The arts are among God's gifts to humankind; they "enrich" the world, and they point to God as the giver of all good gifts (James 1:17). These principles, says Keller, are true even for non-Christians through whom God's common grace can still shine. In fact, Keller notes that non-Christians may sometimes "do great work—even better work—than Christians."[7]

To support that claim, Keller emphasizes a "thick" view, as opposed to a "thin" view, of the doctrines of sin and of common grace. By the term *thick*, he means a robust view of these doctrines, not a *thin* or shallow view of them. "Our thick view of sin will remind us that even explicitly Christian work and culture will always have some idolatrous discourse within it," he writes. "Our thick view of common grace will remind us that even explicitly non-Christian work and culture will always have some witness to God's truth in it."[8]

By contrast, "If we have a thin view of sin, we will feel safe if we remove from our view anything that could tempt us to commit actions of overt sexual immorality, profanity, dishonesty, or violence. By withdrawing such cultural 'texts' from our presence, we may feel less sinful; but we may be fooling ourselves." Still, Keller acknowledges the errors that can result in the culture that fallen men and women produce: "Of course, there is a great deal that is pernicious in popular culture, with its oft-noted glorification of sex and violence. The Bible tells us to flee sexual temptation (1 Corinthians 6:18–20); and a wise person will set wise boundaries."[9] In summary, a thick view of sin reminds us that artifacts made by Christians may not be as good as we suppose; and a thick view of common grace reminds us that artifacts made by non-Christians may not always be as bad as we suppose.

The virtue of prudence is exceedingly important when we consider how to interact with the arts in a fallen world. So, on the one hand, responsible engagement will include sensible limitations. On the other hand, it will avoid utter withdrawal: "Too much emphasis on wholesale withdrawal from culture increases the likelihood of slipping into other more 'respectable' idolatries," warns Keller.[10] How, then, should these principles affect how we engage the arts in a fallen world?

Keller proposes, "We will adopt a stance of critical enjoyment of human culture and its expressions in every field of work. We will learn to recognize the half-truths and resist the idols; and we will learn to recognize and celebrate the glimpses of justice, wisdom, truth, and beauty we find around us in all aspects of life."[11] Of course, these principles are easier said than done, for which reason we will consider a practical approach to engaging the arts in the last section of this chapter.

The points that Keller makes come from the broader Hebrew-Christian tradition, which has held that all truth, whence it comes, is God's truth. In the Exodus account, the Scripture explains that, when the children of Israel migrated from Egypt to the wilderness, God instructed that they "plunder" or "spoil" the Egyptians of their silver, gold, and clothing (Exodus 3:21–22; 12:35–36). This expression means that they took what the Egyptians intended for idolatry and put it toward God-honoring ends.

The church father Augustine (354–430) observed an important principle undergirding these passages: the "spoiling of the Egyptians" illuminates that the children of God may make good use of what unbelievers make to the extent it is true. Augustine explains that Moses "was well aware that true advice, from whatever mind it came, should be ascribed not to man but to the unchangeable God who is the truth. . . . For all truth comes from the one who says, 'I am the truth.'"[12] All truth, as well as goodness and beauty, has Jesus Christ, the *logos* of God, as its fount, even when non-Christians who do not otherwise acknowledge Christ communicate it through their words or demonstrate it through their actions, because truth does not exist except in God.

"A person who is a good and a true Christian," Augustine continues, "should realize that truth belongs to his Lord, wherever it is found, gathering and acknowledging it even in pagan literature, but rejecting superstitious vanities."[13] Thus the disposition we learn from Augustine, as from Keller, is not one of unmitigated saturation in or complete separation from culture but rather one of prudent engagement with culture.

John Calvin (1509–1564) also followed in this tradition. Commentating on Titus 1:12, in which the apostle Paul quotes from a pagan prophet, Calvin wrote, "All truth is from God; and consequently, if wicked men have said anything that is true and just, we ought not to reject it; for it has come from God."[14] God is ultimately the source of all truth and justice.

Similarly, in *Institutes of the Christian Religion*, Calvin wrote: "In reading profane authors, the admirable light of truth displayed in them should remind us, that the human mind, ever much fallen and perverted from its original integrity, is still adorned and invested with admirable gifts from its Creator."[15] Here, Calvin's use of the term *profane* does not refer to the obscene per se but rather to the secular, or that which is not religious or sacred. In other words, Calvin, like Augustine before him, is saying that even non-Christians can display the light of truth.

"If we reflect that the Spirit of God is the only fountain of truth," Calvin continues, "we will be careful, as we would avoid offering insult to him, not to reject or condemn truth wherever it appears."[16] Whereas Augustine links truth to Jesus Christ, Calvin associates it with the Holy Spirit. Both are right. Truth has its origin and definition in the triune God.[17]

As we will consider in greater detail later in the chapter, the Christian can appreciate and even enjoy cultural artifacts insofar as they set forth the good, true, and beautiful because such characteristics have their origin in God Himself. Still, we may understandably question those problematic elements of cultural products—what Augustine referred to as "superstitious vanities" and what Keller describes as "idolatrous discourse" and "perniciousness." However, before considering that question, we will tease out a third motif of biblical theology: redemption.

Redemption: The arts demonstrate redeemed man's obedience to God's creation mandate.

Though we are fallen, God has not left us in our pitiful condition. He has sent forth His Son to redeem what was lost (Galatians 4:4; Matthew 18:11). This redemption includes not only our personal estates but also that of the whole created order and its original function. We see this theme, for example, in the Great Commission in Matthew 28:18–20, which begins as Jesus explains that all authority has been given to Him "in heaven and on earth," a phrase that "obviously recalls Genesis 1:1 and refers to every part of creation," according to Christopher Wright.[18]

Then Jesus tells His disciples to make other disciples by baptizing them in the name of the trinitarian God and by teaching them to observe all He taught. Personal redemption encompasses a renewal of God's original purposes for humankind, which includes the cultural mandate. The Great Commission is a great restoration of God's original intentions in the cultural mandate (Genesis 1:28).

It is no coincidence that the prophecies of Isaiah and John about the new heavens and new earth (Isaiah 65–66; Revelation 21–22) call to mind images of the Garden of Eden. Biblical theology sees the doctrines of redemption and creation as intricately linked. Redemption is the renewal of God's good creation that man's sin has spoiled. John Milton (1608–1674) famously illustrated this point in his works *Paradise Lost* (1667) and *Paradise Regained* (1671). Similarly, Albert Wolters has, more recently, published *Creation Regained*.[19]

These principles mean that redemption affects the way we think about God's cultural mandate and our role as sub-creators and culture makers. In fact, the Scriptures tell us that God is using our work now in His great work of restoration. Paul establishes continuity between the present and future in 1 Corinthians 15, a chapter on the doctrine of the resurrection in which he uses the imagery of a seed. While the fruit of the seed is undoubtedly better than the seed itself, the seed is not inconsequential to the fruit; it is necessary for the fruit. What we do in the present will pale in comparison to what God will reveal, but it is still important.

N. T. Wright beautifully captures this theme, and its application to the arts, in his book *Surprised by Hope*: "What you *do* in the present—by painting, preaching, singing, sewing, praying, teaching, building hospitals, digging wells, campaigning for justice, writing poems, caring for the needy, loving your neighbor as yourself—*will last into God's future*."[20] Paul concludes 1 Corinthians 15 with these words: "Therefore, my beloved brothers, be steadfast, immovable, always abounding in the work of the Lord, knowing that in the Lord your labor is not in vain" (v. 58). The immediate context of Paul's words indicates he is not referring simply to this life but also to the next. Thus Wright, ever imaginative and poignant, writes:

> What you do in the Lord is not in vain. You are not oiling the wheels of a machine that's about to roll over a cliff. You are not restoring a great painting that's shortly going to be thrown on the fire. You are not planting roses in a garden that's about to be dug up for a building site. You are—strange though it may seem, almost as hard to believe as the resurrection itself—accomplishing something that will become in due course part of God's new world. Every act of love, gratitude, and kindness; every work of art or music inspired by the love of God and delight in the beauty of his creation; every minute spent teaching a severely handicapped child to read or to walk; every act of care and nurture, of comfort and support, for one's fellow human beings and for that matter one's fellow nonhuman creatures; and of course every prayer, all Spirit-led teaching, every deed that spreads the gospel, builds up the church, embraces and embodies holiness rather than corruption, and makes the name of Jesus honored in the world—all of this will find its way, through the resurrecting power of God, into the new creation that God will one day make. That is the logic of the mission of God. God's recreation of his wonderful world, which began with the resurrection of Jesus and continues mysteriously as God's people live in the risen Christ and in the power of his Spirit, means that what we do in Christ and by the Spirit in the present is not wasted. It will last all the way into God's new world. In fact, it will be enhanced there.
>
> I have no idea what precisely this will mean in practice. I am putting up a signpost, not offering a photograph of what we will find once we get to where the signpost is pointing.[21]

In some mysterious way, what we do in the present matters for the future. The arts are a means through which the sovereign God in Christ is renewing the world from the effects of the sin of man, for the Scripture tells us that God is summing up *all* things in Christ, "things in heaven and things on earth" (Ephesians 1:10).

They may seem to die like the seed; but by God's power they will live into eternity. Again, the phrase *in heaven and on earth* reminds us of the continuity between the original creation, redemption, and the new creation.

Witness: The arts reflect and shape the world to which God calls us to witness.

Finally, the arts are also valuable because they shape and reflect the world to which God calls us as Christians to witness. We have reviewed how the Great Commission looks back to God's good creation and informs the Christian's self-understanding. Yet the Great Commission also enjoins the Christian to go into an unbelieving world. If God is mysteriously using Christians in His restoration of the world, then we must be "in the world" (John 17:11).

As Augustine explains, members of the City of God are not geographically removed from members of the City of Man but instead live among them and interact with them in the same way that good seed grows along with bad seed in the same field until the time of harvest (Matthew 13:24–30).[22] For this reason, Jeremiah instructed the exiles to "build houses and live in them; plant gardens and eat their produce. Take wives and have sons and daughters; take wives for your sons, and give your daughters in marriage, that they may bear sons and daughters; multiply there, and do not decrease" (29:5–6). Jeremiah then connects these instructions to the broader culture: "But seek the welfare of the city where I have sent you into exile, and pray to the LORD on its behalf, for in its welfare you will find your welfare" (29:7). These passages tell us that God does not want us to retreat or withdraw from the cultures of the world.

By being in the world, we will be among its people, which necessarily will mean we have some exposure to the cultural productions they fashion. Consider that when missionaries prepare to go into a given field, they study its language, history, customs, values, and so forth—its *culture*. They become cultural exegetes. Just as responsible biblical exegesis helps us to read the Scriptures better, responsible cultural exegesis helps us to read the world better.

We see this principle in the New Testament when the apostle John appeals to the concept of *logos* (John 1:1, 14) or when Paul quotes pagan philosophers and poets, such as Aratus (Acts 17:28), Epimenides (Acts 17:28; Titus 1:12), and Menander (1 Corinthians 15:33). These instances demonstrate that the biblical authors had engaged in cultural exegesis and had used the fruit of that work in their witness.

Cultural exegesis is a worthwhile endeavor. By understanding the cultural artifacts that inform peoples' views of life and the world, we can better appreciate them for who they are. After all, people are precisely that: *people*. We do not evangelize empty shells. We build relationships with people who have hopes and dreams and opinions and reasons and hurts and grief.

We increase the quality of our witness by understanding what makes people tick, learning to appreciate people for who they are as divine image-bearers rather than seeing them as means to an end, even if that end (salvation) is a worthwhile one, because people have inherent dignity. The arts can function as the texts of a culture through which the Christian exegete of culture can learn about the non-Christian's beliefs, customs, and questions.

Writing with movies in mind, John Frame mentions another reason for cultural exegesis: "The apostle Paul said that he was not ignorant of Satan's devices (2 Corinthians 2:11). For that purpose, if for no other, we may be called to learn what filmmakers have to say to us."[23] Cultural exegesis teaches us not only about the world of people but also about the devices of the enemy.

In consideration of these principles, we can familiarize ourselves with the cultural artifacts of the world to which we witness. At times, by God's common grace, they will reflect God's goodness, truth, and beauty and, to that extent, we can legitimately enjoy them. At other times, however, they will not reflect these qualities. Yet even then they may be useful insofar as they help us better understand the worldviews of non-Christians and, thereby, improve the quality of gospel witness.

Even so, the Christian who conducts cultural exegesis must do so with prayerful wisdom. Cultural exegesis does not justify or excuse the Christian's substantive engagement with any and every cultural artifact that unbelievers produce. In fact, the mature Christian will positively *not* engage with certain cultural artifacts. Grant Horner writes, "Proximity to evil, real or represented, does not somehow taint the believer," but "this doesn't mean you should expose yourself to everything available."[24] For, as Augustine and Keller explain, much within culture is pernicious and full of idolatry.

In summary, the arts are evidence of the creative, image-bearing capacity of men and women to make and shape culture. However, the arts have been corrupted, along with the rest of the world, by sin, and, consequently, we must engage them with caution. Yet, by God's common grace, they can still convey the goodness, truth, and beauty of God. Still, even when the arts convey badness, falsehood, and ugliness, they can be useful cultural texts for the Christian to understand the world to which he or she witnesses. Having considered the theological foundations for the arts, we turn now to an analysis of the arts before ending with a model for responsible engagement with them.

Analysis of the Arts

Form and Content

Christian analysis of the arts begins with a recognition that all artifacts have both form and content, which must be evaluated according to the Christian worldview.[25] Etymologically, *content* means the "things contained." It refers to the subject matter, the themes, and the message. For example, *The Wizard of Oz* contains themes like good versus evil, courage, maturity, and the importance of home. *Les Misérables* considers the topics of brokenness and injustice, mercy and judgment, forgiveness and hope, and love and redemption. When analyzing the content of a given book or movie or program or song, we should ask what it says about subjects like God, man, love, sex, family, and sin, and then evaluate it according to the values of the Scriptures.

Whereas *content* refers to the subject or message, *form* refers to the techniques or style by which that content is expressed.[26] To analyze an artifact holistically, we will not stop at its content but will also consider the oft-overlooked element of form. Take dialogue as an example: the content is what the characters of a book or movie or television program say and what their words mean, whereas form is how the words are said.

Sometimes we practically ignore questions of form because we act as if it is neutral or inconsequential. Nothing could be further from the truth. Form necessarily communicates something. Form itself conveys content, for which reason media ecologist Marshall McLuhan famously said, "The medium is the message."[27] Jeffrey Overstreet also captures this point: "Style is substance."[28]

Consider movies: a movie with shaky, handheld camera shots and loud, warm color tones often communicates more movement, tension, and aggression than, say, a movie with still shots and subdued, cool color tones. A movie with good CGI (computer-generated imagery) can engross the viewer in an otherwise unbelievable world, but poor CGI results in the viewer not taking the world seriously.

Consequently, as we watch movies and television programs, for example, we should pay attention to their acting and characters, cinematography, dialogue, direction, editing, images and symbols, plot, pace, production design, screenplay, score, script, special effects, and tone.[29] Questions we might ask include: is the acting ridiculous or believable? Is the dialogue hackneyed or fresh? Is the production quality low or high? In other words, are the technical aspects of the movie excellent?

Other genres of the arts, whether architecture, literature, music, photography, or something else, have different elements of form to consider. The point is that, in every genre, form is important because it is not neutral but necessarily communicates something. Additionally, the better the form of the artifact, the more culturally significant and enduring it will likely be; the poorer the form, the less culturally significant it will be.

While good content does not negate the need for good form, neither does good form diminish the importance of good content. We should strive for both. As Darrell Holley explains, "Moral excellence presented in a technically un-excellent manner says that that morality is slight, unimportant, negligible, perhaps even untrue; moral excellence presented in a technically un-excellent fashion is satire; the style pokes fun at the words and changes the meaning."[30] Overstreet remarks similarly, "Much of what passes for 'Christian art' in recent decades is, in fact, simplistic, didactic, a message wrapped in mediocrity. Clunky narratives. Obvious poems. Cliche-heavy lyrics sung to derivative music."[31] Christians, who sometimes settle for mediocre form, must remember its importance.

Yet, just as poor form can cheapen an otherwise rich message, good form can also elevate an otherwise ungodly message. "We should realize that if something untrue or immoral is stated in great art," Francis Schaeffer wrote, "it can be far more destructive and devastating than if it is expressed in poor art or prosaic statement."[32] Just as Christians are not immune to the dangers of bad form for good content, they are also not immune to the dangers of bad content for good form.

Contemporary entertainment culture offers many examples of this phenomenon because some Christians increasingly derive their values more from the music and movies of pop culture than from the Scriptures. However, it is not because God's Word fails to present an ethic that can shape our engagement with the arts and entertainment, which Holley has referred to as the Christian critical tradition (see chapter six).

The Christian Critical Tradition

Christians should engage with and analyze the arts according to the objective values the apostle Paul presents in Philippians 4:7–8, aiming to dwell on the peaceful, true, honorable, right, pure, lovely, commendable, excellent, and praiseworthy rather than on the violent, false, dishonorable, wrong, impure, horrible, reprehensible, poor, and disgraceful.[33] Are the form and content of a given artifact characterized by the former qualities or the latter ones?

For example, Pieter Bruegel the Younger's *The Four Seasons, Spring* is a beautiful painting about the creation and stewardship of culture resulting from subduing the earth, ruling over its creatures, and forming human bonds and society. (Readers may see this image on the dust jacket of this book.) These themes are evident in the painting as men and women till the ground, water the vegetation, build and inhabit structures, practice animal husbandry, dance, and so forth. To use the language of Paul, *The Four Seasons, Spring* is noble, excellent, and true to reality. By contrast, Pablo Picasso's cubism is often not good or true or beautiful, either in its form or its content; its form is often incoherent, and, when it is coherent, its content is often violent, impure, and disgraceful.

Of all the values of the Christian critical tradition, excellence in form can be the most challenging to grasp. What precisely is technical excellence? Holley writes, "The work must be spoken well of by those who are in a position to know."[34] This principle means we must consult the experts, sometimes referred to as critics, of the field in question.

However, we must be careful and prudent when we consider what the critics have to say about a work because many of them are not Christians and, consequently, do not analyze a given artifact from a Christian perspective. Therefore, with respect to statements they make about values such as goodness and truth and beauty, we must consider their worldviews (like we would when interacting with someone in any other field). While we should not mindlessly accept what the art critic says, we should not simply dismiss him or her either. Sometimes, non-Christian critics get form right and content wrong. Yet even when we do not agree with everything they say, they are experts in their fields, competent and trained and helpful.

Modern Art

The prior reference to the cubism of Picasso raises the question of modern art. How ought the Christian to think about modern art, and how do the principles of the Christian critical tradition inform the topic? Thinkers such as Hans Rookmaaker, Francis Schaeffer, and Roger Scruton have all criticized the phenomenon of modern art (and, by extension, postmodern art). Rookmaaker, in his book *Modern Art and the Death of a Culture*, shows how modern art is anarchic, irrational, and nihilistic—how it, in a phrase, contributes to the death of a culture.[35] Likewise, Schaeffer has observed how the art of post-impressionism became increasingly fragmented and hopeless.[36] Such fragmentation, he argued, represents a "complete break with the art of the Renaissance which had been founded on man's humanist hope."[37] Scruton, in his excellent introduction *Beauty*, wrote about how "art became the enterprise through which the individual announces himself to the world and calls on the gods for vindication. Yet it has proved singularly unreliable as the guardian of our higher aspirations."[38] In short, much within the art of modernity and postmodernity has become absurd, incoherent, and stifling.

Stephen Hicks has similarly argued that, with modern art, "art became ugly." It became a quest for the brutal truth (as interpreted by a people with modernist philosophical and aesthetic convictions), not a quest for beauty. Whereas Schaeffer criticized post-impressionism, Hicks criticizes reductionism, which eliminated "the third dimension, composition, color, perceptual content, and the sense of the art object as something special."[39] Hicks also observes how postmodern art has continued the themes of modernism but has developed its own characteristics. Postmodern art has become obsessed with self-referential and ironic content; it cannot take itself seriously. Postmodern art pursues deconstructionist ideologies, employing a hermeneutic of suspicion to practically everything, especially to that which characterizes tradition or the West. Postmodern art affirms social realities and denies natural or objective realities; for example, it views realities through subjective categories, such as power, money, and sex (e.g., gender identity or racial identity), and denies (functionally if not literally) objective realities. Finally, postmodern art promotes nihilism, focusing on the bizarre, the perverse, and the strange (e.g., entrails, blood, unusual sex, urine, and feces).[40]

The trajectory of modern (and postmodern) art goes explicitly against the sensibilities of the Christian critical tradition. It also indicates a move away from realism in art, or representational art, because, quite literally, it does not represent the world as it is. For example, deconstruction and fragmentation are not peaceful but chaotic. Utter brutality is not true. To be sure, sin has made aspects of our world ugly, but a Christian aesthetic does not wallow in that ugliness. Rather, we look for ways in which the God of redemption is restoring brokenness. Reductionism does not cohere with the world as it really is—as God has made it—which is with dimension and composition and color and content. Nihilism is not pure or lovely or praiseworthy. Ordinary, everyday people do not generally enjoy these elitist art movements; they believe in universal truth (of some kind), and they do not enjoy the bizarre.

The Christian understanding of art is more like the Japanese art of *kintsugi*, which is a form of restoring broken pottery with an adhesive mixture of powdered gold or silver so that the dish retains its shape, except that, now, it is more beautiful than it was to begin with because it has veins of gold and silver running through its frame. With kintsugi, there is brokenness, but there is also restoration. The fundamental problem with the art of modernism and postmodern is that it has brokenness without restoration, despair without hope.

Isn't the message what really matters? Isn't beauty in the eye of the beholder?

Notwithstanding the principles that Paul puts forward in Philippians 4:7–8 or the problems with modern art, some Christians still adopt a relativistic aesthetic, especially with respect to form. "Aren't these things just a matter of taste?" they ask. "I like rap, my father likes rock, my grandfather likes country. Isn't the message what really matters?" Some have even wondered, "Isn't beauty in the eye of the beholder?"

That way of thinking stands positively at odds with the Christian critical tradition, and it demonstrates a postmodern, non-Christian worldview. In the words of Paul Munson and Joshua Farris Drake, "No movement in history has been more hostile to beauty than postmodernism."[41] If we insist that beauty is in the eye of the beholder, then we have no basis to judge some art as ugly. However, the apostle Paul did not believe that such qualities are relative.

The Christian view of beauty recognizes that beauty is objective. "Jesus assumed that beauty is more than preference but something objective and important," write Munson and Drake, "so much so that it ought to play a role in the disciples' ethical decision making."[42] Hence, as Christians, we cannot believe that beauty is in the eye of the beholder because Jesus did not believe that proposition.

Remember, a Christian view of the arts recognizes that form itself has meaning, and, consequently, is not neutral or relative. "Such concepts as beauty and form are not religiously neutral," says Frame.[43] Just because we call a rock song *pure* or a rap song *lovely* does not mean they, in fact, reflect the qualities of purity or loveliness. Such values have an objective meaning, both in terms of form and content, external to the shifting whims of human personality, cultural sensibility, and societal pressure. A question we must ask, then, is whether a particular genre or medium can convey a particular value or virtue in a manner that does that value or virtue justice.

Munson and Drake caution Christians against aesthetic relativism, or the belief that beauty is simply subjective: "The end of aesthetic relativism is aesthetic immaturity. Mind you, this describes more than nonbelievers. It also describes Bible-believing Christians who have adopted the world's aesthetic relativism, which is in fact aesthetic rebellion."[44] Aesthetic relativism, whether regarding content or form, is worldliness.

The fact that form is not neutral but communicates something significant can be illustrated through musical examples. Mourners would not generally play circus music at funerals (except in cases of funerals for clowns perhaps) because that musical form communicates a whimsicalness that does not fit the occasion of a funeral. Similarly, artists would not with seriousness sing, "It Is Well with My Soul," with its lyrics, "When peace like a river, attendeth my way," to the style of thrash metal because that form is, by its nature, not peaceful and would undermine the song's message.

Intuitively, we know that form is not neutral because we have all experienced how different styles of music stimulate us in different ways. One style of music inspires foot-tapping, another encourages body-gyrating, and another provokes headbanging. Some styles move us to contemplation while others cause us to sway our bodies. In sum, form is not simply neutral or relative because it is not valueless. Contained within a given form are values that are either consistent with a Christian worldview or not. Having considered a theological foundation for and introduced art analysis, we now turn to how we should engage the arts and entertainment with Christian sensibilities.

Engaging the Arts and Entertainment

For practically everyone, the arts and entertainment are, for good or for ill, part of the air they breathe. They are inescapable. How, then, can the Christian interact meaningfully with movies and television shows and songs while also being cautious about their dangers? Here are several practical ways to engage the arts and entertainment.

Begin with a solid theological foundation. Yet recognize that art analysis is complicated because practically nothing is wholly good or wholly bad. Legitimately enjoy culture that is consistent with the good, true, and beautiful. However, guard against the danger of enjoying the bad, false, and ugly. By so doing, we can avoid the one extreme of compromise and resist the other extreme of withdrawal. We can exegete culture that does not reflect Christian values but must do so with great care and wisdom, ensuring we do not exchange exegesis for enjoyment. Through the course of this section, we will look to each of these principles.

1. Begin with a solid foundation.

If we are going to analyze the arts and entertainment responsibly, we must have a sure foundation. Otherwise, we will build our house on sand rather than on rock (Matthew 7:24–28). Knowing God's Word is crucial. We should examine culture through the motifs of creation, the Fall, redemption, and witness as well as through the Christian critical tradition.

The doctrine of creation demonstrates that the arts have value in themselves because they result from divine image-bearing and from man's obedience to God's cultural mandate. However, the doctrine of the Fall reminds us that they are full of pernicious artifacts that do not comport with God's goodness, truth, and beauty because all people are sinners; yet God's common grace abides so that people and products are not as bad as they could be.

The doctrine of redemption shows us that God desires to redeem fallen men and women so that they produce and engage with the arts and entertainment in a God-honoring way. Even though the Christian is being redeemed, the reality of sin means that the Christian's cultural artifacts are not fully good. At the same time, the reality of God's common grace means that the non-Christian's cultural artifacts are not fully bad.

The Christian critic will learn to analyze not only the artist's beliefs and intentions but also the form and content of the artist's work, observing its characteristics and values. The Christian critical tradition teaches us that some things are objectively peaceful, true, honorable, right, pure, lovely, reputable, excellent, and praiseworthy, and that some things are not (Philippians 4:7–8). These standards teach us to distinguish between what is and what is not consistent with the Christian worldview.

Thus we should always examine the worldview of a given movie or program or song or book or clothing article or image. Frame says that doing so is paramount: "That is the element that is most culturally influential (often in a destructive way), and it is often most central to the [artist's] purpose."[45] What does a given artifact say about things like God, man, life, death, sexuality, sin, despair, loss, happiness, and hope? Christians and non-Christians alike ask these big worldview questions—what F. Leroy Forlines refers to as the "inescapable questions of life."[46] On a basic human level, we can relate to these questions and the quest they inspire because we all ask them, even if we do not always agree with the answers that people propose.

2. Recognize the complicated nature of art analysis.

The difficulty, of course, is that most cultural products have elements that are both praiseworthy and blameworthy. Consider the types of movies and programs and songs the critics love: technically excellent artifacts that often promote non-Christian morality. Now consider the stereotypical Christian cultural artifact: it lacks not only good form, having subpar production value, for example, but often even good content, exchanging dynamic themes for cheap sentimentalism and simplistic moralism.

This stereotype was not always true of Christian artists. We can find all kinds of examples of excellent art produced by Christians, or by people who identified themselves as Christians, in decades and centuries past, such as the poetry of John Donne or George Herbert or Gerard Manley Hopkins or T. S. Eliot, or the painting of Albrecht Dürer or Pieter Bruegel the Elder or Rembrandt, or the music of Johann Sebastian Bach or George Frideric Handel, or the fiction of Fyodor Dostoevsky or George MacDonald or Flannery O'Connor. The problems of contemporary Christian art notwithstanding, we see some exceptions to this general rule, whether in terms of the hymn writing (i.e., poetry) of Keith and Kristyn Getty or Matt Boswell or Bob Kauflin, or in the writings of Wendell Berry or Andrew Peterson.[47]

Exceptions aside, many artifacts lack in being good, true, and beautiful, where others lack in being commendable, excellent, and praiseworthy. Yet in a world of sin where God's common grace still abides, most works will be neither wholly good nor wholly bad, whether produced by Christians or non-Christians. How, then, do we engage with the arts and entertainment in such a world? Must we choose between good content and good form? Additionally, how do we responsibly engage with bad content or bad form?

3. Enjoy culture that is consistent with the good, true, and beautiful.

We can legitimately enjoy culture that is consistent with the Christian worldview in terms of quality of form and content. Such artifacts may or may not have been created by Christians but still display truth and inspire joy. In the words of Forlines, "We do not have to reject everything that society provides."[48] As previously noted, Augustine and Calvin taught that all truth has its origin in God Himself and, consequently, the Christian ought not to reject it. Similarly, Basil the Great (330–379) remarked that Christians may learn "true virtue" from pagan poets and lore insofar as they reflect truth.[49]

Consider that many people resonate with that story, told time and again, of good beating of evil. Think of (spoiler alert!) Jimmy Stewart's George Bailey persevering through the hostility of Mr. Potter in *It's a Wonderful Life*. Or consider Harrison Ford's Indiana Jones defeating the Nazis in *Raiders of the Lost Ark*. Or recall Mark Hamill's Luke Skywalker destroying the Death Star and thwarting the evil Darth Vader (at least, for a time) in *Star Wars*. We resonate with this theme because it is true, and we can legitimately enjoy such stories and even learn things from them.

Rarely will a single medium, such as film, be exclusively characterized by a single type of culture: high, folk, or pop. In other words, the form and content of movies and music and television programs, as well as architecture and fashion and sculpture, may or may not contain the qualities that are consistent with the Christian critical tradition. For example, movies that are scripted and edited in such a manner that the dialogue of their characters does not extend beyond shallow remarks and short quips reflect different cultural values than movies with scenes of dialogue that last five or ten minutes. Clothing that will be outdated in a few years reflects different cultural values than clothing that can be worn for years and even decades; the timeless is higher than the trendy.

One complication from these principles with which we must reckon concerns pop culture. J. Matthew Pinson spends much more time with this question in the next chapter. For now, though, consider the pop culture artifacts of decades past. Now realize that there are many more untold examples of these artifacts you have never heard of precisely because they were insignificant and thus were resigned to the dustbin of history—here today, gone tomorrow.

Consider also that the Scriptures instruct Christians to uphold values such as tradition, continuity, and permanence. If we are not careful, an uncritical diet of pop culture will implicitly undermine our call to constancy and to intergenerational relatedness since many of these works divide us into distinct affinity groups. For example, just consider how people from different generations tend to watch different movies and television programs, listen to different music, and wear different clothes.

And yet, while much of pop culture is fleeting, it is not universally or equally insignificant or divisive. Contemporary history suggests that some of it may unite generations and endure beyond the moment. Yet perhaps part of the reason some works of pop culture have endured and have broad appeal is that they harken back to something older, something higher, through their characteristics of folk and high cultures. These forms of culture do not exist in mutually exclusive, hermetically sealed categories. They sometimes overlap, with pop culture bleeding over into folk culture and folk culture bleeding over into high culture; just think about certain bands or singers or styles of music. Therefore, mature analysis of the arts requires careful, reflective thinking and nuance.

Whatever the case, we can genuinely enjoy artistic works that do not undermine the Christian virtues in their form and content. Perhaps this principle means we may prudently engage with the very best of pop culture. But we should not utterly immerse ourselves in it, and we should not interact exclusively with it. We should not drink too deeply from the well of pop culture because the diet it provides of the trendy, short-lived, and fleeting undermines biblical virtue. Also, we should give attention to artifacts that can bear the scrutiny of sustained reflection and push us toward higher, more historic artifacts than cheap, transitory ones.

Some might wonder, "What if a given artifact demonstrates godly values in its form and content, but I just don't personally like it? For example, what if I just don't enjoy fantasy stories like, say, *The Chronicles of Narnia* or *The Lord of the Rings*, or what if I just don't like folk culture or high culture, even though I've tried to enjoy them? Can there be legitimate differences of opinion?" Indeed, we have legitimate differences of opinion sometimes. These may result from God-given differences of personality or from the tastes we have cultivated through the years.

However, subjective differences that are intrinsic to the nature of art analysis do not mean that artistic merit and quality of form is merely a matter of personal preference. It does not mean that aesthetic relativism is true. Personal subjectivity is not tantamount to ontological relativity because objective standards still exist outside of the subjective self. A given artifact may be good, even if we have not developed the taste for it, just as coffee may be good, whether or not someone recognizes it as such.

A Christian analysis of the arts and entertainment will thus recognize that a spectrum of opinion may exist but will not forsake the objective ideals. And, as I discuss at greater length below, Christian reflection of the arts will also push us outside our comfort zones so that we might come to enjoy better, higher things to which we might be unaccustomed.

4. Guard against enjoying the bad, false, and ugly and disliking the good, true, and beautiful.

We must be careful not to become self-deceived and come to enjoy the bad or to disdain the good. Self-deception can work in either direction. We will enjoy what we value. Accordingly, we must learn to value the right things. In the words of Forlines, we must learn to view sin as bad and righteousness as good:

> We must not buy the devil's propaganda that sin is more enjoyable than righteousness. We are made for righteousness. Sin is a poisonous diet that will lead to serious malfunction in this life and damnation in the life to come. Sin is like ocean water to [a] thirsty man on a life raft. At first it is pleasant, but then it leads to serious consequences. To drink is to sacrifice

the future on the altar of the immediate. Such a decision is the choice of one the Bible calls a fool. . . . Righteousness is the diet for which man is designed. . . . Hungering and thirsting after righteousness is a must for the one who is in the pursuit of ethical truth. . . . It is imperative that we have a deep conviction that righteousness is good and sin is bad.[50]

We learn to hunger and thirst for righteousness through the ordinary means of grace that God has given us such as Bible intake and meditation, prayer, and Christian community. We learn to enjoy the good, true, and beautiful by following a diet of culture that reflects those values. Even if we do not enjoy good culture at first, we can in time learn to do so, in the same way people learn to appreciate good food and come to dislike bad food.

Just as we must take care not to enjoy the bad, we must also train ourselves not to disdain the good. In *The Last Battle*, the great lion Aslan invites the self-sufficient dwarves to a glorious feast with the choicest foods and finest drinks. However, they deceived themselves into thinking "they were eating and drinking only the sort of things you might find in a stable." Aslan remarks, "They will not let us help them. They have chosen cunning instead of belief. Their prison is only in their own minds, yet they are in that prison; and so afraid of being taken in that they cannot be taken out."[51] Just as we can learn to like good food, even though we do not enjoy it initially, we can also deceive ourselves into liking bad food. The same is true of culture: we can learn to like good culture, or we can deceive ourselves into liking bad culture.

Part of what makes art analysis challenging is that it involves categories not only of *right* and *wrong* but also of *good* and *bad*. Hence analysis of the arts is (pardon the pun) more of an art than a science. And while the categories of *right* and *wrong*, and *good* and *bad*, may be distinct, they also overlap. In the words of Forlines, "Holiness cannot ignore ideals. We may be able to distinguish between the right and the good, but when we cease to uphold the good, given enough time, we will cease to uphold the right."[52] For this reason, a Christian analysis of the arts will avoid simplistic conclusions about the merit (or lack thereof) of a given artifact based simply on whether it presents right or wrong morals but will also examine whether it does so in a good or bad manner.

5. Avoid the extremes of either compromise or withdrawal.

Because of the difficulties inherent to engagement with the arts and entertainment in a sinful world, we must guard against compromising the faith. "No part of human experiences has been more subjected to the influences of sin than the area of pleasure and entertainment," proposes Forlines. We must remain faithful to God's Word in our ideals, character, and morals.[53]

At the same time, we must also guard against withdrawing from the cultures in which we find ourselves. Evangelical leader Carl F. H. Henry criticized the posture of withdrawal, referring to it as the "uneasy conscience of modern fundamentalism," because fundamentalists, in the first half of the twentieth century, had effectively withdrawn from faithful cultural witness.[54] God has not called us to cocoon ourselves from the cultures of the world because they unavoidably form the backdrop of the lives of believers and unbelievers alike. Yet, in appropriately engaging the culture, we should avoid two common errors.

First, we should avoid an anything goes, laissez-faire, no-holds-barred cultural ethic in which we engage with practically anything and everything. Russell Moore refers to Christians who do so as "*South Park* Evangelicals." These are "culturally libertarian hipster right-wingers" who enjoy "the crude humor of the R-rated cartoon *South Park*" and "wish to distance themselves from their dour fellow conservatives by assuring liberal opinion-makers that they can be both right-wing and cool."[55] Here, Moore uses the example of *South Park* to illustrate the broad category of people who are too indulgent or permissive in their engagement with works that are edgy, smutty, and vulgar, lacking in refinement and good taste.

Such people are often guilty of what Forlines called short-list legalism, seeming to believe that something is permissible if the Bible does not explicitly prohibit it.[56] However, the Scriptures are more than explicit commands; they also give principles and paradigms for our lives that we apply carefully and prayerfully. Neither artistic excellence nor so-called incarnational living negates our call to godliness and purity. As mentioned above, holiness cannot ignore ideals.[57]

The second error is to swear off secular and non-religious artifacts altogether and to replace them with Christian ones. If the first error is one of compromise, this one is one of withdrawal. Moore refers to those who choose this approach as "off-brand evangelicals," who "take trends in pop culture and reproduce them in Christian dialect for use within the Evangelical subculture, with the hope of making it more attractive not only to those outside but to those within."[58] Whereas *South Park* evangelicals may be guilty of short-list legalism, off-brand evangelicals are often guilty of long-list legalism, piling rules atop already-existing laws.[59]

At the same time, in critiquing off-brand evangelicalism, we must still take biblical boundaries and spiritual standards seriously. "A person is not a legalist simply because he has deep convictions," explains Forlines.[60] God has called us out of darkness into light as a holy people to proclaim His excellencies (2 Peter 2:9).

Like *South Park* evangelicalism, off-brand evangelicalism also has its problems. "To avoid non-Christian influence altogether," says Frame, "we would have to live as hermits."[61] However, we all live in a world with cultures. Even if we could live as cultural hermits who consume only explicitly Christian works, we would not avoid the real problem because, as Keller reminds us in his discussion of thick versus thin views of sin, explicitly Christian culture is still tainted.[62]

Besides, God has not called us to forsake the world. He has called us to be in the world but not of it (John 15:19; 17:14–16). Pinson captures this idea well when he writes we must learn to "withdraw from the world in our values, attitudes, priorities, and habits" (2 Corinthians 6:17) and to "permeate the world with our presence in it and our active engagement with it" (Mark 16:15).[63] Serious Christian witness means not separating ourselves from the cultures of the world while also not succumbing to their godlessness.

Augustine illustrated this middle way between the utter rejection and utter captivation of the world. He contended that Christians should not reject the literature and music of non-Christians because, through them, Christians may learn "something of value for understanding holy scripture" that "may help us appreciate spiritual truths." Still, Christians should exercise caution to reject "pagan superstitions" and avoid being "captivated by the vanities of the theatre."[64] Whenever we read a book or look at an image or watch a movie or listen to a song or wear an article of clothing, we will sometimes observe themes of beauty, goodness, justice, redemption, truth, and other such qualities even from non-Christians.[65] Yet we must avoid being lulled into a false sense of security and evaluate the work holistically.

6. Exegete culture with care and wisdom.

A final reason not to forsake the cultures of the world is because, through them, we better understand the people with whom we form relationships and to whom we witness. "How can we pray for a world we know nothing about?" Frame asks. "We must not seek to isolate ourselves from the world, but rather to be 'salt' and 'light' in our fallen culture, to carry out our Lord's Great Commission." Consequently, we must learn to "live amid secular (=anti-Christian) influence without ourselves compromising the faith."[66]

Remember that sometimes the artifacts of the world will cohere with the good, true, and beautiful, such as those books and movies that we can legitimately enjoy. We can use such points of Christ-culture intersection to build bridges with those to whom we are witnessing, as Paul did at Mars Hill (Acts 17:22–34). However, such artifacts will sometimes, even often, not cohere with the good. Understanding problematic cultures is not tantamount to enjoying them. As Christians we should not find joy in works that celebrate sin and unrighteousness. Still, they can serve as texts by which we study the world in which we live. The arts are like a window into the soul of the culture: the view is not always pretty, but it reveals to us our mission fields.

Still, being in the world but not of it can be challenging. As mentioned above, if we are not careful in our effort to exegete culture, we could end up enjoying its problematic elements. To avoid this danger, we might err on the side of caution rather than that of license. "The problem comes when a person wants to live on the outer edges of what is right," writes Forlines. "He is more interested in not giving up too much than he is in not giving up enough."[67] While we can enjoy what is consistent with the good, true, and beautiful, we should not enjoy what is not.

But sometimes we are like Paul in Romans 7 doing not what we want to do but what we hate to do (vv. 14–25). We must constantly guard against this temptation and repent when we succumb to it. For this reason, we should engage the arts and entertainment not as lone rangers but rather with prayer and accountability in a community of mature Christians. Additionally, we must constantly challenge ourselves to desire what is consistent with biblical values. In addition to the virtues of the Christian critical tradition, we can also consider the fruit of Christ and His Spirit (Ephesians 5:9; Galatians 5:22–23): righteousness, truth, love, joy, peace, patience, kindness, goodness, faithfulness, gentleness, and self-control.

At times, this goal may mean making hard decisions not to listen to certain songs or watch certain movies or programs, decisions that may be difficult when some in our peer groups paint us as legalistic and self-righteous. So be it. While we should not be sanctimonious (but rather humble) about our personal convictions, our allegiance is not to people but to a Person, Jesus. Willingly partaking in a steady diet of poor language, senseless violence, and sinful sexuality is simply not spiritually healthy. Instead, our cultural diet should consist overwhelmingly in Christian fruit.

Conclusion

God wants us to be in society and to create, engage with, and renew culture. Not all Christians will interact with the arts and entertainment in the same way, but, whatever the manner of engagement, we must engage these spheres Christianly. In Christ every thought is being taken captive (2 Corinthians 10:5), and all things are being summed up (Ephesians 1:10), including the arts and entertainment.

To the extent God has created you to do so, enjoy these cultural spheres, using Christian discernment and wisdom toward both form and content. In the words of Horner, reclaim "the lost art of discernment."[68] Refine your tastes according to objective standards of the Christian critical tradition as presented in Philippians 4:7–8 and analyze the arts and entertainment by them.

Train your affections and mind to enjoy what is consistent with the Christian worldview. Yet exercise great care and vigilance to guard against the threat of spiritual compromise. Discuss your initial reflections and questions about a given work with trusted friends and family as iron sharpening iron (Proverbs 27:17) and thereby grow in Christian discipleship and community. And, in "whatever you do, do all to the glory of God" (1 Corinthians 10:31).

CHAPTER EIGHT

The Christian and Popular Culture

J. Matthew Pinson

A Moment of Truth

I experienced a "moment of truth" shortly after the Amish school massacre that occurred in 2006. A psychologist wrote that we must realize how much more horrifying these murders were to the Amish school children who witnessed them than they would have been to "normal" American school children, who will witness more than 16,000 murders on average via video media by the time they reach the age of eighteen.[1] I said to myself, "If that's what it means to be a normal American child, then I don't want my children to be normal."

Now please understand that I am not saying we should never watch television—or Netflix or YouTube or some other streaming service. I am simply saying we have become so accustomed to immersion in electronic media that we do not realize that children watching 16,000 murders by the time they are eighteen is what is truly abnormal. I am saying that Christians need to be more careful and critical about their immersion in and engagement with the popular culture around them.

Christ Transforming Culture

As I said in chapter one, the church's most important challenge in our time is to discern how to be in the world but not of the world, how to bring about transformation in our lives and the culture around us through the values and priorities of Christ's kingdom. This posture will avoid a Christ against culture model (not in the world, not of the world) and a Christ-of-culture model (in the world and of the world). It will also avoid what too often characterizes evangelical Christianity: a mentality of "not in the world but of the world"— mimicking the secular culture while retreating into an evangelical enclave that shuts us off from genuine cultural engagement. In short, as writers like Thomas Oden and Marva Dawn have said, we must be against the world (*contra mundum*) to be for the world.

Being in the world but not of the world, being motivated by the attitudes and values of the kingdom of Christ rather than the kingdoms of this world, will mean that the very cultural products we create, and our consumption of the cultural products others create, will be transformed. Restoring culture necessarily involves transforming it. As a result, cultural products we create and consume will be different—and not only different in the message we communicate but also different in the *way* we communicate that message. Our kingdom orientation will radically transform our *content* and our *form*.

Form and Content

Notice those two words: form and content. The form or style of a cultural product communicates things just as the content does.[2] In music, for example, the content (substance, message) consists of the lyrics, whereas the form (style) consists of the musical, aesthetic, and cultural characteristics of a song or genre of music. Form also includes the cultural context of a given genre and the meaning ascribed to it by its creators.

Ancient wisdom held that the style or form of what is being communicated is often just as important as—and sometimes more important than—the message (content or substance). Therefore, premodern people placed emphasis on eloquence and rhetoric, the *way* one says something, not just on the content of *what* is said. In other words, the way we communicate something, the form we use, also communicates something.

Modernity, however, has driven a wedge between form and content. A radical separation of style and substance became widespread in philosophical circles by the late twentieth century. Philosophical conservatives do not subscribe to this dualism.[3] Instead, they believe that form communicates things just as content does.

Those evangelicals who believe that style is relative are the first self-conscious conservatives in history to be cultural or aesthetic relativists. They say, "It doesn't matter what the methods are, as long as the message doesn't change." When we talk about the arts and entertainment (as discussed in chapter seven) in the specific context of popular culture, we are talking about form. All Christians agree that content must comport with biblical commands. Where we need discernment and wisdom is in the subtle ways the *forms* of culture can militate against the Spirit of Christ.

While we take medium seriously, we also recognize that different media—whether paint or sculpture or prose or poetry or film or television—can all serve as vehicles for values usually associated with pop, folk, or high culture. In other words, we should avoid thinking of poetry and prose as being media only of high or folk culture; these media may also serve as vehicles for popular culture. Likewise, we should avoid thinking of television and cinema as being mediums only of popular culture; they, too, may serve as vehicles of high and folk culture. We must find ways to engage all these media in appropriate ways to the glory of God.

Taking Our Cues from the Kingdom

Christian writers like Ken Myers, Marva Dawn, T. David Gordon, and others advocate that Christians return to creating and consuming cultural products that take their cues from kingdom values that transform the arts and entertainment, science, education, politics, and other expressions of contemporary culture.[4] This goal involves a working out of the ramifications of the riches of the Christian tradition for contemporary culture, not just turning our backs on our cultural inheritance and wolfing down the products of a superficial, rootless, and empty culture that has resulted from the values of consumerism.

This ideal involves being *in* the culture but not *of* the culture. It means seeing the impact of culture on Christian faith, which involves more than whether a certain cultural product violates an explicit biblical command (legalism). It also calls for *discernment* about how popular culture and its contexts and products subtly undermine our ability to engage in faithful Christian discipleship and worship so that we can serve as countercultural witnesses to Christ in the world. Yet to create a Christian culture that can offer transformation—rather than just imitation—of secular culture, we must understand why the culture around us is problematic for the thinking Christian. We must ask how immersion in pop culture makes it hard to engage in Christian discipleship and worship.

Of course I am not saying that all engagement with any popular culture is wrong. As Myers says, "You can enjoy popular culture without compromising Biblical principles as long as you are not dominated by the sensibility of popular culture, as long as you are not captivated by its idols."[5] We can enjoy the very best of popular culture, as I suggest below. However, our problem is not mere engagement; it is utter immersion. So often we do not enjoy it in the way Myers recommends but are instead dominated by its sensibilities.

This sort of discernment is difficult because Christians today are so accustomed to thinking legalistically. As Leroy Forlines says, there are two kinds of legalism: long-list legalism and short-list legalism.[6] The legalism we object to most often is long-list legalism, the pharisaical kind that has a long list of extra-biblical prohibitions that are strictly enforced and viewed as sinful when violated. Yet I think that, for early twenty-first-century Christians, the temptation is not long-list legalism but rather short-list legalism. This kind requires a chapter-and-verse—a "Thou shalt not"—to refrain from a particular activity, rather than thinking in terms of principles and the embodiment of the true, good, and beautiful.

In contrast to short-list legalism, Christian discipleship in Scripture is more about wise living—living to please God out of love for Him, not just keeping commands. The biblical mindset for discernment regarding popular culture is not "Thou shalt not." Instead, it is more like Old Testament themes such as growing in wisdom and New Testament themes such as "'All things are lawful,' but not all things are helpful. 'All things are lawful,' but not all things build up" (1 Corinthians. 10:23).[7] Old Testament scholar Derek Kidner argues that godly living in the Old Testament takes its cues not only from the clear-cut moral commands in the law and the prophets but also from the discernment of the wisdom literature, which "summons us to think hard as well as humbly; to keep our eyes open, to use our conscience and our common sense, and not to shirk the most disturbing questions."[8]

So our aim is "to keep our eyes open," to think hard and use wisdom when it comes to our interaction with the culture around us. Our goal is to view it critically, not naively. When we do these things, we can flourish better as the human beings God created us to be, living more authentic, satisfying, and fulfilling lives of Christian discipleship as individuals, families, and churches.[9] First, however, we need to get some idea of how principles of Holy Scripture should come to bear on our analysis and critique of pop culture—how Christian virtue should shape our cultural lives.

Christian Virtue

Let us discuss how Christian virtue—what Scripture teaches about the true, good, and beautiful—should shape our understanding of culture and our lives within it. We are not accustomed to doing this. Modern biblical interpretation has tended to drive a wedge between creation and spirituality. Culture is a matter of creation—created people creating objects and practices for the enjoyment of humanity. However, we tend to abstract creation and created things from spiritual things. Understanding human beings' four basic relationships can help us with this connection: (1) our relationship to God, (2) our relationship to others, (3) our relationship to ourselves, and (4) our relationship to creation.[10]

The way we moderns too often interpret the Bible and its virtues applies them to the first three relationships but not to the fourth. However, Holy Scripture teaches—and the Christian tradition has believed—that Christian virtue not only touches spiritual or interpersonal issues but also influences our relationship with creation, our relationship with culture and cultural products. How we relate to created cultural products—like a television series or a musical style or a political party or a painting or an iPhone or pollution—is connected to Christian virtue. We must bow to the lordship of Christ and take every thought captive to His obedience (2 Corinthians 10:5) in these "creational" areas (the fourth basic relationship) as well as in the more "spiritual" things covered by the other three basic relationships: loving God, caring for others, and having a Christ-like self-image.

Thus, when we look at Christian virtues—like patience or moderation or modesty or excellence or humility—we should not think of them *only* as "spiritual" virtues: patience with people, moderation in the ways we treat fellow believers, modesty as in keeping "everything covered up," excellence in feelings and spirituality, humility in our self-image.

The Christian virtues also compel us to think, for example, in terms of whether binging too many television programs causes us to be impatient, whether the music we listen to on Spotify embodies and encourages the virtues of moderation and balance and harmony and order, whether our body language exudes modesty even when we have "everything covered up," whether we value excellence and skill in what we do and the things we create and the way we dress, whether our worship services are characterized by humility or by the glitz and glamor of entertainment values. These are just a few examples of how we can think of Christian virtues in ways that account for that fourth basic relationship: our relationship with creation and thus with culture.

In chapter six of this book, E. Darrell Holley is perceptive in his application of Christian virtue to the evaluation of cultural products and works of art, arguing that we should use Philippians 4:8 to evaluate popular culture. Myers is right when he argues that this passage is not saying we should meditate on what we merely "*think* is lovely, or whatever we *feel* is admirable." Rather, we need to "give sustained attention to whatever is *objectively* true and noble and right."[11]

Myers rightly argues that the apostle Paul's admonition to "set your minds on things that are above" (Colossians 3:2) causes us to want to engage with works of art that reflect a sense of the transcendence of God. This admonition also applies to excellence. When we root our view of culture in things above, in transcendent things, we aspire to excellence, to nobility, to virtue. We want the church—and our own lives as its members and our families' lives—to be an outpost of the kingdom and its royal values. Thus excellence is related to what Philippians 4:8 calls honor or nobility. Living like royals will cause us to live our lives in an excellent way.[12]

This brief discussion gives just a few examples of Christian virtues that we must consider as we evaluate how we relate to the culture around us. Other more obvious virtues such as patience, transcendence, depth, community, avoidance of covetousness, decency, order, intergenerational faithfulness, endurance, rationality, passing on our inheritance to future generations, and submission to authority could be discussed, along with other biblical teachings. We will limit our discussion to just a few of these. Again, our aim here is to ask ourselves: how does my consumption of culture encourage or discourage these virtues in my life and the life of my family and church?

High Culture, Folk Culture, and Popular Culture

Before moving on to a more thorough discussion of popular culture, it will be helpful to reflect on the differences between high culture, folk culture, and popular culture and on how well these different forms of culture can be vehicles for Christian virtue.

These are Ken Myers's three categories of culture in modern-day industrial societies: high culture, traditional or folk culture, and popular culture. The best way to define each type of culture is to give examples of each. In music, high culture's best-known form is classical music. Folk culture's best-known forms would probably be Scots-Irish/Celtic music, bluegrass, and the early folk-gospel music of both black and white Americans. Pop culture's best-known forms are rock and hip-hop.[13]

Myers uses the analogy of food: gourmet food would correspond to high culture, traditional home cooking would relate to folk culture, and fast food (restaurants or frozen dinners in the microwave) would correspond to pop culture. He uses this analogy to point to the subtle ways that the culture with which we surround ourselves shapes our sensibilities in a way that affects our spiritual perceptions. As Myers says,

> Most people would agree that fast food has deficiencies that the other two categories do not, not simply in nutritional value or in taste, but in the *ethos*, the way the food is served, consumed, and experienced. Most young men of moderate means trying to make a positive impression on a young woman do *not* treat her to a meal at the nearest Burger King. . . . Now, if every meal you ever ate was from a fast-food joint, would that affect your outlook on the meaning of meals? If there was never any elegance or grace, any ritual or decorum as part of your meals, if all the food you ever consumed was delivered to you by a person in a funny-looking hat, and was wrapped in cardboard or Styrofoam, would that affect your impressions of the Biblical metaphor of the Marriage Supper of the Lamb?[14]

Myers provides a useful list that compares traditional cultures—both high and folk—with popular culture. (One thing Myers makes clear is that some individual cultural products blur these distinctions. For example, some things that might normally be considered pop culture show evidence of being self-consciously indebted to high culture or folk culture or both. Hence, as I stated above, I am not suggesting an absolute ban on all products of popular culture, but we must recognize nuance because some of them are better than others.) Keep in mind, as you carefully read this list, that it describes tendencies or generalizations. Keep in mind also how the biblical virtues we considered above, and that Holley discusses in chapter six, should shape the way we interact with culture and cultural products, not just with interpersonal spirituality.

POPULAR CULTURE	TRADITIONAL AND HIGH CULTURE
Focuses on the new	Focuses on the timeless
Discourages reflection	Encourages reflection
Pursued casually to "kill time"	Pursued with deliberation
Gives us what we want, tells us what we already know	Offers us what we could not have imagined
Relies on instant accessibility; encourages impatience	Requires training; encourages patience
Emphasizes information and trivia	Emphasizes knowledge and wisdom
Encourages quantitative concerns	Encourages qualitative concerns
Celebrates fame (celebrity)	Celebrates ability
Appeals to sentimentality	Appeals to appropriate, proportioned emotions
Content and form governed by requirements of the market	Content and form governed by requirements of the created order
Formulas are the substance	Formulas are the tools
Relies on spectacle, tending to violence and prurience	Relies on formal dynamics and the power of symbols (including language)
Aesthetic power in reminding of something else	Aesthetic power in intrinsic attribute
Individualistic	Communal
Leaves us where it found us	Transforms sensibilities
Incapable of deep or sustained attention	Capable of repeated, careful attention
Lacks ambiguity	Allusive, suggests the transcendent
No discontinuity between life and art	Relies on "Secondary World" conventions
Reflects the desires of the self	Encourages understanding of others
Tends toward relativism	Tends toward submission to standards
Used	Received[15]

We need to stress that pop culture does not get its essence from being popular! This point is sometimes lost on people but is key. For example, some relatively recent movies—such as the ones based on C. S. Lewis's *The Chronicles of Narnia* or J. R. R. Tolkien's *The Lord of the Rings*, or Jane Austen's *Emma* or P. L.

Travers's *Mary Poppins*—do well at the box office but also respect the time-honored values of high culture and folk culture and tease out their ramifications for the modern day (in a way that would please traditionalists like Lewis, Tolkien, and others).

These examples illustrate that no one artistic medium, whether film or painting or print media or sculpture or something else, is automatically a specific type of culture. It may be pop culture or folk culture or high culture, depending on characteristics that the form and content of the medium in question contain. It is not just large numbers of people liking something that makes it typical of pop culture.

Instead, popular culture comes from mass-produced cultural products that are designed to be consumed. These characteristics are at the heart of pop culture. Most of it is not meant to be lasting or enduring or important. It is designed for the market and targeted at specific age groups and affinity groups. Like cars and pop songs, no one expects most of the artifacts of popular culture five years from now to be anything like they are now. In fact, much of the pop music from five or ten years ago is laughed at by the adolescents of today. This example is just one of many ways in which popular culture differs from high culture and folk culture.

Consumerism

If we are to understand popular culture at all, we must see that it results from consumerism. Rod Dreher gives some of the traits of the consumerism that underlies and is woven into the very fabric of popular culture. He correctly observes that it glorifies "individual choice," "welcomes technology without question," and "prizes efficiency." Consumerism urges people "to find and express their personal identity through the consumption of products."[16]

Consumerism glorifies individual choice, which marketers capitalize on. Yet television executives, whose success depends on advertising, do not want us to "think too hard about our choices" because, if we did, we might not buy what they are selling. Consumerist societies place the emphasis on efficiency, *not* on the classic virtues of truth, goodness, beauty, and permanence. A product's being quick and cheap (even if it wears out quickly) is more important than its being good and true and beautiful and thus enduring.[17]

An even greater problem with consumerism, however, is how it shapes our identities. We allow what we buy to become tied up with our identity. It is what marketers call being a part of an "affinity group." Thus, sadly, the identity of so many people is not shaped, as in the past, by things like family, church, beliefs, tradition, community, patriotism, and learning. Rather, our identity is shaped by executives in far-off places like New York and Tokyo and Hollywood who have something they want to market to our affinity group. And we buy what our affinity group or our "generation" is supposed to want to buy.

Our identity becomes tied up in a "tribe" that is not natural and organic but that is man-made, indeed made by the market. The sad thing is that these "tribes," these "affinity groups," are not enduring, not sustainable like traditional social institutions. They will be shuffled around and thrown off and left behind when the next fad emerges. Holy Scripture urges that we shape our identities—our "selves"—by the transcendent, enduring, and eternal. Immersion in pop culture too often shapes our identities by the fads of this passing evil age.

Overall, popular culture cannot exist without consumerism, and consumerism cannot exist without popular culture. This leads John Seabrook to define pop culture as "the culture of marketing and the marketing of culture."[18] The consumerist orientation of pop culture tends to foster greed, envy, and covetousness—the desire to have things that belong to other people, the desire to have an identity other than our own because of our unhappiness, the desire to have more material possessions. As one of Wendell Berry's characters, old Jack, asked, "Shouldn't it be 'strange, unreal' to us . . . 'that a whole roomful of people should sit with their mouths open like a nest of young birds, peering into a picture box the invariable message of which is the desirability of Something Else or Someplace Else?'"[19]

As psychiatrist Richard Winter remarks, too often popular culture "breed[s] in you dissatisfaction and discontent with your house, your car, your body, your clothes," and we might add, your relationships, "in other words, to stimulate in you a desire for more than you have. In old-fashioned biblical language it inspires you to covet. It promises you satisfaction, peace, meaning, and happiness, but only if you get your needs met now."[20]

Technology

Consumerist societies welcome technology and technological products without any critical assessment or limits. Modernity has an uncritical, naive approach to technology.[21] We eagerly welcome any and every technology as if it could not possibly have any problems, as if we could not possibly need to limit it.

Yet we are not this way with nature. We know that the creation is under a curse. We know that some things in nature—like poison ivy or tigers or tornadoes or jellyfish or too much sun—will hurt us, even kill us. Consequently, we properly govern and limit and plan our exposure to nature. We are careful about nature and are critically minded about it. *Just as with popular culture, it is not this way with technology.*

The human family has done a poor job coping with technology. We have failed to be critical of it, to be wary of it, though some strides are being made in more recent years.[22] We have failed to limit its control over our lives. For these reasons, we spend more time with devices than we do with people. As Neil Postman has said in his excellent book *Technopoly*, we have structured our whole society, our whole way of perceiving reality, to serve technology.[23] Scripture, however, tells us to take dominion over the creation. We have not taken dominion over technology. It has taken dominion over us, and this is intertwined warp and woof with the dominion of pop culture over Christians. Our taking dominion of technology will mean using it as a tool and then putting it down—not making it the air we breathe and the reality we serve.[24]

Of course, we all acknowledge the benefits of modern digital technology. The answer to the problem of our immersion in digital technology is obviously not prohibiting it. Instead, it is carefully limiting it. More and more studies are showing how spending too much time "connected" to electronic media is harming us. For this reason, the American Academy of Child and Adolescent Psychiatry recommends that young children not have more than one hour of screen time per weekday and three hours per day on weekends.[25]

Researchers do not limit this advice to children. Those such as Maggie Jackson, in her book *Distracted*, are showing how overuse of electronic media and "multi-tasking" is making it harder for adults to pay attention—to learn and communicate and bond with real people. Mark Bauerlein, who headed a major literacy study at the National Endowment for the Arts, talks in his book *The Dumbest Generation* about how literacy, reading, and the arts are declining sharply in proportion to time spent with electronic media.[26]

This development is especially important for families. For, as T. David Gordon comments, "Every technological development has an opportunity cost because once we spend even part of our day using a technology we once did not use, some of the things we once did with our time we no longer do."[27]

We should heed the counsel of Matt Markins, who pleads with adults to "go counter to [their] culture," unplug, and invest face-to-face time in their children's lives: "Take a long hard look at the model you are following. Are you just going through the motions every day? Do you find yourself plopped on the couch at the end of the day in front of the TV as a family . . . just because you can't think of anything else to do? Maybe you are on the couch while your kids are all in their rooms and you feel disconnected as a family. If you desire to raise spiritual champions, I challenge you to do something different."[28]

The New, Immediacy, and Impatience

Another characteristic of most popular culture is its idolatry of the new. Richard Stivers is right when he says that mass media and pop culture "create a world of the eternal present, a world in which everything is constantly changing, a world in which our purpose as consumers is always to seek new experiences."[29]

This quest for the new contrasts to traditional high and folk cultures—including the cultures of ancient Israel and historic Christianity—which emphasized the importance of ancient truths and manners and folkways handed down from generation to generation. As C. S. Lewis asked, "How has it come about that we use the highly emotive word 'stagnation,' with all its malodorous and malarial overtones, for what other ages would have called permanence?"[30] Yet the quest for the new is linked to the dominance of the machine and mechanization in modern society and to the high value attached to efficiency and speed in our society. But we should resist letting machines and speed and efficiency dominate our cultural and spiritual lives.

Our culture's addiction to novelty and speed has led to an infatuation with the here-and-now, which fosters impatience. This mentality goes against the biblical admonitions to base our lives on "things that are above" (Colossians 3:2) and to let "steadfastness have its full effect" (James 1:4)—in other words, transcendence and patience.[31]

The Bible talks about divine wisdom and understanding as qualities that are attained by a slow, disciplined, patient meditation on the Word of the Lord. Getting wisdom takes much time and effort. Scripture compares godly people to objects in nature, like deeply rooted trees that require cultivation and time to become full-grown.[32] If we are to become the mature, whole, and complete people God is calling us to be, we must engage in slow, patient, careful reflection. We must cultivate ourselves like a gardener cultivates the soil over long periods of time so that he can have a good crop.

Nothing ultimately worth having is quick and instant. Things worth having—whether a solid friendship, personal spiritual growth, a college degree, a deep and strong relationship with one's spouse, church growth, or organizational change—take time. They take disciplined patience.

Yet typical pop culture is too much about having everything quickly, instantly, and immediately. Because we are addicted to speed, we are also addicted to instant things and immediacy. With our high bandwidth, we simply cannot tolerate a website's taking five seconds to pop up on our screen. We want it in one second. Since we must have everything right now, we begin to focus on the now, the immediate, the up-to-the-minute. We become focused on the here-and-now. This mindset too often predisposes us to ignore the past and what we can receive from tradition. And we ignore the effects that our present decisions will have on future generations.

Our addiction to speed and novelty and the immediate is also taking away our ability to create things of beauty. That is why new movements, such as the "slow food movement," have arisen. This movement seeks to emphasize the careful selection, planning, cooking, and serving of food in the context of family relationships and hospitality to one's neighbor. These practices go against the grain of our culture, which is more apt to grab a quick bite through the drive-through or pop a frozen dinner into the microwave.

This cultural tendency away from patience is why fewer and fewer children are learning to play musical instruments and sing. Why practice hard and take music lessons when you can sing to the radio? Too often the people who really get the kudos on television are not people who have poured countless hours into discipline and patience and practice to master an art or craft.

Everything around us is speeding up our lives and pressuring us to be impatient people who are addicted to speed. Yet God is calling us to patience, not just interpersonally, but with the created order, and thus in our cultural lives. The creation of things that last—whether a novel or a song or a painting or a garden or an organization—takes time and effort and patience and careful cultivation. Understanding the ancient virtue of patience will change the way we look at the world around us.

In cultural pursuits, cultivating the virtue of patience will shift us away from a fast, quick, "fifteen-minutes-of-fame" approach to one that encourages the true, the good, and the beautiful. In business, it will lead us away from get-rich-quick schemes and show us that discipline and patience give the greatest return on investment. It will show us that organizational change—including change and growth in churches—takes time and effort and lots of patience.

Again, tied to our quest for the new is our quest for instant gratification. Pop culture usually discourages delayed gratification, which is "at the heart of the contemporary concept of 'emotional intelligence.'"[33] Such deferred gratification, psychologists tell us, is a mark of emotional maturity. Scripture concurs. However, the opposite of deferred gratification is immediacy, which goes hand in hand with our addiction to novelty, speed, and the here-and-now. You can see how this mindset fits in with consumerism and materialism. Yet pop music and most bingeworthy television shows—not just in their content but in their very form, their very style—encourage instant gratification. They encourage speed, quickness, newness. The here. The now.

This addiction to speed and quest for the new, this immediacy and lack of deferred gratification, probably relate to why popular culture is so often a *diversion*. Or, as C. S. Lewis would say, popular culture is most often *used* rather than *received*.[34] So pop culture does not tend to encourage sustained reflection. It is, as Myers says, pursued casually, often to "kill time," rather than pursued deliberately, like traditional cultural activities. It "relies on instant accessibility," whereas high and folk culture "requires training."[35]

Creating Culture, Not Consuming It

We said a moment ago that the products of popular culture are, by and large, designed for consumption. They are designed to become quickly obsolete. Most of the artifacts of popular culture are not deliberately and carefully created to last, to be handed down to subsequent generations as prized possessions, like the products of high and folk cultures are. Pop culture—like the mass media that has spawned it—too often causes people to be *consumers* of culture, *not creators* of it. Media studies professor Mercer Schuchardt has aptly said, "The number one advice I give to my students is to be a culture creator, not a culture consumer.... You have to have time to create, and to create, you have to get rid of those things that steal your time. TV is the great time-stealer in America."[36] As Andy Crouch reminds us, evangelical Christians need to hear this advice in a time when we tend more to mimic secular culture than to create culture.[37]

Being consumers of culture, rather than producers or creators of it, makes people passive, not active. Too much pop culture entertainment makes people passive. In fact, Winter points out, "The word *amuse* comes from the French word *amuser*, which means 'to stare fixedly'! The most common amusement and entertainment is found as we stare at a screen."[38] For this reason the phrase "couch potato" found its way into the English language in the 1970s.[39] Yet the passive self is an unfulfilled and immature self, a self that is not shaped by the pattern of scriptural teaching but more by the spirit of the age.

Prior to the age of mass media, people created culture, not only in their work but in their leisure time. People's leisurely activities were "participatory and interactive." Sheet music sales were much higher prior to the advent of recording devices. People were learning how to sing and play musical instruments rather than just listening to them on a machine.[40]

Let me pause and say how much I enjoy my Apple Music and Spotify playlists! I am not downing recorded music. I just want to offer some insight into our cultural situation so that we can be wiser in our interactions with popular culture. I fear that Christians are too easily taking an "if you can't beat 'em, join 'em" approach to the amount of time we spend with *machines, consuming*, as opposed to the amount of time we spend with real *people, creating*.

Albert Borgmann and other philosophers of meaning point to two kinds of things or two kinds of reality: (1) commanding reality and (2) pliable or disposable reality. These two kinds of things, or two kinds of reality, are illustrated in the contrast between a musical instrument and a digital device that plays music.[41]

Playing a traditional musical instrument is a "commanding thing." It commands attention, concentration, and so on. People who play musical instruments give their attention to an instrument through painstaking practice and hard work. This intentionality requires the attention of the body—disciplining oneself to hold the body in a certain posture, training one's eyes to read music, "transpos[ing] the visual information rapidly and easily into those bodily maneuvers the instrument will register. Music performed on an instrument in our presence captures our attention.... And the instrument, while it produces sound, reveals a person too, the grace or the strain or the fervor of the one who plays the instrument."[42]

Borgmann contrasts this active engagement with the passivity of listening to a stereo: "A stereo produces music as well or, in fact, much better, i.e., with the supernatural sonority and consistency that no live performance can sustain.... Is a stereo a commanding piece of reality?... As a thing to be operated, a stereo is certainly not demanding. Nor do we feel indebted to its presence the way we do when we listen to a musician. We respect a musician. We own a stereo."[43]

Research shows that "musical instruments are rarely played in American homes, on the average three minutes or so a week, a seventh or eighth of the time that is spent on listening to recorded music." This observation is interesting, given the plethora of recent studies that show that playing music increases people's intelligence. However, the move from performing music to listening to recorded music has also tended to foster individualism and to erode human community.[44]

Individualism and the Erosion of Community

The researcher Borgmann asked people to rate the objects in their homes regarding how much the objects helped them orient to themselves and how much the objects helped them orient to others. Television ranked number one, and digital music-listening devices number two, in helping people orient to themselves.

It is no wonder that Robert Putnam, in his celebrated book *Bowling Alone*, says that, compared with 1975, 33 percent fewer Americans eat together regularly, 45 percent fewer people have friends over regularly, and 58 percent fewer people are members of clubs and social organizations.[45] By 1990, "72 percent of Americans didn't know their neighbors.... Rarely do families today sit down together for a meal, and when they do, the television is usually on in the background. Even more rarely do families get together and make music or play games."[46]

One reason for these social shifts is that media consumption now takes up so much time. Each member of the family goes in different directions, attached to different devices. Teenagers, for example, spend an average of more than seven hours a day on screens.[47] We are clearly a "generation immersed in media."[48] Contrast this media immersion with what Wendell Berry says in *What Are People For?*

> There used to be a sort of institution in our part of the country known as 'sitting till bedtime.' After supper, when they weren't too tired, neighbors would... visit each other. They popped corn... and ate apples and talked. They told each other stories... about each other, about themselves, living again in their own memories and thus keeping their memories alive....
>
> But most of us no longer talk with each other, much less tell each other stories. We tell our stories now mostly to doctors or lawyers or psychiatrists or insurance adjusters or the police, not to our neighbors for their (and our) entertainment. The stories that now entertain us are made up for us in New York or Los Angeles or other centers of such commerce.[49]

Marva Dawn reminds us of the work of the French sociologist Jacques Ellul, who showed that "the rise of the technological milieu is paralleled by a corresponding *decrease in skills (and time!) for intimacy.*" This is why Americans spend *minutes* a day, not *hours* a day, talking with their spouses and children.[50] This erosion of community and decrease in human intimacy results in radical individualism and even a "culture of narcissism," as Christopher Lasch discussed in his book of that title. Lasch correctly argues that popular culture is helping to create a society of narcissists: people who are self-focused and concerned more about themselves than others. This narcissism is the bane of the unfulfilled, immature self, which is at odds with the kind of self that the Spirit is calling human beings to be.[51]

Tradition and Authority

These themes point to another important feature of much contemporary popular culture: the casting off of tradition—mass cultural amnesia and the accompanying exaltation of youth. This period is the first time in world history that a culture has ever been marked by these characteristics. Far from following the ancient reading of the commandment to honor our fathers and mothers (Exodus 20:12), modernity has cut us off from our past.[52] The only societies that still seem to place a high premium on respecting the past, honoring one's ancestors, and highly esteeming tradition are premodern and third-world societies that have not been impacted by industrialization and globalization.

Yet we need to understand that the continuity of past, present, and future is part of the very fabric of Scripture. Covenant faithfulness unto a thousand generations undergirds the story of God's people. Up until now, Christians have emphasized the importance of receiving an inheritance from our grandparents' grandparents so that we could hand it down to our grandchildren's grandchildren. But this intergenerational connection is almost absent among my generation of low-church evangelical Christians. Someone has dropped the ball.[53]

However, we are also witnessing a reaction against this loss, especially among some Millennials and Generation Z. As Dreher says, more and more of them are "burned out by the junkiness and ephemerality of mainstream culture" and "feel compelled to seek out the transformative wisdom in simpler, more traditional, more natural ways of living."[54]

We have much work ahead of us to rid ourselves of our cultural and religious amnesia, to recover the riches of the Christian inheritance, and to pass that down unscathed to our children. If we are to maintain faithfulness through the generations and perpetuate the faith once delivered to all the saints (Jude 1:3), we must recover the ancient Christian notion of the *communio sanctorum*, the communion of saints. This concept refers to the great body of believers past, present, and future. In the way we live out the faith in our own lives and in the lives of our families and churches, we must maintain continuity with that great cloud of witnesses that has gone before us (Hebrews 12:1). Only in this way will we be faithful to Scripture and able to hand down that inheritance unscathed to future generations.[55]

Yet most contemporary popular culture firmly resists this notion; it is not about intergenerational faithfulness but about segmenting the generations so that they can be sold things more easily. Neil Postman argues that modern culture's rebellion against tradition and authority has left a vacuum in the shaping of values. Into the vacuum comes what he calls "Technopoly," which "casts aside all traditional narratives and symbols that suggest stability and orderliness." Two necessary ingredients of technopoly—marketing and entertainment—demolish traditions and intergenerational ties because they mess up marketing strategy. Music executives, for example, segment the generations because it is in their best interest to keep tastes changing so they can generate more sales.[56]

YOUTH CULTURE AND THE REVOLT AGAINST TRADITION AND AUTHORITY

Tied to the concept of tradition is the concept of authority. Most contemporary popular culture has arisen out of what is known as youth culture. The concept of youth culture has its origin in the latter half of the twentieth century. Recognizing that there are some exceptions to this general rule, the mainstream of today's pop culture had its birth in the late 1960s when the countercultural movements sought to free themselves from the authority of the establishment of American society.[57]

Thus the rock bands of the 1960s and 1970s saw themselves as heralds of a new self-consciousness that embodied rebellion against the authoritative social structures of the 1950s. *Rolling Stone* editor Jann Wenner illustrated this point in an article from 1971: "*Rolling Stone* was founded and continues to operate in the belief that rock 'n' roll music is the energy center for all sorts of changes revolving rapidly around us: social, political, cultural, however you want to describe them. The fact is for many of us who've grown up since World War II, rock 'n' roll provided the first revolutionary insight into who we are and where we are and where we are at in this country."[58]

The leading rock musicians of the late 1960s and 1970s saw their art as reflecting the deep consciousness of the counterculture of the Sixties. They saw themselves as revolutionaries, rebelling against the political, social, and sexual views of previous generations. Their music was one of revolt against tradition and authority. These characteristics caused many of the early critics of Christian rock to chide it for trying to marry a rebellious form of music to the gospel.

The early Christian rock musicians denied that the style of their music could be characterized as rebellious. Rather, they argued that it was energetic.

Eventually, however, Christian rock musicians, such as the band Audio Adrenaline, began to agree that the form of their music does communicate rebellion. Yet they said they were rebelling in the same way that Jesus rebelled against the authority of His day.[59]

An important aspect of the rebellion against received tradition and authority that originated in this counterculture was a revolt against rationality. This theme is seen in Charles Reich's widely celebrated 1970 book, *The Greening of America*. He called the new mentality "Consciousness III": "In contrast with Consciousness II, which accepts society, the public interest, and institutions as the primary reality, III declares that the individual self is the only true reality. Thus it returns to the earlier America: 'Myself I sing.' The first commandment is: thou shalt do no violence to thyself." As Ken Myers says, Consciousness III was "profoundly irrational, and was to be mediated by rock, which had injected a pulsing new energy into the culture." Reich exclaimed:

> Not even the turbulent fury of Beethoven's Ninth Symphony can compete for sheer energy with the Rolling Stones. Compared to the new music, earlier popular songs seem escapist and soft, jazz seems cerebral, classical music seems dainty or mushy; . . . the driving, screaming, crying, bitter-happy-sad heights and depths and motion of the new music adds a dimension unknown in any earlier western music. The older music was essentially intellectual; it was located in the mind and in the feelings known to the mind; the new music rocks the whole body, and penetrates the soul.[60]

Like Reich, Robert Pattison, author of *The Triumph of Vulgarity: Rock Music in the Mirror of Romanticism*, celebrates rock music's movement away from rationality and toward the body. He argues that, in this way, it is rooted in Romanticism, which is itself a revolt against reason. Thus, like Romantics such as Jean-Jacques Rousseau, the rock musicians of the 1960s and 1970s sought to celebrate the irrational, sensate, physical, and primitive. They wanted to throw off the shackles of polite Western civilization and embrace the primitive with its rawness and sexuality.[61]

This approach to music contrasts starkly with ancient musical thought. Plato, Aristotle, and other ancient thinkers argued that music had a profound social role in calming the animal passions so that the higher self, guided by reason, might rise to the sublime.[62] Traditional Christian thinkers agreed with these sentiments, starting with the church fathers, as Calvin Stapert has demonstrated in his book *A New Song for an Old World: The Musical Thought of the Early Church*.[63]

By contrast, Romantic thinkers such as Rousseau and Friedrich Nietzsche said that music's role was to enliven the passions so that the wild, Dionysian inner spirit of humanity could take precedence.[64] Such thinking was at the forefront of the architects of the rock music subculture in the 1960s and 1970s.

These thinkers and artists were not talking primarily about the words or the content communicated. They believed that the music itself, even without any words, represented a new consciousness that was rebellious, uncivilized, irrational, primitive, passionate, raw, and sexual.

Christians need to discern, carefully and prayerfully, the forms of music in which they immerse themselves and invite their children to immerse themselves, and the forms of the music to which they wed the gospel. We need to ensure that Christian virtue is informing the music we listen to day in and day out—in both form (music) and content (words).

Not everyone will agree on the details of the application of this principle. Yet thinking critically about popular aesthetic and cultural forms demonstrates wisdom rather than the naiveté that results from cultural forms that we never bother to think about or question. Such discernment will be tedious and difficult, and we might be tempted at times to be embarrassed by our conclusions because they are so out of sync with popular opinion. But we must remember that we are resident aliens, strangers in a strange land, living in an outpost of the kingdom, the church (1 Peter 1:10–21), placed by the King in this present evil age to transform it and not to be subtly transformed by it (Galatians 1:4; Romans 12:2).

The Image: Television and Video Media

Hand in hand with this rejection of tradition, authority, and rationality comes a shift from a word-based culture to an image-based culture. In his penetrating book *Amusing Ourselves to Death*, Postman made a very persuasive argument for why people should strictly limit their intake of digital media. He analyzed the nineteenth-century Lincoln-Douglas debates, where hundreds of adults with grade-school educations sat through several hours of tedious, intellectually rigorous debates. Yet now political debates are limited to an hour or two, and candidates' remarks are kept to two minutes each. Worse still, what we hear on the news about these debates consists of five-second sound bites chosen from one of the two-minute comments.[65]

Postman argued that television and video media in general are taking away our ability to think and reason. (These authors' use of "television" is synonymous with what today we would describe as Netflix or YouTube or some other streaming platform.) Dreher echoes Postman in the following observations: "By its very nature, television technology teaches us to experience the world as a series of fragmentary images. It trains us to prize emotions and stimulation over logic and abstract thought. We are conditioned to expect quick resolution to problems, and to develop evanescently short attention spans. We expect the world to be entertaining if it is to hold our attention."[66]

Marva Dawn is correct when she says that too much digital video technology stifles the imagination, limits intelligence by causing children to have smaller brains, and makes people less motivated to think. Vast amounts of research support these conclusions. And when we think of Dawn's first problem with television, YouTube, etc.—that they waste so much time, taking valuable time away from human family and other relationships, evangelism, discipleship, and worship—it compounds the problem.[67]

What are Christians to make of the move from a word-based culture to an image-based culture, where more and more people are image-oriented and less literate and cannot think in linear, logical ways? Does this tendency serve the interests of the church and the historic Christian gospel? Myers sums up the argument against the move to an image-based and away from a word-based culture this way: images "communicate immediately and intuitively." They are "scanned in a subjective pattern." Words, on the other hand, "communicate through abstraction and analysis. Words communicate in linear, logical form; something communicated in words can thus be judged to be true or false. But an image cannot be true or false."[68]

As Myers explains, "A culture that is rooted more in images than in words will find it increasingly difficult to sustain any broad commitment to any truth, since truth is an abstraction requiring language. Words offer commands and prohibitions. Images establish feelings of resonance. Images remind us of things. They involve recognition more than cognition."[69] These are precisely the reasons for the shift to widespread literacy in those Reformation countries that believed images should not be used in worship but that the church service was to be a service of the Word.[70]

Michael Horton has some penetrating things to say about this emphasis on words that we as Christians, people of the Book, need to hear: "It is important for us to realize that it is not only the message of the Word but the method of preaching that God has promised to us for salvation and growth."[71] Elsewhere he says, "One of the remarkable achievements of the Reformation was that instead of capitulating to the ignorance of the people by relying on pictures and icons as 'the books for the unlearned,' the Reformers insisted that they be elevated in their abilities so that they could read Scripture [and] find new opportunities to advance their own calling. . . . Instead of fatalistic accommodation, the Reformers resisted and in fact turned back the night."[72]

Horton believes that explaining Christianity "in terms the average person can understand" is important. However, he rightly disagrees with the image drivenness of much contemporary Christianity—that we must "begin with pictures" or images rather than the Word in communicating the gospel:

> not because it is somehow beneath us but because the Old Testament saints, Jesus, and his apostles refused the idolatry of the eye and instead concentrated on the preaching of the Word. 'So then faith comes by hearing, and hearing by the word of God.' . . . It is hardly for elitist reasons that Christians

are called people of the book. To be sure, the book is not an end in itself but is meant to lead us to Christ. Jesus certainly used colorful metaphors and parables, but these are figures of speech and genres of discourse, not pictures.[73]

These important concerns about violating the Second Commandment regarding the use of images in worship and shifting from a word-centered culture to an image-centered culture must not lead us to a denigration of visual arts such as painting, sculpture, theater, and film. Authors like Myers and Horton offer valid concerns about the image displacing the word and the overuse of digital video technology in contemporary culture. However, as explained in chapter seven, we should avoid jumping from their legitimate concerns to the invalid conclusion—which neither of them would affirm—that the visual arts are improper or poor vehicles for truth, goodness, and beauty.

Discipleship and Worship

What is the upshot of this critique of popular culture for individuals, families, and churches in the areas of discipleship and worship? I believe it will lead us to the conclusion that, at the very least, immersion in pop culture makes Christian discipleship and worship difficult. Thus we should avoid that immersion. To the degree that certain styles and individual artifacts of pop culture militate against the Christian virtues discussed in this chapter, we need to avoid them. We should be more cognizant of the fact that too much media exposure—even to what does not have morally objectionable content—can drain us of our capacity for full-orbed lives of discipleship and worship.

Recall Myers's illustration of high, folk, and popular culture as gourmet food, traditional home cooking, and fast food. Marva Dawn's discussion of those categories as applied to worship shows how immersion in pop culture makes it hard to engage in thinking Christian discipleship. In one of her books, she discusses an individual who criticized her use of Myers's food illustration. A strong advocate of the use of pop styles in worship, this writer said that most people today would *prefer* Burger King to a fancy French restaurant and that traditional home cooking is not an option because it is disappearing. Then he said, "Most advocates of contemporary worship, including me, would opt for Burger King; in a given week it feeds a lot more people, and the food meets the needs. . . . Which kind of food service do you think Jesus and Paul would choose?"[74] Dawn responds to this question with a series of questions and answers, expanding on the comparison of worship to the consumption of fast food:

1. *Isn't the gospel sometimes hard to digest?* . . . [The] Lord . . . says, "For my thoughts are not your thoughts, nor are your ways my ways." . . . Ours is a Christ who repeatedly says, "Woe to you!" . . . That can be very difficult to stomach.

2. *Doesn't discipleship cost a lot in time and money [like gourmet food]?* . . . don't we have a Christ who told a rich man to sell all he had, who warned those who wanted to turn back home that they weren't fit for the kingdom? . . . If our worship is not costly in terms of time, participation, and commitment, how will we teach what discipleship means? The medium must match the message.
3. *Which kind of food service did Jesus choose?* Since he participated faithfully in worship at the Temple and the local synagogue, in the ritualized festivals and feasts of Judaica, we could compare his choices to both home cooking and gourmet food. And what kind of "food service" does Paul signify when he urges us to "seek the things which are above"? Which kind of food service will give us "a foretaste of the feast to come"?
4. *We have to ask why the home cooking of tradition in worship is disappearing.* Is the heritage that could enfold us in the language of faith practiced through the ages no longer important? Why have we lost the traditions that link us to people of faith throughout time and space?
5. *Which need does Burger King food meet besides the need for speed?* If our worship is like Burger King, how will we form the habits and practices, the customs and manners of being the people of God . . . profound meditation, awe-full silence, reflection on meaty doctrines, musical depth, memorization of extensive texts, steadfast intimacy with the true God, the continuity of the Church, genuine community, earnest repentance, grieving lament, discipled cross-bearing, timeless truth, the beauty of holiness, and faithful goodness? Will we learn those if our worship is like Burger King food?
6. I'm not advocating only one (French) gourmet restaurant. I am advocating a plethora of them. . . . *Will we learn diversity at Burger King?*
7. No matter which kind of food service our worship resembles, we must ask *whether it meets our genuine needs*—the needs of our lonely, decentered, hopeless, postmodern world. . . . What is good for us and our neighbors? What will really contribute to growth in faith? As we eat, are we growing stronger or just fatter?[75]

These insights on how popular culture can make authentic discipleship and worship in this present age difficult are profound.

The result of the influence of the problematic characteristics of pop culture on worship results in a "worship style that lacks theological substance, invites passivity, and fosters an easy-listening consumerism that provides neither music nor words that will help worship participants remember deep truths." Yet these are practical concerns, not mere theoretical ones: "One of the dire consequences of adopting this quick-fix technique is that *the real problems*—namely *failure to educate* concerning the meaning and practice of worship, *failure to understand* the real idolatries that keep people from participating in the Church, and *failure to equip the priesthood of all believers for outreach to the world—remain unaddressed.*"[76]

Dawn is obviously not saying that churches should sing only older music. She advocates for the use of a diverse cadre of old and new music to tie together the past, present, and future. However, she believes that churches should use songs with theologically deep lyrics reminiscent of classic hymnody and with music that does not bring entertainment, human-centeredness, and a consumer mentality into the church.[77]

Conclusion

So how should the Christian respond to popular culture? There are no easy answers, but I believe we must squarely face the inconsistency of full-orbed Christian discipleship and worship with immersion in popular culture. To do this we must understand popular culture. We must develop a critical mind to it. We must become more self-critical regarding our intake of it.

Eric Brende writes, "The goal is not to get rid of technology, but to limit its use 'to restore a more integrated life.'"[78] I agree with Dreher when he says that we must put our families on a "strict mass media diet."[79] Barry Raper, ministry program coordinator at Welch College, put his students in one of his courses on a twenty-four-hour media fast—what I call a media detox. His students said that this twenty-four-hour fast changed the way they looked at technology and media and pop culture and renewed their hope that they could connect more closely with God.

When my children were young, they would sometimes read a magazine that Focus on the Family published for eight-to-eleven-year-olds, *Clubhouse*, which had a story in each issue about a make-believe boy they called "Average Boy." In one issue, Average Boy's father sees that he and his siblings are spending too much time on electronic media and declares, "We're unplugging for a week! No video games, computers, TV, or iPods." After unplugging, Average Boy walks outside "and was suddenly hit by an unidentified blinding light." He says, "Panic gripped me until I realized this strange new thing was the sun. I guess I remembered the sun, but I hadn't seen it since getting a Wii" (Remember, this magazine was published when my children were young!). He proclaims, "I never realized that most of my ideas come from Google and not from my actual brain."

Average Boy concluded by giving some sound advice to his pre-teen readers: "So as summer starts, I hope you unplug and go crazy! Don't waste your days sitting inside playing video games and watching TV. Go outside. The graphics are super-realistic!"

This brief advice from a children's magazine goes far in helping us to think about how to "cut the cord" of our dependence on popular culture and tap into more normal ways of life. But the advice is not just good for children; it is good for us all. And if we do not begin modeling a more beautiful, interesting, holistic life of Christian culture making, not just consumption, before our children, they will never know how to live such lives themselves. In some ways, the advice my nine-year-old child got in three pages of a Focus on the Family magazine is all the advice we need to reign in this menace of the dominance of pop culture and electronic media over our lives.

A friend asked me recently, "What advice do you give families who want to limit their immersion in pop culture and electronic media and live more authentic lives?" I jokingly said, "I say, 'Stop it!'" (I had heard this from a psychologist friend.) Of course, I was joking. Yet we do need to discover and develop deeper, richer, and more authentic cultural products and practices so that our lives can truly be worship and praise to God "according to his excellent greatness" (Psalm 150:2b). And thankfully more and more resources exist that support this ideal. However, as in the *Clubhouse* advice, this journey will begin with simply unplugging, becoming self-critical of the large number of hours we spend plugged in, buzzed out, and disconnected from our families and communities, and saying to ourselves, "Stop it!"

Dawn is right when she says, "*We can and must set limits* on our families' use of media. Quentin Schultze suggests a three-to-one ratio of family interaction/relational activities to media consumption. Without imposing such limits, he warns, we reverse the worldwide, ageless habit of parents teaching their children the wisdom of their faith and heritage, and we allow the children instead to float aimlessly—without a sense of who they are or what life is really for." Schultze is correct when he says that we Christians need to "win our children back from the media."[80]

If we are to achieve some success in these goals, it will involve helping our children develop a critical mind toward the products, styles, and media of pop culture. It will involve keeping some of those unhealthy products, styles, and media (unhealthy in form *and* content) out of their reach. It will involve a severe cutting back of the time spent on television, the Internet, video games, smart phones, and other electronic media. And it will involve replacing those hours with hours spent in discipleship and worship and learning and growing together as a family and the creation of a kingdom-shaped culture. What is more, when we wean ourselves off our dependence on popular culture, the riches of the Christian cultural tradition await us and can enhance our lives, making it less difficult for us to live lives of authentic Christian discipleship and worship.

CHAPTER NINE

Language and Literature

Montgomery F. Thornsbury

Christians have always been people of the Word and thus of words. They inherited this ancient obligation from their Hebrew forebears to whom God first entrusted His verbal revelation. Christians, like the Hebrews who preceded them, have developed a thoroughly literate and literary culture around the concept that words matter because God has chosen the medium of the written word to reveal Himself most clearly. Simply put, Christians value language and literature because God values language and literature.

The aim of this chapter is to introduce foundational concepts of the Christian view of language and literature and to demonstrate how a whole constellation of values revolves around the truth that in the beginning was the Word.

The Logos

In the prologue to his Gospel, John recounts the creation of the world with special emphasis on Christ's participation in it. John writes, "In the beginning was the Word, and the Word was with God, and the Word was God. He was in the beginning with God. All things were made through him, and without him was not any thing made that was made" (1:1–3). Note that John calls Christ "the Word," which is translated from the Greek *Logos*.

Whatever the case of the exact origin of *Logos*, or the significance of John's use of the term, which Bible interpreters have debated throughout Christian history, one of its implications is that Christ is the fulfillment of every word ever spoken by God. According to John Calvin, Christ as the Logos "heartily declared to us all that can be comprehended and ought to be pondered concerning the Heavenly Father by the human mind."[1]

John's Gospel, and other relevant New Testament passages, furnish the historic-Christian doctrine of the Logos, which Ronald Nash has summarized neatly:

> The New Testament ascribes three distinct but related functions to the Christian Logos which make it possible to speak of Christ as the cosmological Logos, the epistemological Logos, and soteriological Logos. This is simply another way of saying that Jesus is a necessary condition for the

existence of the world, for human knowledge, and for human redemption. Without Jesus, the world would never have come into existence and would not exist now; without Jesus, the human animal would never have become a creature capable of knowledge; and without Jesus, human beings would never have been redeemed from sin.[2]

Christ's function as Redeemer is probably the most well-known, and justifiably so. But when we understand the larger picture of Christ as the Logos, we see that Christ mediates and reigns over the complex intersection of meaning and the human ability to know that meaning and to express it in words. Christ's cosmological (relating to the universe) and epistemological (relating to knowledge) functions illustrate the centrality of the doctrine of the Logos to the Christian understanding of language and literature.

The Cosmological Logos

In terms of His cosmological function, Christ embodies the fixed value and purpose of everything in the world, which is to say that He embodies every command of creation uttered by God the Father. When God created the world, He did so through words. What had been formless and void became ordered creation at God's commands for the light to be distinct from the darkness, for the waters to be distinct from the dry earth, and for the animals to exist according to their own kinds. With words God also created man in His image, set man above the animal life, and differentiated man from woman. Christ as the cosmological Logos was and is and will always be the essence of these commands. Therefore, creation will always operate according to an implicit order, and human nature will always have a fixed definition in Christ.

On the level of individual words, the linguistic implication is that everything we could possibly name already has a definition within God's whole design for the universe. Vern Poythress concludes, "Meaning is in God's mind. And it is articulate meaning, in accord with the Word, the Logos. . . . Human thought and human expression never create meanings out of nowhere. They are reflective of divine meanings."[3]

We should not interpret this principle to mean that the definition of every English word is locked away in a divine dictionary in heaven. However, the fact that Christ is the essence of the universe's order means that our attempts at making sense of the world through words are not futile endeavors. The words *man* and *animal*, for instance, have distinct meanings when we use them because the differences between humans and animals are aspects of true reality that came into existence when God created the world. The same could be said for the words *man* and *woman*; the meanings of these words are distinct because men and women are, according to God's commands, distinct. Words have meaning because the things they name have fixed meaning.

Stories too obtain meaning only because of Christ's cosmological role. A common understanding throughout much of the history of Western literary criticism has been that literature reaches its purpose when it both delights and instructs us.[4] On one hand, good stories delight us when they reflect the Logos of the created world. This point does not mean that all stories must be realistic and can never be fantastical. But good stories hold up a mirror to the warts and glories of human nature and to the true constitution of the universe. Static characters, for instance, who never change are far less compelling than dynamic characters who reflect complex human psychologies and who readily engage our innate desires to empathize and sympathize with other people.

On the other hand, good stories instruct us when they reflect what William Faulkner called "the old verities and truths of the heart, the old universal truths lacking which any story is ephemeral and doomed."[5] Poet T. S. Eliot called these the "permanent things"—unchanging ideals such as love, honor, and pity which also find their essence in the Logos.

Edmund Burke, the great conservative British parliamentarian and philosopher, believed that literature informs what he called "the moral imagination," the place in the human mind where the delight and instruction of great literature meet and influence our ethical faculties.[6] According to Burke's concept, stories offer us true human experience in the form of images in our minds inspired by the author's arrangement of the characters, setting, plot, and themes of his story, and these images are not morally neutral.

The redemption of Achilles in Homer's *Iliad*, for example, is not simply a picture of a prideful man becoming a humble one; Achilles's transformation beckons us to place ourselves at the center of his experience and to probe our own shortcomings. Homer offers us no direct moral teachings, but he does offer images of honor and cowardice in action and of the real human results of either regarding or disregarding permanent things. Literary critic R. V. Young puts the point succinctly: "Literature, then, is less concerned to assert what is right and wrong than to evoke the experience of good and evil."[7]

The Christian reader is not finished when he has read a work, enjoyed it, and come to what he thinks is a sufficient grasp of the author's intended meaning. His task is complete only when he has considered the work's contribution to the moral imagination by asking the following questions of the author's message. Is it true? Is it beautiful? Is it good?[8]

Because Christ is the Logos, the quality of a work's meaning matters. This value judgment also forms the foundation for the Christian appreciation for classic works of literature that have stood the test of time precisely because of the quality of their meanings. Whether they be pagans, like Homer and Plato; or Christians, like William Shakespeare and John Milton; or non-believers, like Edward Gibbon and Aldous Huxley, authors who reflect the truth, beauty, and goodness of the Logos, albeit sometimes dimly, are of particular interest to Christians.

The Epistemological Logos

Yet how can we be sure that human words can communicate meaning at all? The best place to begin answering such a question is with the simple recognition that God has chosen human words as a means to reveal Himself. Because God trusts human words to convey meaning, so can we. But what about human words that the Holy Spirit has not inspired? How can we trust that the words of everyday conversation communicate our meanings or that the words of the *Iliad* actually give us insight?

Remember that in Christ, the cosmological Logos, "all things hold together" (Colossians 1:17). This truth applies to the reality we perceive daily as well as to the reality of intangible ideals such as love, honor, and pity. In His epistemological function, Christ unifies reality and ideals and makes the world coherent so that human beings can sufficiently perceive meaning and represent it in words.

John concludes his prologue dedicated to the Logos by stating, "We have *seen* His glory, glory as of the only Son from the Father, full of grace and truth" (John 1:14b, italics added). The principle John establishes here is that the truth about reality and ideals that the Logos embodies is not beyond human ability to see it. Moreover, that Christ Himself is the Word demonstrates that words serve as *the* bridge between objective meaning and subjective understanding; in this way, Christ as *Logos* is the bridge between ontology (what is real) and epistemology (what we know). So, yes, words are trustworthy to convey meaning.

What is more, words are a prerequisite for human knowledge altogether. If language ceased to exist tomorrow, the human ability to perceive and communicate meaning would also cease to exist. Richard Weaver, in a chapter on the power of the Word writes, "To discover what a thing is 'called' . . . is the essential step in knowing, and to say that all education is learning to name rightly, as Adam named the animals, would assert an underlying truth."[9]

Until the late nineteenth and early twentieth centuries, the importance of the Logos in the grand scheme of understating the intersection of language and knowledge had been honored throughout the tradition of scholarship and education in the West. Yet as modernism produced more and more skepticism of revealed religion, particularly of the Christian religion, the Western approach to knowing truth changed, and so too its approach to words changed.

THE POST-WORD WORLD

Malcolm Muggeridge has written that the trajectory of Western society since modernism should be thought of as a death wish. Modernism's attempt to grasp the unity of the universe on the supposition that material is where existence begins and ends, according to Muggeridge, established a "Logos in reverse," which heralded that "in the beginning was the flesh, and the flesh became Word." The result blurred "the edges of truth, the definition of virtue, [and] the shape of beauty," offering no grand design from which people—let alone their words—could obtain ultimate meaning and purpose.[10] The modernist Logos, it turns out, was no Logos at all, and its failure precipitated postmodernism's complete rejection of logocentric thinking and the viability of words. Because our world is a post-*Word* world, it is also a post-word world.

The Rise of Linguistics

The year 1916 marked one of the most significant shifts in how language is studied. The event that carved this shift was the publication of Swiss linguist Ferdinand de Saussure's *Cours de linguistique générale* (*Course in General Linguistics*). Whereas scholars had traditionally studied language alongside the various disciplines of the humanities, Saussure proposed a more scientific approach to the study of language.

Earlier Hebrew, Greek, Roman, and Christian scholars had believed that language is a means by which humans name, categorize, and understand a world that is a product of creation and has coherence and meaning from the get-go. For this reason, the traditional study of language, known as philology (or "love of logos/words"), was concerned primarily with the pursuit of understanding texts, such as the Bible and classical literature. The philologist's purpose was to use the study of language not as an end in itself but as a way to understand the rich meaning that exists and can be known and shared through great literature.

What made Saussure's study so groundbreaking was that he moved the focus of language study from the written word to actual speech and the psychological characteristics that bring speech about. In fact, he wrote disapprovingly of philology and called it "too slavishly subservient to the written language."[11] Saussure advocated that the study of language be undertaken as a science concerned with the way in which underlying cognitive structures explain the make-up of individual words and utterances. More importantly, Saussure was concerned with the way in which cognitive structures explain the perception of meaning in language.

Saussure claimed that language is non-referential, which is the idea that words bear no fundamental connections to the things they name. He wrote that the meaning of a given word is not "determined merely by a concept or meaning for which it is a token," or representation, but can be ascertained only "by contrast to other words."[12] For instance, the concept represented by the word *man* can be understood only in terms of its not being the concept represented by *animal*. The concept of *hot* can be understood only in terms of its not being *cold*.

Blue can be understood only in contrast to *yellow*, and so on. In this way, Saussure argued that such individual concepts do not have meanings unto themselves but obtain perceivable meanings only in the context of a structure of differences.

The ramifications of this position are subtle but significant and must not be overlooked. Instead of believing that words represent a universe of meaning that is embodied in Christ, words, according to Saussure, represent structures of meaning in our own heads. Instead of the definition of *man* issuing from a concept of human nature rooted in the Logos, the word *man* has a meaning established merely by its position in a structure of opposing concepts. The result is aptly summarized by Francis Schaeffer's analysis of another similar course of study: "Although it defines words using reason, finally language leads to neither value nor facts. Language leads to language, and that is all. It is not only the certainty of values that is gone, but the certainty of knowing."[13]

Saussure never aimed at destroying the certainty of knowing; his intellectual descendants, known as the structuralists and poststructuralists, would do much of that. However, Saussure did attempt to make sense of human language based on observable linguistic data alone or based on the Logos in reverse. His work opened the door to a questioning not only of language's ability to communicate objective meaning but also of the whole nature of reality itself, sowing the seeds of some of the most foundational ideas of postmodernism.

Derrida and Deconstruction

In the middle of the twentieth century, French philosopher Jacques Derrida used Saussure's concept of structural difference to form the basis of his theory of deconstruction. Derrida agreed with Saussure that language is nonreferential and that contrasts among linguistic concepts explain the perception of meaning in language; but he also held that these contrasts and the meanings they establish are entirely the result of the ideological programing of a given *discourse community*, a deconstructionist term for a group that shares both language and beliefs.

The words *man* and *animal* are contrasted in the discourse of conservative Christianity, for instance, to support the "merely ideological" assumption that humans have a distinct nature from that of animals. To complete Derrida's troubling calculus, man as the image of God is true enough for the discourse of conservative Christianity, but it is not true for everyone else.

Derrida made such claims on the basis of two fundamental ideas. First, Derrida believed that linguistic concepts have so many potential contrasts and associations that stable meanings are never actually achievable. The concept signified by *man*, then, has so many connotations that settled meaning is always deferred. To put it another way, Derrida believed that language was in a constant state of self-deconstruction—hence the name of his theory. Second, because

Derrida believed, along with Friedrich Nietzsche, that "God is effectively dead," Derrida vociferously attacked the whole concept of Logos and what he called the "logocentrism" of the West. Because of this second key idea, Derrida held that an ultimate definition of *man* could never intervene to settle the potential endless string of contrasts and associations because no such ultimate nature exists.

Derrida explained that discourse communities have overcome the chaos intrinsic to language by inventing structures of difference that establish the illusion of stable meaning and communication. These structures of difference—often discussed in terms of binary oppositions such as man v. animal, man v. woman, civilized v. uncivilized, good v. evil, etc.—are purely the products of the beliefs and values of a discourse community.

Critically, Derrida also claimed that these binary oppositions represent privileged hierarchies. He meant that, in any given binary opposition, the dominant discourse(s) (often identified by deconstructionists as Christianity, capitalism, and "the patriarchy") prefers one concept over the other to the disadvantage of a particular marginalized social group. In short, Derrida argued that, wherever there is a semblance of meaning in language, there is a manifestation of "the will to power," a term used by Nietzsche to describe man's singular motivation to conquer all others.

Feminist literary and cultural critics using the methods of deconstructionism would say that the West has historically privileged the concept of man over that of woman to the detriment of women. Marxist critics using the same methods would say that capitalism and the classical tradition have privileged high culture over low culture to the detriment of the working class. And the examples from contemporary critical theory could go on. However, the truth remains that such assumptions and methodologies render language as nothing more than a cruel and oppressive tool and humans nothing more than brutish political animals who constantly attempt to gain power with every word.

The Christian view of the relationship of language and meaning is not Saussure's view, and it certainly is not Derrida's. Because we believe the Word embodies the fundamental order and meaning of the universe, we believe that our words have stable meanings that can reflect the truths of reality and ideals, not just the interplay that concepts of meaning have in our heads. Because we believe the human soul is made up of more than animalistic will, we believe that language and literature aspire to higher purposes than marginalization.

Indeed, the implications of Derrida's insidious theory help us understand that a concept of language is incomplete without an understanding of how language relates to human nature. Therefore, to complete our discussion of the Christian concept of language and literature, we must pick up again at the beginning in Genesis, giving special attention to the relationship of human nature and God's good design for language.

The Two Principles of Language

In the beginning, God spoke Adam into existence and, in the same breath, bestowed Adam with an intellect, heart, and will like His own. Genesis 2 relates how God then placed Adam in the garden of Eden and brought him the beasts of the field and the fowl of the air. Adam named the animals so that the first act of human creation was one with words. The next account of human utterance is Adam's praising God for the gift of Eve. Thereafter, though, Adam and Eve are seen speaking only to explain their disobedience.

From these verses, Noah Webster, in the introduction to his famous *American Dictionary*, concludes, "If we admit what is the literal and obvious interpretation of this narrative . . . it results that Adam was not only endowed with intellect for understanding his Maker . . . but was furnished both with the faculty of speech and with speech itself, or the knowledge and use of words."[14] Webster explains that the language of humanity's first parents could not have been extremely complex but that language was nevertheless the immediate gift of God, who endowed language simultaneously with reason at Eden.

These important facts of creation identified by Noah Webster reveal that language goes to the core of our humanity and, thus, reveal God's ordained purposes for language and literature. The rest of this chapter will discuss those purposes by considering the two principles of language: (1) language is a universal gift given by God; and (2) language communicates thought.

Principle 1: Language is a gift.

Webster argues, "We may infer that language was bestowed on Adam, in the same manner of his other faculties and knowledge, by supernatural power."[15] The account of God's gift of language to man is both a factual claim about the state of Adam at creation and a universal principle about language and human nature. Adam, as many in the Christian tradition have interpreted him, is a map for human nature. What is true for Adam is true for all of us. *The New England Primer* reminds us, "In Adam's fall, we sinned all."[16] We can apply the same logic to the issue of language. Because God gifted Adam with language, we may infer that all people have the capacity for language and that language is a gift exclusive to humans.

God created humans to be verbal beings, just as He Himself is a verbal being. Because God speaks, we speak. In this way, language is a constant reminder of our being made in the image of a word-loving God. More specifically, the gift of language is an aspect of God's provision for human fulfillment. God has endowed humans with the capacity to use language so that they can worship Him and know Him through words. Not all human beings will worship and know God, but the fact that everyone possesses verbal faculties is a supreme testament to the grace of God.

Language as Culture

Another aspect of God's grace through the gift of language is that He has enabled human communities to develop languages, as well as the myths and literatures that go with them. At the heart of any community is culture, and at the heart of any culture is a language and its literature.

In his excellent defense of America's cultural heritage, which has the English language and literature as its center, Russell Kirk quotes Thomas Sowell on the nature of human culture: "Cultural features do not exist merely as badges of 'identity' to which we have some emotional attachment. They exist to meet the necessities and forward the purposes of human life."[17] No cultural feature is more necessary and more suited for the purposes of life than language and literature, and that is no accident. The close relationship of language and community is by divine tactic, revealed in God's own use of language.

According to Vern Poythress, "the Trinitarian character of God is the deepest starting point for understanding language" because "the persons of the Trinity function as members of a language community among themselves."[18] In multiple passages throughout the Bible, the members of the Godhead commune with one another through words. Poythress draws special attention to Christ's high priestly prayer to the Father in John's Gospel.[19]

Another example is the crucial verse in Genesis that describes the bestowal of the *imago Dei*. God says, "Let *us* make man in *our* image, after *our* likeness" (Genesis 1:26a; italics added). Here, God uses language both to externalize His thoughts and to share His thoughts with the other persons of the Trinity involved in speaking the universe into existence. God uses language to accomplish the vital functions of community, and so do we.

By virtue of reading this chapter, you yourself are participating in the verbal culture of the English-speaking peoples. Each word is the result of a long line of speakers using certain words to denote certain meanings. Idioms and special turns of phrase likely originate from literature, often from Shakespeare or the English Bible.

The eight parts of speech, the most fundamental building blocks of organization that help you decipher what you read, are made by human hands and passed down to us to meet the need of stable communication. Language is a cultural feature that unites us with speakers and writers of the past to serve our needs in the present. Our charge is to receive our verbal culture faithfully and to preserve it for future generations.

Language as Gift

A key feature of our English-speaking inheritance is the illustrious body of English literature, the full social and civilizational effect of which is explained by Kirk:

> The language and the literature transmitted to America from Britain carried with them certain assumptions about liberty and order, as expressed through law; also certain assumptions about the human condition, "of moral evil and of good." . . . The body of English literature produced on either shore of the Atlantic still instructs us in what it is to be fully human, the reason restraining will and appetite. . . . The great literature of yesteryear is the communication of the dead to the living; it is the bequest of vanished generations to the generation now quick. Without that inheritance, you and I would be straying in a dark wood, in peril of mires and pitfalls. Through enduring literature, wisdom—the wisdom of the species, the intellectual bank and capital of *homo sapiens*—survives the tooth of Time the Devourer.[20]

The English literary tradition is much more than a collection of stories that entertain us, although English literature can often be quite entertaining. Works from the likes of Geoffrey Chaucer, William Shakespeare, and John Milton fulfill the real human need of making that which is universal local; that is, such works communicate permanent things to a particular people who speak a particular language and who share a particular culture. For example, the virtue of honor, when it is reflected in great English literature, is no mere abstraction but, instead, is animated by characters who look like us and talk like us: they speak our language in more ways than one.

On this point the deconstructionist would have us to believe that the English literary tradition—far from being a transmitter of permanent things—is just another exercise of brute power cloaked in the pleasantries of poems, stories, and songs. But thinking of the history of English literature as an endless parade of dead white males who wrote what they did to reinforce rigid power structures is far too jaded a position for a person enjoying the divine gift of language.

Instead, we should celebrate and preserve our cultural inheritance with thanksgiving, not simply because it is ours but because, at its best, it is true, and its truth makes our lives and the lives of those around us better. We know that human language can aspire to such life-enriching effects because God, in whose image we are made, uses language to similar ends within the divine community of the Trinity. Furthermore, the apostle Paul reminds us that thinking on culture that is true, honorable, just, pure, lovely, commendable, and excellent is not an occasion for narrow-minded ideological skepticism. No, thinking on what is worthy of praise, Paul says, brings us the peace of God (Philippians 4:8–9).

Language, though, like all innate aspects of human nature, is flawed and can be abused. Words can be used for lies and slander, and stories can be untrue and impure. The account of the Tower of Babel and the confusion of languages in Genesis 11 makes the corruptibility of language abundantly clear. Nonetheless, language is one of God's greatest gifts to humanity and no clearer evidence of this gift can be found than the fact that language and literature are central cultural features among peoples all over the world. Another evidence of language's importance is the fact that God through language has given us a means to express our individual humanity.

Principle 2: Language communicates thought.

Once again, we turn to the father of the American dictionary for the biblical and theological foundation of our second principle of language. Webster believed that an appropriate reading of Genesis reveals "that Adam was not only endowed with intellect for understanding his Maker . . . but was furnished . . . with the faculty of speech."[21] Adam's immediate use of his faculty of speech together with his intellect for understanding means that language and reason are complementary faculties for us as well.

We have already concluded that the meanings of human words are reflective of divine meanings embodied in the Logos. In addition to this critical understanding, the fundamental relationship of language and reason helps us understand how humans communicate meaning through words in the first place and why we must take a scrupulous approach to usage and interpretation.

Human verbal culture began when Adam used his newfound gifts of language and reason to name the animals of Eden. Since then, words have conveyed meaning only because humans have willed to express meaning through words. Cicero observed that man, as a rational being, "perceives the connections of things, marks their causes and effects, traces their analogies, links the future with the past, and, surveying without effort the whole course of life, prepares what is needful for the journey."[22]

These marvelous abilities inspire and enable man both to use language and to mean something by his use. If, suddenly, animals developed the capacity to inflect their breath so that they seemed to possess a language, they still would not have anything to say due to their "being swayed by sense [or instinct] alone," due to their lacking the factory of meaning that is human reason.[23]

Ultimately, language is the outward expression of a complex inner self that has its origin in the mind of God. Therefore, the complementary faculties of language and reason work together in the human mind only because they have existed together in God's mind forever. Because God speaks, we speak. Because God thinks, we think. And because God has expressed His thought through speech, so do we. Our love of language rests not on a mere fascination with letters, sounds, and words but on a respect for human beings and their thought behind language.

Much of the Christian approach to language and literature is founded on a respect for other people and their thoughts represented in words; this foundation is an extension of simple Christian neighborliness.[24] We can manifest this approach in our own lives in two ways: first, we can take care to use good diction and grammar so that others can understand us well; and, second, we can take care to understand others, particularly those whose voices persist only in the pages of great books, by employing a method of interpretation that aims to discover the author's original thought.

Usage

Communicating thought through language abides by the same principles of communication in all acts of human culture. All culture requires standards to convey meaning coherently. Cultures need standards for the same reason that nations need laws: humans are imperfect and require rules of conduct to live together. The standards of a language, especially its grammatical standards, are not unlike the traffic signs and lights that govern when, where, and how a person can drive a car. If it were not for a mutually recognized set of traffic laws, we could not live peaceably together on the roads because they would be unsafe to use.[25]

Similarly, if a language lacks the force of precise grammar and good dictionaries, that language is far less likely to support coherent communication among its speakers. If we have an interest in the thought that words convey, we must be interested in the grammars and dictionaries that govern good usage.

One consistent threat to the precision of the English language has been the phenomenon of language change. Take, for example, the matter of *uninterested* and *disinterested*.[26] Until the last few decades, *uninterested* and *disinterested* had two completely different and useful meanings. *Uninterested* has meant "having no interest," so one might be uninterested in a baseball game. *Disinterested*, on the other hand, has meant "free of bias." One would hope that a judge is disinterested in the cases he hears.

Recently, though, these two words have become synonyms, meaning "having no interest." The original meaning of *disinterested* has been all but lost. Christians should lament such a loss, not because we desire to be language snobs but because such careless usage renders the English language less able to communicate thought well. Christians, who believe that the transmission of thought is a part of God's original design for language, must care for the preservation of useful distinctions among words. We must also be concerned with the preservation of good grammar, not for the sake of merely having and enforcing rules but for the sake of order and understanding one another well.

For the Christian who finds himself speaking and reading the English language, these principles mean valuing what E. Darrell Holley calls "traditional English grammar," which itself "values tradition; it values logic; it recognizes the innate language capabilities of man as a manifestation of the imago Dei; it recognizes the importance of beauty, order, and excellence; it values charity for one's neighbor which will manifest itself in a concern for communication; and it certainly is connected with an appreciation of the logos—whether that is the logos of Holy Scripture or even the logos of Shakespeare or the U. S. Constitution."[27] Our belief that meaning exists, that we can know it, and that we can share it through human thoughts and words compels us to an appreciation for the seemingly insignificant details of language.

Interpretation

Interpretation is another task that deserves special attention in relation to the principle that language communicates thought. Overall, the interpretation of novels, poems, laws, and even the Scriptures abides by the same fundamental principle at play in the simple communication between two friends. In all these instances, the goal is to understand the thought or intent of the person speaking or writing. When we interpret written words, particularly whether they were written yesterday or a thousand years ago, the object of our task is the discovery of the author's original intentions for choosing the words he did.

This approach to interpretation might seem self-evident enough. However, our post-Word world works ever against this basic Christian supposition. Before dealing with two fallacies that predominate the post-Word approach to interpretation, we should understand why the author's intentions constitute the only logical criterion for understanding what a given text means.

To illustrate the role of authorial intent in the larger context of what words mean, picture a target with a bullseye. In the middle is the meaning of the word and surrounding that meaning are three concentric circles of determinative influence; that is, each of the three concentric rings surrounding the middle contributes to the overall meaning of the word.

The first and outermost ring is the Logos. Remember, human words have meaning only because they name a meaningful and ordered universe created by God. The ultimate meaning of anything that is signified with a human word is fixed by the Lord of creation. The second ring is history. No aspect of the world can be named without long histories of human verbal cultures that bring us particular words to express particular things. The third and innermost ring of determinative influence is the user. The meaning of a given word is finally determined by the intention of the author or speaker using it.

For example, let us say that someone has used the word *tree* to convey the meaning of "a perennial woody plant."[28] The word *tree* in this instance means what it does for three reasons. First, according to the Logos, trees actually exist and constitute an aspect of God's good creation. Second, according to history, the English word *tree* has developed from the Proto-Indo-European root *deru*, meaning "sturdy."[29] *Deru* changed to *treow*, from which we have the present form *tree*, which English speakers have used to refer to a woody plant for over a thousand years. Third, according to the user, he has intended to use the word *tree* to signify a thing with leaves and branches rather than one of the other several senses of *tree* in the English language.

That the author's intention is the final determinative influence on the meaning of a word does not imply that a person can use a word such as *tree* to signify whatever he wants—say a dog. To call a dog a tree is obviously absurd. Here, the speaker is limited by the linguistic conventions that have developed during the history of the English language, throughout which it has never been the case that the word *tree* has represented "a domesticated carnivorous animal."[30] The importance of authorial intent means that *understanding* is key to the discovery of any verbal meaning, whether in a conversation or in one of Shakespeare's sonnets—understanding why the author wrote, to whom he wrote, in what genre (with its various norms and conventions) he wrote, and so forth.

The approach to uncovering the author's intention varies according to the literary and historical contexts of his utterances. One would not interpret a poem the same way he interprets a law. Nor would one interpret a fifth-century Greek poem in the same way he interprets a twenty-first century English poem. Each interpretive task demands particular knowledge. However, the aim always remains the same, which is to find, as best as possible, what the author originally thought, so to speak, when he wrote what he did.

While this approach to interpretation has gone by various names over the centuries, it is best known today as the historico-grammatico method of interpretation. I am not hereby referring to a reductionistic method of interpretation that has its origins in the Enlightenment but to a method of interpretation that the church through space and time has followed through the millennia. The aim of this interpretive method is the author's intention behind his using certain words, which it reaches by means of history (by understanding the historical, cultural, and biographical context of the author) and grammar (by understanding the linguistic context of his utterances, including, for example, the history of his language and relevant literary conventions).

As valid as the historico-grammatico method may seem to Christians who believe that God has designed language for the purpose of conveying thought, its focus on obtaining the intentions of the author holds little allure for those philosophers and critics who question language's ability to communicate any meaning, let alone the author's thoughts. These bastions of our post-Word world instead locate the focus of their interpretive methods elsewhere and thereby invalidate their approaches. Such invalid approaches abound in modern literary studies. Yet two fallacies have wreaked more havoc than others:

Fallacy 1: "The text means whatever the reader thinks it means." The first fallacy of interpretation that warrants our consideration is the reader-response method. As its name suggests, the misplaced aim of this interpretive method is to discover what a text "means" by understanding the way in which readers respond to certain passages in texts. Practitioners of the reader-response method claim that the meaning of a text is not primarily in the author's intention but is, instead, in some aspect of the reader's response.

Not all advocates agree on exactly what aspect of the reader's response constitutes the meaning of the text. However, all of them agree that the text and/or the author's contribution to it offer no standard for what is and what is not a valid interpretation. Stanley Fish, a scholar known as the father of this method, has written, "No reading, however outlandish it might appear, is inherently an impossible one."[31] Accordingly, because nothing about the text or the author guides proper interpretation, the only criterion left for determining what a given text means is the reader's response and, because such responses invariably differ, there is really no limit to what a text can mean.

E. D. Hirsch, a literary critic who has ardently defended the historico-grammatico method and criticized reader-response methodology, summarizes the illogic of such a stance: "None of the expansive benefits [of reading great literature] comes to the man who simply discovers his own meanings in someone else's text and who, instead of encountering another person, merely encounters himself."[32]

For the serious Christian reader, merely discovering himself in the process of reading falls short of honoring God's design for human language. When we read, we must be careful to extend the same neighborliness to the author that we would extend to a friend: we must show interest in the author's intent. Even in our methods of interpretation, we have an opportunity to love God and to love our neighbor.

Fallacy 2: "The text means whatever a dominant discourse has conditioned us to think it means." Michel Foucault, another thinker whose ideas bore similarity to those of Jacques Derrida, once asked, "What is an author, anyway?" He responded by saying the author is an ideological construct that was invented in the eighteenth century to apply salve to our sad need for authority, a need resulting only from our greed and desire to protect our own private property.[33] His view is, of course, false, but it illustrates the fundamental inadequacy of the approach to interpretation that has come to be known as critical theory.

Because the author is dead to the cultural and literary critics who subscribe to critical theory, authorial intentions are anathema. The only focus left for reading, then, is furnished by the methods of deconstruction, a postmodern approach to language and literature covered earlier in this chapter, and the ideology of Marxism, one which sees every facet of the human experience, including literature, through the paradigm of struggle between oppressors and the oppressed.

Deconstruction holds that what we perceive as meaning in a piece of literature is actually the ideological programing of the dominant discourse within which the work resides. The methodology of critical theory is guided by a search for the binary oppositions in a text that reveal the ideological programming implicit in it.

The binary of good versus evil might reveal the ideological programming of the dominant discourse of Christianity. The binary of ugly versus beautiful might reveal the sinister programming of the patriarchy. Rich versus poor is surely indicative of capitalism's influence. The final aim of critical theory's analysis of these binaries is to root out and deconstruct a text's ideological programing, hoping both to undermine the binaries themselves (e.g., demonstrating that good and evil are not quite as opposite as we have been programmed to think) and to bring to light the way in which powerful voices have manipulated language to suit racist, homophobic, misogynist, or classist ends.

Critical theory, while it aptly understands that literature both reflects worldview and makes demands on our ethical faculties, looks more like political activism than literary criticism. The result is not only the rejection of the idea of the author but also the abuse of the author, using his work as a blank canvas to make political statements and, in the case of biblical and classical works, to destroy traditional notions of life and morality.

Significance

Key in understanding the historico-grammatico response to these two fallacies is knowing the difference between a text's *meaning* and its *significance*. Hirsch writes, "Meaning is that which is represented by the text; it is what the author meant by his use of a particular sign [or word] sequence; it is what the signs [or words] represent. Significance, on the other hand, names a relationship between that meaning and a person, or a conception, or a situation, or indeed anything imaginable."[34] The verbal meaning of a work does not change; it is always the author's intention at the point of writing and publishing. The significance of a work, however, does change and can take on various applications.

Take the following example as another way to think about the difference between meaning and significance. Imagine a room full of kindergarten-age children being read aloud a book about a young boy who loses his father to war. Imagine too that one of those children had recently lost a father or a loved one in a combat circumstance—or in any circumstance for that matter. That one child is going to experience the book differently than the other children. For this child, the meaning of the book is not different than it is for the other children who have not experienced such a loss; but the meaning of the book has a unique connection or significance for the child, a special poignancy given his life experience.

When a reader-response critic observes either a unique response or a pattern of response to a particular passage among readers, he has not found the meaning of the text, only a significance or a series of significances drawn out by the readers. When a critical theorist discovers the workings of capitalist ideology in a piece of literature, he has either made it up out of thin air or has discovered a legitimate aspect of the social and historical context of the work. But, again, he has not discovered the actual meaning of that text. He has discovered a potential significance of the author's message.

Hirsch concludes that the "only compelling normative principle [for interpretation] that has ever been brought forward is the old-fashioned ideal of rightly understanding what the author meant."[35] This view does not mean we are uninterested in the significance of literature. But whenever we seek to read the Bible well or great literature well, or whenever we seek to understand our neighbor well, we must extend Christian neighborliness and endeavor to understand the author's thought first and then base any application or significance on that thought.

Conclusion

You probably began reading this chapter with some idea of the demands that Christianity places on the words you speak. You were probably aware of Solomon's frequent exhortations that wise men and women guard their mouths, or of the Psalmist's plea to keep one's lips from telling lies, and of Paul's characterization of Christian love as avoiding filthy and foolish talk. In the realm of biblical truth, it is obvious that words matter. Our choice of words is a matter of devotion to God and of love toward one another. Yet seasoning one's mouth with salt is not the only application of the fundamental Christian truth that God cares about words.

The realities of our post-Word world make it incumbent on us that we embrace words and the historic-Christian understanding of language and literature. We must remember that, because Christ secures the meaning of the universe, our words have meaning, and literature gives us insight. In addition, because language communicates thought, proper grammar and precise interpretation are concerns native to Christianity. Finally, the benefits of language and literature are not happenstance but are aspects of God's grace for the purpose of His glory and our joy.

CHAPTER TEN

Labor and Vocation

Matthew Steven Bracey

Work affects everyone.[1] No matter the job, we must work to make a living and put food on the table. However, work is not fundamentally utilitarian. Rightly understood, work is a vocation from a good God. In fact, the word *vocation*, from the Latin *vocatio*, means "calling." God has *called* Christians to a host of vocations.

Sadly, college students and working adults alike sometimes fail to view secular jobs as sufficiently spiritual when compared to church jobs. Such wrongheaded thinking can lead to apathy or even despair. Laypeople need to appreciate the true significance of their work. For this reason, pastor Tom Nelson talks about the "extraordinary ordinary work" of the church's laypeople. Ministers need to help congregants see the significance of their work. Ministers occupy a unique role to help laypeople bridge the "Sunday-to-Monday gap."[2]

All Christians are co-laborers in God's kingdom. Whether the child of God is behind the pulpit or on the mission field, behind the tractor or on the football field, he or she can rejoice in his or her God-given work. We should reject the false sacred-secular dichotomy, value the spiritual significance of all God-given vocations, and empower people to engage their vocations Christianly. To establish these truths, we will first examine some theological foundations of work.[3] Next, we will reflect on a wider view of vocation. Finally, we will meditate on some practical considerations for labor and vocation.

Theological Foundations

Creation

Work has not resulted from the Fall—the curse on work, yes, but not the call of work. In fact, human work has resulted from God's ordering of the world. The creation mandates make this point plain: "Be fruitful and multiply and fill the earth and subdue it, and have dominion over the fish of the sea and over the birds of the heavens and over every living thing that moves on the earth" (Genesis 1:28). Since the beginning, God has tasked humans to steward the earth and rule over its creatures.

Genesis 2 further clarifies God's instructions: "The LORD God took the man and put him in the garden of Eden to work it and keep it" (v. 15). The word *work* means "to cultivate," related to the word *culture* (the subject of this book). So, while *culture* includes the stuff of history and politics and economics and science, as well as the arts and technology and sports, *culture* refers, at root, to work.

Leroy Forlines argues that because of the creation mandate all God-given vocations have value: "One of the important aspects of exercising dominion over the earth is the cultivation of the soil to produce food, raw materials for clothing, and a number of other products. . . . The exercise of dominion over the earth and its inhabitants is a divine command. . . . When seen as a divine service, housekeeping, the everyday chores of life, and the work-week take on a new sense of value."[4]

Similarly, Albert Mohler connects divine creation to human purpose: "God has made us able to work—to manipulate things, to cultivate the ground, to manage herds, and to invent microprocessors," and "He has allowed us through labor to understand at least part of our purpose in life—to fulfill a vocation."[5] Both Forlines and Mohler remind us that any labor resulting from obedience to God's instruction has dignity and purpose. Although this teaching may expand one's view of God's vocational calling, it is not without limits. For example, God will never call someone to a profession that inherently violates His character and the moral law: hitman, loan shark, mobster, prostitute, psychic, and the like.

Undoubtedly, the way work manifests itself in individuals' lives differs according to their God-given propensities and strengths. God creates each person with unique gifts and talents, interests and personalities, likes and dislikes (Psalm 139:13; Jeremiah 1:5). These God-designed characteristics impact our choices for jobs and careers. Gene Edward Veith, Jr., writes, "The doctrine of vocation has to do with the mystery of individuality, how God creates each human being to be different from all of the rest and gives each a unique calling in every stage of life."[6] Our work matters; God creates us with it in mind.

Carl F. H. Henry masterfully links the themes of creation and individuality: "Through his work, man shares the creation purpose of God in subduing nature, whether he is a miner with dirty hands, a mechanic with a greasy face, or a stenographer with stencil smudged fingers."[7] Contemporary cultures sometimes demean blue-collar work in favor of white-collar work. However, neither biblical Christianity nor the mainstream Christian tradition affirms any such vocational hierarchy. Everyone from the apostle Paul (Ephesians 4:28) to the early church father Augustine to the English clergyman Thomas Adams affirmed the dignity of manual labor.[8]

Whether someone works primarily with brooms or computers or hand tools or heavy machinery or medical instruments, that person pursues a noble task when it reflects God's design for him or her. In the words of Jim Mullins, God created "the butcher, the baker, and the biotech maker."[9] Part of our task is to discern God's vocational calling on our lives.

Fall

However, work is not fully what God intended for it to be. We must deal with the curse of work. Through Adam and Eve, sin entered the world, affecting everyone and everything, including you, me, and our work. In the Garden of Eden, the crafty serpent tempted Eve with the fruit of the tree of the knowledge of good and evil, which God had forbidden (Genesis 2:16–17; 3:1–7). She succumbed to the serpent's temptation, and Adam succumbed to hers (3:6b).

Man sinned because he mismanaged the serpent and the fruit, each of which, significantly, were the objects of man's work. God created humankind for certain ends, including ruling over the animals and subduing the earth, or working it and keeping it (1:28; 2:15). However, by listening to the serpent, Adam and Eve transgressed God's regal command to exercise dominion over the beasts (3:1). Rather than ruling over the serpent, they let it rule over them. By eating from the forbidden tree, they did not subdue the earth as God intended. Hence man's Fall has occurred partly because of the failure of Adam and Eve to work the ground and rule over the animals according to God's design. Because of this failure, God has cursed work itself: "cursed is the ground because of you" (3:17). Now, the pursuit of work lacks the unmitigated blessing for which God intended it.

When God confronted Adam about the mismanagement of his vocation, Adam deflected responsibility and blamed both Eve and God Himself: "The *woman* whom *you* gave to be with me, she gave me fruit of the tree" (3:12, italics added). God created the institution of marriage for the purpose (among others) of the husband and wife's cultivating the earth and ruling over the animals together—of *working* together—under God's lordship.[10] Yet, instead of obedience before God, we see disobedience; instead of unity between husband and wife, we see disunity.

This background explains how the Fall of man has upset what Forlines calls the "four basic relationships" within the context of work: relationships to God, self, others, and created order. As Christians, says Forlines, our relationship to God is "primary" and "gives direction to all other relationships."[11] Our Creator has called us to work as stewards and viceregents. However, all too often, we do not subdue the earth and rule over the animals according to God's designs.

Because our relationship to God is compromised, our relationships to self, others, and the created order are likewise undermined within the context of work. We work with wrong motives and for wrong ends. We work begrudgingly and, consequently, fail to engage in work with joy and excellence. Or we work for gold or glory rather than for God: "Work becomes selfish."[12]

Similarly, our relationships to others are damaged. Like Adam, our relationships with our co-workers (including our spouses) are damaged. We yell at our spouses. We use people as means to an end, failing to honor them as divine image-bearers having worth in themselves. We lie, cheat, and steal: "We envy the success of others," says Bethany Jenkins, "thinking we deserve the promotions they receive. We tell white lies to our managers."[13]

Finally, our relationship to the created order is harmed because the ground itself is cursed. Work carries with it drudgery and frustration and loss. It can be fruitless, pointless, selfish, and even idolatrous.[14] Instead of bounty, we experience famine; instead of fruit, we get thorns. Instead of the garden, "it's a jungle out there!"[15]

Thankfully, work does not reflect these qualities intrinsically. Although sin has darkened it, God's common grace shines through. Timothy Keller explains, "Work will still bear some fruit, though it will always fall short of its promise. Work will be *both* frustrating and fulfilling."[16] If the frustration of work reminds us of the Fall, the fulfillment of work reminds us that our Creator is also the Restorer.

Restoration

God, being rich in mercy (Ephesians 2:4), seeks to restore what is lost (Matthew 18:11), including the intended ends for work. Although God alone may provide rescue, man attempts to save himself by his work, which we see even in Adam and Eve. They compromised their call to work the ground and rule over the animals (Genesis 2:9, 17; 3:2–3, 6), thereby learning shame. Prior to the Fall, "the man and his wife were both naked and were not ashamed" (2:25). After the Fall, "the eyes of both were opened, and they knew that they were naked" (3:7a).

Consequently Adam and Eve sought to cover their shame by working: they subdued the earth (1:28), or cultivated the ground (2:5), by "sew[ing] fig leaves together and made themselves loincloths" (3:7b). However, their hard work could not save them. For this reason, God, after confronting them, "made for Adam and for his wife garments of skins and clothed them" (3:21). God covered their shame in a way they could not.

God alone saves man from himself. Our hard work cannot save us. As the apostle Paul explains, "For by grace you have been saved through faith. And this is not your own doing; it is the gift of God, not a result of works, so that no one may boast" (Ephesians 2:8–9). This marvelous gift follows from "the working of [God's] great might that he worked in Christ when he raised him from the dead and seated him at his right hand in the heavenly places" (1:19b–20). Whereas Adam and Eve surrendered to the tempter in the garden (Genesis 3:1–7), Jesus Christ resisted him in the desert (Matthew 4:1–11). Just as God covered the shame of Adam and Eve, He will also cover the shame of those who receive His gift of faith and will restore their work according to God's work in Christ.

Significantly, God does not sanctify our work in solitary existence. In the words of Greg Forster, God does not call us to "go it alone—even the Lone

Ranger had Tonto."[17] Rather, God restores our work within a community, the body of His Son, the church.

The Church

The church upholds the individual's dignity against two poles: the collectivist pole in which the person is subsumed and the atomist (individualist) pole in which the group is sacrificed. Just as the human body is a composite of different parts (e.g., feet, ears, and eyes), the church is one yet composed of distinct members, each with their own strengths and functions. The Trinitarian God has given varieties of gifts and services and activities, and He "empowers them all in everyone" (1 Corinthians 12).

Although Paul applies this analogy directly to spiritual gifts, the principles undergirding this passage apply more broadly to our vocational gifts. Veith thus refers to the church's composition as a "divine division of labor."[18] God endows us with unique interests and talents and callings, which are cultivated within the Christian community.

Hence Dallas Willard and Gary Black, Jr. describe the "local church" as a "glorious beachhead of the kingdom of God where disciples of Jesus the Christ are trained to receive divine empowerment, responsibility, and blessing." Further, the local church participates in "training individuals to be ambassadors of good and light in every area, every corner, and every aspect of our shadowy world."[19] The gathered church on Sunday then becomes the scattered church throughout the week, having been empowered as ambassadors for Christ's kingdom (2 Corinthians 5:20).

Augustine envisioned that Christians belong to the City of God, and its members live by the ethic of King Jesus. Non-Christians belong to the City of Man, and its members live according to the spirit of the age.[20] Often times, the scattered church lives and works within the City of Man among non-Christians, much like wheat and tares grow in the same field (Matthew 13:24–30, 36–43), or sheep and goats roam in the same land (25:31–46).

By working in church vocations and non-church vocations alike, Christians fulfill the multifaceted mission of the church: the pursuit of excellent work unto good ends as they serve as salt and light to the people around them (Matthew 5:13–16; Colossians 3:23–24). God chooses to use us in all our respective spheres of work and influence as vessels through which He accomplishes His kingdom purposes.

A WIDER VIEW OF VOCATION

Hitherto we have considered the vocation of work, but now we will expand that usage, speaking more precisely about our many *vocations* rather than simply our *careers*. Previously, we reviewed the creation mandate in Genesis 1:28. The commands to be fruitful, multiply, fill the earth, subdue the earth, and rule over the animals signify the vocations to which God has called humanity. We have seen how work results from humanity's obeying God's command to subdue the earth and rule over the animals. However, the creation mandate also reveals our vocations to God, family, society and state, and church.[21]

God

God's primary vocation on peoples' lives is that they would know Him, their Creator and Redeemer. First, God has the authority to direct us because He is our Creator. The prophet Isaiah explains that God "created the heavens and stretched them out," He "spread out the earth and what comes from it," and He "gives breath to the people on it and spirit to those who walk in it." Consequently, He may command His people: "I am the LORD; I have called you in righteousness" for the purpose of being "a light for the nations" (42:5–7).

Second, God has the authority to direct us because He is our Redeemer. The apostle Peter describes God as "him who called you out of darkness into his marvelous light" who is "not wishing that any should perish, but that all should reach repentance" (1 Peter 2:9; 2 Peter 3:9). God has a claim on our lives because He is our Creator and Redeemer, and He desires that we would repent of our sins and walk in the marvelous light of His righteousness.

This vocation is the foundational calling that gives structure and shape to every other vocation we receive. By loving God with our whole beings, we can better love our neighbors in whatever vocational context (Deuteronomy 6:5; Leviticus 19:18): family, society, and church.

At times we will go through difficult seasons in our vocations. Jesus never promised that the Christian life would be easy; He says just the opposite. Jesus pleads we would build our lives on the sure foundation of God's Word so that, when the winds and rains and floods come, our structures will stand (Matthew 7:24–27). The brick and mortar of the Christian life come from the regular practice of the spiritual disciplines informed by a right relationship with God.

Family

Mankind's second vocation is his or her biological and/or adoptive family, which exists because men and women have been fruitful and multiplied.[22] This vocation differs fundamentally from the others because we do not choose it, whereas the others result from an exercise of human agency. The vocation of family demonstrates that God sometimes calls us to things we have not necessarily chosen for ourselves. We choose our spouses by God's will, but we do not choose our parents, siblings, children, or extended families. Yet God calls on us to honor our parents, to keep our siblings, and to care for our children, whether they are biological, adopted, or spiritual (Exodus 20:12; Genesis 4:9; Deuteronomy 6:7).

A central ethic for properly stewarding our vocations is that of neighbor-love, "Love your neighbor as yourself," which flows from love of God (Mark 12:29–31). The command to love our neighbor gives us an important principle for vocation. In whatever vocational context, the neighbor is not some abstract other but rather is a concrete relation. For example, in society and state, the neighbor is the clerk at the store, the runner on the greenway, and the teacher at school—not to mention one's literal neighbor. In the church, the neighbor is the pastor, the deacon, and the fellow congregant. Likewise, in the family, the vocational neighbor is mom and dad, brother and sister, son and daughter, and so forth.

Precisely how neighbor-love applies within each familial context will depend on the relationship. The godly stewardship of loving one's parents will differ from that of loving one's children. Passages such as Ephesians 5–6, Colossians 3–4, and Titus 2 trace out the implications of these differences. But the underlying point is that God calls us to view the families within which He has placed us, and the specific people that comprise those families, as vocations. They are not inconsequential inconveniences; we should not disregard them or take them for granted.

Instead, we must think seriously about the love of parents, children, and siblings. Admittedly, unique complications can result from circumstances of abuse or divorce; accordingly, we must pursue this vocation with prudence. But, generally, our family members, whether Christian or not, are our neighbors whom God has called us to love. In addition, this vocation gives us the opportunity to interact with people with whom we might not otherwise associate because of differences in career, geography, politics, religion, or something else. One might consider, for example, the brother-in-law who lives in another state or the aunt who votes differently from you or the cousin who is an atheist.

Society and State

A third vocation follows from the second. The fruitfulness of men and women has resulted in their filling the earth, which has resulted in the establishment of communities, societies, and political bodies. Consequently, some theologians have even referred to this component of God's creation mandate as His "political mandate."[23]

Although we may be tempted to take this vocation for granted, the societies in which we live are not inconsequential; within them we pursue our other vocations. Neither are they accidental because the sovereign God has placed us within them, whether in the United States or the United Kingdom, Japan or Jamaica, or Bulgaria or Belgium. No one community or society is like any other. In addition, the societies in which we live will change at different stages of our lives, according to circumstances of family, school, and employment.

Society, and all it involves, is a vocation from God not to ignore but to steward. In the words of Jeremiah, God calls us to "seek the welfare of the city" (Jeremiah 29:7).[24] Yet the precise way in which we engage this calling will differ according to our circumstances because all societies are distinct in terms of their histories, cultures, and politics. But whatever our engagement looks like, it should occur under the lordship of Jesus Christ.

Some Christians have resisted the political implications of this vocation because they associate them with historical or contemporary sins. However, such complications do not justify withdrawal from this vocation. The histories of our families and churches also include regrettable chapters, yet still we engage them with Christian love. The vocations of society and state have resulted from God's creation mandate. Consequently, sinful manifestations within them are incidental not inherent to them. Sinful distortions of God's creations do not destroy the thing itself because God is a God of restoration not of obliteration.

As before, a key ethic here is that of neighbor-love. Within societies, our neighbors are those with whom we practice community—at home, church, work, the marketplace, and even the voting booth. For example, seemingly ordinary acts, properly understood, are acts of love of neighbor. Even something as simple as obeying road rules demonstrates a love of the neighbor because by so doing we help to maintain order rather than create chaos, thereby decreasing the likelihood of accident, harm, and even fatality to the societal neighbor.

Likewise, the act of voting may also signify an act of neighbor-love. Voting for a preferred candidate or party (or a less problematic one) is not mere partisanship; it is the prudent stewardship of vocation. Elections have consequences because officeholders promote and enact policies that affect our societal neighbors. Christians must recognize that the election of certain candidates or parties has real-world implications for real people. Issues surrounding abortion, adoption and foster care, big tech, creation care, drug use, food, immigration, marriage, medicine, poverty, religious liberty, school choice, sex trafficking, and the like are not abstract political points. Such topics impact real people either for the cause of neighbor-love or neighbor-harm.

Unquestionably, this vocation is rife with complication and controversy. However, Christians' failure to engage it with a biblical ethic means that a higher percentage of non-Christians will engage it with a non-biblical ethic, resulting in bad policies for the abused, addicted, exploited, trafficked, unborn, vulnerable, and so forth. For these reasons, we must take our vocation to society and state seriously.

Church

A final vocation is our spiritual family, the church. Taking its imagery from the procreative mandate (family), the church is an important means by which the triune God is redeeming sinful man and restoring his capacity to obey the creation mandate as God intended. Through the church we learn how to steward the earth and rule over its animals within the context of our families and societies in a God-pleasing way. We also learn how to love God and neighbor, whether in our families, jobs, or communities.

Our church neighbors include our fathers, mothers, brothers, and sisters in the faith: pastors, deacons, teachers, music leaders, laypersons, and so on. We practice neighbor-love toward them by obeying the "one another" passages throughout the Scriptures: greet and rejoice with one another; comfort and weep with one another (Romans 12:15; 16:16; 2 Corinthians 13:11); love one another with brotherly affection; outperform one another in showing honor (Romans 12:10); pray on one another's behalf (1 Thessalonians 5:25); live peaceably with one another (Romans 12:16; 2 Corinthians 13:11); and seek one another's good (1 Thessalonians 5:15).

Just as our biological or adoptive families bring us into contact with people and circumstances that test our sanctification, our spiritual families do the same. However, such circumstances do not excuse our mutual assembling (Hebrews 10:25). Jesus calls us to confront problems and to seek forgiveness (Matthew 5:23–24; 18:15–20; 2 Corinthians 13:11). Just as God, in Jesus Christ, has achieved reconciliation with sinful men and women (vertical), He also calls us to seek reconciliation with our spiritual brothers and sisters (horizontal) (Ephesians 2).

Having reviewed key theological foundations of vocation and expanded our view of vocation, we turn now to examine practical considerations.

PRACTICAL CONSIDERATIONS FOR LABOR AND VOCATION

1. Bridge the sacred-secular divide.

Christians sometimes dichotomize sacred (church) and secular (non-church) jobs, seeing church jobs as superior to non-church jobs. Christians who do this might even appeal to passages such as 1 Timothy 5:17, which reads, "Let the elders who rule well be considered worthy of double honor, especially those who labor in preaching and teaching." However, Paul is not arguing for the intrinsic superiority of pastoral work (as important as pastoral ministry truly is) compared to non-pastoral work. Rather, he is explaining that pastors should be financially paid their worth. Sadly, because of such harmful dichotomies, some Christians in non-pastoral vocations underestimate the significance of God's call on their lives. But in the words of Willard and Black, "We have no desire to elevate pastors or priests above any other profession."[25]

The sacred-secular division has resulted in two errors. First, people sometimes think that secular jobs are non-religious or even anti-religious. This mistake occurs because people conflate *secular* and *secularism*. However, *secularism* refers to the absence of religion, whereas *secular* refers to the world but not necessarily to the non-religious. A secular vocation occurs in the world but not in the church; however, this does not mean that Christians cannot engage it with religious sentiment. For example, in medieval Europe, prior to people's conflating *secular* with *secularism*, many Christians worked in secular vocations as butlers, clerks, cooks, cottars, knights, miners, porters, shoemakers, and watchmen. Likewise, most contemporary Christians work in secular vocations and should pursue their secular vocations under the lordship of King Jesus.

The second error correlates church vocations with the sacred and non-church vocations with the secular. However, this mistake treats the secular vocation as if it is not also sacred. In fact, *sacred* means "holy" or dedicated to God. In the words of Dorothy Sayers, "It is the business of the Church to recognize that the secular vocation, as such, is sacred."[26] In sum, a sacred vocation is any work, whether non-secular or secular, to which God has called someone.

2. Expand your view of ministry.

Just as people have associated church vocations with the sacred, they have also associated them with "the ministry." Undoubtedly, the pastoral office is a noble calling (1 Timothy 3:1). However, ministry extends beyond church offices and church walls and includes non-church jobs. The word *ministry* means "service." Whether inside or outside of the church, Christians serve God and people through their God-given vocations.

We observe the application of this principle in Jesus' ministry as recorded in the Gospel of John. In John 9, Jesus states, "As long as I am in the world, I am the light of the world" (v. 5). Then, the very next verse narrates His healing of the man born blind by giving him sight. Being the light of the world means being and working among the people of the world. Being the light of the world means engaging in healing ministry. Yet note that Jesus stated, "As long as I am in the world." Shortly before ascending to heaven, Jesus stated to His disciples, "As the Father has sent Me, even so I am sending you" (20:21). Because the Spirit of Christ indwells them (16:7–11), Christians are now the light of the world within their vocations, which includes, as we see in John 9, healing ministries.

Numerous ordained ministers have remarked rightly about a broader view of the ministry. For example, Ken Riggs observes, "I do not believe the Bible makes a distinction between those whose livelihood is paid by the church and those who are supported by other means." A view of vocational ministry that confines it to the church is too narrow. "I am convinced there are many good believers who . . . have never come to grips with the fact that what they do as a means of making an income is also their ministry." The reason God's children have not thought of their secular jobs as ministry is because "they have assumed the 'ministry' meant you were a preacher or a missionary. They should not be blamed for that, however. They have learned that!"[27] Thus pastors must be mindful of their teaching.

Pastor Tom Nelson argues along similar lines that some pastors are guilty of "pastoral malpractice" for not helping congregants see the divine significance of their Monday-to-Friday jobs.[28] He emphasizes the importance of pastors "narrowing the Sunday-to-Monday gap" by demonstrating the "robust theology that informs work."[29] Likewise, pastor Eugene Peterson contended, "if Christian ministry is reduced to the work of pastors and the people who help them . . . there is not much integrity in praying, 'Thy Kingdom Come.'"[30] Rather than distinguishing between sacred and secular jobs, or designating church jobs alone as vocational ministry, perhaps we should speak in terms of church work and secular work, recognizing that all jobs within God's sovereign economy are vocational, sacred, and ministerial.

3. Honor church work and secular work alike.

Whether we are called to work in the church or the world, God has given us our vocations. Consider the example that Jesus provides: He called Simon Peter and Andrew, and James and John, to leave their nets and to follow Him (Matthew 4:18–22). Similarly, He told the rich young ruler: "sell what you possess" and "come, follow me" (19:21). Undoubtedly, Jesus calls some people to change their vocations, but He does not instruct everyone to that effect. The Gerasene demoniac "begged [Jesus] that he might be with him" but Jesus told him, "Go home to your friends and tell them how much the Lord has done for you" (Mark 5:18–19). Hence our vocations, whether professional or personal, vary.

Or consider Jesus' interactions with tax collectors. To Matthew, Jesus said, "Follow Me," and "he rose and followed him" (Matthew 9:9). Yet, when other tax collectors asked, "Teacher, what shall we do?" He replied, "Collect no more than you are authorized to do" (Luke 3:12–13). Likewise, when soldiers asked, "And we, what shall we do?" Jesus replied, "Do not extort money from anyone by threats or by false accusation, and be content with your wages" (3:14).

In Luke's Gospel, Jesus did not tell the tax collectors to leave their booths, though Matthew left his; and He did not tell the soldiers to drop their swords, though He would tell Peter to drop his (Matthew 26:52). Likewise, when He interacts with the centurion about his sick servant, He did not tell him to leave his profession (Luke 7:1–10). Again, vocation is bigger than our jobs; vocation is, in a manner of speaking, all of life, personal and professional.

Jesus' interactions with different people who had different ideas about their callings demonstrate that God calls us to all kinds of vocations according to His will. Sometimes God calls us to change direction in our lives from fishing nets and tax booths to mission work or preaching ministry. Other times He calls us to stay the vocational course, not to drop our swords or leave our administrative posts but to tell our friends what we have seen and heard.

Sometimes students are tempted to think that their student vocations do not bear equal significance to workplace vocations, or people engaged in secular work are tempted to believe that their vocations are not as important as church vocations. However, a biblical theology of vocation dispels these notions. Speaking specifically against the sacred-secular dichotomy, C. S. Lewis, a professor of medieval literature, wrote, "Before I became a Christian I do not think I fully realized that one's life, after conversion, would inevitably consist in doing most of the same things one had been doing before: one hopes, in a new spirit, but still the same things."[31] All people are called to follow Jesus, but their unique God-given callings will not all be the same.

The English Puritans rightly honored church vocations and secular vocations alike. For example, Joseph Hall stated, "The homeliest service that we do in an honest calling, though it be but to plow, or dig, if done in obedience, and conscience of God's Commandment, is crowned with an ample reward; whereas the best works for their kind (preaching, praying, offering evangelical sacrifices) if without respect of God's injunction and glory, are loaded with curses."[32] Perspective and motivation matter immensely. When we follow an "honest calling" in obedience to God's leading and in consideration of His glory, we follow a good path. Even church work can dishonor God when pursued in the wrong manner or for a wrong end.

Likewise, William Perkins argued that "washing dishes" and "wiping shoes" may please God just as much as "preaching the Word of God." "He is spiritual which is renewed in Christ . . . and whatever is done within the laws of God . . . however gross they appear outwardly, yet are they sanctified."[33] John Dod spoke along similar lines: "Whatsoever our callings be, we serve the Lord Christ in them. . . . Though your work is base, yet it is not base to serve such a Master."[34] Even jobs appearing on the television program *Dirty Jobs*, such as crime scene cleaners, garbage pit technicians, pig slop processors, sewer inspectors, and the like—jobs that are unattractive by the world's standard—are attractive in God's management.

Kentucky farmer Wendell Berry illustrates how God providentially leads us even in seemingly ordinary callings. In his novel *Jayber Crow*, the protagonist, a barber, looks back on his life's work and says, "Surely I was *called* to be a barber. . . . It looks to me as though I was following a path that was laid out for me . . . and I have this feeling, which never leaves me anymore, that I have been *led*."[35] We should not develop inferiority complexes regarding our jobs. God gives us our callings, and, consequently, they are honorable.

These principles should empower all Christians to pursue God's call on their lives, whatever it is, with confidence. Whether as an athlete like David Robinson, an author like Flannery O'Connor, a composer like J. S. Bach, an entrepreneur like J. C. Penney, a lawyer like Thomas Helwys, a playwright like Dorothy Sayers, a philosopher like Alvin Plantinga, a preacher like Martyn Lloyd-Jones, a professor like C. S. Lewis, a restaurateur like Samuel Truett Cathy, or a statesman like William Wilberforce, Christians who follow God's call on their lives pursue a holy service. The providence of God, the supremacy of Christ, and the power of the Spirit reach even there.

4. Find an appropriate church-work balance.

People whose vocational ministry does not occur within the local church often find the church-work balance difficult. On one hand, pastors want God's people to spend more time in the church and at church functions. On the other hand, people with secular vocations are often exhausted from following God's will for them in the world and, at some point, must rest in obedience to the command of Sabbath (Exodus 20:8–11; Deuteronomy 5:12–15). How can we best navigate the tension that can arise between pastors and congregants because of these challenges?

Pastors may rightly challenge their congregants about their church commitment. But, in so doing, they should avoid creating a false sense of guilt within their congregants who cannot participate in everything the church offers. Pastors should recognize that congregants' secular jobs are their God-given ministries. Similarly, congregants may rightly pursue their jobs in the world as their service (ministry) before God but should also not forsake assembling with believers (Hebrews 10:25) and serving the church (Galatians 6:10). In addition, congregants should not confuse or conflate their God-given ministries in the secular workforce with the Bride of Christ.

Gene Veith offers some helpful advice. To congregants, he explains, "We indeed have a calling to serve in our local churches, but it must be emphasized that our so-called 'secular' vocations are actually 'holy offices' where we are to serve our neighbors and live out our faith." To pastors, he says, "Churches should not demand so much 'church work' from their members that it takes away too much time from their primary vocations."[36] Imbalance creates overwork and burnout.

An additional sphere of culture that complicates this question is that of family. We must learn to balance not only church and work but also family. Some people, for example, have idolized work so much that they do not give adequate attention to their churches; others have idolized church so much that they do not give proper attention to their families. With respect to all these spheres, we must find balance between the poles of idleness and idolatry. Idleness makes too little of our callings, but idolatry makes too much of them. The idolatry of any of these spheres will result in idleness in the others. Somehow, we must practice "faithfulness and fruitfulness" within all our vocations.[37]

We must not treat the vocations of work, church, and family as if they are at odds with one another. Properly understood, they do not compete with one another but rather complement one another. People within secular vocations attend and serve the church to learn and worship and to rest. But then the church empowers and sends its people to love their families and serve their co-workers better than before.

5. Recognize that God sanctifies you in Christ by the Holy Spirit within vocation.

Church vocations and secular vocations have meaning because God has called us to them for specific *purposes*. Whereas the considerations discussed above criticize the artificial divisions of vocation, the following points will introduce readers to the manifold purposes of vocation, beginning with that of sanctification. God's sanctification of His children takes place in the hustle-and-bustle of ordinary life: family, church, community, and (yes!) work.

The apostle Paul considers this point in his epistle to the Ephesians. He "urges" readers to "walk in a manner worthy of the calling to which you have been called" (4:1) by practicing the virtues of burden-bearing, encouragement, forgiveness, gentleness, goodness, holiness, humility, kindness, love, patience, peace, purity, righteousness, tenderheartedness, truth, and unity in how they think, talk, and act (4:2–3, 17–32; 5:1–21). Each of these virtues applies to all of life's vocations, including employer-employee relationships generally (6:5–9).[38] Specifically, Paul mentions that Christian employees should not steal from their employers but rather work with honesty and integrity (4:28).

Christian commentators have also spoken to the theme of sanctification within vocation. For example, Charles Kingsley memorably commented on how God uses workplace circumstances to cultivate virtue: "Thank God every morning when you get up that you have something to do which must be done, whether you like it or not. Being forced to work, and forced to do your best, will breed in you temperance, self-control, diligence, strength of will, content and a hundred virtues which the idle will never know."[39] Likewise, workplace circumstances test our virtue. As Dietrich Bonhoeffer explained, "Every day brings to the Christian many hours in which he will be alone in an unchristian environment. These are times of *testing*."[40] In sum, God sanctifies us within the vocations to which He calls us.

6. Pursue excellence in your work, or "serve the work."

A key virtue to which God calls us is excellence in our work. Yes (as we will consider hereafter), we serve other people through our work. But fundamentally, we serve God through it and, therefore, should pursue excellence in it. Consider these passages from Paul:

> Bondservants, obey your earthly masters with fear and trembling, with a sincere heart, as you would Christ, not by the way of eye-service, as people-pleasers, but as bondservants of Christ, doing the will of God from the heart, rendering service with a good will as to the Lord and not to man, knowing that whatever good anyone does, this he will receive back from the Lord, whether he is a bondservant or is free (Ephesians 6:5–8).

> And whatever you do, in word or deed, do everything in the name of the Lord Jesus, giving thanks to God the Father through him. . . . Whatever you do, work heartily, as for the Lord and not for men. . . . You are serving the Lord Christ (Colossians 3:17, 23–24).

Ultimately, we work in Jesus' name and, consequently, should serve heartily with a sincere heart and good will.

Leroy Forlines follows Paul in recognizing that work is service unto God, deserving of excellence. Forlines appeals to the creation mandate, arguing that it "makes the labor in fulfilling this command a divine service. Since it is a divine service, it must be done well."[41] Likewise, Dorothy Sayers bases our call to vocational excellence on Genesis 1: "man, made in God's image, should make things, as God makes them, for the sake of doing well a thing that is well worth doing."[42] Hence we should pursue excellence in our work because it results from God's instructions and because we bear the image of the one whose work is always excellent.

One of the ways we do excellent work is by engaging it with what Forlines calls our "total personality." Good work will engross our minds, hearts, and wills.[43] Sayers similarly explains that excellent work will be the "full expression of the worker's faculties, the thing in which he finds spiritual, mental and bodily satisfaction, and the medium in which he offers himself to God."[44] By pouring ourselves into our work, we offer ourselves to God. This concept is significant for Sayers (whose remarks we will examine over the following pages), leading her to coin the curious expression of "serving the work."

We best serve God in our work by serving the work. Serving the work means giving it our best; it means excellence before God. We aim to serve the work even before serving the neighbor. If we place the neighbor before the work, and hence God, then we "falsify the work." For one, the work will not receive our full attention and, therefore, will suffer: "Work that is not good serves neither God nor the community; it only serves mammon." Second, it becomes an occasion for egotism: "You will begin to bargain for reward, to angle for applause, and to harbor a grievance if you are not appreciated."[45]

Third, if we place the neighbor before the work, work loses its intrinsic value and takes on a utilitarian function. People-pleasing restrains vocational integrity. Sayers, a playwright, gives this example: "Nine-tenths of the bad plays put on in theaters owe their badness to the fact that the playwright has aimed at pleasing the audience, instead of at producing a good and satisfactory play." We might consider any number of movie franchises that forfeit artistic merit for short-lived popularity and cheap profit. Then, the very masses that praised the franchise, in time, condemn it: "The work has been falsified to please the public, and in the end even the public is not pleased. As it is with works of art, so it is with all work."[46]

In sum, "the only way to serve the community is to forget the community and serve the work." In this way, we leave the good of the community to the goodness of the sovereign God, who uses our work to His ends. However, the call to serve the work in no way invalidates the call to love the neighbor; it means simply that love of neighbor must not come before love of God. In Sayers's words, "the second commandment depends upon the first," and, "without the first, it is a delusion and a snare."[47] We serve God best by serving the work.

Sayers rightly criticizes the church that fails to emphasize workplace excellence but confines its vocational instruction to moral behavior ("don't get drunk," "come to church"). The "very first demand" of the "intelligent carpenter" is that "he should make good tables." She imagines the carpentry that would have come from Jesus' shop: "No crooked table legs or ill-fitting drawers ever, I dare swear, came out of the carpenter's shop at Nazareth. Nor, if they did, could anyone believe that they were made by the same hand that made Heaven and earth."[48] Undoubtedly, the church should teach about morality, yet also it must teach about excellence. Otherwise, it will settle for the poor witness of mediocrity.

7. Do not settle for mediocrity.

Sayers observes that Christians often settle for mediocrity in the name of piety, giving examples from the church and from secular work. For example, the church in its architecture, art, music, hymns, prayers, sermons, and devotional books will "tolerate, or permit a pious intention, to excuse [something] so ugly, so pretentious, so tawdry and twaddling, so insincere and insipid, so *bad* as to shock and horrify any decent draftsman."[49] Good intentions do not excuse shoddy work. If any institution should lead the way in excellence, it is the church of God.

Sayers also gives examples of mediocrity in secular work: "The worst religious films I ever saw were produced by a company which chose its staff exclusively for their piety. Bad photography, bad acting, and bad dialogue produced a result so grotesquely irreverent that the pictures could not have been shown in churches without bringing Christianity into contempt."[50] Such examples, whether from the church or from the world, demonstrate a failure to serve the work. Piety minus excellence equals "a living lie" because God desires our excellence. "A building must be good architecture before it can be a good church," she argues, and "a painting must be well painted before it can be a good sacred picture."[51]

That God can accomplish His work through mediocre or poor work speaks only to God's sovereignty, not to any irrelevance or relativity of excellence, which has its foundation in Him. Still, God clearly condemns hypocrisy (Isaiah 1:12–17). Thus our work, whether in the church or in the world, should exhibit both sincerity and excellence. But these standards must not drive us to elitism. Rather, we should cultivate a spirit of humility about ourselves and grace toward others.

8. Make money.

Of course, serving the work does not exclude making money. While the love of money is the root of all kinds of evil (1 Timothy 6:10), money itself is not evil. Money serves important purposes, such as providing for our families, giving tithes and offerings, practicing charity, and enjoying God's good gifts. Yet we must not let money corrupt our hearts.

John Wesley suggested three rules for money: gain all you can (industry), save all you can (frugality), and give all you can (charity).[52] We cannot give except we save, and we cannot save except we gain, and we cannot gain except we work. "For religion must necessarily produce both industry and frugality; and these cannot but produce riches."[53]

Wesley viewed money as "an excellent gift of God, answering the noblest ends." In order of priority, Wesley spoke first of providing for oneself and family, followed by giving to the church and then to the broader community. "In the hands of his children, it [money] is food for the hungry, drink for the thirsty, raiment for the naked: It gives to the traveler and the stranger where to lay his head."[54] Yet he warned against industry and frugality without charity because the "essence of religion" will decrease and "pride, anger, and love of the world" will increase.[55]

Like Wesley, Forlines also interprets the Bible to present material gain as a divine blessing. "Many sincere people feel guilty about having things of high quality," says Forlines, but that is a "false sense of guilt."[56] With money, we provide for ourselves, our churches, and those in need. Also, like Wesley, Forlines expresses concern about the spiritual loss that can result from material gain: "The rich person who lacks righteousness is poor. The poor man who has righteousness is rich." Consequently, he submits that the "majority of people are better off if they are somewhere between poverty and wealth."[57] In sum, the call to excellence may produce material affluence, but material gain should not result in spiritual poverty.

However, Sayers might challenge Wesley and Forlines: "We should ask of an enterprise, not 'will it pay?' but 'is it good?'" as well as "what is the work worth?"

"Is it useful?" and "Does it exercise man's faculties?"[58] Undoubtedly, Sayers brings a different emphasis to the topic of vocation than Wesley and Forlines do, but they each contribute meaningfully to the topic of money. Labor is not merely or even primarily about money, but also it does not neglect money because, by it, we support our families, love our churches, and serve our communities.

9. See the "masks of God" in your vocations.

The Protestant Reformer Martin Luther described secular vocations as the "masks of God" by which God teaches us to depend on Him and cares for the world at large. On the point of dependence, Luther wrote:

> God could easily give you grain and fruit without your plowing and planting. But He does not want to do so. . . . You are to plow and plant and then ask His blessing . . . . What else is all our work to God—whether in the fields, in the garden, in the city, in the house, in war, or in government—but just such a child's performance, by which He wants to give His gifts in the fields, at home, and everywhere else? These are the masks of God, behind which He wants to remain concealed and do all things.[59]

God does not need our work; it is like a child's. Yet He graciously uses it in the hopes that we will learn dependence on Him.

In addition, secular vocations are the "masks of God" by which He cares for the world. A Lutheran theology of vocation emphasizes how God cares for the world—feeding, clothing, sheltering, and supporting them—through the vocation of ordinary, human labor.[60] For example, we pray, "Give us this day our daily bread" (Matthew 6:11), and God answers that prayer not only by providing seeds and soil and sun and rain and crops but also by gifting farmers and factory workers and truck drivers and retail clerks to get that food from the ground in South Dakota to our tables in Tennessee. Whether it is producing food, building shelter, or a thousand other things, all honorable work is a "mask of God" through which He works in us and through us.

10. Find opportunities to witness and contribute to human flourishing.

Finally, our work is a means by which the sovereign God invites people to Himself and brings about human flourishing. In his epistle to the Romans, Paul uses the language of "transformation" when he instructs Christians to be transformed by renewing their minds according to God's will (12:2). Over time their personal transformation manifests in how they interact with people in their churches (12:3–13) and communities (12:14–21)—in other words, in their church vocations and secular vocations. Hence transformation is about evangelical witness; it is about letting our "light shine before others, so that they may see [our] good works and give glory to [our] Father who is in heaven" (Matthew 5:16).

Additionally, as the Reformed tradition has emphasized, God uses the effects of Christian transformation to produce human flourishing more broadly. As Christian workers are transformed, their work will also be transformed, and, as their work is transformed, the culture and society around the work may also be transformed. To be clear, this teaching does not refer to the inevitable and wholesale change of specific society; rather, it refers to the progressive change of people being renewed in Christ and the way it impacts their daily lives.

Slowly but surely Christian transformation will change how people engage their work, interact with coworkers, shape workplace policy, respond to workplace challenges, and so forth. God's children are cultivated according to Christian virtue within the body of the local church but then disperse into their vocational spheres of influence, whether as entry-level employees or middle management or senior management. With time, our sovereign God may use small changes throughout the workforce, brought about by His spiritual transformation in us, to impact cultures and societies. Thus, in the words of John Bolt, we may contribute to "human flourishing" and "real-world shalom."[61]

Conclusion

A rich and robust theology undergirds vocation. Although God has created us to work, sin has corrupted God's good design. Thankfully, God in Christ is restoring His call on our lives. Yet God's call extends beyond our jobs and includes our relating rightly to Him, family, society, the state, and the church. Christian theology teaches that God calls us to all kinds of sacred vocations, both secular and non-secular, which are our ministries before God that deserve excellence not mediocrity. Through our work, God graciously sanctifies His children, cares for the world, invites people to Himself, and brings about human flourishing. Whatever God's calling on your life, learn to see it through the lens of faith and recognize your vocational significance within God's economy.

CHAPTER ELEVEN

Technology and Innovation

Christopher Talbot

Sophia is a humanoid robot created by a Hong Kong-based company known as Hanson Robotics. She was fully activated in 2016 and since then has made quite an impact on pop culture. The Internet is replete with videos of Sophia in interviews and on display. She has appeared on *60 Minutes* and *The Tonight Show*, as well as in a handful of other notable venues. *Forbes* and the *Wall Street Journal* have profiled her as well. What makes Sophia unique is her advanced artificial intelligence. She uses facial recognition and data processing to interact with others and to imitate them. Thus her interactions have eerie human likeness.

While you may think onlookers are amazed by her advanced technology (some certainly are), most are concerned. While the technology on display is innovative and amazing, a first-blush impression of Sophia is often characterized by unease. The robot's ability to perceive the world around it comes off as concerning and makes one wonder what may be next in the queue of innovation.

Of course, we can easily speak hyperbolically about technology and innovation and their influence on culture. Collectively we are obsessive about new technologies (see any Apple event), yet we are still anxious about their powers. We love new trinkets and gizmos that make life supposedly easier: we download new apps, buy roaming robots to vacuum our houses, and look for new "wearable tech." Still, we become quickly apprehensive about technology. Movies like *2001: A Space Odyssey*, *The Matrix*, or even *Wall-E* illustrate our communal concern for the far-reaching potential of technology. In this digital age, we feel like we are on a balancing beam.

As Christians thinking about technology and innovation, we are often of two minds. In the words of Craig Detweiler, "Technology is most effective when we fail to notice it, but our faith in technology is so pervasive it is often blind."[1] We enjoy and appreciate the ease that new technologies provide. At the same time, we have some concern about where current technological innovations could be heading, even if that concern is in the back of our minds. Fortunately, our theology and Christian worldview are not silent on this subject.

Since technology has an inherent posture toward innovation, it cultivates certain ideologies within us, whether for good or ill. As believers in the gospel of Jesus Christ, we must develop a theological posture toward how we engage various technological tools, as well as toward the innovation of future technologies. What should that engagement look like? Should we accept wholesale the tools and technologies around us? Should we be Luddites, casting off all technologies as evil? Or can we find a more biblical way forward?

Defining Technology

Technology is not the easiest term to define. What we often imagine when we think about technology is only a fraction of the category. Our minds often go to electronic objects that make our lives easier and more efficient. Smart phones, televisions, computers, and tablets all easily fit into this category. Additionally, we appropriately think of technology as future-oriented. Thus we think of technological possibilities like flying cars, androids, or Nike shoes with automatic laces. While technology and progress are not synonyms, they walk hand in hand. For many of us, technology is always looking forward to the next invention.

However, technology does not have to include wires and circuits. I appreciate W. Jackson Watts's definition of technology: "Technology is a manmade tool, composed of both manmade and natural materials, designed for the purpose of supporting, sustaining, or extending some aspect of human culture."[2] This definition expands the category appropriately. Chairs, cups, glasses, and hymnbooks are all "technologies" by this definition. We must remember that clarification as we move forward: technology is not just electronic innovation.

We must also note that Jesus, through whom the created order was made, interacted with the creation at a human level. Jesus was a craftsman who was involved in working with and building from wood and stone. Certainly, Jesus was innovative. He, the agent of creation, made use of the "technologies" of His day.[3]

Since our God is the Creator of all and Jesus gave us an example of working a human trade, then we—being made in His image—are to reflect that creative image. We are what J. R. R. Tolkien called "sub-creators."[4] We take the things of the earth and *do* things with them. We make things. We create ballads and burritos, gardens and gearboxes, clothing and coffee.

For this reason, technology and innovation are not simply sciences but also arts. As Detweiler argues, "Perhaps we need to recover the art of technology."[5] Maybe we have focused too much on the scientific aspect of technology and innovation and forgotten the artistic side of this sphere of culture. Jacques Ellul expands on these problems: "New kinds of production appear because new machines have been created, or because men have discovered fresh ways of exploiting matter hitherto unknown. It seems to make no difference that man may not *need* these new products, that these new creations may be absolutely useless. The means beget another means."[6] Ellul was concerned that, in our technological society, we have replaced the ends with the means: we pursue progress for the sake of mere progress. We have forgotten that technology is an art; we have thought of it only as a science to be conquered. Progress seeks only to move forward, regardless of expression.

Yet art reveals the assumptions we have. Good art encourages reflection.[7] It manifests our values in the things we create. The Christian recognizes that art should embody what is true, honorable, just, pure, lovely, commendable, and excellent (Philippians 4:8), as chapters six through nine of this book demonstrate.

Christians must recognize that technology and innovation result from the creation mandate. As recorded in Genesis 1:28, "And God blessed them. And God said to them, 'Be fruitful and multiply and fill the earth and subdue it, and have dominion over the fish of the sea and over the birds of the heavens and over every living thing that moves on the earth.'" God has called Adam and Eve—and, by extension, us as the sons of Adam and daughters of Eve—to exercise care and stewardship over the world. God enlists us as vice-regents of this world. He calls us to do something with the stuff of creation.

In creation, God created something out of nothing. In our *sub*-creation, we take the raw materials of that something and make them into something else—culture—which can bring God glory. For this reason, Andy Crouch defines *culture* as "what we make of the world."[8] As human beings, we make new technologies and innovations, yet we do not pursue this aim simply for the sake of progress. Instead, as Christians, we should seek to display our Christian worldview in our creations. This posture is different from simply putting a "Jesus sticker" on the things we make; it includes more than that. It means displaying a level of excellence and creativity that can come only from the Creator God when we make technology.

However, this call to create can easily go awry. While we should aim to bring order to chaos, we are tempted to control and exercise power for pride's sake. Thus technology and innovation can demonstrate obedience to a biblical command, and/or they can tempt our vanity and glory. Often, technologies enable our temptations and aggravate sins that are already present in our lives.

Consider how the "seven deadly sins" can directly relate to social media platforms and technologies: lust (Tinder), gluttony (Yelp), greed (LinkedIn), sloth (Netflix), envy (Instagram), pride (Facebook), and wrath (Twitter).[9] I am not suggesting that these sites are evil in and of themselves, but they can easily display the hidden evil in our hearts. They can enable sins and temptations that were already present.[10] Thus Christians must think critically about their engagement, both personally and corporately, with various technologies, especially those of a social nature.

Finally, although we attempt to define technology, technology often defines us. It shapes us in profound ways. Technology, like the form and content of other cultural products, is not neutral. Its very form is embedded with values, and it exercises power over the user. As Neil Postman noted, "Technologies create the ways in which people perceive reality."[11] They change our habits and practices.

We should not be blind to how our tools and technologies affect us and our greater culture. Consider how terms that we previously used exclusively to describe the conditions of men and women or of machines are now used interchangeably: computers get *viruses*, people *compute*, life can be *hacked*, and so forth. The line between man and machine is blurred. Christians, then, must think clearly on how we should approach this area of culture.

The Development of Technology and Its Effect on Culture

Neil Postman has written a classic analysis of technology's effect on culture in his book *Technopoly: The Surrender of Culture to Technology*, in which he offers significant insight into the slow effect that technology has on a particular culture. Postman argues that the progression exists in three tiers. In his words, "I find it necessary, for the purpose of clarifying our present situation and indicating what dangers lie ahead, to create still another taxonomy. Cultures may be classified into three types: tool-using cultures, technocracies, and technopolies."[12]

First is the tool-using culture: "The main characteristic of all tool-using cultures is that their tools were largely invented to do two things: to solve specific and urgent problems of physical life, such as in the use of waterpower, windmills, and the heavy-wheeled plow; or to serve the symbolic world of art, politics, myth, ritual, and religion, as in the construction of castles and cathedrals and the development of the mechanical clock."[13]

Postman notes that the defining characteristic of technology (or tools) in this kind of society is that its creators did not intend to challenge the integrity and structure of society. To be sure, a tool-using culture is a technological culture. We may be tempted to think that a tool-using culture is impoverished in some way, but that is simply not the case. A tool-using culture can be technologically advanced and societally complex. Yet the *defining* characteristic of such cultures is that the tools do not control the culture; instead, the culture determines the use of the tools.

The second type of culture is technocracy. A significant shift occurs when a culture moves from a tool-using culture to a technocratic one. "In a technocracy, tools play a central role in the thought-world of the culture," writes Postman. "Everything must give way, in some degree, to their development. The social and symbolic worlds become increasingly subject to the requirements of that development. Tools are not integrated into the culture; they attack the culture. They bid to *become* the culture. Consequently, tradition, social mores, myth, politics, ritual, and religion have to fight for their lives."[14]

Postman uses both the printing press and the telescope as examples of technologies that can deeply affect the presuppositions of a culture.[15] Rarely would someone argue against the positive impact that these inventions have had. These changes have radically reoriented the way we think about the world; the invention of the telescope led to the verification of a heliocentric view of the galaxy rather than a geocentric one. Sometimes, though, such drastic reorientations have had regrettable consequences; the invention of the printing press largely abolished any element of an oral culture, for example.

While a technocracy adopts technologies that affect the culture, it nonetheless wrestles with the tension between the tools and surrounding culture but does not suggest a clear master. Also, technocrats are concerned with truth but not with "progress." "They were not concerned with the idea of progress," Postman states, "and did not believe that their speculations held the promise of any important improvements in the conditions of life."[16] This characteristic distinguishes a technocracy from the last tier of Postman's taxonomy.

The third category is technopoly, or "the submission of all forms of cultural life to the sovereignty of technique and technology."[17] In a technopoly, culture lives, moves, and has its being in subservience to technology. Technology and innovation are no longer means to an end but ends in themselves. In technopolies, a culture's citizens no longer use technology; technology uses them.

Contrasting the second and third tiers, Postman explains, "Technocracy does not have as its aim a grand reductionism in which human life must find its meaning in machinery and technique. Technopoly does."[18] In a technopoly, worth and happiness are found in the innovation and use of technology. "Technopoly, in other words, is totalitarian technocracy."[19] Postman argues that the United States was exceptionally ready to become a technopoly. The ethos of American character, the audacity of capitalists in the late nineteenth century, and the success of twentieth-century technology provided a perfect foundation for the rise of a technopoly.[20]

Early in the twentieth century, two authors wrote novels that hypothesized how our technological culture would end in oppression. George Orwell published *Nineteen Eighty-Four* in 1949, illustrating a world where external forces would oppress man. "Big Brother" would control man's behaviors and even his thoughts. Seventeen years earlier, Aldous Huxley had published *Brave New World*. He took a different perspective from Orwell; as Postman noted, "Orwell warns us that we will be overcome by an externally imposed oppression. But in Huxley's vision, no Big Brother is required to deprive people of their autonomy, maturity, and history. As he saw it, people will come to love their oppression, to adore the technologies that undo their capacities to think."[21]

Postman favored Huxley's interpretation to Orwell's: man would experience greater oppression from his amusements than from society. Admittedly, the external forces of society and the state are indeed strong; but so are those internal forces of man's slavery to his amusements. "Orwell feared that the truth would be concealed from us. Huxley feared the truth would be drowned in a sea of irrelevance. Orwell feared we would become a captive culture. Huxley feared we would become a trivial culture.... Orwell feared that what we hate will ruin us. Huxley feared that what we love will ruin us."[22]

Just as the early church father Augustine had warned us many centuries before, our disordered loves can undo us. Loving things in the wrong order—chiefly, not loving God first and foremost—will lead to our dismay. Mankind was not created to place an ultimate and primary love on technology and entertainment.

Postman's taxonomy offers a helpful rubric for understanding the ways in which technology and culture work with and against one another. Technology is not neutral. It affects us and promotes certain ideologies over others. As Christians who take seriously our sanctification, we must learn to consider these ideologies carefully.

The Ideologies of Modern Technologies

One of the most prevalent misconceptions about technology is the assumption that it is inherently neutral. Most people, both Christians and non-Christians, assume that a given technology is neutral in its ideologies and presuppositions. We quickly argue that "what matters is how you use it." However, that is not the case. Every technology has an inventor who holds certain views of the world around him or her, which translate to the technology in some way—sometimes conspicuously and sometimes inconspicuously.

What is more, the technology of the modern era shares a common ideology. Consider these words from Dietrich Bonhoeffer: "The technology of the modern West has freed itself from every kind of service. Its essence is not service but mastery, mastery over nature. A wholly new spirit has produced it, the spirit of violent subjection of nature to thinking and experimenting human beings; and when this spirit dies out, it will come to an end. Technology has become an end itself. It has its own soul; its symbol is the machine, the embodiment of violation and exploitation of nature."[23]

Ellul would sound the same note as Bonhoeffer: "The tool enables man to conquer. But, man, dost thou not know there is no more victory which is thy victory? The victory of our days belongs to the tool. The tool alone has the power and carries off the victory."[24] The effects and ideologies of technology on the human person are numerous. Whole volumes have been written on these topics. While this chapter is too brief to offer an exhaustive list of how technology influences ideology, two areas are especially prominent: first, technology promotes individualism, and second, it provides a deficient anthropology.

Individualism

Repeatedly we see how technologies affect the individual person, a point that is further exacerbated in our individualistic age. No one needs to tell us that individualism is a real issue, but this form of interacting with the world around us manifests itself profoundly in our current culture. While individualism may not be new, its current expressions are.

Our current understanding of individualism boasts a strong "network" dynamic. Arguably, this form of individualism, compared to other forms of it, gives the impression that it connects individuals to a larger community. We live in a culture of "friends" and "followers." However, this impression is more of a façade than a reality.

Although networked individualism has a variety of social implications, it nonetheless represents a move away from traditional community structures—the family, neighborhood, church—and a move toward "personalized communities embodied in me-centered networks."[25] Andrew Zirschky argues that this form of individualism began in the Industrial Revolution. Without the rise of modern technologies, this current form of disembodied networking would not be possible. Zirschky writes,

> As with any social system, networked individualism demands that its inhabitants behave in certain ways in order to be socially successful. Those who lived in the era of door-to-door community had to conform to social expectations or face being shunned by the village. Those who lived in the era of place-to-place community had to attend group meetings, services and functions, or face being cut off from community. And when we consider networked individualism, we find four demands placed upon teenagers. Meeting these demands can have negative effects.[26]

Zirschky argues these four demands call students (and indeed all participants) to (1) create a personal network, (2) keep the network engaged, (3) grow the network large, and (4) be socially selective.[27] They require people to focus more on the management and sustainability of the network itself rather than on those who comprise the network. In other words, people in the throes of networked individualism are concerned about being connected, not always about those with whom they connect.

As Samuel Baker notes, "The notion of 'networked individualism'—a predominantly digital social construction of oneself—only underscores a particularly problematic trend in post-familial relationships, whereby an over-reliance on gadget-mediated relationships strains interpersonal presence."[28] Networked individualism is more than an orientation around media; it is a significant shift in the very social configuration of our culture.[29] It is a move away from traditional, embodied communities.

With new technologies come new ways of interacting with those around us. Undoubtedly, many have attempted to use the technological mediums and messages that come through them appropriately but are nonetheless profoundly affected by them. One of the common themes of networked individualism, as well as expressive individualism (which I defined, in chapter two, as hyper-subjective self-determination), is the inherent effort to propagate one's own work. In a sense, it is like works-based righteousness; but instead of focusing on tithing, it may focus on tweeting.

These forms of individualism constantly call those engulfed in them to do more and try harder, whether through maintaining connections with virtual friends to stay informed or through constructing a certain form of themselves for others to affirm and even envy. These types of individualism will never fully satisfy people caught in their clutches.

People engrossed by this individualism are being robbed of authentic, accountable community—especially of that which is available to them within the body of Christ. They are being deprived of the realization that the humbled self leads to a much more contented life than what we might call the expressed self. A student who is networked and expresses himself but who is not communally loved or deeply affirmed is like a "child who wants to go on making mud pies in a slum because he cannot imagine what is meant by the offer of a holiday at the sea."[30] As Christians, we stand ready to offer a better and more fulfilling way to those who are tempted by these expressions of individualism.

Deficient Anthropology

A second problem with contemporary technological influence is that it contributes to a deficient anthropology. We might think of numerous science fiction works in which people are not what they seem; perhaps they are aliens disguised as humans or human-like robots. Science fiction often (maybe ironically) causes us to ask the question: what does it mean to be human?

The way we think about personhood directly affects ministry, spiritual formation, and church practice. Ours is a culture of technological sophistication and consumerism. Hence, more than ever, we must think critically about what being made in God's image means for how we view people. For example, do we primarily view people as consumers, the mere recipients of goods? If so, then corporations are right to see people as part of certain demographics at the mercy of economic and social trends, as well as means to an end as purchasers of products.

In our technological age, we may also be guilty of thinking of people as machines. We treat people as data points to be processed for our human program to reach its highest efficiency. Or maybe we think of people as a means to further innovation; that is, people become part of the process to help one progress toward a future goal.

However, both examples (man as consumer, man as machine) fail to grasp the fullness of personhood. Full-orbed anthropology has far-reaching implications. Human beings are more than a means to an end. They are certainly more than categorized consumers or data points. They are more than screen-watchers or tool-users. Human beings are God's workmanship (Ephesians 2:10) whom He created in His image. Our ministries and methods, then, should reflect that truth, and we should work to minister to the whole person.

First, we must consider the anthropological question of what being human truly means. I would affirm F. Leroy Forlines's articulation of the "total personality" (Genesis 1:27; 3:6).[31] People possess multiple dimensions in personhood: mind, heart, and will.[32] God did not create us as mindless machines; we are more than robots. As Forlines says, "We are not mere instruments being used by God."[33] God created us to think, feel and act.

Second, though designed and created in God's image, each person is now depraved because of man's Fall. Total depravity has corrupted each component of a person's total personality. However, the prospect of redemption through the gospel offers hope from the curse of sin. For this reason, Carl F. H. Henry affirmed "an anthropology and a soteriology that insists upon man's sinful lostness and the ability of God to restore the responsive sinner."[34]

The gospel engages and transforms man's thinking, feeling, and acting. Forlines teases out the anthropological dimensions of this redemption:

> The mind, heart, and will are involved in saving faith. With the mind, the truth about sin, Jesus Christ, and salvation is comprehended objectively. The content of the truth is grasped and understood. With the heart, what is grasped objectively by the mind is grasped subjectively. The truth about sin becomes real. Conviction takes place. The truth about Jesus Christ and salvation becomes real. The reality of the truth conditions the heart for action to follow. The emotions are definitely involved in the experience of faith and the total Christian experience. We feel what we believe. We are not emotional blanks. Emotions are a part of the human personality by creation. Emotions need to be based on truth and disciplined by truth, but emotions must not be downgraded. With the will there is the commitment of the personality to Jesus Christ. We receive Jesus Christ. The will can act only where there is a prepared mind and heart. The will, out of the prepared mind and heart, sets in action the response of faith. What is objectively perceived by the mind is subjectively felt by the heart, and subjectively appropriated by the will.[35]

Forlines explains that no part of the human person is left untouched when one receives the gospel. Thus, as we talk and engage with people, we should appeal to their total personalities: minds, hearts, and wills (Matthew 22:35–40).[36]

Whether you are a student in the student center, an employee in the workplace, a teacher behind a lectern, or a preacher behind the pulpit, you must talk with people and interact with them holistically.

To be a Christian is not to become more than human but to become fully human. Believers are the new humanity (Colossians 3:9–10). "We are persons being transformed in our basic, inner nature into the likeness of Jesus Christ," says Forlines.[37] As we interact with people, whether believers or non-believers, we should always treat them with dignity and respect. People are not machines. They are not tools to be used. They have inherent worth.

Simple practices can demonstrate our conviction on this point. We can place greater emphasis on embodied interactions over digital ones. We can talk to people face-to-face.[38] We can enjoy meals together as a family or with friends. Such actions help to bolster communal interactions. We might also choose to write hand-written letters rather than emails on occasion because doing so demonstrates a level of thoughtfulness. The list goes on, but we can see how small practices, over time, can stem the influence of an overly technological society.

Technology and Innovation: Considering the Eschaton

As we continue to think about technology, we should look toward the eschaton, or the summing up of all things in Christ (Ephesians 1:10)—God's plan for the end of the world. Technology has an inherent posture toward innovation. In fact, it even cultivates certain forward-looking ideologies within us, whether for good or ill. As Christians, we should develop a particular posture toward how we might engage various tools, as well as toward the innovation of future technologies. I contend that a biblical eschatology rightly orients our thoughts and practices concerning technology and innovation.

Though the roots of technology and innovation lie with the dawn of man, our focus on them has increased particularly since the Industrial Revolution. Because of the increase of new tools and technologies since then, we can easily become fascinated with wondering what new things might come next. Each passing day seems to deliver new promises of technological sophistication and innovation. How much longer do we need to wait for flying cars and food replicators?

This anticipation is further exacerbated in consideration of our roles as consumers living within a consumerist culture. Michael Goheen and Craig Bartholomew explain, "A consumer culture is one in which increasingly the core values derive from consumption rather than the other way around." We are tempted, all around us, with bigger, better, and more efficient tools and technologies; invariably, they affect our values, hopes, and habits. As Christians we must take care in how we interact with the ideologies of consumerism and technological progress. Further, "A consumer culture is . . . one in which freedom is equated with individual choice and private life."[39] As one can see, consumerism and expressive individualism naturally go together.

Technology and innovation are inherently future-oriented. While they may appropriately borrow from the past, their posture is forward-looking, toward what can be done next. Technologists, engineers, and inventors want to build newer and more innovative technologies that will push us toward progress. Progress is not bad per se, so long as it conforms with the good, true, and beautiful (as examined in chapter three under canon ten of classical conservatism). However, Dr. Ian Malcolm from *Jurassic Park* offers a sober warning: "Your scientists were so preoccupied with whether or not they could that they didn't stop to think if they should."[40]

As we engage with technology, we must think about how we should orient ourselves toward this ever-changing world. We must develop a biblically-centered posture. Since technology and innovation are already forward-looking, Christians should look beyond their culture's immediate future to the culmination of all future events at the end of time.

This principle means we should consider technology in the context of the eschaton: "The Christian hope of Christ's return . . . has direct cultural pertinence. Societies and cultures run up against the problem of destiny that is also the problem of destination," writes Geoffrey Bromiley. He then asks: "What is the goal of humanity, or of our specific portion of it? Where are we finally heading even here on earth? Does the race have a goal?" and then adds, "But cultures also take into account the larger question of orientation, direction, and purpose to which Christianity supplies the answer of the coming of the kingdom."[41]

Because we take a Christian interpretation of culture and history, we can capture a long-term view of our inventions and creations. Our eschatology challenges our thoughts, attitudes, and habits. Again, Bromiley writes, "Either explicitly or implicitly, eschatology confronts every culture with new thinking, and the culture responds either by resisting the thinking, by developing its own variations upon it, or by offering alternatives."[42] Orienting ourselves according to our eschatology helps us not to sacrifice long-term blessing for short-term convenience.

As we invent and consume technologies, we should ask ourselves: How does this technology bring glory to God? Does it have transcendent, lasting value? Will it further man's common good? Can its bad use be replaced by good use? Does its form undermine its content? How does my eschatology affect the way I use this technology?

With the eschaton will come the fulfillment of all cultures. Remember, history began with a garden which God called man to cultivate. The garden, of course, was made of raw materials: seeds, dirt, rocks, and so forth. But God called Adam and Eve to cultivate this raw material. The sons of Adam and daughters of Eve have been called to follow suit. In their work of cultural stewardship, they have built myriad technologies through the ages: pencils and cups and books, as well as lamps and computers and smartphones.

These are all examples of sub-creation, the results from men's and women's subduing the earth and ruling over the animals. Of course, we know that God will refine all our cultural products at the end of time. All things, including our cultural artifacts, will undergo a deep restoration and culmination.

This last point leads Andy Crouch to ponder: "It's a fascinating exercise to ask about any cultural artifact: can we imagine this making it into the new Jerusalem?"[43] Do any of the artifacts we use or have a hand in creating seem transcendent enough to have a place in the end of time?

Of course, as Crouch observes, nothing will make it to the new heavens and the new earth without "being suitably purified and redeemed."[44] But these questions provide a helpful rubric by which to test our technological pursuits. Crouch notes, "This is, it seems to me, a standard for cultural responsibility that is both more demanding and more liberating than the ways Christians often gauge our work's significance."[45] These principles should challenge how we engage with technology.

Francis Schaeffer noted, "Christians have two boundary conditions: (1) what men *can* do, and (2) what men *should* do. Modern man does not have the latter boundary."[46] But the modern Christian *should* have this latter boundary. Navigating the technological age can be difficult for believers, but our rich theology of hope and restoration can help us to think biblically and critically about our engagement with the world around us, including its technologies and innovations.

CHAPTER TWELVE

Christianity and Science

Ian Hawkins

Conversations about the intersection of the Christian faith and science can be some of the most difficult and tedious discussions that one can have in our society. Many people, both Christians and non-Christians, have avoided these topics for years, which is part of the problem. For too long, evangelicals have avoided discussing these topics in their families, churches, and public lives. I am often surprised by how many people have questions regarding the interaction of religion and science yet avoid these topics unless prompted to speak about them.

What is it about these subjects that causes us to avoid them? Perhaps we feel inadequately equipped to converse intelligently about them. Perhaps we wish to avoid interpersonal conflict. Or perhaps we just have too many unanswered questions regarding the intersection of these topics. I hope to encourage readers to engage these topics—in life, in church, and in community. In addition, I hope to encourage the church to help equip the saints to address these ever-present issues in a biblical manner.

I have discovered that many Christians have made one of two errors in addressing these issues: some have compromised the gospel to satisfy their need to reconcile faith with science, while others have disengaged completely from these questions to avoid conflict. Undoubtedly, those who are wary about the dangers of falling prey to the world's thinking have some valid concerns. However, by ignoring these issues altogether, they have left the scientific discipline entirely to people who have used their platforms to ridicule God's Word and to propagate the myth of war between Christianity and science.

Readers may be surprised to learn that Christianity and science have enjoyed a long history of working together and of mutually laying groundwork for growth in many areas.[1] The popular notion that they are at war with one another is simply false. Even so, we hear talk of this alleged war seemingly from every quarter. Most often it comes from those on the extremes, whether anti-religion or anti-science. The history and philosophy of science demonstrates that this "war" between Christianity and science rests on a false dichotomy. In fact, those scientists who wanted to eliminate the influence of religion from their field first championed this false conflict and then wrote history books to support this ruse.[2]

However, for ourselves and our children, we as Christians must work to lay a solid foundation built on Scripture for pursuing scientific understanding for the glory of God. In this chapter, I aim to accomplish two goals: (1) to give readers a broad foundation on the issues related to these subjects; and (2) to encourage readers to engage these areas rather than avoiding them.

Foundations of Christianity

To build a solid foundation, we must first begin by understanding our *a priori* beliefs, or those beliefs and ideas we have assumed beforehand. Philosophers generally acknowledge that all human beings process information by filtering it through a view of the world they already have. For instance, children perceive the world believing that their senses (e.g., sight, smell, or touch) are giving them an accurate and real picture of what the world is like. No child feels a hot stove and then decides that his senses are deceiving him and, therefore, ignores the hot stove.

These *a priori* beliefs help form our worldviews. Each discipline has *a priori* beliefs. The discipline of science, for instance, believes that the world is knowable and intelligible and that it is regular, consisting of patterns that people can observe and know. These beliefs are vital in scientific knowledge. Why would we seek to know about the weather or the human body or about how we could cure cancer if we do not believe that the world has laws and regularities about it that allow us to know and study it? So, we begin by stating our *a priori* beliefs so that we are clear about our starting points.

We will begin with four foundational points about the intersection of Christianity and science. First, and most importantly, God is the final authority in all things. Second, He has communicated Himself by His Word, which is infallible and inerrant in all that it affirms and which we must properly interpret to understand what He is teaching us about the world and ourselves. Third, we are fallible creatures, meaning that our knowledge and understanding, whether theological or scientific, are limited. Thus we must approach these topics with humility, though, regrettably, I find very little of this on either side of the proverbial aisle. Humility does not prevent us from forming conclusions and even having certainty in our convictions about the correct way to interpret or understand a subject or a biblical passage. However, humility does cause us to have charitable and respectful discussions with others who may differ from us. Fourth, all truth is God's truth, including that which science makes known. As a result, we should demonstrate confidence, not fear, when we pursue scientific knowledge because it accords with God's purposes on earth.

Foundations of Science

Over the past fifty years, scholars have produced a groundswell of work to explore the reasons for the growth and development of science to its present form. This work on the history and philosophy of science, from scholars such as Edward Grant, Rodney Stark, and Stanley Jaki, has shown that a Judeo-Christian view of the world has played a significant role in laying foundational principles that helped science to flourish in Western culture.[3]

For instance, Jaki observes that science fully developed only in the Christian West, even though Chinese, Egyptian, Islamic, and Greco-Roman cultures had dabbled in scientific endeavors and even had invented machines. The reason for such development results from specific foundational principles of Christianity that are absent in the religions of these other cultures. For instance, Christianity teaches that God has created a world that is stable and governed and logical.

This view contrasts with the belief often found in the aforementioned cultures that people are subject to the ever-changing whims of the gods who are constantly at war. How could someone come to study science if he or she believes that the gods are always causing unpredictable turmoil in the world? Only a religion having a presupposition of an orderly and unchanging creation that is governed and sustained by a logical God who does not change nature's laws on a whim could provide a sure foundation for someone to think that experimental science could be a worthwhile endeavor. Such Christian concepts laid the foundation on which medieval theologians built.

Galileo

Europe's Rediscovery of the Ancients

Most books discussing the history of science begin with the ancient Greeks and Romans.[4] Medieval European scholastics, as they increasingly interacted with Islamic scholars because of the Crusades, rediscovered these Greek and Roman writers, including Archimedes, Pythagoras, Plato, Aristotle, and Ptolemy. Islamic scholars had inherited these writings from the early Christian church fathers and had even made some scientific discoveries themselves from A.D. 700 to 900.[5]

Europeans who read these Greek and Roman writers during the 1100s to the 1300s discovered many topics of interest in the arts, the humanities, and the sciences, which spurred them to develop schools and universities. The church was particularly important in developing these institutions and encouraging the study of these topics. Sometimes scientists adopted accurate conclusions, but other times they came to wrong conclusions, at least as we judge them today.

One such major error was their adoption of a Ptolemaic cosmology, which teaches that the sun and planets revolve around the earth (known as the geocentric model of the universe). Unfortunately, during this period, many theologians interpreted passages from the Old Testament with this theory in mind. Later, though, Ptolemy's theory of an earth-centered universe came under scrutiny when Nicolaus Copernicus (1473–1543) proposed a sun-centered universe (known as the heliocentric model).

However, when Copernicus's book proposing his theory was published, a colleague added a foreword to it to indicate that Copernicus's theory represented a hypothesis for predicting the positions of the stars and was not intended to portray a true account of the heavens. In doing so, the book's publication was much less controversial than it could have been, and it was widely read and accepted—until the Galileo affair.

The Galileo Affair: An Overview

Some scholars have overdramatized the story of Galileo Galilei (1564–1642), presenting it as the first battle of an apparent war between science and religion. The reason for this interpretation is that the church declared Galileo as a heretic for his support of a heliocentric universe to the point that he was placed under house arrest for publishing the *Dialogue Concerning the Two Chief World Systems* (1632).[6]

Scholars adopting the science-versus-religion interpretation of the Galileo affair often fail to mention several important facets of the story. First, Galileo was an extremely antagonistic and bombastic individual who made enemies quickly. For instance, in his *Dialogue*, he named the character representing the Roman Catholic Church's position on the universe as *Simplico* (or Simpleton). Second, the broader context of the Protestant Reformation created challenges for the church and society. Protestants spoke regularly of rejecting certain church traditions that did not, they believed, comport with Scripture—a position the Roman Catholic Church rejected and formalized at the Council of Trent (1545–1563). Thus, in refusing to reject some mistaken traditions, the Roman Catholic Church held tightly to an interpretation of Scripture that assumed a geocentric model of the universe.

A third facet—and perhaps the most important one—is that Galileo ignored the work of previous scientists who had demonstrated problems with Copernicus's model. For example, Tycho Brahe (1546–1601) had demonstrated that an updated model of an earth-centered universe could have been viable based on the data that was available to them at the time. In addition, Johannes Kepler (1571–1630) observed certain flaws in Copernicus's model, which scientists today have acknowledged. Galileo was aware of Kepler's work but ignored it because he believed in Copernicus's model. This observation does not remove those issues with the church, but it shows that the Galileo affair was not simply a controversy of science versus religion. Rather, it was a scientific question about how to interpret the available data. Galileo put forth one theory and did not interact with other theories that, at the time, could neither be proven nor disproven.

Lastly, some of the reasons for Galileo's status as a heretic had nothing to do with science. The church did not dismiss alternative theories per se; it was deeply interested in science. For that reason, the church had not dismissed Copernicus or deemed him a heretic and was perfectly willing to use his ideas as theories. At the time, the church held that the earth was stationary, not moving or rotating, but this view resulted from the church's acceptance of the theories of Ptolemy and Aristotle and theologians who had read Scripture from that perspective.

Galileo's heretical status is also ambiguous because he was supposedly told, during an inquisition in 1615, that he could not teach or believe in heliocentrism, which he agreed to do. When he was brought to trial for heresy in 1633, he was convicted of suspected heresy by the inquisition, but there was debate within the church on this charge. Galileo was placed under house arrest, but he still had many clergy who agreed with him and housed him. Eventually he went back to his home and continued writing. Several of his books were published after his inquisition trial.[7]

The Galileo affair matters so much because it has taken on a life of its own. Critics of religion have incorrectly told it as the first battle between science and religion, and each successive generation has retold the tale. However, the historical context demonstrates several important points an honest assessor will consider.

First, theologians prior to Copernicus had interpreted Scripture according to the Ptolemaic science of their day. This fact shows that the church is not anti-science; rather, it has engaged science at least since the medieval period. Second, the debate about Copernican heliocentrism was not fundamentally a debate of science versus religion; it was a debate about the extent to which the church has the final authority to interpret Scripture that occurred against the backdrop of the Protestant Reformation and Council of Trent. Finally, Galileo is not an example of the church's holding back science. If anything, he is an example of the church's disagreeing with an interpretation that, at the time, was not validated on other scientific theories.[8]

Lessons from the Galileo Affair

These three important parts of the story indicate that the science-versus-religion interpretation of the Galileo affair is simplistic and inaccurate when compared to the full story. The real story also reminds us: First, we must distinguish between Scripture itself and our interpretation of Scripture. The Galileo affair demonstrates that the church had interpreted Scripture to support the then-current scientific thinking of Ptolemy (and Aristotle before him). So, when Copernicus and Galileo proposed a new scientific theory, later religious critics attacked Scripture itself rather than the geocentric interpretation of Scripture. But the two are not the same.

Additionally, we must recognize that we interpret the Scriptures with a different (scientific) background than the biblical authors who wrote them. Still, God inspired the biblical authors to write truthfully in a manner that reflected their experience. For example, when Joshua 10:12–14 recounts that the sun and moon stood still, it does not mean that Scripture supports a geocentric theory of the universe. The biblical authors did not write in view of our modern scientific theory. It means that the sun and moon appeared to stand still to Joshua and is an example of phenomenological language, meaning that the passage reflects how things appeared.

Third, the notion that scientists are always seeking truth no matter their prior beliefs is simply not true. Galileo presents a good example of this point; he believed in a heliocentric universe but ignored or else denied conflicting data from Brahe's geocentric model and Kepler's heliocentric model. Thomas Kuhn addressed this very issue in the 1960s when he illustrated how leading scientists often refuse to question certain beliefs even when conflicting evidence exists and how, regrettably, scientists often change their beliefs only after the alternative becomes undeniable.[9] Such examples show that even scientists are limited by their biases.

Finally, we must be careful about how we interpret Scripture so as not to wed our interpretation inescapably to the scientific thinking of the day. History has demonstrated, time and again, that current scientific models become unfashionable and new data changes old theories. We must also be humble about our interpretation of Scripture and our interpretation of science—to say nothing of our limited cognitive abilities. In short, we must recognize that we are not omniscient.

These points do not mean we cannot clearly interpret Scripture or science; sometimes differences of interpretation are superficial and can be reconciled by a clear and honest engagement with the historical and grammatical facts. However, we should always give grace and practice humility toward people who hold different interpretations because, sometimes, the historical and grammatical data is not clear.

Isaac Newton

While the Galileo debate was happening in Italy, the foundations for modern science were being laid in England. Francis Bacon (1561–1626) was not much of a scientist, but he was a proponent of science, and he established a method of study known as the inductive method that later thinkers would use to formalize scientific inquiry. One such thinker was Isaac Newton (1642–1727), an Englishman who transformed science from a fledgling curiosity to a serious pursuit.

Newton made many scientific discoveries, but his theory of gravity is the most well-known. This discovery cemented science as an important discipline because people began using it to predict phenomena previously unknown. For example, about twenty years after Newton's death, scientists observed that the planet Uranus was not in the position it should have been. However, other scientists, using Newton's theory of gravity, predicted that the planet Uranus was being affected by some other previously undiscovered planet; in time, scientists discovered another planet, Neptune.[10] The notion that theories of science could accurately predict things, such as the existence of planets that scientists did not know existed beforehand, made a huge impression on the scientific and popular imagination.

Newton believed that science is valuable for several reasons. For one, he believed it is eminently useful to people. Because men and women can build on the information it yields, the discipline of science is worthy of financial investment, a sentiment he shared with Francis Bacon. Newton emphasized experimental science as the most useful method of inquiry, making it the preferred scientific method going forward.

Also, Newton believed that science helps people learn about the cosmos God created. He suggested, for example, that the forces of gravity and motion provide evidence of God's hand in sustaining life. However, other skeptical scholars and philosophers used his ideas as a foundation for the theory that the forces of nature can explain, in and of themselves, the wonders of the world and that the universe is more like a machine. In fact, some people began to believe that science would lead to people's understanding the universe in its totality; Voltaire, a critic of Christianity from the French Enlightenment, believed that claim.[11]

Instead of seeing the handiwork of God in the normal operations of nature, these skeptics began suggesting simple laws of nature that did not require divine activity or intervention. Consequently, some people, such as Voltaire, advocated Deism, a belief which generally holds that a god has created the world so that it can function on its own but is now distant from it and not interacting with it. According to this way of thinking, people are responsible for themselves since they will not receive any help or intervention from a higher being (perhaps because this being is uncaring). Such ideas would lead, in time, to the many revolutions that littered Europe from the late-1700s through the mid-1800s, and such ideas continue to pervade our thinking to this day.

To summarize, Newton's success gave many people the confidence to believe in new things—some good and some bad. People began to believe that science can lead to greater knowledge (and it has). Sadly, many began to believe in a mechanical world that does not require God's operation in it. Finally, people began to take these ideas and to propose sweeping changes to society, resulting in violent revolutions. After Newton, the next significant figure we are going to consider in the history of science is Charles Darwin.

Charles Darwin

Overview

Charles Darwin (1809–1882) was born in England approximately eighty years after Newton's death into a world where Newton's scientific theories were commonly held. Like Galileo before him, Darwin is relevant to the discussion of the relationship between science and religion. However, his ideas of evolution and natural selection took on significance because of the broader cultural context within which he presented them.

At the time, many thinkers were theorizing about new progressive ideas. Jean-Baptiste Lamarck, Robert Chambers, and even Erasmus Darwin (Charles's grandfather) published theories about the natural origins of the universe.[12] The theories of Georges Cuvier and Charles Lyell each proposed extending the age of the earth.[13] These ideas laid the groundwork for Darwin's.

After studying at Cambridge for ministry in the Anglican Church, Darwin sailed around the globe in the early 1830s. These journeys led him to hypothesize a theory about the origins of nature, which he developed over the course of subsequent decades. He finally published the theory in his book *On the Origin of Species* (1859), feeling compelled to do so when he learned that Alfred Russell Wallace was proposing a similar theory. Darwin later expanded on his views in *The Descent of Man* (1871).[14] As Darwin's theory became popular, radicals appropriated it for their social revolution against religion, using it to promote deleterious ideas, policies, and practices, including communism, racism, sexual perversion, and the like, which eventually manifested in eugenics and even Nazism.[15]

Darwin lived during a tumultuous social period with revolutions sweeping Europe that often pitted the young against the old. Consequently, when Darwin published his theory, younger scientists more readily accepted it than did older scientists, until, eventually, the older scientists died off.[16] One merit to Darwin's theory is that, at that point in history, it better explained the data than the outdated creation models of the time did.

Scientists were asking questions like: Do fossils not provide evidence for an older earth? Where did fossils come from? Why did these animals become extinct? How are all animals seemingly adapted specifically for their surroundings? How did plants and animals come to be different across the world if they all came from the ark? How does creation science explain how animals came to be on islands that formed more recently due to volcanic activity? Today, scientists who affirm creationism and intelligent design have good, scientific answers to these questions and others like them, but, when Darwin published his theory, they did not because they were relying on outdated ideas. Models of creation were in a state of flux with the recent discovery of the fossil record, as well as with Carl Linnaeus's proposal of a narrow concept of species.

Darwin published in a world that did not believe nature created itself and that did believe organisms were fixed in their natures so that they produce offspring only like themselves. However, many Christians believed these propositions in a distinctly Aristotelian manner. When the West had rediscovered the writings of Aristotle centuries beforehand, his ideas seemed to agree with how people had interpreted Genesis from the beginning, and, as a result, people had interpreted Genesis through an Aristotelian lens. We saw something similar happen with the Galileo affair in which people conflated the words of Scripture with an interpretation of Scripture. Consequently, Darwin's theories appeared to call into question not only Aristotle but also Genesis. In fact, Darwin's ideas really called into question belief in the *fixity of species*. Did God separately create each species? Or did each species result from a natural random evolutionary process?

Prior to Darwin's birth, William Paley had published *Natural Theology: Or, Evidences of the Existence and Attributes of the Deity* (1802), which was based on Aristotelian science and convinced even Darwin when he voyaged around the world in the 1830s.[17] However, when Darwin published his theories several decades later, he challenged the arguments of contemporary natural theology by providing a natural explanation for the existence of living organisms.

Perhaps some of the most important implications of Darwin's theory were the ideas that humans are not fundamentally different from animals and that morality merely reflects social norms. To be clear, neither Darwin nor his immediate defenders touted moral relativism, but his theory opened the door to it that others would certainly walk through. If Newton's theory opened the door for Deism (even though he was not a Deist), Darwin's theory opened the door for atheism. Atheism resulted in the rejection of any presumed supernatural authority over man: men and women may do as they please if they come from the random processes of nature and therefore have no soul or responsibility.

Yet even those people who did not embrace atheism but still adopted Darwinism began to think differently about God's activity. No longer was God required for the development of any species, including humans; He was required only for the first act of creation. Instead, Darwin's theory posits that individual species have come about by chance rather than by divine design. As a result, man lacks purpose, and he is free to choose his own morals and paths.

Responses to Darwin

Responses to Darwin's books varied in the second half of the nineteenth century. Reaction in the United States was somewhat delayed because of a civil war. Social and theological debate on Darwinism finally gained momentum in the early twentieth century. As alluded to previously, social Darwinism manifested itself among many liberals and progressives in the development of eugenics. This movement resulted in attempts (some of which, regrettably, were successful) to sterilize people of certain ethnicities, such as African Americans, American Indians, and Latinos, as well as people displaying mental or physical disabilities or poverty. (In Europe, social Darwinism played a role in the rise of Nazism.)

On the other hand, many Christian fundamentalists in the United States responded to Darwinism by rejecting the sciences altogether and adopting an anti-intellectualist posture so that their children did not pursue academic degrees in the sciences. This development resulted in serious problems because the field became overwhelmed with people who were not sympathetic (and were often hostile) to Christian orthodoxy.

Fortunately, during the second half of the twentieth century, various groups and organizations of Christians began to emerge that pursued these questions of science. For example, Henry Morris formed the Institute for Creation Research in which scientists could defend creationism on scientific grounds. Such scientists would take both Genesis and science seriously. Morris believed in interpreting Genesis literally and supported young earth creationism. He published books such as *The Genesis Flood* (1961, co-authored with John Whitcomb) and *The Genesis Record* (1976).[18] Morris's organization began a movement that spread across the globe as other young earth groups have sprung up around the world in response to Darwinism.

However, old earth groups have also formed. An important old earth organization is Reasons to Believe, founded by Hugh Ross in 1986. Rather than coming to science as a Christian, as Morris had done, Ross, as a student, came to Christianity through science. Unlike Morris, he believes in an old earth and interprets Genesis through that lens. This group has grown considerably since its inception and has played an important role among Christian evangelicals debating the theory of evolution.[19]

The BioLogos Foundation is another major scientific organization. It approaches issues of science from the perspective of evolutionary creationism. This group argues from science and Scripture that God used evolution as the means by which life was created. BioLogos was co-founded by Francis Collins, who led the Human Genome Project and headed the National Institutes of Health (2009–2021) amid the COVID-19 pandemic.[20]

Another response to Darwinism has come from the intelligent design movement, which bears particular importance due to its widespread dissemination. This movement, which welcomes both young earth and old earth creationists, began in the 1990s when several scientists and academics came to believe that the theory of Darwinian evolution, as it was then proposed, fell short of the scientific data from the previous half century. Important scholars from this movement include Stephen Meyer, Michael Behe, and Philip Johnson.[21]

Interestingly, several high-profile cases have demonstrated how scientists supporting the theory of intelligent design have been bullied or denied tenure by other scientists.[22] Thus, in many ways, scientists who affirm Darwinian evolution have adopted the dogmatism they claim the Roman Catholic church possessed during the Galileo affair.

Since the mid-twentieth century, both young earth and old earth groups have demonstrated an interest in Christians engaging matters of science. Sadly, in the decades following the release of Darwin's publications, many Christians did not engage in any real scientific debate but instead ignored and even derided debates about Darwinism and evolution. Thankfully, more recent history shows an increased interest from evangelicals to engage in these debates. All of this leads us to ask: how should we as Christians engage the sciences?

How Should Christians Engage Science?

So far, we have observed how Christians and the church have responded to debates within the scientific community. The background context, which includes the ideas of Galileo, Newton, and Darwin, gives us a clear picture of what has happened historically. All too often, people debating the relationship of Christianity and science demonstrate ignorance about the past. Key to these debates are the issues of authority and truth. Does science determine truth? Is the Bible inerrant, infallible, and authoritative? How should the Scriptures be interpreted?

At the beginning of this chapter, we reviewed some foundations for Christianity and for science. Though God is the ultimate source of truth, the discipline of science may, nonetheless, reveal His truth; hence science should not frighten us. We believe that God's Word and God's world are consistent; consequently, they will reveal the same truth, if we interpret them properly. The problem, often, is not God's Word or His world but rather our interpretations of them.

At the same time, we must recognize that not everyone begins with these *a priori* beliefs, and we must interact with them in grace and kindness. We must also recognize that disagreements do not mean that the Bible is wrong or that science is wrong; instead, disagreements demonstrate differences of interpretation of the biblical Word or of scientific data. Thus people generally have taken one of three broad positions concerning the relationship between Christianity and science.

Scientism

First is metaphysical naturalism, methodological naturalism, or scientism.[23] It begins with the *a priori* assumption that nothing exists outside the natural world—the universe is a closed system. For this reason, people should believe only in the natural world. Accordingly, truth ("fact") is determined only by what people can empirically verify. The discipline of science in this view rests on these premises.

Because "science" trumps all other truth claims, it should not admit theories arising from other premises, especially from religious ones. Science is the only way by which people may know the facts. This view of science has pervaded the academy for approximately a century, and people like Richard Dawkins and Daniel Dennett have popularized it for the masses. Additionally, some disciplines not otherwise associated with science have become more scientific in nature in terms of how their leaders govern the disciplines.

Nevertheless, scholars of the history of science, and of the humanities more generally, as well as scholars from the intelligent design movement, have rightly criticized this view of science and exposed its weaknesses.[24] Even secular scholars have found fault with the presumption of scientism. It feigns objectivity, but, as philosophers have observed, it does not begin from nowhere; it begins with *a priori* beliefs that are not subject to scientific experimentation. If we begin assuming that science can accept only what can be empirically verified or naturally explained, then we cannot accept science itself because it cannot be empirically verified or naturally explained.

By contrast, when medieval theologians began studying nature, they took seriously naturalistic explanations for phenomena within a greater framework of knowledge. They correctly viewed science alongside the other disciplines, rather than above the other disciplines. This posture meant that the study of nature and discovery of natural explanations expanded their view of God and His work instead of diminishing it.

If advocates of scientism want to limit scientific methodology to empirical means only, then they should acknowledge the immense limitations of science. Instead, all too often, they offer grand conclusions about being, knowledge, and ethics, that exceed the proper bounds of their methodology.

Fideism

A second view of the relationship between Christianity and science is fideism. This view represents the opposite extreme of scientism. In many ways, scientism and fideism are opposite sides of the same coin, with each excluding the main emphasis of the other. Fideism, when applied to science, contends that we should avoid science because a secular mindset has corrupted scientific endeavors. This position has characterized some fundamentalists (going back to the fundamentalist-modernist controversy of the early twentieth century), but this characterization has begun to change in more recent history.

Even if this view is held by a minority of people, it has pervaded the thinking of many. For example, we see it clearly when the teachers in some religious schools purposefully omit teaching about challenging theories, such as Darwinian evolution, and encourage their students not to pursue degrees in the sciences for fear that they would lose students to atheism. Admittedly, that concern is a valid one, but the answer is for the church to prepare students for these challenges.

Not engaging these areas over the course of the past century has resulted in a serious problem: the church has forfeited valuable influence in the sciences so that scientism largely defines the discipline. Atheists fill our universities because many Christians have adopted a posture of scientific fideism. I do not recommend either extreme—either scientism or fideism—when considering the relationship between Christianity and science. Rather, I recommend a middle way.

Integrationism

I believe we can take Scripture and science seriously, integrating the truths of God's Word with His world. Many Christians have suggested models for how the relationship between Christianity and science should work. We will not consider them here because there are too many of them. However, I do want to summarize two important aspects that are pertinent to this discussion. The first concerns the interpretation of Scripture, and the second concerns the interpretation of science. At times the two appear to conflict, but, in actuality, they do not because they each exhibit God's revelation. Even apparent contradiction is the exception and not the rule. In many scientific disciplines, such as chemistry, engineering, mathematics, and physics, Christianity and science have practically zero conflict. Nevertheless, how do we resolve tensions when they do appear?

Creating Some Guidelines

Before we consider some of the questions that arise from the Scriptures and science, I will offer some guidelines to help us approach them well. We could refer to these guidelines, which most Christians throughout history have believed, as our *a priori* beliefs. We will begin with Scripture's teachings about the creation before considering some principles about science.

Scripture

The whole of Scripture testifies to the doctrine of creation.

1. God created the world out of nothing (*ex nihilo*) (Genesis 1:1; Hebrews 11:3; Revelation 4:11).
2. God's creation was good (Genesis 1:4, 10, 12, 18, 21, 25, 31).
3. God created humankind in His image according to His likeness (Genesis 1:26–27).
4. God gave men and women the mandate to subdue the earth and rule over its animals (Genesis 1:28).

5. God created the institution of marriage (Genesis 2:23–24; Mark 10:6).
6. The biblical authors appeal to creation theology for various propositions:
   a. God is the Creator (Colossians 1:16; Hebrews 11:3).
   b. God the Creator has great authority and power (Job 37:14; Jeremiah 32:17).
   c. Jesus Christ is the agent of creation (John 1:1–5; Colossians 1:15–17).
   d. God, the Creator of the heavens and earth, deserves our worship (Psalm 33:4–11).
   e. The created order provides evidence for God's existence (Psalm 19:1; Acts 17:24–28; Romans 1:18–21).
7. The creation is the first part in the grand narrative of Scripture, followed by the Fall, redemption, and new creation.

These points establish a simple understanding of how the Scriptures clearly define the creation and its importance. Additionally, no true interpretation of scientific data will conflict with these points.

Science

In addition, I want to offer some principles about science that we can use when we consider the data of scientific evidence.

1. When rightly interpreted, both Scripture and science do not come into contradiction.
2. The Bible is not a scientific textbook but, when it does recognize things about the physical world, it is accurate.
3. Human reason, while corrupted by sin, is an important tool for examining data (Isaiah 1:18; Acts 17:17).
4. We cannot deny that scientific data exists, but we can acknowledge that our interpretations of the data may be incomplete, depending on a whole host of factors, and that a comprehensive model of scientific interpretation will consider multiple lines of evidence.

Interpreting Scripture

In this section, we will first consider some biblical passages that appear to conflict with the scientific data. Genesis 1–11 includes the creation of the world, a talking serpent, the Fall of man, Nephilim, a worldwide flood, and the Tower of Babel. Should we read these passages literally or allegorically? Some interpreters have suggested treating these chapters as allegorical in nature to eliminate any conflicts that seem to arise between these stories and scientific data. However, we cannot support that hermeneutic because it gives improper authority to the interpreters of science, and it relegates God's Word only to spiritual matters.

The main passages that generate tension regard the creation and flood narratives. The problem with interpreting these stories allegorically is that later biblical passages do not treat them in that manner but instead speak of them as occurring in the time and space of history (Isaiah 54:9; Hebrews 11:3). How then should we interpret them? Excluding allegorical interpretations, there are two major interpretations: (1) a literal twenty-four-hour day, six-day creation event with a young earth and worldwide flood; and (2) a long period(s) of time somewhere in the creation event with an old earth and a local flood.

Young Earth

Let us first consider the young earth interpretation of Genesis 1–11, the view I personally hold. The Hebrew word *day* (*yôm*) has generated much controversy through the years. Although the biblical authors sometimes use the Hebrew word *day* to refer to longer periods of time, such as when they refer to the "day of the LORD," they never use it in this way while also using words like *evening* and *morning* in the same context, such as in Genesis 1:5, "And there was evening and there was morning, the first day."[25]

The usage of such terms means that interpreting *day* as referring to a literal twenty-four-hour period is the best reading of Genesis 1. Additionally, Exodus later states that the LORD made heaven and earth "in six days" and then rested on the "seventh day" to give man a pattern for how to live (20:11; 31:17). The underlying point of such verses requires a literal reading. After all, men and women do not allegorically occupy twenty-four-hour days and seven-day weeks; they literally occupy them. No astronomical event has given us this formula for a week; the Hebrew-Christian Scriptures alone have provided it.

The early chapters of Genesis not only describe a literal twenty-four-hour day, six-day creation event but also the Fall of man. A long period of time during the creation event would require death (the death of animals), but Genesis 3 tells us that the origin of death is the sin of man. In fact, the first animal death we see occurred when the LORD God made garments of skin for Adam and Eve (v. 21); we know that Adam and Eve did not eat animals as food because God instructed them to eat from plants (2:15–17), and God did not give animals as food until after the flood of Noah (9:1–4).

In addition, passages about the new heavens and new earth describe them as a state in which pain, destruction, and death no longer exist (Isaiah 11:6; Romans 8:20–22; Revelation 21:4). Significantly, the new heavens and new earth reflect the Garden of Eden (Genesis 2:9; Revelation 22:2). These connections mean the biblical authors did not believe that death or destruction of any kind characterized the beginning of time.

This picture runs counter to that which is painted by those advocating for the lapse of a long period of time within the creation event. Specifically, the image they promote includes wide-ranging death and destruction, such as the (practical) extinction of dinosaurs by meteors. But that picture is quite different from the one that Scripture presents.

Old Earth

We must also understand the view that favors long periods of time that coincide with scientific ages. Followers of this view believe in an old earth, as opposed to a young earth, and offer various interpretations of Genesis to substantiate their views. For example, one view is that the word *day* is literal, but a lengthy period exists between Genesis 1:1 ("In the beginning, God created the heavens and the earth") and 1:2 ("The earth was without form and void, and darkness was over the face of the deep. And the Spirit of God was hovering over the face of the waters"). Another view is that the word *day* is literal, but a lengthy period exists between each twenty-four-hour period.

Another view is that the word *day* (e.g., day seven) is not a literal twenty-four-hour period but is a lengthy period of time. Old earth supporters may also interpret references to "lights" in the heavens (e.g., moon, sun, and stars) metaphorically so that they do not delineate actual time (history). In this way of thinking, the creation story of Genesis 1–2 is literary, not historical.[26] At times, some of these views may overlap with one another but not always.

I have given reasons previously for why I believe that a literal twenty-four-hour-day creation with a young earth is the best interpretation of these verses. Yet we should be saddened by the vitriol that some Christians express toward one another because of differences of interpretation regarding the age of the earth, and we should respond respectfully and charitably to people with whom we disagree. While holding to our convictions with integrity, we should also recognize that we are finite and fallible.

Evaluation of the Biblical Evidence

I have presented a young earth interpretation of Genesis and an old earth interpretation. Which one fits best into the guidelines I established previously? Given the foundational points regarding a doctrine of creation, the young earth interpretation fits within the boundaries we have listed in a much more cohesive way. For instance, Genesis declares that God created a good world and that death, disease, and destruction followed from the effects of sin. However, an old earth interpretation of Genesis would require that animal death, disease, and destruction exist prior to sin, which, in essence, reduces the doctrine of sin to a spiritual condition with a less profound (of no) effect on the physical creation. By treating the Fall as a mere (or near mere) spiritual issue, some thinkers have interpreted cultural issues surrounding same-sex unions and transgenderism differently than orthodox Christians, who see these issues as resulting from sin.

Reasons such as these establish a good case for believing in a young earth. Even so, well-meaning Christians will disagree about some of these questions, sometimes even in the churches we attend. We can hold strong convictions while also showing grace to those with whom we disagree.

INTERPRETING SCIENTIFIC DATA

Old Earth

Having reviewed some of the key biblical passages and the interpretive issues surrounding them, we will now consider questions related to the scientific data according to an old earth interpretation of the creation event. One question supporters of this view must answer concerns evolution. To what extent do species evolve? Has God created specific species, or did He create generic kinds (Genesis 1:11–12, 21, 24–25) that then evolved into specific species, such as a cat kind that then evolved into lions, tigers, and cougars? Where is the boundary between God's direct actions and the evolutionary process?

Whether an interpreter reads Genesis 1–2 assuming long periods of time or assuming metaphorical images, he or she faces difficulty with the question of human evolution. Much debate has arisen within theological circles concerning the historical nature of Adam and Eve and questions arising from the discovery of so-called pre-human fossils. Whereas young earth interpreters believe in a literal Adam and Eve, old earth proponents vary considerably in their views: from one view saying that God used evolutionary means to produce Adam and Eve and then gave them a soul later to another view saying that God specially created Adam and Eve apart from the evolutionary process.

Old earth proponents generally consider only scientific evidence for their views since such interpretations go beyond the biblical text. Additionally, such groups generally have no qualms with the dating methods of the fossil record or with any other data being used to explain the earth's history. In their minds, such data does not present a problem with Scripture if one interprets the early chapters of Genesis according to a theory that does not require a literal reading, such as day-age theory or gap theory. However, as I have suggested, the scientific data does not require such interpretations.

Young Earth

An additional problem with which old earth interpretation must reckon concerns the history of biblical interpretation. Specifically, the most prevalent interpretation of Genesis throughout the history of the Hebrew-Christian tradition coincides with the young earth interpretation. However, these remarks about hermeneutics do not mean that all Christians from earlier times agreed exactly on all matters related to the early chapters of Genesis. Reading young or old earth interpretations into some historical Christian thinkers can be anachronistic.

Three questions are of vital importance in young earth creationist research. First, proponents of a young earth interpretation generally question old earth interpretations by rightly calling into question the dating methods most scientists use. Recently, the Institute for Creation Research published findings in the field of radiometric dating that indicate that current methods lack full integrity and, consequently, require readjustments; significantly, such readjustments would fit with a young earth model.[27] Scholars such as Russell Humphreys and Jason Lisle explore these issues in their publications on the subject.[28] This research, however, is highly debated; thus young earth scientists must continue pursuing lines of research that are promising.

Second, young earth creationists must also contend with questions related to the fossil record and geologic column. Generally, they appeal to the biblical record of, and to scientific evidence for, a cataclysmic worldwide flood. Understanding flood geology is crucial in explaining the scientific data from a young earth perspective. Lines of evidence for a worldwide flood include the existence of polystrate fossils that go through several layers of the geologic column, the lack of evidence of erosion between layers in the geologic column, and the existence of rapidly buried fossils with bent rock layers. In some cases, the available evidence presents conflicting data, indicating that scientists do not completely understand flood geology. However, research by scientists such as Timothy Clarey point to further ways forward.[29]

A third issue for young earth creationists concerns the questions surrounding the existence of human-like fossils. Typically, these scientists either group such fossils with extinct apes or else identify them as belonging to the human lineage. Todd Wood, who was trained as an evolutionary biologist and has done extensive research in this field, has published his findings cogently arguing that the evidence indicates clear distinctions between ape-related and human-related fossils.[30]

Young earth interpretations demonstrate the most straightforward reading of Genesis. However, like any scientific theory, they come with difficult questions when we consider the scientific data, though these difficulties are not insurmountable as young earth creationists do good work. Yet this field warrants still more research. If the history of science teaches us anything, it is that our current scientific models are constantly in flux.

Evaluation of the Scientific Evidence

Just as we evaluated the young earth and old earth interpretations against the biblical evidence, we will do the same with respect to the scientific evidence. Even without the testimony of the Scriptures, the straightforward scientific evidence indicates the following:

1. The universe was created out of nothing.[31]

2. The universe appears to be designed because thousands of physical operations are governed by specific factors that would otherwise destroy life.[32]
3. The first living cell formation appears to break every chemical and physical law, meaning that, at this point in time, science cannot explain it without recourse to a designer outside the system.[33]
4. The theory of random mutations appears to lack significant power to explain our current living systems.[34]

These points establish the logical conclusion that a God who is a designer exists and created the world. But could this God have used evolution as the means by which He created the world? The work of many within the intelligent design community, including Michael Behe, Stephen Meyer, and Douglas Axe, limits the use of evolution to small changes—microevolution rather than macroevolution.[35] Additionally, thinkers promoting an old earth interpretation of the data point to several lines of evidence to support their position, including starlight, radioactive dating, and the depth and magnitude of the fossil record. According to the guidelines we established previously, we cannot dismiss these lines of evidence. In many respects, people subscribing to an old earth base their positions on these data points.

Even so, young earth creationists have proposed several answers. For example, young earth creationists point to the recent discovery of tissue in the bones of dinosaurs and other creatures.[36] Many scientists have believed that dinosaurs are so old that their bones would not have any tissue remaining. So incredulous were people when this evidence was first provided, that it took several years before they were satisfied that the findings were true. Old earth and young earth creationists are still working through questions related to this evidence: What was the condition of this tissue? Could the tissue have lasted for millions of years? How we interpret scientific data is an ever-changing challenge for people who believe in a young earth or an old earth. However, my point is that a young earth interpretation of the data can be scientifically respectable.

Taking both the biblical evidence and the scientific evidence together, I believe the young earth position is the most tenable. I am not suggesting that my position is without any challenges, but I am suggesting that, in the aggregate, it has less challenges than other positions. I believe that the young earth position is scientifically plausible, and it fits the biblical evidence the best.

Getting Involved

In this chapter, we first considered important foundations of Christianity and science. We then reviewed key figures in the history of science, including Galileo, Newton, and Darwin. Third, we examined three models for the relationship of Christianity and science: scientism, fideism, and integrationism. Finally, we answered questions that invariably arise with interpreting Scripture and the scientific data. This final section of the chapter functions also as a conclusion in which we will contemplate three reasons for why Christians should stay engaged with the fascinating subject of science.

Subdue the Earth and Rule Over the Animals

One reason we should engage in scientific debates is that it is man's responsibility to subdue the earth and to rule over the animals: "And God blessed them. And God said to them, 'Be fruitful and multiply and fill the earth and subdue it, and have dominion over the fish of the sea and over the birds of the heavens and over every living thing that moves on the earth'" (Genesis 1:28).

God-honoring stewardship and viceregency (see Matthew McAffee's discussion of these concepts in chapter four) means we should know something about the earth, its creatures, and the best way to use them properly—and we learn these things through science. Here, I use *science* in a broad sense rather than a narrow one. So, whether we like science or not, we must recognize that scientific knowledge is pertinent to the endeavors to which God calls us.

How can we steward something we do not know? How can humanity be fed if we do not know the best ways to grow produce? How can we care properly for animals without understanding ecosystems and environments and our impact on them? How can we contribute meaningfully to a discipline we know nothing about? Why have a secular people (in the contemporary world) without a Christian worldview stewarded this field of knowledge better than Christians?

Some people may assume we as Christians can get by in life with little to no knowledge of science; however, that assumption is faulty and causes us to falter in our responsibility to care for the world. While the industrialization of the world has provided some important benefits, it has produced many detriments as well. In addition to wreaking havoc on the natural world and social order, it has contributed to economic specialization so that vast swaths of people can avoid learning about certain subjects, including science. Christians have thus avoided science because they live in the wake not only of the fundamentalist-modernist controversy but also of economic specialization resulting from industrialism.

However, the Christian retreat from this discipline has resulted in a vacuum so that the field is ruled predominantly by secular scientists. Sadly, in some cases, these scientists steward the knowledge of God's world better than Christians do. In his book *The Quest for Truth*, Leroy Forlines points us in a better direction. He reminds us that our relationship with the created order is one of the primary relationships to which God has called us.[37] As a result, we must take seriously God's call to steward the knowledge of the world and its creatures.

Meditate on God's Attributes

Secondly, the study of science assists us in meditating on God's nature. In Romans 1:20, the apostle Paul demonstrates the connection between the created order and God's attributes, explaining that God's "invisible attributes, namely, his eternal power and divine nature, have been clearly perceived, ever since the creation of the world, in the things that have been made." Study of the world leads us to a greater study of God; in this way, science contributes to worship because it teaches us more about God's worth. To demonstrate this claim, we will consider two examples, one macroscopic and another microscopic.

By understanding the size of the universe, we observe the vast differences between God and man; God has set the moon and stars in place (Psalm 8:3). God's majesty and transcendence makes His care of human beings more significant: "what is man that you are mindful of him, and the son of man that you care for him?" (8:4) The psalmist David establishes the utter contrast between God and man by use of the word *yet*: "Yet you have made him a little lower than the heavenly beings and crowned him with glory and honor" (8:5).

David then explains that the glory and honor of men and women is seen in God's call that they steward the world and its creatures (my previous point from Genesis 1): "You have given him dominion over the works of your hands; you have put all things under his feet, all sheep and oxen, and also the beasts of the field, the birds of the heavens, and the fish of the sea, whatever passes along the paths of the seas" (8:6–8). Hence study of the heavens and of the stars teaches us more about the majestic God.

A second example of how science teaches us more about God comes from the world of microbiology. The smallest particles teach us about the sheer complexity and design of God's creation. For example, the DNA polymerase is responsible for copying the instructions that tell the cell how to make things. This microscopic system properly recognizes the needed parts, installs them in the correct order, and replaces any mistakes that occur, all while existing in an environment surrounded by other parts that, if combined, would cause mutations in the system.

Amazingly, this system makes, on average, one mistake for every 10,000 bases. This extremely accurate system functions in a truly difficult environment, making it more efficient than most man-made systems. To the extent it does make mistakes, we blame the effects of sin and total depravity rather than God. In any case, the study of the microscopic world, like the study of the heavens, teaches us much about our great God. "O LORD, our Lord, how majestic is your name in all the earth!" (Psalm 8:9)

Expand Your Vision of Divine Restoration

A final reason we should engage in scientific debates is that it expands our vision of divine restoration. Because all things are being summed up, or united, in Jesus Christ, things in heaven and things on earth (Ephesians 1:10), we must take "all things" seriously in the present, including scientific knowledge.

We can observe this theme from the writings of people like Hugh of St. Victor (c. 1096–1141). When scholars first began establishing universities in Europe, many early educators gave defenses for education in general and for universities particularly. In his *Didascalicon*, Hugh of St. Victor argued that "the intention of all human actions is resolved in a common objective: either to restore in us the likeness of the divine image or to take thought for the necessity of this life, which, the more easily it can suffer harm from those things which work to its disadvantage, the more does it require to be cherished and conserved."[38]

Hugh of St. Victor was explaining that the proper *telos*, or goal, of human education is the restoration of God's kingdom. This restoration occurs by limiting the destructive effects of sin throughout the world and restoring the perfect image of God in human beings. The pursuit of science has unquestionably played a significant role in this vision.

Consider the ways in which men and women have used medicine and technology to mitigate the effects of sin. Regrettably, sinful men and women have used these means to ill effect, but the point remains they have used them to good effect too. While our sovereign God will not fully restore His kingdom until Jesus returns and He sums up all things in Him, He is nonetheless currently using the scientific knowledge of medicine and technology to bring physical healing to sick people, clean water to remote villages, nutritious food to impoverished people, and so forth.

God invites us—you and me—to be a part of this story, but it will require that we know something of how the sovereign God is working through people and their work, whether they recognize it as such or not. Undoubtedly, God's callings—God's vocations—on our individual lives will not all look the same. We must discover what God would have *us* to do. But, in some way, God has called each of us to steward His world, and understanding science can help us in that endeavor.

CHAPTER THIRTEEN

The State and Public Life

Montgomery F. Thornsbury

The Common Good

Greek Roots

At the beginning of the fourth century B.C., Greece was not a nice place to live. Athens was particularly chaotic. The cause of the disarray was a successive cycle of governments quickly taking control and then dissolving just as quickly. A leader or leaders would establish a democracy, but then an especially charismatic elected official would curry enough favor and power to declare himself dictator. A group of powerful men would then depose the dictator, after which an oligarchy, or rule by the richest and most powerful, would wield power for a while until the entire process repeated itself again.

Disgusted by this never-ending cycle of social and political turbulence, the Greek philosopher Plato wrote *The Republic,* the first systematic treatment of a proper political philosophy, which takes the form of a dialogue. If you are not familiar with the genre of dialogue, think of it as a type of drama in which the characters ask and answer philosophical questions.

The Republic was Plato's attempt to answer the question, "What would society be like if its leaders constituted it on a stable concept of the good rather than on the unstable competition of self-interest?" Plato responded to this question through the discussion of characters in the dialogue. His most important interlocutor was Socrates, Plato's teacher whose real-life murder had resulted from the political upheaval of the day.

At the outset of his interlocutors' discussion of the ideal form of government, Socrates lays down an important principle: "Our aim in founding the State [is] not the disproportional happiness of one class, but the greatest happiness of the whole; we [think] that in a State which is ordered with a view to the good of the whole we should be most likely to find justice, and in the ill-ordered State injustice."[1] Philosophers through the ages have abbreviated Socrates's principle of concern for the good of the whole as "the common good." By asking what is the common good, Plato, through Socrates, was also asking, "What do humans fundamentally need?" "What brings about human flourishing?" and "How can the constitution and laws of a state bring about that flourishing?"

Plato recognized rightly that determining the good for human society is not just a matter of power. More fundamentally, it is an issue of knowing the societal applications of the virtues of the good, true, and beautiful. We inherit from Plato the understanding that all public and political questions, from how to be a good parent to how to be a good president, are ultimately worldview questions. While Plato did not get everything right when answering the broad questions that we are considering, he got much of it right, including the importance of appeals to theology, morality, and tradition.

Hebrew-Christian Roots

Understanding the Hebrew-Christian approach to the common good begins with understanding the right perspective of what people need. By understanding that God has made the family as the bedrock of society (Genesis 1:28; 2:24), we know that society is oriented from the bottom up and not the top down. By understanding that God is the source of all authority (Genesis 1:1; Matthew 28:18), we know that proper human authority is a wonderful gift of God's common grace that we should not resist for "light and transient causes."[2] By understanding that God has created man in His image (Genesis 1:26–27), we know that human life is dignified and realizes its greatest potential when people are free to live as God has made them to be. By understanding that man has a fallen nature (Romans 5:12), we know that man is prone to destructive behavior and given to abusing his authority and freedom.

Through the prophet Jeremiah, God commanded the Israelites whom He had exiled into pagan Babylon to care for themselves and their families. He tells them to build homes, plant gardens, and get married; in other words, God tells the exiles to make culture. Then God adds one last command: "But seek the welfare of the city where I have sent you into exile, and pray to the LORD on its behalf, for in its welfare you will find your welfare" (29:7).

Though we are not exiled Israel, our present social and political situation can seem sometimes like exile. God's exhortation to Israel supplies an important principle for us as well. Peter tells us we are sojourners and strangers in this life (1 Peter 2:11). As we face a culture that seems belligerent to belief in objective value and habituated to moral and ethical disorder, our duty is to build houses, plant gardens, and grow families. We make culture for the benefit of the city to which God has called us by seeking its welfare—its common good.

Most likely, God has called a majority of those reading this chapter to the political context of the United States or an English-speaking country in the West. Therefore, much of the second portion of this chapter will concern the way in which the Christian concept of the common good has already exercised an outsized influence on the American approach to society, law, and politics. We will see that, thanks to this influence, our primary ethic of creating public and political culture is one of conservation—conserving those aspects of our social, legal, and political institutions that Christian ideals have helped shape (see chapter three).

Conservation does not remain in the past but extends into the present and future. Thus we seek the welfare of the city by influencing the present public and political order both by supporting candidates, and even by lobbying for legislation, that reflect the values of the Christian concept of the common good. While this approach may seem narrow-minded, know that the Christian view of the common good is not just *a* view of what brings about human flourishing. It is *the* view of what brings about human flourishing because it is based on the truth of God's Word and the witness of Christian doctrine. Any other view is far less likely to bring about justice, order, and freedom.

God and Society: The Primacy of the Family

Our survey of the Christian concept of the common good begins with the recognition that God has designed society to work. We must first define two terms that people often use synonymously but that are not, in fact, the same.

The first term is *politics*, a word with Greek origins that refers to the formal governance of a city or a people. Perhaps you have assumed, from the outset of your reading this chapter's title, that it would concern itself exclusively with political things. Indeed, the "state" aspect of this chapter deals with the topic of formal governance or politics, but this chapter concerns more than that narrow topic.

The second term *public life* refers to a much broader category of inquiry than formal governance. The word *public* derives from Latin and relates to people in general, not just to those who are governed by a formal state. We will use *public life* to describe aspects of human existence that deal with life among people, whether political or (more often the case) nonpolitical. Public life comprises cultural aspects such as literature, art, religion, customs, and traditions—all of which provide identity and critical moral and ethical insights.

A key contention of this chapter is that *public life produces political life*. That is, public life should inform political governance, and the most important responsibility of politics is to protect public life. Rod Dreher has made this point in connection with our present political situation: "Culture [or public life] is more important than politics, and neither America's wealth nor our liberties will long survive a culture that no longer lives by . . . eternal moral norms necessary to civilized life."[3]

The Familial Creature

If society were a house, politics is the outer surface of brick protecting the inner structure of public life—both resting on the foundation of family. However,

Aristotle wrote in his treatise *Politics* that man is a political animal, meaning that human society is "crowned" by and reaches its fulfillment in the state, or in the exercise of political power.[4] Aristotle explained that society began with the family, which produced the village, which then produced the city, which then necessitated the state, which is the end or *telos* of all human relationships. Aristotle's observation that the family is the source of society is true enough.

However, the Christian understanding of society inverts Aristotle's final analysis. The family, much more than the state, is the crown of human society, which God Himself ordained. Man is not merely a *political animal*, a term Aristotle used. Man is a *familial creature* with affiliations that go deeper than civic bonds that are purely political, legal, or economic. Because of this fact, man is also a cultural creature since culture arises out of the needs of the vast interconnected web of family units that we call human community.

Scripture attests to the primacy of the family in the Christian concept of society. Genesis 1 recounts that God created human beings. Genesis 2 then tells how man, possessing the tools both to understand and to communicate with God, entered into community with his Creator. Yet, seeing that man should not steward the earth alone, God created the family (v. 18). God commanded that "a man shall leave his father and his mother and hold fast to his wife, and they shall become one flesh" (v. 24). From this first union the entire human race has sprung. It follows that, because a family first sustained human society, families continue to sustain societies.

The nineteenth-century Dutch theologian and politician Abraham Kuyper explored some of the central implications of the primacy of the family. He wrote, "A child born from his parents is thus what guarantees the organic unity of the human race, and produces within it the organic points of intersection constituted by family, kinship, tribe, and nation."[5] The family, Kuyper argued, provides society not only with people but also with basic social relationships that begin with loyalties among kin and that branch out to produce the national loyalties on which entire cultures depend.

Authority in Society

Kuyper also wrote that authority in society depends on God's delegation of authority to the family: "Another element grounded in the birth of children from their parents is authority—in such a way, in fact, that authority within the family is directly connected to the high authority of the government and even to the highest authority that resides in the very sovereignty of God."[6]

In the political manifesto of his Anti-Revolutionary Party, Kuyper illustrated the bigger picture of the suffusion of God's authority throughout creation and society: "Sovereign authority flows out from God Almighty to all parts of his creation—to air and soil, to plant and animal, to a person's body and a person's soul, and in that soul to one's thinking, feeling, and will; and further, to society in all its organic spheres of scholarship and business; and finally, to families, to rural and urban communities, and to the sphere that encompasses all these spheres and has to safeguard them all: to the state."[7]

God's authority animates the created order, including plant and animal life, as well as human life down to the individual person (Genesis 1:28). The logical progression of this order is that God delegates His authority throughout the organic constitution of society, beginning with the family and passing to local communities and then to the state. Kuyper believed that God had designed society to function in this way in order to establish and sustain human society, which would then produce flourishing for communities and individuals. However, Kuyper also understood that fallen man could easily upset this balance of delegated authority.

The Spheres of Sovereignty

Notice Kuyper's specific reference to "organic spheres" in the quotation above. Kuyper conceived of the just share of God's authority throughout society by envisioning a series of interrelated cultural spheres that work together. At the same time, these spheres exercise their own special share of delegated authority from God. Just as plants and animals exist after their own kinds (Genesis 1:11–12, 21, 24–25), so the spheres of culture exist after their own kinds as well (1:28). Kuyper never identified a hard and fast list of these spheres. But, as examples of spheres of sovereignty, he pointed to the family, the church, the village or local community, business, education, and the state.[8]

Thus, according to Kuyper, God's Word, which is the clearest revelation of God's plan for society, grants certain reserved powers to certain members of society. For instance, God gives the family the authority to perform the most fundamental social task, the rearing of children. If another sphere, such as the church or the state, undertook to rear children in ways that parents normally do, then it would challenge God's plan for the delegation of authority on earth. Such an overreach would represent a social injustice.

Another category of Kuyper's taxonomy of authority in society is God's appointing the state as the protector of public life. More precisely, Kuyper understood that the state exists to protect each sovereign sphere's ability to exercise its own God-ordained authority: "Political authority operates alongside many other authorities that are equally absolute and sacred in the natural and spiritual world.... Every attempt by political authority to try and rule over those other areas is therefore a violation of God's ordinances."[9] Thus the sphere of state does not exist over the other spheres of culture but rather alongside them. God gives authority as a grace to us, but He has established clear limits to that authority.

A just society exemplifies a delicate balancing act of mutually dependent spheres, all expressing their rightful authority in accord with God's design. This picture begins with the protection of the family against the encroachment of other spheres. In addition, it is achieved by rendering to Caesar what is Caesar's and respecting the rightful authority of governmental powers (Mark 12:17).

Still, Kuyper clearly indicated that this societal sphere could possibly wreak the most havoc on the balance of society, which is a fundamental problem of placing too much power in the state. In this way, Kuyper's reflections on the French Revolution exemplify his conservative sensibilities: because power should be prudently restrained, localized expressions of power are preferred over centralized expressions of power—points that are consistent with canons eight and nine of classical conservatism as presented in this book's third chapter.

The Problem of Centralized Government

For Kuyper, the French Revolution represented one of the most unfortunate epochs of human history. Kuyper understood that the sphere of the state could relate to the rest of society in one of two ways: either top-down or bottom-up. Kuyper's preference, consistent with God's prescription in Genesis 1–2, was clearly bottom-up, with society welling up from the family. The French Revolution, though, had precipitated a top-down governmental state of affairs; it had inverted the order put forth in the earliest chapters of Genesis. It inspired a form of government that "impels to ever greater centralization as soon as the possibility for it arises."[10]

Kuyper used the term *centralization* to describe the abandonment of local control and the growth of nationalized bureaucracies in the wake of the French Revolution. This centralization not only abrogated power from more local forms of government to a central government, but it also destroyed the entire balance of society. When a central government seizes control of a local one, it takes away the sovereign authority of that local government. This act of tyranny inevitably produces other and perhaps greater seizures of rightful authority by the central government, or even by a local government that has had its correct purposes frustrated.

Overall, Kuyper contended, "the smaller parts come first, and those things of smaller dimensions form and make up the larger nation. So the parts do not arise from the nation, but the nation arises from the parts." Kuyper used simple logic to prove his point about the importance of respecting the authority of the smaller spheres of society: "In fact, if we descend still lower and go down to families, it is true even there that the village is composed of families and not that the families are cut from the village. The family was there first, and only then could the village take shape. Finally, if the village vanished there would still be families;

but if the households were to disband the village too would come to an end."[11] Thus we see that centralized government threatens the family.

For these reasons, Kuyper continues, "We shall maintain, over against the fiction of the all-competent, all-inclusive, and all-corrupting state, the independence given by God himself to family and municipality and region as a well-spring of national vitality."[12] Kuyper's approach highlights several Christian principles: (a) the family is the foundation of society; (b) the state is instituted to protect the family, as well as the rightful authority of the various spheres of society; and (c) the local government is better than the centralized government.

Centralized power of any sort, whether by government, business, church, family, or individual, inevitably becomes corrupt and brings imbalance to society. Rod Dreher has illustrated this point effectively in his books *Crunchy Cons* and *Live Not By Lies* in which he examines the challenges associated with Big Business, Big Government, and Big Tech.[13] An aversion to centralized power is not merely one plank in the political platform of American conservatives; it is an aversion that is native to the Christian conservative tradition. If we believe that the family is in fact the foundation of society, then we must believe that "small is beautiful," to borrow the title of E. F. Schumacher's wonderful book on economics.[14]

The sovereign authority exercised in the context of public life, which is the life of the family, church, business, school, and other spheres, is just as important as the authority exercised by formal political powers. The Christian concern for the common good is characterized by a concern for the correct exercise of authority in society. Balanced society means just society, and just society is good for our souls and promotes human flourishing.

However, the fallen nature of man complicates the realization of balanced society and the common good in the sinful actions of both individuals and groups (of individuals). The next section of this chapter will thus detail the ways in which the Christian understanding of human nature further influences our concept of the common good.

Man and Society: The Balance of Order and Freedom

Genesis 3 relates the Fall of man. In disobeying God's strictures not to eat the fruit of the tree of the knowledge of good and evil, our first parents introduced sin into the world and, in so doing, conditioned man for chaos. In Genesis 4, sin brings chaos to humanity's first family when Cain kills Abel in a fit of rage (4:1–15). Then God asks Cain, "Where is Abel your brother?" and Cain infamously responds, "I do not know; am I my brother's keeper?" Clearly, the Fall had passed from Adam and Eve to their sons, and, in one of the first recorded effects of the Fall, we see that sin works ever to destroy every human connection, the family first and foremost.

We see that the fallen nature of man has implications both for the individual in his need for redemption and for society in its need for order. At the same time, the psalmist declares that God has "crowned [man] with glory and honor" (Psalm 8:5). We know also that man is made in the image of God and that he is possessed of an inherent dignity (Genesis 1:26–27), a dignity that realizes greater and greater potential when he is free.

Here is yet another balancing act of any just society. Order and freedom are the indispensable principles that at once depend on one another and exist in constant tension. Without order, or a check on passions, liberty becomes libertinism, for, to quote Socrates, "an excess of liberty is an excess of slavery," which turns out to be the tyranny of self.[15] Conversely, without freedom, man is servile and subject to the tyranny of the state or principality. Neither extreme is ideal or conducive to the prosperity of the whole.

Thus justice requires a transcendent moral code to define the exact limits of order and freedom. This moral code will also explain the parameters of right and wrong behavior and the nuances of character and virtue. Therefore, the proper balance of order and freedom does not originate from the state, although the state and its laws and its means of law enforcement contribute to this balance. Instead, it originates in the moral foundations of public life, which, in turn, effect political order and freedom.

The Eternal Contract

Edmund Burke, the eighteenth-century British statesman and philosopher introduced previously in this book, explained the sources of order and freedom by comparing society to a contract, "the eternal contract of human society." In his *Reflections on the Revolution in France*, Burke observes: "Society is indeed a contract.... It is to be looked on with reverence.... It is a partnership in all science [or knowledge]; a partnership in all art; a partnership in every virtue.... As the ends of such a partnership cannot be obtained in many generations, it becomes a partnership not only between those who are living, but between those who are living, those who are dead, and those who are yet to be born."[16]

For Burke, society transcends the here-and-now and functions as a binding agreement among the past, the present, and the future. The practical application of Burke's observation is that the social and political participant who seeks the common good must think of himself as being beholden not only to those who are living but also to those who are already dead and to those who are not yet born. To the dead, he owes deference and respect, a piety that humbly receives what Burke called the wisdom of ages. To the living, he owes a knowledge of needs, both material and immaterial. To the not yet born, he owes the good deposit he has received from the past and cultivated in the present to be passed on into the future.

Burke's admonition that our ancestors ought to inform our contemporary society goes beyond simply "keeping their memories alive." Rather, Burke upheld a strict but not uncompromising adherence to the beliefs and customs of those who have preceded us. Such a social and political ethic may seem hopelessly narrow-minded in our age of near constant change and unfettered "progress."

Nevertheless, the inheritance of time-tested beliefs and traditions, according to Burke, is both reasonable and rational. It is reasonable because inheritance has governed human society forever. Only since the Enlightenment have philosophers and political thinkers conceived of society any differently. Inheritance is also rational because the ideas and customs that survive the fire of human experience, often over the course of centuries, prove to be vital and to bring vitality to our shared lives.

This inherited knowledge is the product of the culture of public life, and it comes to us in the form of the beliefs, habits, customs, literature, and art of our families, our churches, our local communities, and our national community—the trove of human experience that is the Western tradition. In many ways, this inheritance is the subject of this book because, as Christians, we should live in view of the past, present, and future within the various cultural spheres in which God has placed us. Public life, therefore, is cumulative. From these sources we obtain *an* order, a moral order, from which balanced society and freedom spring.

We owe the prudent stewardship of the benefits of society, both public and political, to the not yet born. Our charge is to know this order and to preserve it through education and through the conservation of the aspects of our public and political life that bear the influence of this order. Whether you are from Kentucky or California, it behooves you to learn and to conserve the unique culture and traditions that govern your home's way of life, especially those that lead to the common good. And in light of Kuyper's thinking, we are led to value our local communities and to think of them as "the well-spring of national vitality." Yet, in addition to considering our local backgrounds, we should also reflect on our common national background.

American Order

Russell Kirk, in his book *The Roots of American Order*, wrote, "Seeking for the roots of [American] order, we are led to four cities: Jerusalem, Athens, Rome, and London. In Washington or New York or Chicago or Los Angeles today, the order which Americans experience is derived from the experience of those four old cities."[17] Kirk is saying that the American knowledge of moral right and wrong and of the nuances of character and virtue is the inheritance of the culture of Western civilization. From Jerusalem, we gain the eternal truths of the Old and New Testaments. From Athens and Rome, we gain the philosophical observations of Plato and Aristotle, the imaginative insights of Sophocles and

Virgil, and the memorable lessons of the Roman republic. From London, we gain our fundamental identity through the English language, the body of English literature and culture, and English history.

For lack of space, a thorough treatment of all four of the "old cities" that have produced American order is impossible. However, understanding the influence of Jerusalem and London, the two cities which loom the largest, is indispensable to understanding both how public order produces political order and how Christianity has exercised outsized influence on American political institutions, such as the American practice of common law and the Constitution. We will begin by considering the development of the Anglo-American legal doctrine of the supremacy of law. This doctrine teaches that both rulers and subjects are beholden to the same laws, and it illustrates well how English culture and law has mediated the influence of Jerusalem onto America.

The Supremacy of Law

Mark David Hall has written convincingly that the best way to understand the Christian character of the American founding and American political institutions is to think of its character in terms of influence. In *Did America Have a Christian Founding?* he argues that Christianity unequivocally influenced all the founders, but he is clear to argue that, by that claim, he is not saying they were all sincere Christians who practiced orthodox Christianity and always acted like Christians.[18]

On the matter of such influence, Kirk wrote that the Hebrew-Christian concepts of human nature and divine law taught the founding fathers the "sanctity of law": that "certain root principles of justice exist" and that "law is a means for realizing those principles, so far as we can." Kirk then moved from a discussion of justice to one of sin, writing, "A conviction of man's sinfulness, and of the need for laws to restrain every man's appetite, influenced the legislators of the colonies and of the Republic."[19] Christianity thus supplied the founders with a coherent view of human nature and a respect for both eternal and temporal law, lessons that came to the founders by way of the dominant culture of the overwhelmingly Christian colonies, as well as by way of the ingrained assumptions of the political institutions of England.

Given that the War for Independence was predicated on American separation from English rule, some might find strange the claim that the model of English law and government influenced the founders of the United States. However, as M. E. Bradford, scholar of early American political literature, wrote, "both for the outlines and the details" of America's legal and political order, the founders "went primarily to the example they knew best: to the history of the English constitution in whose name they had recently achieved an independence ironically outside of the protections of that authority."[20]

The War for Independence was not a revolution to bring about a new political order. It was a conflict to reclaim key aspects of the English constitution, such as the rights of life, liberty, and property. The colonists thought of themselves as Englishmen who had inherited these rights that the English Parliament had unjustifiably revoked. By choosing to model America's political order on England's, the founders extended the influence that Christianity had already had on England's laws and politics to the fledgling American republic.

The Anglo-Saxons and the Common Law

The influence of Christianity on the English constitution, which is made up of several charters with kings and acts of Parliament, began in the late sixth century. Until then, England had been an island of warring pagan kingdoms, remembered today as the Anglo-Saxons. The year A.D. 597 marked the arrival of Augustine of Canterbury, the first Christian missionary to these brutal peoples. In a span of only one hundred years, much of the island was at least nominally Christianized.

Early codes of law provide excellent evidence of the way that Christianity manifested itself in the English political order. Nick Spencer, in his exploration of the influence of the English Bible on English politics, argues that the legal codes of Anglo-Saxon kings such as Wihtred of Kent and Alfred the Great of Wessex, though almost never effective as law, were nonetheless important. Specifically, their significance owes to their invocation of Christian principles and, in the case of Alfred's code, their direct citation of the Old and New Testaments.[21]

For example, Alfred quoted the Ten Commandments and placed harsh penalties on theft, murder, and adultery. Although Alfred and his fellow Anglo-Saxons were incapable of enforcing many of their laws, later regimes better suited to legal administration would take portions of the Anglo-Saxon codes and enforce them in a manner that was common to every corner of the island. Laws such as Alfred's eventually helped spawn the common law, a system that still protects the life, liberty, and property of Americans today.

The Anglo-Saxon codes are also significant as markers of the moment when English kings came to recognize the importance of man-made law based on the assumption that a higher law exists to which they are subject in the final judgment. Spencer writes that the most important principle that Christianity has taught English kings is that they will "have to give account of their actions before the King of Kings. 'Whether you will or not, you will always have him as judge,' Alcuin warned Ethelred."[22] (Alcuin of York was a scholar and clergyman who advised King Ethelred.) Christianity thus taught the Anglo-Saxons that law matters to God, embedding the idea that law is king into English political culture.

Magna Carta

English kings would have to learn the lesson of the supremacy of law repeatedly because they frequently breached either the laws of the land or the laws of the universe. One of the most important of these lessons, a rebuke to King John, was enshrined in the text of Magna Carta in 1215. Early in his reign, King John had lost vast swaths of English land in northern France and, as a result, had levied high taxes on his nobles to pay for a war to reclaim the lost territory.[23] The nobles balked and with the help of Stephen Langton, an especially political archbishop of Canterbury, forced John to assent to a litany of rights due to the English church and the nobles.

Their demands reflected the basic legal assumptions of the common law. The king agreed that he would not imprison the nobles without a trial, that he would not deny them a fair and speedy justice, and that he would not arbitrarily seize their land. While the stipulations of Magna Carta concerned the exclusive relationship of the king and his nobles, the Christian idea that the power of political rulers should be limited would continue to take shape through the development of English common law and politics.[24]

The Influence of Parliament

The success of the nobles and the church in consistently holding English kings to the supremacy of law led to the creation of Parliament, the forerunner of many state legislatures and the United States Congress. Parliament's first power was to reissue charters either based on or bearing resemblance to Magna Carta. In other words, the English Parliament grew into a body of elected and unelected officials who held the monarch accountable to law.

Parliament's influence reached its zenith in the period following the Protestant Reformation, which emphasized biblical teachings concerning human depravity and dignity and the importance of law. The political and legal effects of the Reformation in England led to an increased interest in the aspects of the English civic tradition that already radiated Christian influence. For instance, the Reformation's criticism of the abuse of power in the church (what some called "prelatical tyranny") naturally led to criticism of the abuse of power in politics. Therefore, aspects of Parliament's authority related to checking arbitrary power came to be wielded with unparalleled strength after the Puritans (who wanted to make the already Protestant Church of England even more Protestant) gained control of Parliament in the seventeenth century.

In 1628, the Puritan-led Parliament rebuked King Charles I for imprisoning citizens without recourse to trial and for dispossessing landowners of their property by exacting high taxes and forcing them to house troops. Like King John, Charles had justified his questionable actions on the basis of funding an expensive foreign war. The parliamentarians, bolstered by the Reformation's ethos, would not have this justification and forced Charles I to assent publicly to the Petition of Right, the formal list of complaints against the king. His assent, though, did not last long. Almost as soon as Charles had approved the Petition, he reneged on it and dissolved Parliament without their consent. The English Civil War ensued with Parliament on one side and Charles on the other. The parliamentarians won, and, on a cold January morning, Charles was executed for being a "tyrant, traitor, murderer, and public enemy to the good people of the nation."[25]

By 1688, in rebuke of one of Charles's descendants, Parliament stipulated that kings and queens of England must assent to the English Bill of Rights. Among these rights were protections of life such as habeas corpus (or the right to avail oneself of a court of law if arrested), protections of liberty (such as the freedom of speech for Parliament and the freedom to bear arms for Protestants), and protections of property (such as the freedom from arbitrarily levied taxes).

Like Magna Carta, the Petition of Right and the English Bill of Rights drew heavily from the common law and dealt exclusively with the relationship between Parliament and the crown. However, in another resemblance to Magna Carta, the ramifications of the Petition and the Bill of Rights would be felt more broadly than the parliamentarians ever could have imagined.

The American Colonies

In 1607 the first permanent English settlement was established in what is now known as Virginia. With the establishment of Jamestown in the New World came English people, and with English people came English culture, and with English culture came English law (and hence Christian influence). Almost as soon as initial settlements were founded, colonists, according to their royal charters, set up courts of law that heard and settled disputes according to the common law. By 1619, Virginia had established its House of Burgesses, a legislative body closely mirroring the English Parliament.

The text of the Mayflower Compact, which was signed in 1620, provides perhaps one of the clearest indications that, from the earliest period of English settlement, colonists transplanted to America a respect for English law and the supremacy of law. The Compact declares the intent to "constitute, and frame, such just and equal Laws, Ordinances, Acts, Constitutions, and Officers, from time to time, as shall be thought most meet and convenient for the general Good of the Colony; unto which we promise all due Submission and Obedience."[26]

Along with the desire for law and the processes to make and enforce law came the understanding that everyone, governors and subjects alike, had the duty to obey those laws. Any other approach, the colonists knew, would tend toward tyranny. Fortunately, when the problem of the abuse of power did arise, colonial America was not without keen expositors of English law and its Christian foundations, one of which was not a politician or lawyer but was instead a churchman.

On January 30, 1770, Boston minister Jonathan Mayhew delivered an election sermon entitled "A Discourse Concerning Unlimited Submission and Non-Resistance to the Higher Powers." The date was not inconsequential: it was the one-hundredth anniversary of the execution of English King Charles I. Mayhew was the son of a long line of Puritans reaching back to those who had originally opposed Charles during the English Civil War; therefore, he felt very keenly the importance of reminding his congregants of Charles's misdeeds when some in England and in the colonies began venerating Charles as a Christian martyr.

Furthermore, the year 1770, to many colonials like Mayhew, seemed alarmingly like 1215, 1628, and 1688. The Sugar and Stamp Acts had levied high taxes; the Quartering Act had forced colonial households to board troops in private dwellings; and the Declaratory Act had voided the legal authority of laws passed by colonial representative bodies. To Mayhew, the obvious overreach on the part of the British king and Parliament also demanded attention.[27]

In this sermon, Mayhew took Romans 13 as his text. In it, the apostle Paul identifies God as the source of all authority and then declares, "Therefore whoever resists the authorities resists what God has appointed" (v. 2). Mayhew explained, "The apostle here enforces the duty of submission to the higher power."[28] Mayhew, though, drew attention to the nuance that Paul's exhortation is "not in favor of submission to all who bear the title of rulers, in common; but only, to those who actually perform the duty of rulers, by exercising a reasonable and just authority, for the good of human society."[29]

Paul's qualification of authority as punishing the bad and upholding the good, Mayhew contended, is key:

> If rulers are a terror to good works, and not to the evil; if they are not ministers for good to society, but to evil and distress, by violence and oppression; if they execute wrath upon sober, peaceable persons, who do their duty as members of society; and suffer rich and honorable knaves to escape with impunity; if, instead of attending continually upon the good work of advancing the public welfare; if this be the case, it is plain that the apostle's argument for submission does not reach them.[30]

Mayhew thus argued that Paul's definition of authority disqualifies those who act in such a way that is contrary to just laws or to the eternal law of God. Mayhew's reasoning may seem somewhat shocking, but it was not outside the Christian doctrine that had guided the development of English law. Stephen Langton, the archbishop responsible for key passages of Magna Carta, had written on the application of Romans 13 that "when a king errs, the people should resist him as far as they can; if they do not, they sin."[31]

Mayhew ended his sermon with what was effectively a review of the provisions of the Petition of Right and the English Bill of Rights. Mayhew understood, it seems, that if the colonists were going to gain a redress for the grievances caused by the abuse of power, they would have to resist King George III and Parliament according to the principles of the common law and the processes and institutions that had resulted from the doctrine of the supremacy of law. It turns out that such a sentiment was on the minds of many other colonials in 1770. Mayhew's sermon was distributed so widely that it came to be known as "the morning gun of the revolution."

Mayhew's sermon was far from the only impassioned restatement of the supremacy of law and the English constitution in colonial America. Many of the founders held a tacit understating of these things by virtue of their growing up in the English colonies in America. However, Mayhew's sermon does illustrate the central contention that public life produces political order. In the case of the doctrine of the supremacy of law, the influence of Jerusalem (to use Kirk's terminology) provided clear definitions of the source and purpose of law, the limits of power, and the importance of everyone's being subject to the same laws.

While this influence was slow and required recapitulations by generation after generation of citizens, churchmen, and politicians, it resulted in key Anglo-American laws and freedoms, judicial processes, and political institutions, all of which bear the mark of Christianity and, what is more, would not exist but for the influence of Christianity.

While we cannot say that the United States has an established Christian church, we can say that its Bill of Rights protects life, liberty, and property; we can say that its judiciary is founded on basic principles of the common law such as habeas corpus; and, crucially, we can say that the Constitution balances and limits power and grants the authority of Congress to make laws to which everyone is beholden.

These aspects of American government represent the Christian character and influence of America's political order. Our principal duty as Christians who desire to realize the common good is to protect these laws, freedoms, processes, and institutions that bear witness to the truth and justice of the Bible and Christian doctrine. We must receive these aspects of our political order from our ancestors, avail ourselves of them in the present, and conserve them so that future generations will inherit the blessings of liberty.

The story of American order teaches us that political order is reliant upon moral order. This is true of all nations and of all public and political traditions. Law cannot exist outside the scope of definitions of right and wrong and of the nuances of character and virtue. This observation is true for the Christian, Buddhist, capitalist, Marxist, and anyone else. Everyone brings a set of moral assumptions to legal and political action.

Fortunately for us, the set of moral assumptions that has consistently guided legal and political action in the Anglo-American tradition has been a Christian set of assumptions. It is up to us to continue this influence not only for our own sakes but also for the sake of our cities. A Christian understanding of concepts like order and freedom results in an influence in culture and politics that produces the greatest share of human fulfillment.

Freedom and Law

Freedom is the other aspect of society that flows from man's nature, which society must balance with order so that he can achieve justice. Because man is fallen, he needs the order that results from the limits of just laws. Yet, because man is made in God's image, he is dignified and, consequently, is due respect and protection. Christians who are interested in the realization of the common good must have a knowledge of and respect for both order and freedom.

Already, we have seen that moral order arises from public order and that public order creates political order. Now we turn to freedom (a concept previously explored in chapter three on classical conservatism), which is itself a product of political order. We must understand that the origin of all freedoms is law and that true freedom is always attended by duties, meaning that the ultimate purpose of freedom is virtue. All of this becomes clear considering the divine grant of freedom.

In Genesis 1, God creates humanity in His image and, through His command to Adam and Eve, commands all people to be fruitful and multiply, to fill the earth and subdue it, and to rule over the animals (v. 28). We refer to this passage as the *creation mandate* since it represents God's instruction to men and women at the creation.

In this act of eternal law, God has elevated human beings above the animals (Psalm 8:6–8), giving us a means to express our dignity by creating culture through procreation and through work. When man is free to carry out his God-ordained calling, to have a family and serve as steward and viceregent, he is fulfilled and expresses his humanity more completely.

When men and women are free to work and have the fruits of their labor protected from unjust seizure, they are similarly fulfilled. Note that the dignity of man originates from the commands of divine law given before the Fall. It follows that the mechanism of law is valuable not only to restrain men's passions but also to order human life and secure human dignity.

In Genesis 9, the events of which happen well after the Fall, God establishes another covenant of law. This time it is with Noah and with "all future generations" of humanity (v. 12). God reaffirms the dignity of man by commanding again that he be fruitful and multiply. Then God reaffirms the dignity of all human beings by setting a standard punishment for cases of murder. God says,

"Whoever sheds the blood of man, by man shall his blood be shed, for God made man in his own image" (v. 6). Later, God establishes the Sixth Commandment: "You shall not murder" (Exodus 20:13). God leaves nothing to question on the matter of the worth of human life.

These passages clearly demonstrate that all humans possess the right to life. Note, though, that Genesis 9 identifies this right in accord with an attendant duty. If one person takes another person's life in an act of murder, he too must be killed. That law is not to say that if a government does not exact capital punishment Christians should take the matter into their own hands and kill murderers. However, this passage should serve as a principle for us: *human life is dignified, and governments should protect this dignity by punishing those who seek to disrespect it.*

Human law reaches its highest potential when it reflects divine law's restraint on sinful human will and grants human freedom through certain protections. Therefore, just laws will respect the inherent dignity of the human person by protecting the fundamental right to life. Just laws will foster a conducive environment for the family and the other spheres of sovereignty to express their God-given authority. Just laws will encourage work by protecting the fruits of labor. However, we have no guarantee that the populace will enact, enforce, and respect such laws and constituent freedoms. So, for political order and the freedoms it produces to exist, public order must underlie it. Without histories of cultural and political reaffirmation (as discussed in chapter five), just laws and the freedoms they entail cannot long survive.

The Issue of Rights

We have considered how human dignity applies to the Christian approach to law and politics. But many Christian authors are quick to list "natural rights" that are due to man on the sole basis of his being made in God's image. They have reasoned that the universal dignity of all human beings entitles everyone to certain freedoms, freedoms not unlike those listed in the United Nations' Universal Declaration of Human Rights. Among these rights are the rights to privacy, to seek and obtain asylum, to take part in the affairs of government, to receive an education, to get married, and—perhaps most troublingly—to "rest and leisure, including reasonable limitation of working hours and periodic holidays with pay."[32]

As well-intentioned as the Universal Declaration of Human Rights and its various proponents might be, they often abstract rights from the key means that God has given to secure those rights in the first place; specifically, they neglect to recognize the roles of tradition and culture and law as the sources of the rights we enjoy today. These proponents' concept of rights often mistakes desires for rights. In response to the Universal Declaration of Human Rights, Russell Kirk wrote:

> This lengthy catalogue of "rights" ignores the two essential conditions which are attached to all true rights; first, the capacity of individuals to claim and exercise the alleged right; second, the correspondent duty that is married to every right. If a man has the *right* to marry, some woman must have the duty of marrying him; if a man has the *right* to rest, some other person must have the duty of supporting him. If rights are confused thus with desires, the mass of men must feel always that some vast, intangible conspiracy thwarts their attainment of what they are told is their inalienable birthright.[33]

To criticize the Universal Declaration of Human Rights is not to say that people do not have rights. It is to comment on the ideology that underlies it. The writers of the Universal Declaration made a naive assumption that a person is bestowed rights simply because they said so. This understanding of rights completely misses the fact that God, in His common grace, has given to human beings the means of securing rights for themselves and their posterity: law, which results from the creation mandate in Genesis 1 and which God reaffirmed in Genesis 9. Kirk adds, "God has given man law, and with that law, rights."[34]

The story of American law and order is also the story of American freedom. Over the course of the development of English and American law, certain freedoms such as the rights to life, liberty, and property became enshrined in various legal and political processes and institutions. The rebuke of kings, rooted in the law of God, turned into charters that guaranteed freedoms to certain individuals, freedoms which then became part of a wider expectation of protection.

In the United States, our rights are enshrined in the statutes, legal procedures, bills of rights, and constitutions of the various states and of the federal government. Our rights and the legal and political traditions that have transmitted them to us are heavily indebted to the English civic tradition. Thus the freedoms that Americans enjoy every day have not been simply wished into existence; instead, they have come about through a long and arduous process of both public and political history. For this reason, these rights have credence in our society.

Freedom and Virtue

Because the rights of life, liberty, and property have grown up over the course of centuries, social and political participants in the United States have come to a tacit understanding of both the rights they are owed and the duties that are incumbent on them to respect others' rights. Without such long histories of development, the attempt to establish rights based on theological and/or philosophical principles alone (no matter how true they may be) lacks the consensus of public life, which takes time to accomplish and is required for the guarantee of lasting political freedom.

The truth that political freedom requires a cultural foundation of respect toward others' rights perhaps casts new light on our understanding of Christian missions. Remember, the influence of Christianity on English culture and law began only after the ministry of Augustine of Canterbury and his group of missionaries in England. We should hope that parts of the world that do not enjoy the blessings of liberty will one day do so. However, we should be political realists enough to recognize that such cultures will not gain good laws and freedoms without a religious and cultural foundation that properly defines the limits of power, supremacy of law, and nature of freedom.

Apart from the influence of the gospel, freedom cannot be understood completely. We know that he whom the Son sets free is free indeed (John 8:36). Yet the way in which freedom in Christ came about was long: it was the result of the long story of redemption and eventually cost Christ His life. The nature of our freedom in Christ, too, is not easily reconciled to contemporary notions of freedom as unrestrained desire. We learn from the Scriptures that freedom in itself is slavery to sin but that freedom in Christ is slavery to righteousness and service to others (John 8:34; Romans 6:16–19; 1 Corinthians 9:19).

This paradox alone indicates that Christians cannot conflate freedom and desire. According to the example we have in the gospel, we must understand that freedom has a higher purpose than mere self-fulfillment. In political terms, proper freedom consists in virtue. Or, put another way, appropriate political freedoms make us free to do the right thing. For this reason, we must understand rights as necessarily having ancillary duties. Rights, liberties, and freedoms bring with them the expectations of what citizens will do with those freedoms—that is, what they will do for the sake of the whole and not just for the sake of themselves.

Conclusion

Twenty-first century America bears an unsettling likeness to the tumult that Plato witnessed in Athens so long ago. While we enjoy the benefits of stable representative government, both our public and political lives evince a deep disorder. Doubt of objective values such as goodness, truth, and beauty has produced a public without ordered affections toward what is worthy to be loved and feared. The family, in particular, has suffered much in the wake of the sexual revolution and the present upheaval of biblical concepts of gender and sexuality.

As a result, our political order has been thrown out of balance. The first few decades of the twenty-first century have lacked sufficient definitions of order and freedom. Consequently, we have witnessed the continued growth of a strong, centralized federal government and, at the same time, unprecedented allowances of personal freedom from the constraints of community, tradition, and virtue.

But the path to balanced society runs through the human heart. Neither the rationalism of governmental bureaucracy nor the licentiousness that passes for political platforms such as liberalism and progressivism will bring justice to our imbalanced public and political lives. The renewal of the human spirit, which is the heart, provides the only sufficient means of needed recalibration.

As Christians concerned with the common good, our first priority should be the health of our own families: "to beget children, and read to them o' evenings, and teach them what is worthy of praise."[35] Second, we should be concerned for the health of our local communities because "the smaller parts come first."[36] Third, we should educate ourselves and those under our mentorship according to the sources of our public and political order so that the freedoms we enjoy can continue for another generation.

Know that this suggestion will require a reading of the Old and New Testaments, of Plato's dialogues and Aristotle's treatises, of Virgil's verse and Cicero's orations, of Shakespeare's histories and tragedies just as much as it will require a reading of the U. S. Constitution. Political balance is dependent on public balance.

Direct political involvement, though, is also paramount if we are going to seek the welfare of the city to which God has called us (Jeremiah 29:7). For some, such involvement will look like voting on a regular basis. Let us seek candidates and political platforms that recognize and protect the authority of the family, that uphold the rights of life, liberty, and property, and that want to conserve (conservatism) the laws and political institutions that bear the influence of Christianity. For others, political involvement may look like getting involved on a campaign or volunteering at a local political party.

While political parties have suffered in the estimation of many Americans lately, know that parties are aspects of our political infrastructure that have served our country well since its inception. And that has not changed. Underneath the less-than-savory depictions of partisan politics on television and social media are people who really care about the common good and who work to bring it about. It behooves us to be a part of that unavoidable aspect of our political context to bring about the uniquely Christian concept of the common good. To do so brings glory to God and flourishing to people.

CHAPTER FOURTEEN

Economics, Wealth, and Poverty

Phillip T. Morgan

In his celebrated 1994 work *The Scandal of the Evangelical Mind*, evangelical historian Mark Noll dourly concluded that evangelicals' "intellectual sterility" had produced "virtually no insights into how, under God, the natural world proceeded, how human societies worked, why human nature acted the way it did, or what constituted the blessings and perils of culture."[1] While Noll's thesis exaggerates the current situation, it is somewhat true.[2] Evangelical Christians have often limited the application of the gospel's power and authority to individual salvation, ignoring its relevance for the rest of life.

In this chapter, we will consider the Christian view of economics. Though intellectual laziness may tempt us to ignore this subject, economics is vitally important to people. This chapter will focus on money and labor, and it will address issues regarding wealth and poverty. We will ground our reflections firmly in Scripture so that we are not vulnerable to the sly whispers of "the cosmic powers over this present darkness" (Ephesians 6:12) or guilty of denying the power of the gospel over all areas of life—economics included.

What Is Economics?

When we consider the subject of economics, we are attempting to describe and explain the accumulated activities and relationships of individuals who labor within a society. At the most basic level, we study the labor of individuals in particular vocations. However, individuals live in community, and the labor of each member relates to the broader society. By expanding the scope of our investigation to the level of society, we perceive ordered patterns of interaction that channel their work.

Lest we forget, men and women carry out each level of human labor in the context of the created universe, which Herman Daly describes as the "vast network of patterns and powers in terms of which all of life's necessities and values are parceled out and exchanged."[3] Seeking to understand these multilayered patterns in relation to the labor of the individual is what we call "economics." As Harry Veryser puts it, "Economics is the science of human action," which is exemplified in how we spend our time and how we manage our reputations.[4] Or, as Greg Forster argues, it concerns not only our money and labor but also our time and reputation.[5]

People have understood the patterns of economics differently and have developed various economic theories. Free-market economics and socialism are the two dominant theories active in the modern world. Advocates build each approach on distinct theological and philosophical understandings of the world. Unfortunately, they are "more often deployed as surface-level expressions of political identity."[6] Because we want to avoid this reckless approach to participating in public discourse and governmental policy, we will consider how each of these economic philosophies align with our theological commitments.

THEOLOGICAL FOUNDATIONS

Creation

In the beginning, God created man in His image and gave him work. The opening narrative of Scripture shows Adam and Eve living in an "agrarian temple" before God. God commanded them, as caretakers of the garden and rulers of the world, to tend to the created order He placed under their stewardship and viceregency. He also allowed them to use their wisdom and creativity to work out that command in specific circumstances (Genesis 1:26–28). This dynamic teaches us that individual liberty and work are good.

Sin

However, sin has subjected all of creation to its harmful effects (Romans 8:20–22). Adam and Eve retained their individual liberty after the Fall, but sin darkened their understanding, making them prone to immorality and wickedness (Ephesians 4:18). As God confronted the guilty pair in the garden, He doomed them and their work to pain and frustration (Genesis 3:17–19).

Even though God placed a "curse upon the ground because of man's sin," He also "blessed and glorified the labor of man."[7] Since that fateful day in the garden, work has brought marred blessing: suffering and gratification, consternation and joy, temptation and satisfaction.

After Adam and Eve walked past the flaming sword of the cherubim out of the garden, sin continued to grow and affect their lives. Before long, a division developed among the laborers of the world. Certainly by 3000 B.C., when Ur and Egypt began to develop as societies (if not before), a clear distinction had emerged between rulers and priests and everyone else. Important people did not work with their hands; slaves did. The division between important labor and unimportant labor has evolved over time, but the basic assumptions remain.

Vocation

However, as chapter ten on labor and vocation explains, all vocations are valuable if they are not inherently immoral (such as prostitution). Adam and Eve were farmers in the garden before the Fall, highlighting the goodness of agricultural work. Time and again in Scripture, God worked through common folk to effect His plans, such as shepherds (e.g., Abraham, Jacob, and David), farmers (e.g., Noah, Gideon, and Elisha), fishermen (e.g., Peter, James, and John), and craftsmen (e.g., Bezalel, Oholiab, and Hiram). Jesus grew up working with His earthly father Joseph who was a craftsman (Mark 6:3). In addition, as Martin Luther noted, God has divinely called all believers to different but worthwhile vocations; consequently, all believers' vocations ("callings") are important: "God milks the cows through the vocation of the milk maids."[8]

Since labor is good, and all God-given vocations signify divine callings, Christians have a special duty to carry out their work with excellence. Our first parents were given the task of cultivating the garden, making "it a better place, a well-tilled place, a managed place."[9] Paul explained that, even though we have left the garden, we must perform whatever work to which God has called us as "for the Lord" (Colossians 3:23). Laziness and shoddy work are not just bad business practices; they are immoral business practices (Proverbs 15:19; Matthew 25:26).

Hard work and diligence often bring wealth, which many in our society regard with suspicion or contempt. However, Scripture clearly shows that acquiring wealth through trade is good. Paul explains that the Law teaches that the plowman, thresher, soldier, and even minister ought to labor with the expectation of receiving profit (1 Corinthians 9:3–10). Wealth is a good blessing (Genesis 13:2; 1 Chronicles 29:26–28; 2 Chronicles 1:11–12; Job 42:10) unless man uses it for sinful purposes.

After all, God is the source of wealth (Psalms 24:1; James 1:17). Creation itself is the outpouring of His abundant wealth as a gift. Meditating on the abundance of creation, Annie Dillard writes, "The world is fairly studded and strewn with pennies cast broadside from a generous hand."[10] In different instances throughout the Bible, both the just (e.g., Abraham, Job, and Joseph of Arimathea) and the wicked (e.g., Nabal, Ahab, and Annas) possessed wealth.[11] Therefore, wealth itself is a good thing created by God but can be affected by our actions, whether righteous or wicked.

Wealth and Stewardship

We must also consider how we accrue wealth. The Bible clearly states that God honors private property. The Eighth Commandment and Tenth Commandment (do not steal; do not covet) both imply the justice of private property by stating that taking someone else's property or even desiring to take it is wrong.[12]

God gives all people the property they possess as stewards, and neither society nor the government nor anyone else has any claim to it.[13]

Transferring and acquiring wealth under honest terms of commerce is appropriate, but God clearly states that He punishes fraud and theft (Exodus 20:15; Leviticus 19:36; Proverbs 16:11). As Protestant Reformer John Calvin noted, God also expects governments to punish unjust market activity (Romans 13:2–3).[14] Wealth that is sought through "theft or government extraction creates moral *decay* that can be seen in individual lives and in broader social institutions," writes Chad Brand.[15]

Proper stewardship of creation is another important aspect of our efforts to acquire wealth. In the garden, God issued a regal command, granting to man dominion over His creation (Genesis 1:26–28). God reaffirmed man's vicegency with Noah after the flood (9:1–7). God calls man to rule in His place in a manner that glorifies Him and reflects Christ. Through our capacity as sub-creators under God, we can cultivate the universe so that it reaches its fullest potential.[16]

However, when we rule as authoritarians, we horribly abuse the creation, forcing it to obey our desires without regard for the ecological harm that ensues. The role of a steward is intrinsically temporal, meaning that the King will eventually return to rule over His kingdom. Good stewards will be lavished with reward, but wicked and lazy stewards will suffer great wrath (Matthew 25:14–30). Therefore, we must carry out all labor and wealth creation with a firm commitment to govern justly.

Labor applied to property results in products we can exchange for other objects. As we determine what we are willing to part with in exchange for the object of our desire, we assign that object a value. While this fact may seem obvious, it has been misunderstood by many and led to many wrong conclusions in economic theory.

For the moment, we need only to affirm that economic values are relative in nature. They are set by the needs and wants of the buyer and seller of any given product.[17] In fact, Scripture illustrates this point. When Jesus explained to His disciples that the widow who dropped two small copper coins in the offering box at the temple gave more than all the wealthy who had put in large sums, He was highlighting the relative nature of value (Mark 12:41–44).

Though wealth is a gift from God, poverty is not necessarily a function of His wrath, as we just saw in the example of the poor widow. But Scripture clearly says that sins such as laziness will often result in poverty and should be discouraged (Proverbs 19:15; 1 Timothy 4:8). However, Solomon also explained that the righteous may be poor and that their lot is better than the wicked who are rich (Proverbs 15:16; 17:1). God commanded the Israelites to treat the poor justly but without favor and to assist them in their need (Exodus 23:3, 6, 11).

Perhaps one of the most poignant examples of the righteous living in poverty can be found in the book of Hebrews. As the writer of Hebrews came to the end of his reflection on the heroes of the faith, he despaired of finishing the list, instead commending those who, among other things, "went about in skins of sheep and goats, destitute, afflicted, mistreated—of whom the world was not worthy—wandering about in deserts and mountains, and in dens and caves of the earth" (11:37–38). The poor may be righteous, and God cares for them, just as He cares for the wealthy.

A sound economic philosophy will derive its strength from this solid biblical foundation. From our quick overview of Scripture's teachings on the various aspects of economic theory, we find that God calls all people to work with excellence in all vocations so that they may enjoy His creation in worship before Him. The wealth accrued from honest labor is a good gift from God that we have a responsibility to use rightly.

Yet poverty is not a sin or necessarily the result of sin. In addition, God cares deeply for the poor, even identifying with them in the person of Jesus Christ (Matthew 8:20). With these foundations, we can think more deeply about economic systems and their effect on societies.

FREE-MARKET ECONOMICS

Free-market economics developed in the West based on that culture's Hebrew-Christian and Greco-Roman foundations. While we can discern the earliest glimmerings of this economic philosophy in medieval Europe, the free market came into its own in the eighteenth and nineteenth centuries largely because of the seventeenth-century British and Dutch development of limited liability organizations and joint-stock companies.[18]

Sometimes people refer to free-market economics as capitalism, but, as Ronald Nash has pointed out, the free market's most prominent critic, Karl Marx, coined the term *capitalism*, which is inherently ideological.[19] We will address the philosophical position of free-market economics in relation to our theology before considering the Marxist critique of it. The overall framework for this discussion is deeply indebted to Nash's fourfold characteristics of economic freedom: liberty, rules, risks, and rewards.[20]

Liberty

Advocates of free-market economics argue that it is morally and socially beneficial to honor personhood by protecting individual liberty within the limits of law. Governments often engage in interventionist economic policies for one reason or another but never without harming economic health or individual freedom.

Ancient civilizations such as Sumer and Egypt practiced command economies where the ruler had claim to all property within the realm. The mercantilist policies of European colonialism also engaged in interventionism by strictly constraining the legal economic actions and trading partners of their colonies. The most common form of interventionism in the modern world is socialism, but these other historical examples continue to exist in the world.

Adam Smith, who is widely considered the "founder of economic science," first articulated the benefits of a free-market system in his seminal work, *An Inquiry into the Nature and Causes of the Wealth of Nations* (1776). Within the pages of *The Wealth of Nations*, as it is more popularly known, Smith argued that government should limit its role in society to international defense, the preservation of justice and order, and the erection and oversight of public works and institutions.[21] In this way, the government preserves social order while also allowing for maximum individual liberty. Smith's work was a "long overdue diatribe against the principles and policies" of government economic intervention.[22]

Smith and other free-market advocates, rather than looking to governmental regulation, believe that healthy societies will protect individuals' liberty to make their own economic decisions. Such policies will intrinsically protect (a) freedom of thought, (b) private property, (c) freedom of labor, and (d) political freedom. Yet each of these liberties is situated within the context of nation-states in competition rather than to a borderless global market.

First, freedom of thought serves as the catalyst for economic exchange and growth in a free-market economy. Determining the relative value of goods demands freedom of thought on the part of the buyer and the seller. Working together in negotiation, they determine the true value of any product within a specific circumstance.[23] Products in high demand will have a high value, unless too many of them are available in the market. Conversely, undesirable products will have a low value, even if they are relatively rare.

The many economic exchanges of a community create a market that reveals its true needs. Freedom of thought allows entrepreneurs to study market values and invest their capital (e.g., money, labor, land, tools, and knowledge) where they think it will be most productive. When governments try to impose prices on goods, they create a false market that, like all lies, they cannot indefinitely sustain.[24] Rather than building a healthy market, such governments create market bubbles that eventually burst, resulting in economic downturns; think of the housing market collapse of 2007 that led to an extended economic recession.[25]

Second, the free market protects the liberty of private individuals to hold and use private property. Those who own property have the freedom to transform and/or transfer property as they see fit within the limits of justice. As Pope John Paul II explained, we may utilize the "things of this world as objects and instruments" by using our "intelligence and freedom" and, as a result, fulfill one of our God-given purposes.[26] We may use entrepreneurial competence to produce goods for exchanges. Or we may decide to exchange our property for other property we value more highly. However, all these prospects must occur within the context of justice, meaning that we may not take advantage of others, such as by theft or fraud.

Free-market advocates are committed to the free entry of anyone or any group into the competition of the market. When one person or company controls the entire market for a specific product or service, they have created a monopoly on that product or service. However, monopolies are not naturally occurring. Left unregulated, "the process of the market is enough to insure sufficient competition."[27]

When governments begin regulating and licensing businesses, barriers are raised against entry into the market, which gives "earlier entrants a monopolistic advantage."[28] These kinds of policies unjustly favor the wealthy and influential. For this reason, free-market economists are averse to any unnecessary governmental regulation of the market.

Governments engage in healthy economic regulation when they resolve conflicts, such as when they ensure that contracts are honored. However, governments engage in harmful regulation when they create rules that are policy-driven and influenced by interest groups, which arbitrarily benefit one group over another. For example, in 1955, the federal government passed the Smith-Lever Act, which claimed to encourage the development of agriculture but, in fact, drove family farms that were "too small or too unproductive, or both" to abandon their farms to large, mechanized agribusiness corporations.[29]

The freedom of labor is a third liberty protected by free-market economics. This freedom leads to different people's pursuing unique (specialized) forms of labor within the broader context of a community. Noting that men do not live "independent of one another," the Greek philosopher Plato argued that, in the process of producing the "necessaries of life," men would inevitably divide and specialize their labor. Because people have various "natural endowments and talents," nature suits them to "serve the community in different ways."[30]

Two and half millennia later, Adam Smith observed the same principle, arguing that the division of labor "occasions, in every art, a proportionable increase of the productive powers of labor."[31] Both men realized that the division of labor would increase the overall quality of products because men and women hone their natural skills through specialization.[32] However, Smith further perceived that this process also saves time that is otherwise lost in moving between different activities, leading to the development of "specialized tools."[33]

Fourthly, economic freedom fosters political freedom for all people in a society. Smith noticed that peoples' freedom to enjoy the fruit of their labor further encourages them to apply themselves to their occupations, cultivating skill, talent, and ingenuity appropriate to those occupations.[34] With increased competence comes confidence, strength, and courage. Further, as people hone their abilities and receive and keep the benefits of their hard work, wealth accrues, even among "the lower ranks of the people."[35]

Over the next two hundred years, Smith's theories were validated by the economic policies of many Western countries, which increasingly sought to protect peoples' economic freedoms, resulting in unimaginable increases of personal wealth for all levels of society. Sociologist Rodney Stark summarizes this rise in wealth in this way: "Today the average person in a Western nation enjoys a standard of living sixteen times as high as in 1700, and lives nearly three times as long. In fact, an infant born today in the Republic of the Congo [which has largely benefited from the economic freedom of the rest of the world] can expect to live twenty-five years longer than a baby born in France in 1800."[36] The economic freedom that developed in the West has given people unprecedented access to food and water, health care, and clean and safe housing.[37] The result has produced a booming global population.

Rules

Such extreme expansion of wealth seems impossible to many people. They assume that free-market economies exist as a zero-sum game in which every dollar that someone makes was taken from someone else. Though some Darwinian thinkers have defended free markets, many have popularized this perception of economics. They argue that the world exists in a constant battle for the survival of the fittest.[38]

However, the relative nature of value means that economies consisting of free people can exist as win-win games; an exchange of goods can leave both parties satisfied. Further, the more opportunities a person has to trade, the better he can maximize the relative value of a particular good.

Sometimes we practice this economic principle at gatherings around Christmas time. Though the game has various names and sets of rules (e.g., Dirty Santa, White Elephant, or Yankee Swap), participants usually select gifts at random and then trade them among the other participants with everyone seeking to end the game with the optimal gift. The gift items remain the same, but they are valued differently by the participants. Trading goods allows people to exchange something they value less for something else they value more. If these trades are completely voluntary, both parties will benefit from a trade. The more people and the more gifts that are involved, the better the odds are that everyone will find a gift he really likes.

Though larger markets generally provide the greatest opportunity for economic satisfaction, the reality of geopolitics prompts us to see the need for some limitations. Smith argued that small markets limit the profitability of the division of labor and the opportunity for trade.[39] Therefore, Smith advocated for a free global market in which participants can trade goods between countries without unnecessary government-enforced trade barriers. However, Smith's ideas were situated within the framework of competing sovereign nation-states.

The twenty-first-century global economy is intertwined with current globalist political ideologies. Many economists and politicians argue that global economic integration is the only way forward for economic development and growth.[40] In this global market, any individual could invest in any business in the world without regard for national or local barriers. However, several problems arise in this scenario. For one thing, global free markets militate against national and sub-national sovereignty and individuality.[41] Relationships between countries might then assume a coercive nature; the market is then no longer truly free.

Another problem is that global free-market policies often exchange long-term benefits for short-term gains, thereby harming workers in first-world and third-world countries alike in the long run. For example, first-world countries like the United States may export jobs, especially manufacturing jobs, to third-world countries where manufacturers can produce products more cheaply and then import them back to the wealthier nation. From one perspective, such policies provide similar goods at cheaper prices for consumers and much-needed opportunities for poor people in third-world countries. However, from another perspective, these policies leave wage laborers in countries like the United States struggling to find work without significant retraining, thereby upsetting the established economy. Additionally, the jobs that were exported to third-world countries may not remain in those countries. If it is not financially advantageous for a business to base itself in a given country, it will move on, potentially leaving workers in those communities in worse shape than they were before the business arrived.

Perhaps pre-industrial skills and traditions have been lost over the course of time so that, when a business leaves, local workers cannot turn to traditional forms of labor and, without good opportunities, live in greater poverty than they did even before the business arrived in the first place. Perhaps local tyrants or gangs fill the economic vacuum that is left by the business's exit so that local communities are, again, in worse shape than they were beforehand. Such outcomes do not always occur, but they may occur as the unintended consequences of poorly executed global free markets.[42]

Some economists issue calls to replace imports with locally made products as a response to globalism, but other economists (mistakenly) dismiss such calls as hopelessly misguided.[43] Preserving the nation-state and local economies is a good and worthwhile goal. Daly has suggested, among other things, legally limiting the activities of foreign investments to stall some of the worst abuses of globalism.[44] While Daly's idea is good, it places the onus for fixing the problem on governmental bureaucracy. A better approach is for each person to take part in solving the problem by purchasing locally-sourced goods as often as possible—even if doing so costs a little more.

Risks

Free markets also promote individual economic liberty by preserving the individual's choice either to take risks or to avoid them. Investment and saving are both important aspects of business, requiring wisdom to ascertain the proper balance between the two. Sometimes, as the Roman poet Horace noted, "It is better for me to expand my little income by contracting my desires."[45] In other circumstances, as we see with the wise woman of Proverbs 31, spending, and even the prudent accumulation of debt, can be deployed to grow a business profitably and justly. The protection of an individual's ability to make his or her own investments rewards entrepreneurial competence and punishes entrepreneurial foolishness.

Competent investing requires wisdom, but no amount of prudence can overcome the problems created by bad market information. Prices signify relative value—the needs and wants of people in the market economy. If demand is high for a given product that is in short supply, the price of the product will rise. On the other hand, when people in the market do not have a strong need for a product, demand sinks along with the price of the item. As we can see, prices provide important information for entrepreneurs as they make decisions about investment and resource allocation in their businesses.

Interest rates on financial loans are perhaps the most important price indicators in the market. Banks lend money at interest, based on their appraisal of the health of the economy and their assessment of risk when granting these loans. When banks perceive inequalities in the market that predict economic downturns, they begin to raise interest rates to hedge against risk. For a variety of reasons, governments and/or large, powerful banks sometimes attempt to regulate the market through artificially manipulating interest rates.

Such actions disconnect prices from supply and demand and, instead, reflect an artificial financial market that rises and falls at the whim of the government. Thus governmental "tampering . . . negates the market's vital informational function" and engages in deception.[46] Without accurate price information, businesses "overexpand their investment and production activities, which [creates] unsustainable levels of economic activity (booms), which eventually [require] correction in the form of production cutbacks and layoffs (slumps)."[47]

Even though free-market advocates argue that government intervention in the market is destructive, they affirm the government's responsibility to punish wickedness. The economic laws and rules of a community provide a "framework" which informs "agents in the market which actions are legal."[48] Economic laws are important because, as Horace's contemporary Virgil warned, "To what extremes will you not drive the hearts of men, accurst hunger for gold!"[49] The government should engage the market by fairly enforcing general laws. This action promotes commercial justice.

Problems arise when governments abandon their duty to commercial justice in an attempt to achieve specific social or political purposes (such as socioeconomic equality) through coercive power.[50] As economist Henry Hazlitt notes, "Some of these specific interventions may indeed 'remedy' this or that specific 'evil' in the short run, but they can do so only at the cost of producing more and worse evils in the long run."[51] Nash argues that only two actions produce "deviations from the market ideal": statist interference and defects in human nature (such as craving security over risk and competition).[52]

When governments sacrifice commercial justice for political gain or social manipulation, their power expands while individual liberty contracts, and the market is adversely affected. Perversely, many political leftists base their argument for the necessity of increased governmental involvement in the market on the market volatility that was caused by governmental intervention in the first place.[53]

Rewards

Protecting the honest rewards of risk-taking in the market (winning and losing) is an important aspect of commercial justice. Investors who place their wealth at risk in the market should receive the appropriate reward for their work.

The Christian tradition supports the principles underlying this point. One of the most important Christian theologians, Augustine of Hippo, argued that commerce has a proper role in life and that honestly gained profit is just.[54] But then the great medieval theologian Thomas Aquinas, drawing on Aristotle, modified the Christian understanding of profit when he argued that charging interest loans is immoral. However, he was writing during the medieval period, when many money lenders charged extravagant interest rates, and the feudal economy of the day did not offer many opportunities to make enough money to repay loans. John Calvin rightly pushed back against Thomas, arguing that lenders deserve compensation for the risk involved in loaning money. Still, even Calvin recognized that excessive interest is usury, which is a form of theft and thus immoral.[55]

Adam Smith studied the matter of profit even further and realized that profit motive benefits everyone. As we have noted, the division of labor is a necessary aspect of trade. Smith realized that any person living in an advanced and complex society "requires the cooperation and assistance of great multitudes.... And it is in vain for him to expect it from their benevolence only."[56]

Famously, Smith saw that the motive of profit, not of benevolence, produces all the benefits of a complex economy: "It is not from the benevolence of the butcher, the brewer, or the baker, that we expect our dinner, but from their regard to their own interest. We address ourselves, not to their humanity but to their self-love, and never talk to them of our own necessities but of their advantages."[57]

As Christians we recognize that a healthy self-interest plays a rightful role in our economic ethic. Scripture clearly articulates this same principle. Jesus commands us to love our neighbors as ourselves (Mark 12:31), which requires healthy self-interest. Additionally, God consistently promises blessings for obedience (e.g., Deuteronomy 28), appealing to our self-interest to inspire us to good work.[58]

Economist Paul Heyne correctly argues that, in our pursuit of self-interest, we implicitly (if not explicitly) acknowledge our limitations. Because we lack divine omniscience, our knowledge of others' self-interest is severely limited. To assume otherwise, to presume to rule over an economy, is to claim a type of knowledge and power we do not have.[59]

Finally, market competition also usually drives down the price of goods, which benefits the poorest in society. Some have complained that the profits gained from the free market produce unequal wealth distribution in a society. Clearly, wise investors and entrepreneurs will acquire more wealth than others, but, as we have noted above, denying them the fruits of their labor or risk would be unjust.

Redistribution and Justice

Still, political leftists argue that the government should redistribute wealth to achieve a more financially equitable society. They believe that unequal wealth distribution is itself unjust. Nash rightly observed how such ideas can easily gain popularity: "It is not difficult to organize dissatisfaction with the actual distribution of the market. It is natural to feel moral outrage at the prosperity of the wicked; it is easy to feel envy at the prosperity of the righteous. If some have more than others, it is natural for discontent to arise among those with less."[60]

For these people, the justice of the process of wealth accumulation (abiding by the economic laws) is less important than the equal distribution of wealth, which they perceive to be a form of social justice. However, forced redistribution of wealth is not actually just. Part of the confusion in our society about redistributionist schemes arises from our ignorance of true justice.

Everyone is called to practice universal justice, which means that we should behave virtuously in all areas of life. When people practice virtue (universal justice) in specific circumstances, they are practicing particular justice. Aristotle argued for three basic kinds of particular justice: commercial, remedial, and distributive. We have already seen that commercial justice is concerned with fair economic exchanges, or right business practices. Remedial justice refers to criminal and civil legal proceedings. Finally, distributive justice regards the distribution of some good between two or more people.[61]

We must note that only someone who "is in a situation where he is involved in the distribution of some good or some burden" can practice distributive justice.[62] This condition means that when the government forcibly takes the wealth of one person and distributes it to others, it acts unjustly because the money is not the government's to give. Calvin argued that forced redistribution of wealth by the government or anyone else was legalized theft.[63] Agreeing with Calvin, Nash stated, "No adequate justification for the welfare state has yet been given."[64]

Redistributionist schemes are founded in human pride. Friedrich Hayek explained that such plans for social justice reflect a loss of "faith in a supernatural revelation." People who embrace these plans have replaced communication from God with "a new 'social' religion which substitutes a temporal for a celestial promise of justice, and who hope that they can thus continue their striving to do good."[65]

In essence, Hayek argued that forced redistributionist schemes are part of a secular religion with its own final judgment and acts of benevolence. However, no individual freely engages in benevolent acts under this model. Instead, the government forcibly takes his wealth to redistribute in an abstracted form of benevolence.

To summarize, the free-market economic model draws heavily from the biblical worldview. Free-market economists are committed to preserving man's individual freedom to pursue his vocation and reap the rewards of his work. Individual liberty also allows people to ascertain the best value of goods and to take risks prudently in the market. Governments should articulate and protect the framework of rules that govern just trade but should refrain from unjustly robbing some citizens or subjects to benefit others. Historically, when the state has preserved economic freedom, wealth has spread rapidly, increasing the material quality of life for everyone in society.

The Marxist Critique

The foremost challenger to free-market economics is Marxism. Founded on the ideas of Karl Marx and Friedrich Engels, Marxism provides the intellectual framework for both socialism and communism.

Socialism

Much of the economic and social discontent that underlies modern socialism began to surface during the Industrial Revolution, which first developed in eighteenth-century England because of economic freedom. Industrialization then moved to the European continent, then to the United States, and then to the rest of the world.[66] Although industrialization eventually brought wide-reaching economic benefits (e.g., the standard of living for the average British person doubled between 1750 and 1850), it also destroyed much along the way, including traditional rural society.[67]

For a variety of reasons, mass migration began from the European countryside into overcrowded urban centers. Former peasants became common laborers, living in squalid apartment tenements and working low-paying, dangerous jobs under the command of strangers. Disconnected from their families and home communities, these new urbanites found that the anonymity of urban life bred crime and dissatisfaction with the state and society.

The discontent caused by industrialization took several forms, but the political movement of socialism was the most prominent and influential. Socialists came in many varieties, but all of them looked to redress some of the problems (both real and imagined) of industrialization. Radical egalitarianism, including equality of social activity and wealth distribution, was a primary goal shared by these groups.

Many, like Claude de Saint Simon, Robert Owen, and Charles Fourier, believed that socialist policies would bring about a completely restructured utopian society where people would live in perfect harmony. During the second half of the nineteenth century, socialism gained popularity, especially in excessively repressive, politically unresponsive, or economically underdeveloped areas of Europe like Germany and Russia, and Marx's particular approach to socialism came to dominate the movement.

Karl Marx

Born into a middle-class German family, Marx was highly educated in philosophy. However, because his atheism was a barrier to his advancement in nineteenth-century Germany, he became a journalist for radical and socialist political movements. His radicalism soon brought him to the attention of the German authorities, and he fled his homeland in 1843. For the rest of his life, Marx lived outside of Germany, mostly in Britain (which was, ironically, the center of free-market economics and industrialization).

Marx and his longtime friend Engels worked from Britain to build international support for socialism. The earlier utopian socialists mentioned above strongly influenced them.[68] However, for Marx, so-called democratic socialism was only a halfway point between capitalism and his vision of communism. Both Marx and Engels often wrote of socialism and communism as essentially synonymous.[69] Marx saw his "view of communism as the most rational outworking of a democratic society advocated by the French Enlightenment."[70]

Marx brought together aspects of German Idealism and English economics to form a comprehensive materialist philosophy. William Dennison rightly describes the result as a secular religion that features a state of innocence, sin, salvation, and utopian eschatology.[71] Despite Marx's utopian claims, his philosophy led, in most cases, to social disorder and the unlawful death of thousands of people; in other cases, it led to widespread poverty (see discussion below regarding democratic socialism).

Marx argued that history alone gives meaning to life, but he rejected any spiritual component to reality. He insisted that nothing exists beyond the bounds of the material world. Instead, drawing from John Locke, Marx saw labor and property as central to life and, drawing from Georg Wilhelm Friedrich Hegel, viewed history as an ever-changing dialectic. These views resulted in what we call dialectical materialism founded on property and economics.

In the preface of *A Contribution to the Critique of Political Economy* (1859), Marx asserted that economics and economic relationships are the true foundation of human life. Other aspects of human existence and society, such as religion, law, government, and class structures, are *superstructures* that arise from specific material contexts with the sole purpose of justifying the economic order of the moment.[72] Along these lines, he famously argued that religion "is the opium of the people."[73]

Furthermore, according to Marx and Engels, when the economic order becomes unbalanced, violent revolution results in the birth of a new economic order. In this way, human action, specifically violent revolution, creates and pushes forward history.[74]

Marxism Explained

Contrary to the materialistic worldview of Marx, Christians believe that history presents a metanarrative of God's redemption that encapsulates the state of innocence in the garden, the Fall, redemption in Christ, and the coming kingdom of Christ.

Marx, instead, posited a secularized metanarrative of history that includes roughly five economic arrangements: (1) primitive communism (with no individual property ownership), (2) slavery, (3) feudalism, (4) capitalism, and (5) socialism/communism.

Each of the first four arrangements is a system of exploitation in which one group exploits the labor of another. In each case, Marx argued that any sense of mutual social responsibility was an illusory superstructure. He believed he saw behind the illusion and exposed the exploitation that had remained hidden from everyone who had gone before him. Therefore, he was like a prophet who had received special revelation about the truth of the world.[75]

Free-market economics, or *capitalism*, as Marx referred to it, exploited the weakest in society, much like its predecessors. Here he was specifically influenced by the thinking of political economist David Ricardo, who posited that the value of the labor involved in producing a good was the true value of the good.[76] In this way, Ricardo, and Marx after him, eschewed the idea of relative value, arguing instead that economic values are objective and fixed. If a good sold for more than the value of the labor that went into producing it, Marx argued, then the capitalists who owned, invested in, or operated the company must have exploited the laborers.[77]

Worse, common factory laborers (known as the proletariat) did not receive property as the fruit of their labor. Most of the proletariat owned little more than the clothes on their backs since they worked with someone else's tools and lived in rented apartments. Thus, according to Marx, the free market produced a state of extreme alienation and servitude.[78] In the end, Marx argued that the proletariat would rise up against the bourgeoisie (middle class) and create a new economic system known as communism.

The communist society would be formed by the dictatorship of the proletariat (working class). According to Marx, once the proletariat overthrew their bourgeoisie capitalist overlords, they would abolish all private property, giving ownership of all means of production to the state. Further, the state would take full control of communication, transportation, and credit services. A heavy progressive income tax would redistribute wealth from the rich to the poor and contribute toward eradicating class divisions.

The state would also work to redistribute its citizens geographically, abolishing the "distinction between town and country" and inculcating its values in the society by providing free education for all children.[79] This revolution might begin in specific nations, but it would end in a worldwide revolution that would erase all national borders and destroy all class structures.

The result would be a completely uniform world where the superstructure has disappeared. No one would own property or have specific responsibilities. Each person would be free to work as he chooses, and everyone would receive the same benefits from the state. The family unit would also disappear since it too is a system of exploitation. In the end, individuals lose their individual identity in communal commitment, and the state, religion, and class structures become unnecessary and wither away.[80]

Marxism Critiqued

Marx believed that this utopian kingdom would be the culmination of history. However, Marxist economics is antithetical to biblical Christianity. In short, as theologian Wayne Grudem argues, "Communism enslaves people and destroys human freedom of choice. The entire nation becomes one huge prison. For this reason, it seems to me that communism is the most dehumanizing economic system invented by man."[81] Those who tried to realize Marx's ideas in the twentieth century consistently proved Grudem's argument.

As Rodney Stark has pointed out, "when Marxist regimes appeared in the world, they turned out to be nothing more than the same old command economies. The only difference was that, in comparison with Joseph Stalin and Mao Tse-tung, the Ottoman sultans and the Egyptian pharaohs seemed enlightened and restrained tyrants."[82] Every time they have been applied to government, whether in China, Cuba, Russia, or Venezuela, Marx's theories have ended in mass murder, starvation, and horrifying state control of the individual.

In rough numbers (and all we have are rough estimates because sheer madness reigned in each of these regimes), somewhere around 100 million people were killed by communist governments in the twentieth century.[83] Most of those murdered were the subjects of the governments that killed them systematically as if they were removing problematic numbers on an actuary table.

Even if we were inclined to ignore this mass murder, the economic system still does not work. It is impossible to determine the economic value of a good without a market.[84] Communist governments around the world have systematically starved their people to death as in North Korea, or they have collapsed as in the Soviet Union, or they have begun moving toward free markets as in China.

By the mid-twentieth century, most in the West began recognizing that communism is disastrous and even murderous. However, political progressives in the United States have latched on to democratic socialism as a gentler and more compassionate economic system. Socialists point to some early twenty-first-century European governments, such as Denmark, Finland, Norway, and Sweden as examples of peaceful and successful socialist societies. However, such examples are complicated. Most of these countries have never practiced socialism and are tired of being accused of it.[85]

Denmark, like many Western economies of the twentieth century, embraced a large welfare system, but they never adopted socialism. Interestingly, in recent years, the Danes have even begun to pare back their welfare and unemployment programs because they have found that the benefits resulting from those programs provide more income than numerous full-time jobs. This means that working people are paying taxes to support non-working people who are enjoying a higher standard of living than many of the working people themselves. As a result, such programs have been significantly discouraging employment among healthy working-aged people, and the country's overall economic health has been suffering.[86]

Even those countries that have experimented with varying levels of socialism in the past have abandoned it in favor of much freer economies. Sweden experimented with moderate socialist policies during the 1970s after their lengthy history of free-market practices and small government had earned them the fourth highest per capita income in the world. Over the next twenty years, their government heavily regulated industries, propped-up stagnating sectors of the economy, nationalized healthcare, expanded various welfare and unemployment benefits, and forbade any private competition in education or postal services.

To pay for these services they raised taxes drastically, especially for high-income earners, and began borrowing heavily.

However, these policies created economic depression rather than economic prosperity. The Swedish economy declined significantly while the government ballooned in size so that governmental spending and transfer payments were valued at seventy percent of the gross domestic product. In 1991, when the Swedish people chose to abandon these policies and elect a more market-oriented government, the state was deeply in debt, inflation was high, and the per capita income of Swedes had dropped to fourteenth in the world.[87] Even when the economic turmoil emanating from the Soviet Union at the time is taken into account, Sweden's economy declined in comparison to other European countries like Finland.[88]

However, the change in policy in the 1990s has produced good effects for Swedes over the past thirty years; a conservative think tank, the Heritage Foundation, even ranked Sweden as the eleventh freest economy in the world in 2022. Significantly, Denmark, Finland, Norway, and the United Kingdom all ranked higher in the Heritage Foundation's index than the United States, whose economy has become increasingly burdened by regulation, which came in at twenty-five.[89].

Further, those countries in present-day Europe that might "call themselves 'socialist,' in fact advocate a *partial* socialism—the nationalization of railroads, various public utilities, and heavy industry—but not usually of light industries, the service trades, or agriculture."[90] Still, even "partial socialism," such as Venezuela's attempt to nationalize only certain segments of the economy, end in disaster.[91] Venezuela was one of the richest countries in South America during the mid-twentieth century. However, in 1975, President Carlos Andrés Pérez, who was committed to the idea of planned economies, nationalized the country's massive oil industry and began heavily regulating numerous others. Pérez and those who followed him used the enormous wealth of the oil industry to fund massive government spending and buy political support. As in Sweden, even such moderate socialist policies led to immense governmental debt and rapidly rising inflation.

By the 1990s, when Venezuela's last democratically elected president, Rafael Caldera, took office, inflation was skyrocketing up to one hundred percent with no way to stop it without massive government spending cuts and renewed economic growth.[92] Like with many historical examples, such as Weimar Germany or early twentieth-century Russia, such bad economic and political times made it possible for malevolent demagogues to capture the imagination of a hopeless people. Venezuela was no different. When Hugo Chávez took power in 1999, he promised that he could fix the problems with the economy by further expanding state control. However, his policies made matters only worse, despite enjoying a massive oil boom for over a decade in the early 2000s, during which time he also took control of foreign oil projects in the Orinoco Delta.[93]

Defenders of Venezuela's socialist policies in recent years have tried to emphasize that the current economic and social terrors in that country have resulted from volatile oil prices since the mid-2010s. However, the Venezuelan economy was already teetering on the brink of collapse, and, even if we were to allow the conceit that everything was fine up until that point, why had the socialist policies so unwisely focused all economic growth on a single industry? In either case, the increasingly socialist policies of the Venezuelan government since the 1970s bear the burden of the guilt for the current suffering of their people.

In American politics, open socialists, such as Bernie Sanders and Alexandria Ocasio-Cortez, have gained prominent positions in the Democratic Party of America during the early twenty-first century. In addition to their making direct appeals for economic and social restructuring, they have also used other issues to push forward their socialist agenda covertly. For example, in 2019, Ocasio-Cortez's chief of staff, Saikat Chakrabarti, explained that restructuring the economy was the primary focus of the much-touted environmental policy statement known as the Green New Deal, even though it had been presented to the public as an attempt to address climate change.[94] It does not seem that Marxism is going to disappear any time soon. However, these examples from Denmark, Sweden, and Venezuela give us great pause.

Conclusion

As Christians, we have a duty to think deeply about economics. Whether we realize it or not, we hold an economic philosophy. But we should try to fashion a well-rounded economic philosophy grounded in the biblical worldview. We should promote economic theories and decisions that protect individual liberty and private property, affirm the relative value of goods, and limit governmental power.

Free-market economics has the strongest connection to biblical concepts and has proven to be an incredible source of wealth even for the poor. Utopian systems, such as Marxism, which seek to restructure society and economics radically, reject a biblical understanding of man and reality, and lead to mass social chaos and mass murder, or else widespread poverty. In the end, though, we as Christians must always remember that, while economics is important, true human flourishing is founded on godliness and wisdom rather than on wealth and poverty.

CHAPTER FIFTEEN

Sports and Recreation

Greg Ketteman and Gregory Fawbush

Imagine walking into a place of worship that is filled with a diverse group of men and women—people from distinct backgrounds and nationalities and socio-economic levels—who are gathered for the same reason. As we enter, we make the obligatory monetary offering and quickly find our seats. Over the course of the next hour or two, we sing together and rejoice together and lament together. We celebrate victory because our foe has been vanquished. As a body we believe together, and we encourage one another to persevere in our faith. We have even dressed appropriately, demonstrating by our appearance the reason we have gathered. Now consider this question: have we just described a church event or football game?[1]

To frame a Christian view of sports and recreation is a formidable task. It crosses multiple disciplines, and it is as ancient as it is contemporary.[2] Because this topic is as old as humanity itself, our reflections will begin with some theological considerations to give us a sure foundation before we turn to some challenges associated with this cultural sphere and some responses to those challenges. Our hope is that this chapter will cause readers to take serious stock of how human sin has impacted sports and recreation and how divine grace may restore them.

Establishing Theological Foundations

The role of sports in society often causes intense dialogue among Christians. Jeremy Treat remarks that "some dismiss sports as merely a game, while others worship sports as nearly a god."[3] Treat's observations are right; people tend toward extremes. Treat reminds us, though, that we are not limited to one of two options: dismissal or idolatry. We can find a middle way, but doing so will require our thinking through questions related to sports and recreation in a deeply theological and reflective manner.

The first pages of Scripture provide justification for this cultural sphere. Genesis 1:28 reads, "Be fruitful and multiply and fill the earth and subdue it, and have dominion over the fish of the sea and over the birds of the heavens and over every living thing that moves on the earth." This divine mandate given by our Creator as He ordered the world has resulted in all kinds of culture, which the authors of this book have considered, including history and tradition; the arts, including movies, music, and literature; labor and vocation; science and technology; and politics and economics. This chapter explores another manifestation of "culture making" in sports and recreation.[4] We value these activities because they result from obedience to God's creation mandate.

In addition, God called Adam and Eve—and by extension men and women today—not only to *develop* the created order but also to *delight* in it. Genesis 2:16–17 reads, "And the LORD God commanded the man, saying, 'You may surely eat of every tree of the garden, but of the tree of the knowledge of good and evil you shall not eat, for in the day that you eat of it you shall surely die.'" People often read these verses in terms of what they prohibit, but we should also read them in terms of what they grant. Treat explains:

> Unfortunately, many have focused so much on the prohibition of the one fruit that they have overlooked the invitation to feast upon all the other fruits. The God who abounds in love and kindness created a world of delights and placed his beloved image bearers in it with an invitation to enjoyment. Creation is not merely a resource to be used for productivity, it is a gift to be received and enjoyed. This is where the idea of 'play' comes in, which is implicit in humanity's calling to develop and delight in God's creation. To play is to creatively enjoy something for its own intrinsic good.[5]

Sports and recreation signify not only man's development of the created order but also his delight in it.

However, the first humans perverted God's call to develop and delight in the created order. Rather than enjoying what He gave, Adam and Eve partook in what God had not given, giving birth to sin. Put simply, sin is the perversion or privation of the good, and it has poisoned everything. Consequently, just as the Fall of man has impacted the other cultural spheres discussed throughout this book, it has also impacted sports and recreation in which we see all manner of idolatry and immorality.

Because of humanity's fallen state, men and women take sports and recreation to extremes and use them for self-gratification. Such abuse leads critics to argue that attending a professional ball game or spending the day fishing is wrong. People who do adopt this view have usually done so because they have witnessed other Christians placing a higher emphasis on recreational activities than on sanctification and, as a result, they advocate for total withdrawal. However, an instrumental wrong does not amount to an inherent or intrinsic wrong; in other words, just because people make idols out of things does not mean those things themselves are bad. In short, sports and recreation are not bad in and of themselves.

Though we see much that is wrong with sports, we can also glimpse much that is good with them. Even in a fallen world, God's common grace abounds.

God is not only the Creator and Judge but also the Restorer. He brings restoration to what is ruined and healing to what is broken. As Christians, we can learn to develop and delight in God's created order in a manner consistent with His call and will. We can beware of the idolatries that exist within sports and recreation, we can engage them in way that is restorative, and we can enjoy them in a God-glorifying manner.

The Christian worldview does not promote the elimination of leisurely activities, contrary to what some people may think. We see this point from the first pages of Scripture to the example of Jesus Himself. God Himself took leisure in Genesis 2:2–3, and, because He is our Creator and Redeemer, He instructs our leisure too (Exodus 20:8–11; Deuteronomy 5:12–15). Likewise, Jesus, speaking to the disciples, said, "Come away by yourselves to a desolate place and rest a while," with the evangelist Mark explaining, "For many were coming and going, and they had no leisure even to eat" (Mark 6:31). People were sick and diseased and in constant need of help. The disciples were busy doing God's will but had no time for leisure, so Jesus encouraged them to get away to recharge and refocus.

Having leisure time is vital if we wish to be effective for the kingdom. As we have seen, leisure is a God-given part of the human life, good in and of itself.[6] We should not think of leisure as free time so much as we think of it as hallowed time before the God who gives us rest amid work, merriment amid misery, and even joy amid despair. As Paul Heintzman writes, "To conceive of leisure as free time is both limiting and confusing."[7] When we view leisure only as down time, we misunderstand God's plan for it. God sanctifies our leisure, which sometimes involves sports and recreation—ball games, hunting trips, travel teams, and the like.

Just because people use their leisure time to ill effect does not mean that leisure itself is the issue. And yet leisure, like everything else, can result in problems. Hence, before meditating further on a redemptive vision for sports and recreation, we will consider some of the challenges that come from them in a post-Fall world.

Identifying Challenges

The Sacrosanctity of Sport

One of the key challenges we face in this sphere is the worship of sport. Many people within a secularized culture (and even many within the Christian church) worship at the church of sport. Sport has captured the soul of an increasingly shallow American culture that is no longer anchored in the ideals of the good, the true, and the beautiful.

The church of sport thrives in a culture that is driven by the unrestrained pursuit of consumerism and entertainment. It thrives in a culture that is deeply saturated with the worship of faux-heroes and vacuous idols. It is facilitated by ubiquitous digital gateways, extended adolescence, and superabundant leisure time. Musicians, entertainers, and athletes are reduced to commercialized commodities that millions of Americans emulate. Although the church of sport presumes to meet people's deepest needs, it, sadly, delivers only temporal solutions.

Because so many people worship at the altar of sport, it has become a near sacrosanct subject. As Christians, we may argue vociferously about topics ranging from the doctrine of the end times to the meaning of modesty, but we often resist entering a conversation about the idolatry of sports and recreation. We may discuss problems associated with hostilities and divisions resulting from the competition or rivalry of sports, but we do not (often) question the extent of the engagement itself.

Fanatic loyalty is uncritically accepted and rarely questioned. From the pastor to the Easter-only layman, from parents to great-grandchildren, people see obsessive (and fanatic) participation in sports as the norm. Not to be utterly engrossed in sports may even be considered abnormal. Sports enthusiasts defend their commitments with platitudes like: "What's wrong with golf? It's not immoral," "Involvement in sports keeps young people off the streets," "This sport is part of the fabric of America," and the clincher, "Sports give Christians a platform to demonstrate and discuss their faith." We do not deny that the points underlying these remarks are true, as we have stressed. Sports are not immoral, they result from the creation mandate, they provide opportunities for delight, and they are an important part of our culture.

At the same time, our level of commitment to sports, when compared to our commitment to the church, is sometimes off-kilter. Consider how we may brag about perfect attendance to the home games of our preferred teams but cannot boast about perfect attendance at church, or how we may know more about the order of events and etiquette at the ballpark, golf course, racetrack, or track meet than we do about the order of service and appropriate etiquette at church, or how we may emulate—idolize even—our favorite teams and players over the course of decades but do not know much about the heroes of the faith throughout space and time, or how we may perfectly memorize all types of sports trivia but struggle to commit to memory Bible passages, or how we may sing word-for-word "Take Me Out to the Ball Game" but struggle to remember the lyrics to the "Doxology" on Sunday morning, or how we may expertly define terms like "clean-up batter," "hat trick," "pinch hitter," and "third and inches" but demonstrate uncertainty about the meaning of "the Trinity," "omnipotence," or "salvation by grace."

To be clear, we are not criticizing sports and recreation themselves. We will talk below at length about some of the opportunities we have through sports and recreation. Rather, our point here is to caution against the idolatry of sports to such an extent that we cannot even talk about them honestly and openly, a temptation that is all too real.

The Challenge of Sunday

One of the biggest trends affecting church attendance is that youth sports and other recreational activities often occur on Sundays. This was not always the case. Historically, Sunday was a day set aside for religious observance and family on which people did not conduct business or play organized sports. However, as a secularized cultural ethos has replaced a religious one, extra-curricular activities on Sundays have increased exponentially. Whether they are related to sports, education, careers, or "keeping up with the Joneses," such as boating, camping, fishing, or hunting, Sunday activities are now the norm rather than the exception.[8]

Now, youth sports and other recreational activities effectively compete with Christian worship and church engagement. According to ESPN, 21.5 million youth between the ages of six and seventeen participate in youth sports.[9] Frequently, athletes practice during the week and play games on the weekend, including on Sundays. This development not only takes players away from church, but it also takes their parents and fans away.

For Christians, this trend is problematic. "Do I honor my commitment to my church or to my team?" Christians must conduct thoughtful dialogue on this dilemma, and, in the end, our decisions will reveal our true loyalties. For most families, the prospect of missing work on a consistent basis for sporting events and recreational activities is unacceptable. Sadly, missing church for these functions has become all too commonplace.

Some groups have formed church leagues, adopting a mantra of "if you can't beat 'em, join 'em," but their doing so has not eliminated the challenge of this "rivalry" that has emerged between the liturgies of Christianity and the liturgies of sports and recreation. As Christians our priority on the Lord's Day must be the fellowship of believers rather than the camaraderie of fans. As Hebrews 10:25 explains, Christians should not neglect "to meet together, as is the habit of some," but should encourage "one another, and all the more as you see the Day drawing near."

Just as the smorgasbord of extra-curricular activities on Sundays competes for our time, it also competes for our money. Tithing has dropped as precipitously as church attendance. Self-proclaimed Christians have significantly cut back on their charitable giving to churches and other non-profit organizations. Consider that 247 million Americans claim Christianity but only 1.5 million regularly tithe. Only approximately five percent of self-proclaimed Christians are tithing like they should with an average amount of church attendees giving $17 per week.[10]

Compare these figures to other extra-curricular outlets. The average American family spends $1,145 per person each year on vacation. In 2016, a family of four spent an average of $503 to attend an NFL game. In 2017, twenty percent of Americans spent an average of $1,000 monthly on youth sports with sixty-three percent spending anywhere from $100 to $499 monthly on youth sports.[11]

By no means is spending time or money on leisurely activities and sporting events inherently wrong.[12] We should avoid legalism in our Sunday observances, yet we must also ensure that recreational activities and sporting events not become idolatrous. So often, though, we see this latter tendency more than the former one. A growing number of professing Christians have exchanged the church of Christ for the church of sport, letting it fundamentally shape their rituals, traditions, and values. Exodus 20:3 reads, "You shall have no other gods before me." Few people would ever admit to putting anything before God, but the available data suggests otherwise.

Yes, Christians ought to enjoy fishing, hunting, running, and other activities. However, when these events take priority over church attendance and commitment, then people have placed a temporal god before the eternal God. When someone idolizes sports and recreation—or, for that matter, career, family, or anything else—he or she has exchanged the Creator for a created thing. "But seek first the kingdom of God and his righteousness," Jesus says (Matthew 6:33). We can learn to balance sports and recreation with other noble pursuits. The solution to this problem is not retreat or withdrawal from this cultural sphere but rather Christian engagement. However, before considering what this engagement looks like, we will consider one more challenge.

The Survival of the (Athletically) Fittest

Sports may do more to promote a form of practical Darwinism in popular culture than do the much-maligned college science professors. It is often an extremely effective promoter of the notion of survival of the (athletically) fittest.

The ability of athletes or teams to develop a "killer instinct" to "finish off" the opponent is too often glorified and touted as a positive virtue in sports. Some leading figures in this field do not encourage athletes to cultivate the image of the "nice guy" or the concept of being a "good sport" since "nice guys finish last." American Christians join their secular counterparts in "putting on a game face," worshipping at the altar of "live and let die," and celebrating hard-nosed, "kill or be killed" aggression, along with youth, strength, and speed. Can these prevailing attitudes about sports be reconciled with Christian virtues?

These realities are not a new cultural phenomenon. Roman culture was saturated with cravings for entertainment, competition, and hero-worship, which were fed by life-or-death gladiatorial competition. The barbaric cruelty of these ancient events that captivated Roman culture would stun the participants and fans of today's ultimate fighting competitions. Without the constraints of Christian teachings and practices, these bloody conflicts were "anything goes," "no holds barred," and "fight to the death"—literally. History tells us that the thirst for bloody spectacles coarsened Roman culture and hastened pervasive moral decay that ultimately caused Roman culture to crumble.

At times a macho type of survival of the fittest has manifested in patently immoral behavior. Although there are hopeful signs to the contrary, athletes still get a greater pass on morality than we would like to admit. They celebrate the killer instinct during an athletic contest and then celebrate pride, hedonism, and moral indulgence outside of the athletic arena. Evangelical Christians, desperate for role models who help to justify their faith in sports, overlook a multitude of sins because an athlete mentions his "Lord and Savior" in a speech or her faith in a nationally televised interview. Never mind the reality of the athlete's lifestyle that does everything but honor God and support His church.

Not a Lost Cause

The sphere of sports and recreation carries with it many challenges, as the previous section has shown. In fact, such difficulties have caused some Christians to "throw in the towel" with respect to sports. "Sports is a lost cause," they say. But we are not suggesting the elimination of these activities from our lives or from the broader culture. In fact, we believe they have many good and positive effects.

While we should eschew notions like survival of the fittest and the killer instinct, we can nonetheless appreciate the spirit of competition that sports engender. Competition can create problems in a sin-cursed world, but it can also push us toward greater degrees of excellence. Competition can be serious yet humble and friendly without its being prideful, bitter, and immoral.

The point is that we should recognize some of the dangers that accompany this sphere. As we have seen, some people become so enthusiastic about their sport of choice that they treat the sport as sacrosanct. Others give sports such an outsized influence in their lives that they come to worship at the church of sport, having turned this otherwise noble pursuit into an idol. Still others, having yoked themselves to unbelievers or having succumbed to the spirit of this present evil age (2 Corinthians 6:14; Galatians 1:4), have adopted an ethic of the survival of the athletically fittest, turning healthy competition into a bitter fight.

Leisurely activities and athletic competition are not bad in and of themselves, but because we are fallen, our engagement with them can be idolatrous so that we "amuse ourselves to death."[13] As Christians, we must constantly evaluate our attitudes toward sports and recreation. We should engage these activities with mindfulness, not mindlessness. Beginning with ourselves, we must reflect thoughtfully about these expressions of culture, just like we reflect about other cultural spheres, whether the arts or technology or politics. We must always, through God's common grace and restorative power, fight for a balance in our lives that truly honors God.

Restoring Sports and Recreation

Intrinsic and Instrumental Value

The Scriptures reveal that sports and recreation have intrinsic and instrumental value. Intrinsically, sports have value because, as we explained earlier, they result from men and women developing and delighting in the created order in obedience to the creation mandate. In addition, as the apostle Paul says to Timothy, "bodily training is of some value" (1 Timothy 4:8).

Instrumentally, sports have value because they are the instruments through which we serve God in multiple capacities.[14] Sports provide an opportunity for witness: "You are the light of the world. A city set on a hill cannot be hidden. Nor do people light a lamp and put it under a basket, but on a stand, and it gives light to all in the house. In the same way, let your light shine before others, so that they may see your good works and give glory to your Father who is in heaven" (Matthew 5:14–16). If we as Christians simply dismiss sports and recreation, if we withdraw from that sphere, then we remove from it the light of Christ, and darkness endures and expands.

Other instrumental rewards include holistic health and social interaction. Sports and recreation can improve not only our physical health but also our mental, emotional, and spiritual health. They can boost self-confidence without self-conceit. They can provide positive role models for young men and women and can break down social and economic boundaries.

Excellence without Idolatry

As we pursue the intrinsic and instrumental goods of sports and recreation, we must do so with excellence. The Scriptures repeatedly call us to excellence (Philippians 4:8; 2 Peter 1:3). So, as Christians, we pursue excellence in whatever task to which God calls us, including sports and recreation.

We see many people pursue excellence in their athletic endeavors. In his best-selling book *Outliers*, Malcolm Gladwell examines multitudes of statistical data about the lives of thousands of professional athletes, top-flight attorneys, and wildly successful computer company entrepreneurs. Gladwell shows that the cost of being the best at anything requires a minimum of ten thousand hours of work—in other words, everything a person has. This principle holds true in music, in law, in business, and especially in sports.[15]

We may admire those who have dedicated themselves to being the best in a chosen field, but we must ask, "What price has been exacted for this achievement?" At what point does the Christian's pursuit of excellence in sports compromise his or her commitment to Christ's gospel and church? At times, honest answers to such questions may create feelings of discomfort, guilt, and uncertainty within us, but they will likely depend on God's specific call on an individual's life. Has God vocationally called us to a certain sport for this period of life? If *yes*, then one's level of commitment may warrant the time (and money and energy) he or she spends with it. If *no*, then an over-the-top commitment may not be justified.

Whatever our callings, we must all search our hearts and seek balance in view of God's callings on our lives. Like the psalmist David, we pray to the Lord: "Search me, O God, and know my heart! Try me and know my thoughts! And see if there be any grievous way in me, and lead me in the way everlasting" (139:23–24). And with the Lord Jesus, we remember, "For what does it profit a man to gain the whole world and forfeit his soul?" (Mark 8:36) Whatever the pressures of cultural expectations, we must courageously stand against the idolatry and immorality that can emerge within this sphere, doing everything for God's glory.

The book of Daniel demonstrates what courageous conviction looks like. When the newly enslaved Hebrew youths were confronted with the requirement of eating the king's food in their training to be palace servants, they resisted the cultural pressure to do so and violate their religious convictions. These young men were astute enough to understand the consequences of their choices and, through the grace of God, they withstood the tremendous pressure for them to make the easy, safe choice to "go along to get along" (1:8–13).

We later see these same Hebrew men again refusing to bow to tremendous political and cultural pressure when they resisted worshipping a golden statue, even with the threat of being burned alive in a fiery furnace, because they understood the consequences of their actions (3:8–18). In both instances, God rewarded their wise and courageous choices, demonstrating His care for these young men and His powerful presence in their lives (1:14–16; 3:19–30).[16]

In our culture, answering questions about the Christian's involvement in sports and recreation will require the wisdom and courage of these Hebrew exemplars who are worthy of our admiration and emulation. They refused to engage mindlessly in what the dominant culture dictated to them. Although God delivered them, they were willing even to die for their beliefs: "If it be so, our God whom we serve is able to rescue us from the furnace of blazing fire; and He will rescue us from your hand, O king. But even if He does not, let it be known to you, O king, that we are not going to serve your gods nor worship the golden statue that you have set up" (3:17–18).

We, too, must thoughtfully pursue single-minded obedience to God's claim on our lives, no matter the cost. Again, our obedience will depend on God's unique call on our lives. But whatever our path, God can give us the courage and resolve to withstand the idolatrous and immoral pressures of a secular culture. These Hebrew men demonstrate how to be in the culture but not of it. They accomplished this careful balance by steeping themselves in the Scriptures and applying them to their lives. Likewise, we must fully saturate ourselves in God's Word under the instruction of faithful, godly men and women and apply its truths in our homes, churches, schools, jobs, and sporting events and recreational activities.

Whatever our respective callings, whether we pursue sports leisurely or vocationally, all Christians should consider the application of Gladwell's "ten thousand hours" principle to Bible knowledge and the spiritual disciplines. How many of us aspire to reach the ten-thousand-hour threshold of excellence in our knowledge of Scripture and in disciplines like prayer and fasting or in service to hurting and needy people? On the other hand, how many of us glorify the athlete or performer who has given all to become famous for his achievements but do not honor the Christian who has given all to know God truly and to serve Him? We can pursue and achieve excellence without idolatry, but it will require resolve and courage.

Questions for Thoughtful Believers

Before concluding this chapter, we want to consider questions for thoughtful believers who are navigating their journey through sports and recreation. The authors of "When Church Gets Sidelined by Youth Sports" ask three questions: do we acknowledge God as the Creator of sporting and recreational activities, do we bring glory to the Lord Jesus Christ through them, and do we obey Scripture in them?[17]

These three questions offer a good guide for the Christian thinking through his or her engagement with sports and recreation. As we have seen, these activities have intrinsic value because they are the Creator's gifts to men and women who obey His creation mandate. Sports and recreation also have instrumental value because they are a means of holistic health, social interaction, Christian witness, and the pursuit of excellence. Throughout this overview is an emphasis on obedience to Scripture. Now, in the spirit of these questions, we would like to pose thirteen more.

As we work our way through these questions, readers will note they overlap and build on each other. In addition, we have not designed them with any preconceived agendas but instead intend them to invoke honest answers. As these questions demonstrate, moving toward a Christian view of sports and recreation is not easy, but God will richly reward those who seriously contemplate them and apply them to their lives.

1. *Does participation in sports and recreation qualify as doing "all to the glory of God" (1 Corinthians 10:31)? Can we really participate in these spheres "heartily, as for the Lord and not for men" (Colossians 3:23)?* Unequivocally, we can participate in these activities to God's glory. The Creator has gifted people with abilities and interests, and the Bible values those who have developed and mastered what God has given them. However, due to sin, people can be tempted to exchange the glory of God for the glory of self because temporal rewards can seem more enticing than eternal

rewards. Therefore, we must play the long game for God's glory, avoiding the short game for man's glory.

2. Can mindless, unbridled involvement in sports and recreation be classified as "youthful passions" (2 Timothy 2:22)? Or can our participation in these activities be a means by which we "remember also [our] Creator in the days of [our] youth" (Ecclesiastes 12:1)? In 2 Timothy, Paul contrasts "youthful passions" with the pursuit of "righteousness, faith, love, and peace, along with those who call on the Lord from a pure heart." These "youthful passions" do not refer to the interests we have in our youth; they are vices and contrast with virtue. Hence our engagement with sports and recreation can demonstrate our "youthful passions," but they do not have to. They can also provide a platform on which we practice virtue and remember our Creator in the days of our youth.

3. Does our participation in sports and recreation sow to the flesh or to the Spirit (Galatians 6:7–8)? God gifts us with a life by which we can sow to the flesh or the Spirit. In many ways, this question is like the previous one, except that it uses the imagery of good fruit and bad fruit instead of virtue and vice. God has ordained the law of nature so that we will reap the fruit of what we sow, whether in this life or the next. Sow to virtue, not to vice. Sow to the Spirit, not to the flesh as you engage in sports and recreation. As Paul argues in Galatians, sow to "love, joy, peace, patience, kindness, goodness, faithfulness, gentleness, and self-control" (5:22–23).

4. How can the pursuit of sports promote the pursuit of "righteousness, godliness, faith, love, steadfastness, gentleness" (1 Timothy 6:6–12)? In the fanaticism of our culture's current practice of sport, the practice of virtue—righteousness, godliness, faith, love, steadfastness, and gentleness—can be difficult, but, by God's grace, it is not impossible. We find our ultimate fulfillment and contentment in godliness, not in the glory we may receive from the temporal rewards of athletic achievement. If we seek to fill our deepest needs through sports and recreation, we will be sorely disappointed. However, when we order these activities under the lordship of Christ, they become a worthy means of our growth in godliness.

5. In sports and recreation, are we becoming "lovers of pleasure rather than lovers of God"? Do these activities lead us to "having the appearance of godliness, but denying its power" (2 Timothy 3:1–7)? As we have seen, sports and recreation are gifts granted by the Creator for our enjoyment and pleasure, but they can become idols when we sinfully indulge in them. We can exchange the Creator for the created thing, the Giver for the gift (Romans 1:23). At other times, we may fool ourselves into having only the appearance of godliness but denying its power. Consequently, we engage with sports and recreation with care and avoid self-deception.

6. Do we "walk circumspectly" in our involvement with sports? Are we "making the best use of the time" in these evil days? Are we drunk with sports, or are we filled with the Spirit? Do we speak to one another in sports and games and statistical data or "address one another in psalms and hymns and spiritual songs" (Ephesians 5:15–19)? Christians must live wisely and talk about things that matter. Whether we are making the best use of our time with respect to sports and recreation will depend on God's call on our lives. But whatever that call, we must walk with prudent care, not with drunken intemperance, knowing that our conversations will reflect our lives. We converse about what we enjoy. If our lives and conversations are more about sports and rarely (or never) about the Savior, our priorities are unhealthy. We are not suggesting that discussion about sports and data is off-limits, but we would warn against its becoming our religion.

7. *Can you "let your reasonableness be known to everyone" in your commitment to sports and recreation (Philippians 4:5)?* Many who would call themselves Christians have no concept of reasonableness, or "moderation" as the King James Version translates it. This problem is (almost) as old as Adam and Eve in the garden. It is at the heart of everything that the Fall and sin have damaged. From food to human sexuality to luxury to money to sports, we ruin everything God has given by our intemperance. We overindulge in the good things that the Creator has allowed us to enjoy, making them into idols that threaten our obedience to the true and living God. We crave pleasure and comfort and become idolatrous gluttons, substance abusers, and sports addicts. Rather than engaging sports and recreation with moderation or reasonableness, we engage it with a fervor that far exceeds what is warranted according to our callings. Rather than engaging sports and recreation with balance, we allow them to consume our lives to the point that we neglect the disciplines of worship, service, prayer, Scripture intake, and regular church attendance. Whatever our callings, we must not lose balance and reasonableness in the Christian life.

8. *Whom do we serve when we devote ourselves to sports and recreation (Matthew 6:24)? Do we "seek first the kingdom of God and his righteousness" in our participation in these activities (6:33)?* Our calendars, credit card statements, and checkbooks provide ample evidence of the real object(s) of our affections. We have a problem when we spend more time at the park than at the church or more money on athletics than on tithes and offerings. How we spend our money and time will demonstrate whether we place sports and recreation under or above the lordship of Christ.

9. *Can you "love the LORD your God with all your heart and with all your soul and with all might" (Deuteronomy 6:5) and devote yourself entirely to the pursuit of something else, such as sports?* Depending on God's call on our lives, we may love God with our whole beings while also pursuing something else wholeheartedly because we place it under His lordship. How we order these priorities becomes paramount. To be sure, Jesus tells us that "no one can serve two masters" (Matthew 6:24). Anything that comes to control us is our master, and God is the only master that the Christian should serve. We must navigate this area with care and wisdom.

10. Does the exhortation, "Whatever your hand finds to do, do it with your might" (Ecclesiastes 9:10), apply to sports and recreation? If these activities are worthwhile at all, Scripture exhorts us to do them with all our might. We pursue them wholeheartedly, not half-heartedly. We pursue them with commitment and excellence. However, we should not confuse such exhortations with idolatry or imbalance. As we considered above, we love God with our whole beings, which manifests in the pursuit of excellence.

11. Does physical exercise properly value the body as the "temple of the Holy Spirit"? Is athletic competition a way to "glorify God in your body" (1 Corinthians 6:19–20)? One might argue that, to the extent that sports and recreation promote physical, mental, emotional, social, and spiritual health, the bodily "temple" may be enhanced through them. Hence physical exercise and athletic competition is a means of valuing the holy temple and glorifying the holy God. Exercise provides an opportunity to glorify God for His unparalleled design of the human body as we watch talented athletes stretch the limits of physical performance with power, grace, and accuracy. This awareness should inspire a sense of wonder in all people and especially in believers.

12. Is the command, "Have this mind [of humility] among yourselves, which is yours in Christ Jesus" (Philippians 2:5), compatible with a winning sports ethos? One could argue that the phrase *a winning sports ethos* has carried a positive connotation in the past. However, in contemporary culture, it may reflect a disposition of "killer instinct" or "survival of the fittest" in competition. Neither of these interpretations is compatible with a "turn the other cheek" attitude of the humble servant that Jesus exemplified (Matthew 5:38–40). Having the mind of Christ may be a difficult endeavor in our sports culture, but we may achieve it with God's grace. Still, while the "killer instinct" ethic is problematic, the desire to win is not problematic insofar as it inspires us unto biblical excellence.

13. As we participate in sports and recreation, do we focus our minds on what is true, honorable, just, pure, lovely, commendable, excellent, and praiseworthy (Philippians 4:8)? Today's culture of sports and recreation celebrates some of these ideals in a limited way but it does not celebrate all of them. It generally emphasizes the pursuit of excellence. However, its track record with the other virtues is mixed. Today's sports culture talks frequently about justice, but its understanding of justice is often perverted. It highlights what is commendable and praiseworthy, but it also highlights much that is not and omits much that is. Generally, today's culture of sports does not celebrate truth, honor, purity, and loveliness; in fact, it often tears them down. Much of what defines athletic and recreational cultures minimizes and even mocks these biblical ideals. However, we as Christians must work to ensure that our sports ethic is grounded in these timeless ideals rather than in the passing fads of the world.

Conclusion

We love sports and recreation. Yet we have significant experience with the unhealthy side of this sphere from early ages and from virtually every possible perspective: player, coach, statistician, and reporter. At times, our involvement with sports and recreation has tipped the scale to idolatry, becoming more important than anything else in life, including Christ and His church. We must be sensitive to the personal difficulties that can arise with respect to trying to maintain a healthy balance between sports and recreation and the Christian life.

As we have seen, these activities occupy a place of tension in our culture, especially with the apparent tacit approval of its basest qualities. We can see this reality even within the evangelical church, sadly. These activities have become an American civil religion for millions. Yet we can bring the principles of Scripture to bear upon this sphere.

We have seen that the Bible does not condemn the Christian's engagement with sports and recreation; in fact, it encourages it. It results from the obedience of men and women to the creation mandate. Even in our fallen world, God's common grace abides, and He is making all things new (Revelation 21:5).

God in Christ by His Spirit is restoring what man has ruined. God calls on us to live wise and courageous lives that are guided by biblical truth. We have explicated principles and questions to help readers consider how best to submit to God's call on their lives so that we might all consciously take every thought captive to the obedience of Christ (2 Corinthians 10:5), whether we are on the court, field, or track.

Conclusion

Christopher Talbot

Our exploration through the various spheres of culture that we as Christians inhabit has been extensive but not exhaustive. We could say much more about the areas to which God calls us. Good thinkers have written numerous books that do so. So, while we know that *Christians in Culture* has not said everything it could say about Christian engagement in culture, our hope is that it has produced in readers a desire to engage more deeply—more Christianly—with the culture around them.

Of course, a lingering question remains: where do we go from here? Having read the past fifteen chapters, readers are now equipped with theological and philosophical foundations and paradigms from which to analyze questions related to tradition, history, the arts, literature, popular culture, labor, technology, science, politics and economics, sports and recreation, and more. If anything, readers might feel like they have gained a new understanding of the Christian worldview. However, if this book results only in more knowledge, it has not accomplished its goal.

Instead, we hope that readers would be not only hearers of the Word but also doers of it (James 1:22). In many ways, this short admonition from James, the brother of Jesus, provides the answer we need. Our hope is that you—equipped with all the research presented and challenges issued throughout this book—would be exactly what the title suggests: Christians in culture. Our prayer is that you would live lives of orthodoxy and orthopraxy with equal parts compassion and courage. We pray that you would not only think God's thoughts after Him but also model His kingdom work in your actions. We hope you will display the lordship of Christ in tangible ways in your thoughts, affections, and actions.

We see these aims beautifully demonstrated in an anonymous letter from the second century, the *Epistle to Diognetus*, which clearly describes the Christian in culture. It is lengthy but worthwhile:

> For the distinction between Christians and other men is neither in country nor language nor customs. For they do not dwell in cities in some place of their own, nor do they use any strange dialect, nor practice an extraordinary kind of life. This teaching of theirs has not been discovered by intellect or thought of busy men, nor are they the advocates of any human doctrine as some men are. . . . They dwell in their own fatherlands, but as if sojourners

in them; they share all things as citizens, and suffer all things as strangers. ... They marry as all men, they bear children, but they do not expose their offspring. They offer free hospitality, but guard their purity. ... They pass their time upon the earth, but they have their citizenship in heaven (Phil. 3:20). They obey the appointed laws, and they surpass the laws in their own lives. They love all men and are persecuted by all men. ... They are put to death and they gain life. ... They are warred upon by the Jews as foreigners and are persecuted by the Greeks, and those who hate them cannot state the cause of their enmity.[1]

Of course, we do not live in the second century. We live in a time that is similar yet distinct from that in which these Christian brothers and sisters lived. Our culture has its own artifacts of meaning—ideologies that demonstrate what our culture values and glorifies.

Let us consider the various cultural frameworks in which we find ourselves and faithfully follow the call of Christ to obey Him in all things. Whether that call is planting a garden in the backyard or fundraising for the local crisis pregnancy center or raising children at home or supporting legislation for true human flourishing or creating art for the glory of God, Christ calls us to faithfulness. We hope this book helps you as you engage and seek the restoration of the cultural spheres to which God calls you.

Notes

Introduction

1. Abraham Kuyper, "Sphere Sovereignty," in *Abraham Kuyper: A Centennial Reader*, ed. James D. Bratt (Grand Rapids, Mich.: Eerdmans, 1998), 461, 488.
2. H. Richard Niebuhr, *Christ and Culture* (New York: HarperSanFrancisco, 1996), 227.
3. C. S. Lewis, "Christianity and Culture" (March 1, 1940), in *Christian Reflections*, ed. Walter Hooper (Grand Rapids, Mich.: Eerdmans, 1967), 41.
4. Bruce Ashford, "Lessons from Father Abraham (Kuyper): Christianity, Politics, & the Public Square," *The Ethics and Religious Liberty Commission*, March 6, 2015; https://erlc.com/resource-library/articles/lessons-from-father-abraham-kuyper-christianity-politics-and-the-public-square.

Chapter One

1. This question, with its allusion to Psalm 8:4, is inspired by a subheading in Ken Myers's groundbreaking book *All God's Children and Blue Suede Shoes: Christians and Popular Culture* (Wheaton: Crossway, 1989).
2. Matthew Henry, *An Exposition of the New Testament: In Two Volumes*, vol. 1 (Edinburgh: Hamilton, Balfour, and Neill, 1757), 598 (spelling modernized).
3. For more on inaugurated eschatology, see Russell Moore, *The Kingdom of Christ* (Wheaton: Crossway, 2004) and George Eldon Ladd, *The Presence of the Future: The Eschatology of Biblical Realism* (Grand Rapids, Mich.: Eerdmans, 1994).
4. See Clement of Alexandria, *The Instructor*, in *The Ante-Nicene Fathers*, vol. 2, ed. Alexander Roberts and James Donaldson (New York: Charles Scribner's Sons, 1905).
5. See Rodney Stark, *The Rise of Christianity: How the Obscure, Marginal Jesus Movement Became the Dominant Religious Force in the Western World in a Few Centuries* (New York: HarperSanFrancisco, 1997).
6. J. C. Ryle, *Expository Thoughts on the Gospels. For Family and Private Use*, vol. 3 (London: William Hunt and Co., 1873), 216.
7. Ibid.
8. Ibid., 207.
9. Ibid., 207–08.
10. I owe this concept to F. Leroy Forlines and his strong emphasis on the four basic relationships as he described them in his books *Biblical Ethics: Ethics for Happier Living* (Nashville: Randall House, 1973) and *The Quest for Truth: Theology for a Postmodern World* (Nashville: Randall House, 2000).
11. Abraham Kuyper, "Sphere Sovereignty," in *Abraham Kuyper: A Centennial Reader*, ed. James D. Bratt (Grand Rapids, Mich.: Eerdmans, 1998), 461, 488.
12. See Rodney Stark, *The Victory of Reason: How Christianity Led to Freedom, Capitalism, and Western Success* (New York: Random House, 2007); Rodney Stark, *How the West Won: The Neglected Story of the Triumph of Modernity* (Wilmington, Del.: ISI, 2015); Rodney Stark, *For the Glory of God: How Monotheism Led to Reformations, Science, Witch-Hunts, and the End of Slavery* (Princeton: Princeton University Press, 2004); and Alvin J. Schmidt, *How Christianity Changed the World* (Grand Rapids, Mich.: Zondervan, 2004).
13. See "Changes in Worldview Among Christians over the Past 13 Years," *Barna*, March 9, 2009, https://www.barna.com/research/barna-survey-examines-changes-in-worldview-among-christians-over-the-past-13-years/.

14 Readers may find further discussion regarding the distinction between form and content in chapter six (E. Darrell Holley, "The Principles of the Christian Critical Tradition"), chapter seven (Matthew Steven Bracey, "The Arts and Entertainment"), and chapter eight (J. Matthew Pinson, "The Christian and Popular Culture").
15 Saint Augustine, *On Christian Teaching*, trans. R. P. H. Green (New York: Oxford University Press, 1997), 6, 47.
16 Andy Crouch, *Culture Making: Recovering Our Creative Calling* (Downers Grove, Ill.: IVP, 2013).
17 See Jeff Turnbough, "Understanding Culture: From a Missiological Perspective," *Integrity* 3 (Summer 2006): 65–89.
18 Frédéric Louis Godet, *Commentary on the Gospel of John with an Historical and Critical Introduction*, vol. 2, trans. Timothy Dwight (New York: Funk and Wagnalls, 1886), 335.
19 The classic work on this is H. Richard Niebuhr, *Christ and Culture* (New York: Harper and Row, 1956). Niebuhr's categories are Christ against culture, the Christ of culture, Christ above culture, Christ and culture in paradox, and Christ the transformer of culture. I use the first, second, and fourth categories in this treatment, since I think they are the main categories that have been employed by twentieth- and twenty-first-century evangelicals.
20 Myers, 18.
21 Russell Moore, "Pop Christianity and Pop Culture: Relating Mars Hill to Rolling Stone," *Fusion* 5, no. 3 (2009): 56.
22 Russell D. Moore, "Retaking Mars Hill: Paul Didn't Build Bridges to Popular Culture," *Touchstone* (September 2007).
23 Roger Scruton, *An Intelligent Person's Guide to Modern Culture* (South Bend, Ind.: St. Augustine's, 2000), 1–4. See also T. S. Eliot, "Notes Towards the Definition of Culture," in *Christianity and Culture* (New York: Harcourt, 1949); and Roger Scruton, *Culture Counts: Faith and Feeling in a World Besieged*, Brief Encounters (New York: Encounter, 2007).
24 Scruton, *An Intelligent Person's Guide to Modern Culture*, 1–4.
25 See chapter four by Matthew McAffee: "Creation, Sin, and Renewal."

CHAPTER TWO

1   For instance, consider John Dewey's famous quote: "Democracy has to be born anew every generation, and education is its midwife" (John Dewey, *The Middle Works of John Dewey, Volume 10, 1899–1924: Journal Articles, Essays, and Miscellany Published in the 1916–1917 Period*, 1st ed., ed. Jo Ann Boydston [Carbondale: Southern Illinois University Press, 2008], 139).
2   Søren Kierkegaard, *The Journals of Søren Kierkegaard*, ed. and trans. Alexander Dru (New York: Oxford University Press, 1938), IV, A, 164.
3   Alister McGrath, *Mere Apologetics* (London: SPCK, 2016), 30.
4   The individual's agency and ability to influence the flow of history is a common theme in the work of Francis Schaeffer. He highlights the motif often, but for a brief synopsis see Francis A. Schaeffer, *The Church Before the Watching World*, in *The Complete Works of Francis A. Schaeffer: A Christian Worldview*, 2nd ed. (Wheaton: Crossway, 1985), 168–71.
5   James W. Sire, *The Universe Next Door*, 5th ed. (Downers Grove, Ill.: IVP, 2009), 216–17.
6   See Christopher Talbot, "Communicating the Gospel: The Church's Mission and Ministry," in *The Promise of Arminian Theology: Essays in Honor of F. Leroy Forlines*, ed. Matthew Steven Bracey and W. Jackson Watts (Nashville: Randall House Academic, 2016), 223–26.
7   This account is largely the flow that Schaeffer follows as he maps culture's degradation below "the line of despair." See Francis A. Schaeffer, *The God Who Is There* (Downers Grove, Ill.: InterVarsity, 1968), in *The Francis A. Schaeffer Trilogy* (Wheaton: Crossway, 1990), 8.
8   Gene Edward Veith, Jr., *Postmodern Times: A Christian Guide to Contemporary Thought and Culture* (Wheaton: Crossway, 1994), 29.
9   Ibid.

10 Ibid.
11 Thomas Aquinas, *On the Truth of the Catholic Faith: Summa contra Gentiles*, ed. Joseph Kenny, vol. 4: Salvation, trans. Charles J. O'Neil (Garden City, N.Y.: Doubleday, 1957), 4.1.5.
12 Peter Kreeft, *The Platonic Tradition* (South Bend, Ind.: St. Augustine's Press, 2018), 68.
13 Ibid., 70.
14 Ibid., 70-71.
15 Veith, 32.
16 Michael W. Goheen and Craig G. Bartholomew, *Living at the Crossroads: An Introduction to Christian Worldview* (Grand Rapids, Mich.: Baker Academic, 2008), 70.
17 René Descartes, "Meditations on the First Philosophy," in *The Longman Standard History of Philosophy*, ed. Daniel Kolak and Garrett Thomson (New York: Pearson Longman, 2006), 416.
18 Joshua D. Chatraw and Mark D. Allen, *Apologetics at the Cross: An Introduction for Christian Witness* (Grand Rapids, Mich.: Zondervan, 2018), 203.
19 Ibid.
20 McGrath, 27.
21 D. A. Carson, "Christian Witness in an Age of Pluralism," in *God and Culture: Essays in Honor of Carl F. H. Henry*, ed. D. A. Carson and John D. Woodbridge (Grand Rapids, Mich.: Eerdmans, 1993), 52.
22 See J. P. Moreland, *Christianity and the Nature of Science: A Philosophical Investigation*, 2nd ed. (Grand Rapids, Mich.: Baker, 1989); and J. P. Moreland, *Scientism and Secularism: Learning to Respond to a Dangerous Ideology* (Wheaton: Crossway, 2018).
23 H. R. Rookmaaker, *Modern Art and the Death of Culture* (Wheaton: Crossway, 1994), 50.
24 Chatraw and Allen, 85.
25 Immanuel Kant, *An Answer to the Question: What is Enlightenment?* (London: Penguin, 2013), 1, quoted in Chatraw and Allen, 85.
26 Darrell Holley uses this phrase when he lectures on these men in his World Literature course at Welch College.
27 The full, rightly translated quotation reads, "Religion is the sigh of the oppressed creature, the heart of a heartless world, and the soul of soulless conditions. It is the opium of the people" (Karl Marx, *Critique of Hegel's 'Philosophy Of Right'*, trans. Joseph J. O'Malley [Cambridge: Cambridge University Press, 1977], 131).
28 Friedrich Nietzsche, *The Gay Science: With a Prelude in Rhymes and an Appendix of Songs*, trans. Walter Kaufmann (New York: Knopf Doubleday, 2010), 181.
29 Friedrich Nietzsche, *The Anti-Christ*, trans. H. L. Mencken (New York: Cosimo, 2005), 91.
30 F. Leroy Forlines, *The Quest for Truth: Theology for a Postmodern World* (Nashville: Randall House, 2001), 96.
31 See Richard M. Weaver, *Ideas Have Consequences* (Chicago: University of Chicago Press, 1948)
32 Edward John Carnell, *An Introduction to Christian Apologetics: A Philosophical Defense of the Trinitarian-Theistic Faith* (Grand Rapids, Mich.: Eerdmans, 1973), 226.
33 Ibid.
34 Weaver, 2.
35 Francis A. Schaeffer, *The God Who Is There: The Book That Makes Sense Out of Our World* (Downers Grove, Ill.: InterVarsity, 1968), 16. Schaeffer did not use the word *postmodernity* but clearly understood the idea that has come to be called by that name.
36 Weaver, 3.
37 Schaeffer, *The God Who Is There*, 13.
38 Phillip T. Morgan, "Worldview and Culture in the Thought of F. Leroy Forlines," in *The Promise of Arminian Theology*, 27.
39 McGrath, 32.

40　Charles Taylor, *A Secular Age* (Cambridge: Harvard University Press, 2007), 716–17.
41　Thomas C. Oden, *After Modernity . . . What?* (1979; repr., Grand Rapids, Mich.: Zondervan, 1992), 11.
42　David F. Wells, *The Courage to Be Protestant: Truth-lovers, Marketers, and Emergents in the Postmodern World* (Grand Rapids, Mich.: Eerdmans, 2008), 107.
43　Forlines, 16.
44　Ibid., 14.
45　McGrath, 32.
46　Carnell, 228. Like Schaeffer, Carnell did not use the word *postmodernity* but interacted with the concept before it went by that name.
47　Weaver, 4.
48　Forlines, 14.
49　Taylor, 473.
50　Yuval Levin, *The Fractured Republic: Renewing America's Social Contract in the Age of Individualism* (New York: Basic, 2017), 148.
51　Wells, 77.
52　Greg Forster, *Joy For the World: How Christianity Lost Its Cultural Influence and Can Begin Rebuilding It* (Wheaton: Crossway, 2014), 63.

Chapter Three

1　Roger Scruton, *Conservatism: An Invitation to the Great Tradition* (New York: All Points, 2017), 6.
2　Different scholars may employ different terms to describe the content of this chapter, such as "modern conservatism," which refers partly to the historical period in which Edmund Burke emerged, or "paleo-conservatism," which aims partly to distinguish it from neo-conservatism. However, I would distinguish it from those terms and have adopted the nomenclature of "classical conservatism" for two reasons: (1) many of the themes of the conservatism discussed in this chapter have a basis in the classical period, with roots in Hebrew-Christian and Greco-Roman belief and practice, to which Burke gave expression; and (2) the conservatism discussed in this chapter is distinct from other, less historic forms of conservatism, particularly in its post-Industrial and neo-conservative manifestations.
3　Dreher also refers to Kirk as the "patron saint of crunchy conservatives" and "the paterfamilias of all crunchy cons" (Rod Dreher, *Crunchy Cons: The New Conservative Counterculture and Its Return to Roots* [New York: Three Rivers, 2006], 10, 26, 246). By his reference to *crunchy cons*, also the name of his book, Dreher distinguishes a classical conservatism from a modern one.
4　Kirk suggested six canons in *The Conservative Mind: From Burke to Eliot*, 7th rev. ed. (1953; repr., Washington, DC: Gateway, 2014). Then, about thirty years later with the publication of *The Portable Conservative Reader* (New York: Viking Penguin, 1982), he varied the canons, combining some and adding others. Finally, in *The Politics of Prudence* (Bryan Mawr, Penn.: Intercollegiate Studies Institute, 1993), Kirk laid out ten canons, which forms the model that this chapter adopts.
5　Winston Churchill captured Burke's balance of the prerogative of liberty and the order of truth when he wrote, "On the one hand he [Burke] is revealed as a foremost apostle of Liberty, on the other as the roundtable champion of Authority" (Winston S. Churchill, "Consistency in Politics," in *Amid These Storms: Thoughts and Adventures* [New York: Charles Scribner's Sons, 1932], 40).
6　Jesse Norman characterizes Burke's view as being that "absolute freedom or 'license' is disastrous both for individuals and for the social order" (*Edmund Burke: The First Conservative* [New York: Basic, 2015], 258).
7　Kirk pointed to "belief in a transcendent order, or body of natural law, which rules society as well as conscience" (*Conservative Mind*, 8). He stated something similar in *Reader*: "[C]

NOTES

onservatives generally believe that there exists a transcendent moral order, to which we ought to try to conform the ways of society.... [W]ith few exceptions conservatives recognize the need for enduring moral authority. This conviction contrasts strongly with the liberal's utilitarian view of the state" (Introduction to *Reader*, xv).

8 Classically, many authors understood "divinity" to refer to a theistic deity. George F. Will represents an aberration to this rule. Will authored *The Conservative Sensibility* (New York: Hachette, 2019) in which he reviews "conservatism without theism" (457–511). Dreher, however, writes that traditional conservatives "stand apart from mainstream conservatives in several basic ways, but the thread that ties them all together... is religion.... [I]t gives... the impetus to orient their lives and their efforts toward an ultimate end: serving God, not the self" (*Crunchy Cons*, 180).

9 William Ernest Henley, "Out of the Night that Covers Me" (1875), in *A Book of Verses* (London: David Nutt, 1888), 57.

10 Edmund Burke, *Reflections on the Revolution in France: And on the Proceedings in Certain Societies in London Relative to That Event*, Penguin Classics (New York: Penguin, 2004), 173.

11 Edmund Burke, "Speech on Unitarians' Petition for Relief" (May 11, 1792), in *The Writings and Speeches of Edmund Burke*, ed. Paul Langford, vol. IV, *Party, Parliament, and the Dividing of the Whigs: 1780–1794*, ed. P. J. Marshall and Donald Bryant (Oxford: Oxford University Press, 2015), 491.

12 John Crowe Ransom, "Reconstructed but Unregenerate," in Twelve Southerners, *I'll Take My Stand: The South and the Agrarian Tradition*, 75th anniv. ed. (Baton Rouge: Louisiana State University Press, 2006), 12.

13 Kirk, *Politics of Prudence*, 17.

14 Ibid., *Conservative Mind*, 8.

15 Conservatives and liberals may interpret the natural law differently from one another, but they each affirm that it exists and plays an important role for ethics and morality. In addition, the doctrine of natural law varies from the theory of natural theology. Whereas the former posits that a moral law exists within the state of nature (an ontological claim), the latter holds that man may develop a theology from it (an epistemological claim). Likewise, a broadly Reformed understanding of natural law differs from a Thomistic interpretation of it. While such distinctions are relevant to the topic at hand, further discussion about them is beyond the scope of this chapter.

16 See T. S. Eliot, *The Idea of a Christian Society* (New York: Harcourt, Brace and Company, 1940).

17 Kirk, *Politics of Prudence*, 18.

18 Nicholas Wolterstorff, "Christian Learning in and for a Pluralist Society," in *Educating for Shalom: Essays on Christian Higher Education*, ed. Clarence W. Joldersma and Gloria Goris Stronks (Grand Rapids, Mich.: Eerdmans, 2004), 259.

19 G. K. Chesterton, *Orthodoxy* (Dover, N.Y.: Mineola, 2012), 40; Jaroslav Pelikan, *The Vindication of Tradition* (New Haven: Yale University Press, 1984), 65.

20 See C. S. Lewis, *Surprised by Joy: The Shape of My Early Life* (New York: Harcourt, 1955), 200–01, 206, 209.

21 Kirk, *Conservative Mind*, 10.

22 Roger Scruton, *The Need for Nations* (London: Civitas, 2004), 36.

23 Burke, *Reflections*, 172–73, 183 (spelling modernized).

24 Ibid., 9. See also Kirk, *Politics of Prudence*, 18: "When successful revolutionaries have effaced old customs, derided old conventions, and broken the continuity of social institutions—why, presently they discover the necessity of establishing fresh customs, conventions, and continuity, but that process is painful and slow, and the new social order that eventually emerges may be much inferior to the old order that radicals overthrew in their zeal for Earthly Paradise."

25 Kirk, *Politics of Prudence*, 18.
26 Rudyard Kipling, "Kaa's Hunting," in *The Jungle Books*, The 100 Greatest Books Ever Written (Norwalk, Conn.: Easton, 1980), 27 (italics added).
27 Rod Dreher, *Live Not by Lies: A Manual for Christian Dissidents* (New York: Sentinel, 2020), 113–14, 126.
28 See Yuval Levin, *The Great Debate: Edmund Burke, Thomas Paine, and the Birth of Right and Left* (New York: Basic, 2014), 67.
29 Kirk, *Reader*, xvi; *Politics of Prudence*, 18.
30 Kirk, *Reader*, xvi.
31 Ibid., *Conservative Mind*, 42.
32 Ibid., *Politics of Prudence*, xvi; see also 19–20.
33 Ibid., *Reader*, xvi.
34 Burke, *Reflections*, 183.
35 Ibid., 187–89. As an English conservative, Burke would have supported religious establishment as a matter of law and morality. While the American conservative would not support *legal* religious establishment, owing to the Establishment Clause in the First Amendment ("Congress shall make no law respecting an establishment of religion," U. S. Constitution, amend. I), he or she would support the good moral instruction that issues forth from the institution of the church. Classical conservatism makes room for such differences because it respects local distinctions (that promote virtue rather than vice).
36 Ibid., *Reflections*, 189.
37 Ibid., 188.
38 "The bulk of mankind have neither leisure nor knowledge sufficient to reason right" (Philip Dormer Stanhope Chesterfield, "The World," no. 112 [February 20, 1755], in *The Letters and Works of Philip Dormer Stanhope, Earl of Chesterfield; including Numerous Letters and Papers Now First Published from the Original Manuscripts*, ed. Lord Mahon, 5 vols. [Philadelphia, Pa.: J. B. Lippincott, 1892], 5:338). Likewise, "Most people have neither the time nor the inclination to delve deeply into theories and evidence, much less the expertise to do so effectively" (Thomas Sowell, *The Quest for Cosmic Justice* [New York: Simon and Schuster, 1999], 135).
39 Kirk, *Conservative Mind*, 42.
40 Ibid.
41 Edmund Burke, "Speech on Reform of Representation in the House of Commons" (May 7, 1782), in *The Speeches of the Right Honourable Edmund Burke, in the House of Commons, and in Westminster-Hall*, 4 vols. (London: Longman, Hurst, Rees, Orme, and Brown, Paternoster-Row; and J. Ridgway, Piccadilly, 1816), 3:47.
42 Kirk, *Conservative Mind*, 37.
43 John Randolph of Roanoke, quoted in Kirk, *Reader*, xvii.
44 Thomas Sowell, "Twisted History," in *The Thomas Sowell Reader* (New York: Basic, 2011), 18.
45 Jean-Jacques Rousseau, *Discourse on Political Economy and The Social Contract*, trans. Christopher Betts, Oxford World's Classics (Oxford: Oxford University Press, 2009), 45.
46 Kirk, *Conservative Mind*, 8; see also Kirk, *Reader*, xvii.
47 John Adams, "Letters to John Taylor, of Caroline, Virginia," in *The Political Writings of John Adams*, ed. George W. Carey (Washington, D.C.: Regnery, 2000), 373; John Paul II, *Centesimus Annus*, §13, quoted in Michael Novak, "American Realities and Catholic Social Thought," in *Social Justice Isn't What You Think It Is*, by Michael Novak and Paul Adams, with Elizabeth Shaw (New York: Encounter, 2015), 135; Leo XIII, *Rerum Novarum*, §17, quoted in Michael Novak, "Leo's *Rerum Novarum*," in *Social Justice Isn't What You Think It Is*, 102; C. S. Lewis, "Membership," in *The Weight of Glory and Other Addresses* (1949; repr., New York: HarperCollins, 1980), 163–71; Thomas Nagel, "The Meaning of Equality," *Washington*

University Law Quarterly 1979, no. 1 (January 1979): 28; Michael Novak, "Six Secular Uses of 'Social Justice,'" in *Social Justice Isn't What You Think It Is*, 31; Roger Scruton, *I Drink Therefore I Am: A Philosopher's Guide to Wine* (New York: Continuum, 2010), 166; Roger Scruton, *The Meaning of Conservatism*, 2nd ed. (London: Macmillan, 1984), 63, 86, 103.

48 Abraham Kuyper, *Lectures on Calvinism* (Grand Rapids, Mich.: Eerdmans, 1987), 95, 195.
49 Kirk, *Conservative Mind*, 8.
50 Carl Henry notes this connection in *Christian Personal Ethics* (Grand Rapids, Mich.: Eerdmans, 1957), 102–03.
51 Lewis, "Membership," 168, 171.
52 Ronald H. Nash, *Freedom, Justice and the State* (Lanham, Md.: University Press of America, 1980), 76–77. See also Roger Scruton, *How to Be a Conservative* (New York: Bloomsbury, 2014), 51.
53 Kuyper, *Lectures on Calvinism*, 31, 60; Kirk, *Conservative Mind*, 9; Kirk, Introduction to *Reader*, xvii.
54 U. S. Constitution, art. 1, §9; amend. XIV, §1.
55 Kirk, *Conservative Mind*, 9.
56 Thomas Sowell, *Intellectuals and Society* (New York: Basic, 2012), ch. 4 (italics removed). He also discusses the concept of cosmic justice in *Black Rednecks and White Liberals* (New York: Encounter, 2006), ch. 6; *Intellectuals and Race* (New York: Basic, 2013), 107; and *The Quest for Cosmic Justice*.
57 Sowell, *Intellectuals and Race*, 117 (italics removed). See also Thomas Sowell, "The Money of Fools," in *The Thomas Sowell Reader*, 10–11.
58 Walter Lippmann, *Public Opinion* (New York: Harcourt, Brace, 1922), 18.
59 Kirk, *Conservative Mind*, 8.
60 Ibid., 255.
61 "Because of human restlessness, mankind would grow rebellious under any utopian domination, and would break out once more in violent discontent—or else expire of boredom. To seek for utopia is to end in disaster" (Kirk, *Reader*, xvii).
62 Kirk, *Conservative Mind*, 10.
63 Pelagius (c. 354–418), John Locke (1632–1704), and Jean-Jacques Rousseau (1712–1778) were each thinkers who denied the doctrine of original sin, believing that human beings are not born with innate knowledge or *a priori* ideas but rather are "blank slates."
64 J. D. Vance, *Hillbilly Elegy: A Memoir of a Family and Culture in Crisis* (New York: Harper, 2016).
65 Kirk, *Conservative Mind*, 10.
66 James Fitzjames Stephen, *Liberty, Equality, Fraternity* (New York: Holt & Williams, 1873), 45.
67 Ronald H. Nash, *Poverty and Wealth: Why Socialism Doesn't Work* (Richardson, Tex.: Probe, 1986), 81.
68 Paul Elmer More, "Property and Law," in *Aristocracy and Justice: Shelburne Essays*, 9th series (Boston: Houghton Mifflin Co., 1915), 133–34. "Socialism rests on two assumptions. First, that community of ownership will, for practical purposes, eliminate the greed and injustice of civilized life. . . . Secondly, that under community of control the material productivity of society will not be seriously diminished."
69 Edwin Lawrence Godkin, "Who Will Pay the Bills of Socialism?" (Forum, June, 1894), in *Problems of Modern Democracy: Political and Economic Essays*, 3rd ed. (New York: Charles Scribner's Sons, 1898), 225–49. See also a delightful fable on this topic in Thomas Sowell, "Grasshopper and Ant," in *The Thomas Sowell Reader*, 3–5, also accessible online.
70 Fyodor Dostoevsky, *The Brothers Karamazov*, trans. Constance Garnett (New York: Macmillan, 1926), 22.
71 Kirk, *Reader*, xviii.
72 Burke, *Reflections*, 149.
73 Thomas Aquinas, *The Summa Theologiae of St. Thomas Aquinas*, trans. Fathers of the English Dominican Province (1920), II–II, 66, 2, http://www.newadvent.org/summa/index.html.

74 The same principle holds true with respect to the Tenth Commandment about coveting your neighbor's house (Exodus 20:17; Deuteronomy 5:21).
75 John Calvin, *Institutes of the Christian Religion*, vol. 1, trans. Ford Lewis Battles, The Library of Christian Classics, ed. John T. McNeill (Louisville: Westminster John Knox Press, 2006), 408–09.
76 Chad Brand, *Flourishing Faith: A Baptist Primer on Work, Economics, and Civic Stewardship*, The Oikonomia Series (Grand Rapids, Mich.: Christian's Library Press, 2012), 73–74 (italics removed).
77 Carl F. H. Henry, *Aspects of Christian Social Ethics* (Grand Rapids, Mich.: Eerdmans, 1964), 124, 164.
78 Kirk, *Politics of Prudence*, 22.
79 Kirk, *Conservative Mind*, 10. See Kirk, *Reader*, xvi; and Kirk, *Politics of Prudence*, 19–20.
80 Jay W. Richards, *Money, Greed, and God: The Christian Case for Free Enterprise*, 10th anniv. ed. (New York: Harper One, 2019), 21. Different economists and political philosophers define words like *communism* and *socialism* in different ways and understand the relationship between them in different ways. This sentence reflects the categorization of the economist Richards, as well as the economic tradition that he follows. Thomas Sowell also identifies Russia, China, and Cambodia with socialism. See Thomas Sowell, "The Survival of the Left," in *Barbarians Inside the Gates and Other Controversial Essays* (Stanford, Calif.: Hoover Institution Press, 1999), 104.
81 Kirk, *Politics of Prudence*, 21.
82 Scruton, *The Meaning of Conservatism*, 103.
83 Burke, *Reflections*, 150.
84 Sowell, "The Survival of the Left," 104.
85 See Alexis de Tocqueville, *Democracy in America*, trans. Arthur Goldhammer (New York: The Library of America, 2004).
86 Kirk, *Conservative Mind*, 9. *Leviathan* is an image for the totalitarian state that Thomas Hobbes had previously used.
87 Richards, 21; Sowell, "The Survival of the Left," 104.
88 John Bolt, *Economic Shalom: A Reformed Primer on Faith, Work, and Human Flourishing*, The Oikonomia Series (Grand Rapids, Mich.: Christian's Library Press, 2013), 145–64.
89 Richards, 83–110.
90 Michael Novak, "A Mirage?" in *Social Justice Isn't What You Think It Is*, 46.
91 Robert Nozick, *Anarchy, State, and Utopia* (New York: Basic, 1968), 161. Mark Coppenger discusses this illustration in *Moral Apologetics for Contemporary Christians: Pushing Back Against Cultural and Religious Critics*, B&H Studies in Christian Ethics, ed. Daniel R. Heimbach (Nashville: B&H, 2011), 30–31.
92 For further reflection on income gaps, see Victor V. Claar and Robin J. Klay, "Rich Man, Poor Man, Beggar Man, Thief: Attending to the Poor or Worrying about Income Gaps," in *Economics in Christian Perspective: Theory, Policy and Life Choices* (Downers Grove, Ill.: IVP Academic, 2007), 188–212.
93 Kirk, *Politics of Prudence*, 22 (italics removed).
94 Ibid.
95 Kirk, *Politics of Prudence*, 23.
96 Michael Novak, "Social Justice Isn't Want You Think It Is," in *Social Justice Isn't What You Think It Is*, 24–25.
97 Kirk, *Politics of Prudence*, 23.
98 U. S. Constitution, art. 1, sec. 8.
99 U. S. Constitution, amend. 10.
100 Bruce Ashford and Chris Pappalardo, *One Nation Under God: A Christian Hope for American Politics* (Nashville: B&H Academic, 2015), 39.

101 Kirk, *Politics of Prudence*, 23.
102 Ibid.
103 Ibid., 24.
104 I do not know the source of this anecdote. I first heard it in a lecture given by Russell Moore, who said he heard it from another speaker and was unsure whether it was original with him or not.
105 Kirk, *Politics of Prudence*, 24.
106 The Right Hon. Edmund Burke to the Comte de Mercy (August 16, 1793), in *Correspondence of the Right Honourable Edmund Burke; Between the Year 1744, and the Period of His Decease, in 1797*, ed. Charles William, Earl Fitzwilliam, and Sir Richard Bourke, 4 vols. (London: Francis & John Rivington, 1844), 4:138 (italics added).
107 See Henry Sumner Maine, *Popular Government: Four Essays* (New York: Holt & Williams, 1873).
108 Kirk, *Politics of Prudence*, 25.
109 C. S. Lewis, "On the Reading of Old Books," in *God in the Dock: Essays on Theology and Ethics*, ed. Walter Hooper (Grand Rapids, Mich.: Eerdmans, 1970), 202; C. S. Lewis, Introduction to Athanasius, *The Incarnation: The Treatise* De Incarnatione Verbi Dei, trans. A Religious of C.S.M.V., Popular Patristics Series, No. 3 (Crestwood, N.Y.: St. Vladimir's Seminary Press, 1996), 5.
110 Burke, *Reflections*, 106.
111 Kirk, *Politics of Prudence*, 25.
112 Burke, *Reflections*, 119.
113 Kirk, *Conservative Mind*, 9.
114 Ibid., *Politics of Prudence*, 25.
115 U. S. Constitution, amend. I
116 Dreher, *Crunchy Cons*, 1–2.

Chapter Four

1   All translations in this chapter are the author's own, unless otherwise noted.
2   See JoAnn Scurlock, "Searching for Meaning in Genesis 1:2: Purposeful Creation out of Chaos without Kampf," in *Creation and Chaos: A Reconsideration of Hermann Gunkel's Chaoskampf Hypothesis*, ed. JoAnn Scurlock and Richard H. Beal (Winona Lake, Ind.: Eisenbrauns, 2013), 56–61.
3   Matthew McAffee, "Creation and the Role of Wisdom in Proverbs 8: What Can We Learn?" *Southeastern Theological Review* 10 (2019): 44–46.
4   We must maintain both aspects of this statement. Some recent scholars have attempted to correct the failure to give proper attention to the functional nature of creation (e.g., John H. Walton, *The Lost World of Genesis One: Ancient Cosmology and the Origins Debate* [Downers Grove, Ill.: IVP Academic, 2009], 38–46). One must not, however, overcorrect so as to ignore the fact that God did create the substance or material of creation.
5   For a similar arrangement, see David T. Tsumura, "Rediscovery of the Ancient Near East and Its Implications for Genesis 1–2," in *Since the Beginning: Interpreting Genesis 1 and 2 through the Ages*, ed. Kyle R. Greenwood (Grand Rapids, Mich.: Baker Academic, 2018), 225.
6   Francis A. Schaeffer, *Pollution and the Death of Man: The Christian View of Ecology* (Wheaton: Tyndale House, 1970), 54.
7   See, e.g., Klaas Schilder, *Christ and Culture*, trans. William Helder and Albert H. Oosterhoff (Hamilton, Ont.: Lucerna, 2016); and F. Leroy Forlines, *The Quest for Truth: Answering Life's Inescapable Questions* (Nashville: Randall House, 2001), 141–42, 232–33.
8   See A. R. Millard and P. Bordreuil, "A Statue from Syria with Assyrian and Aramaic Inscriptions," *Biblical Archaeologist* 45 (1982): 135–41.
9   See Umberto Cassuto, *The Documentary Hypothesis and the Composition of the Pentateuch*, with an Introduction by Joshua A. Berman (New York: Shalem Press, 2006), 56–58. For a fuller

discussion, see Peter J. Gentry and Stephen J. Wellum, *Kingdom through Covenant: A Biblical Understanding of the Covenants* (Wheaton: Crossway, 2012), 155–61.
10 Augustine, *City of God*, ed. David Knowles, trans. Henry Bettenson (New York: Penguin, 1972), 688–89; cited by Michael Horton, *Introducing Covenant Theology* (Grand Rapids, Mich.: Baker, 2006), 85.
11 Schaeffer, 60–61.
12 Forlines, 140–42.
13 See Matthew McAffee, *Life and Mortality in Ugaritic: A Lexical and Literary Analysis*, Explorations in Ancient Near Eastern Civilizations 7 (University Park, Pa.: Eisenbrauns, imprint of Pennsylvania State University Press, 2019), 255n291.
14 Schaeffer, 50.
15 Ibid., 51.
16 Forlines, 141.
17 Jacob Milgrom, *Leviticus 1–16*, Anchor Bible 3 (New York: Doubleday, 1991), 254–56; cited in Allen P. Ross, *Holiness to the Lord: A Guide to the Exposition of the Book of Leviticus* (Grand Rapids, Mich.: Baker Academic, 2002), 124.
18 Ross, 123.
19 Virginia Morell, "Why Do Animals Sometimes Kill Their Babies?" *National Geographic*, March 28, 2014, https://www.nationalgeographic.com/news/2014/3/140328-sloth-bear-zoo-infanticide-chimps-bonobos-animals.
20 Herman Melville, *Moby Dick* (New York: Charles Scribner's Sons, 1902), 240. I would like to thank Matthew Bracey for bringing this passage to my attention.
21 Ibid.
22 John Milton, *John Milton: The Complete Poems*, ed. John Leonard, Penguin Classics (London: Penguin, 1998), 197; book IV, lines 205–10, 215–17.
23 J. A. Emerton, *Studies on the Language and Literature of the Bible: Selected Works of J.A. Emerton*, ed. Graham Davies and Robert Gordon, Supplements to Vetus Testamentum 165 (Leiden: Brill, 2015), 465.
24 See Matthew McAffee, "Forlinesean Eschatology: A Progressive Covenantal Approach," in *The Promise of Arminian Theology*, ed. Matthew Steven Bracey and W. Jackson Watts (Nashville: Randall House Academic, 2016), 144.
25 Christopher J. H. Wright, *The Mission of God's People: A Biblical Theology of the Church's Mission*, Biblical Theology for Life, ed. Jonathan Lunde (Grand Rapids, Mich.: Zondervan, 2010), 56.
26 Compare also Deuteronomy 5:15 where Sabbath observance is grounded in the Exodus event. Since God has rescued His people from the slavery of Egypt, they must keep the Sabbath.
27 Schaeffer, 73.
28 Ibid., 90.

Chapter Five

1 Roy Rosenzweig and David Thelen, *The Presence of the Past: Popular Uses of History in American Life* (New York: Columbia University Press, 1998), 9.
2 Russell Kirk, *The Conservative Mind: From Burke to Eliot*, 7th ed. (Washington D.C.: Gateway, 2014), 41, 43.
3 Edmund Burke, *Reflections on the Revolution in France*, in *The Works of Edmund Burke, with A Memoir*, vol. I (New York: Harper and Brothers, 1860), 494.
4 Philip Dormer Stanhope Chesterfield, "The World" no. 112 (February 20, 1755), in *The Letters and Works of Philip Dormer Stanhope, Earl of Chesterfield; including Numerous Letters and Papers Now First Published from the Original Manuscripts*, ed. Lord Mahon, 5 vols. (Philadelphia: J. B. Lippincott, 1892), 5:337–38.

5 Sophocles, *Antigone*, lines 560–62, trans. Richard Emil Braun (New York: Oxford University Press, 1973).
6 Kirk, 45.
7 Sophocles, lines 1291–93.
8 Kirk, 43.
9 Ibid., 42.
10 Jaraslov Pelikan, *The Vindication of Tradition* (New Haven: Yale University Press, 1984), 65.
11 Kirk, 45.
12 Bradley G. Green, *The Gospel and the Mind: Recovering and Shaping the Intellectual Life* (Wheaton: Crossway, 2010), 44.
13 Robert F. Rea, *Why Church History Matters: An Invitation to Love and Learn from Our Past* (Downers Grove, Ill.: IVP Academic, 2014), 23.
14 Ibid.
15 Horace, *Odes*, Book II, X *Recitius vives*, lines 17–18, in Horace, *The Complete Odes and Epodes*, trans. David West (New York: Oxford University Press, 1997), 64.
16 Virgil, *Aeneid*, trans. Robert Fitzgerald (New York: Vintage Classics, 1983), 105.
17 Kirk, 21.
18 F. Leroy Forlines, *Biblical Ethics: Ethics for Happier Living* (Nashville: Randall House, 1973), 27.
19 Rea, 30.
20 Marc Bloch, *The Historian's Craft*, trans. Peter Putnam (New York: Vintage, 1953), 4.
21 Ibid.
22 Matthew Steven Bracey, "Is History 'Bunk'? A Biblical Theology of History," *Helwys Society Forum*, September 10, 2012, https://www.helwyssocietyforum.com/is-history-bunk-a-biblical-theology-of-history/.
23 Green, 35.
24 Ibid., 41.
25 Francis A. Schaeffer, *Escape from Reason* (1968; rev., Downers Grove, Ill.: InterVarsity, 2006), 118.
26 Earl E. Cairns, *God and Man in Time: A Christian Approach to Historiography* (Grand Rapids, Mich.: Baker, 1979), 31.
27 Gordon H. Clark, *Historiography, Secular and Religious*, 2nd ed. (Jefferson, Md.: Trinity Foundation, 1994), 312.
28 Ibid.
29 Ibid., 228.
30 Augustine, *Concerning the City of God Against the Pagans*, trans. Henry Bettenson (New York: Penguin, 2003), 5.
31 Clark, 216.
32 Ibid.
33 Augustine, *On Christian Teaching*, trans. R. P. H. Green (New York: Oxford University Press, 2008), 39.
34 J. Matthew Pinson, "'Renewal through Retrieval': On the Value of Tradition," unpublished lecture presented at the South Georgia Free Will Baptist Heritage Conference, August 6–7, 2010, np.
35 Roger Scruton, *An Intelligent Person's Guide to Modern Culture* (South Bend, Ind.: St. Augustine's, 2000), 23.
36 Ibid., 23–24.
37 See Roger Scruton's analysis of Ferdinand Tönnies's *Germeinschaft and Gesellschaft* in *An Intelligent Person's Guide to Modern Culture*, 24.
38 Ned Smith, "Need to 'Rent-a-Grandma'? Try This New Franchise," *Business News Daily*, June 6, 2011, https://www.businessnewsdaily.com/1049-mature-women-rent-a-grandma-employment-franchise.html.

39 Christopher Talbot, "The Narcissism of Now," *Helwys Society Forum*, September 8, 2013, http://www.helwyssocietyforum.com/the-narcissism-of-now/.
40 Pinson.
41 Ibid.
42 John Burrow, *A History of Histories: Epics, Chronicles, Romances and Inquiries from Herodotus and Thucydides to the Twentieth Century* (New York: Vintage, 2009), 435.
43 William D. Dennison, *Karl Marx*, Great Thinkers (Phillipsburg, N.J.: P&R, 2017), 47.
44 Ibid.
45 Burrow, 427.
46 Jean-Louis Panne et al., *The Black Book of Communism: Crimes, Terror, Repression* (Cambridge: Harvard University Press, 1999), 4.
47 R. Laurence Moore, "Insiders and Outsiders in American Historical Narrative and American History," in *Religion in American History: A Reader*, ed. Jon Butler and Harry S. Stout (New York: Oxford University Press, 1998), 203.
48 See Burrow; Christopher Watkin, *Michel Foucault*, Great Thinkers (Phillipsburg, N.J.: P&R, 2018); and Michel-Rolph Trouillot, *Silencing the Past: Power and the Production of History*, 2nd ed. (Boston: Beacon, 2015).
49 While the specific groups defined as oppressors and victims may change with specific cultural contexts, the basic historical approach remains the same.
50 See Dipesh Chakrabarty, "Provincializing Europe: Postcoloniality and the Critique of History," in *The New Imperial Histories Reader*, ed. Stephen Howe (New York: Routledge, 2010), 55–71.
51 See Howard Zinn, "The Uses of Scholarship," in *Howard Zinn on History* (New York: Seven Stories, 2001), 177–88; and James Green, *Taking History to Heart: The Power of the Past in Building Social Movements* (Amherst: University of Massachusetts Press, 2000).
52 See Burrow, 397; Richard Handler and Eric Gabler, *The New History in an Old Museum: Creating the Past at Colonial Williamsburg* (Durham: Duke University Press, 1997); and Alan Taylor, *American Colonies* (New York: Penguin, 2001).
53 Green, 43.
54 Richard M. Weaver, *Visions of Order: The Cultural Crisis of Our Time* (Baton Rouge: Louisiana State University Press, 1964), 41.
55 Green, 46.
56 Kirk, 46.
57 See Paul Boyer, *When Time Shall Be No More: Prophecy Belief in Modern American Culture*, Studies in Cultural History (Cambridge: Belknap, 1994).
58 C. S. Lewis, *Surprised by Joy: The Shape of My Early Life* (San Diego, Calif.: Harcourt, 1955), 207.
59 For examples of this practice, see Phillip T. Morgan and J. Matthew Pinson, *Light and Truth: A Seventy-fifth Anniversary Pictorial History of Welch College* (Gallatin, Tenn.: Welch College Press, 2018); and Phillip T. Morgan, *Heads Free Will Baptist Church: A Rich Heritage; A Bright Future* (Cedar Hill, Tenn.: Heads Free Will Baptist Church, 2015).

CHAPTER SIX

1 This chapter first appeared as: Darrell Holley, "The Principles of the Christian Critical Tradition," *Integrity: A Journal of Christian Thought* 1 (2000): 153–70. This chapter interacts with the King James Version (KJV), which is public domain, rather than the English Standard Version (ESV).
2 Leon Trotsky, "The Formalist School of Poetry and Marxism," in *Critical Theory since Plato*, ed. Hazard Adams (New York: Harcourt, Brace, Jovanovich, 1971), 827.
3 Georg Wilhelm Friedrich Hegel, "Philosophy of Fine Art," in *On Art, Religion, and Philosophy*, ed. J. Glenn Gray (New York: Harper and Row, 1970), 29–30.

4. Marcel Proust, quoted in H. R. Rookmaaker, *Modern Art and the Death of a Culture* (Downers Grove, Ill.: InterVarsity, 1970), 11.
5. Hegel, 59.
6. Dorothy Sayers, *Christian Letters to a Post-Christian World* (Grand Rapids, Mich.: Eerdmans, 1969), 69–70.
7. Hegel, 25.
8. Ibid., 29.
9. Ibid., 81.
10. Francis A. Schaeffer, *Art and the Bible* (Downers Grove, Ill.: InterVarsity, 1979), 34.
11. Ibid.
12. Ibid., 36.
13. Hegel, 35–36.
14. Rookmaaker, 236. This passage is a contributing source for the idea of the article.
15. John Calvin, *Commentaries on the Epistles of Paul the Apostle to the Philippians, Colossians, and Thessalonians* (Grand Rapids, Mich.: Eerdmans, 1957), 121.
16. Hegel, 44.
17. Cited in Rookmaaker, 236.
18. Ibid.
19. Dorothy Sayers, *The Poetry of Search and the Poetry of Statement* (London: Victor Gollancz, 1963), 72.
20. Henry George Liddell and Robert Scott, *A Greek-English Lexicon* (New York: American Book, 1963), 72.
21. Alexander Souter, *A Pocket Lexicon to the Greek New Testament* (London: Oxford University Press, 1976), 12.
22. Rookmaaker, 236.
23. Ibid., 237–38.
24. Sayers, *Poetry*, 71–72.
25. Alexandr Solzhenitsyn, *Nobel Lecture*, trans. F. D. Reeve (New York: Farrar, Straus and Giroux, 1972), 33–34.
26. Thomas Babington Macaulay, "Minute on Indian Education," in *Speeches by Lord Macaulay with His Minute on Indian Education* (1935; repr., London: Oxford University Press, 1979), 355–56.
27. Ibid., 349.
28. Ibid., 351.
29. Allan Bloom, trans., Introduction to Plato, *The Republic of Plato* (New York: Basic, 1968), xviii.
30. Schaeffer, 48.
31. Ibid.
32. Hegel, 87.
33. Ibid., 37.
34. Schaeffer, 44.
35. Ibid., 51.
36. Rookmaaker, 214.
37. Ibid., 243.
38. Liddell and Scott, 325; James Strong, *A Concise Dictionary of the Words in the Greek New Testament* (Nashville: Royal Publishers, 1979), 23; Souter, 66.
39. Rookmaaker, 239.
40. Ibid., 243.
41. Ibid., 248.
42. Richard Byrd, *Alone* (New York: G. P. Putnam's Sons, 1938), 138–39.

CHAPTER SEVEN

1. See Kenneth A. Myers, *All God's Children and Blue Suede Shoes: Christians and Popular Culture* (1989; repr., Wheaton: Crossway, 2012).
2. J. R. R. Tolkien, "On Fairy-Stories" (1947), in *Tree and Leaf* (New York: Harper Collins, 2001). See also George MacDonald, "The Fantastic Imagination" (1893), in *George MacDonald: The Complete Fairy Tales*, Penguin Classics (New York: Penguin, 1999); and C. S. Lewis, "On Three Ways of Writing for Children" (1946), in *On Stories: And Other Essays on Literature* (Orlando, Fla.: Harcourt, 1982).
3. H. Richard Niebuhr explained that culture "comprises language, habits, ideas, beliefs, customs, social organization, inherited artifacts, technical processes, and values" (H. Richard Niebuhr, *Christ and Culture* [New York: HarperSanFrancisco, 1951], 32). Ken Myers defines culture as "an ecosystem of institutions, practices, artifacts, and beliefs, all interacting and mutually reinforcing" (Myers, xi).
4. See Andy Crouch, *Culture Making: Recovering Our Creative Calling* (Downers Grove, Ill.: IVP, 2008).
5. See R. Stanton Norman, "Human Sinfulness," in *A Theology for the Church*, ed. Danny Akin (Nashville: B&H, 2007).
6. Timothy Keller, *Every Good Endeavor: Connecting Your Work to God's Work* (New York: Dutton, 2012), 191.
7. Ibid., 185.
8. Ibid., 197.
9. Ibid., 193.
10. Ibid.
11. Ibid., 197.
12. Saint Augustine, *On Christian Teaching*, trans. R. P. H. Green (397, 426; New York: Oxford University Press, 1997), 6.
13. Ibid., 47.
14. John Calvin, *Commentary on the Epistles to Timothy, Titus, and Philemon*, trans. William Principle (Grand Rapids, Mich.: Eerdmans, 1948), 300–01.
15. John Calvin, *Institutes of the Christian Religion*, 2 vols., trans. Henry Beveridge (Peabody, Mich.: Hendrickson, 2008), II.2.15:167.
16. Ibid.
17. Many others have followed in this tradition, evident by the aptly titled *All Truth Is God's Truth* (Grand Rapids, Mich.: Eerdmans, 1977) by Arthur F. Holmes.
18. Christopher J. H. Wright, *The Mission of God's People: A Biblical Theology of the Church's Mission*, Biblical Theology for Life, ed. Jonathan Lunde (Grand Rapids, Mich.: Zondervan, 2010), 162.
19. See Albert M. Wolters, *Creation Regained: Biblical Basics for a Reformational Worldview*, 2nd ed. (1985; repr., Grand Rapids, Mich.: Eerdmans, 2005).
20. N. T. Wright, *Surprised By Hope: Rethinking Heaven, the Resurrection, and the Mission of the Church* (New York: Harper Collins, 2008), 193.
21. Ibid., 209.
22. See Augustine, *The City of God against the Pagans*, ed. and trans. R. W. Dyson, Cambridge Texts in the History of Political Thought (1998; repr., Cambridge: Cambridge University Press, 2002).
23. John M. Frame, "Theology at the Movies," *Frame-Poythress.org*, http://www.frame-poythress.org/ebooks/theology-at-the-movies.
24. Grant Horner, *Meaning at the Movies: Becoming a Discerning Viewer* (Wheaton: Crossway, 2010), 58.
25. See Francis A. Schaeffer, *Art and the Bible* (Downers Grove, Ill.: InterVarsity, 1979), 51.

26 See James Mooney, "The Importance of Form: Introduction to Film Studies," *Filmosophy*, January 29, 2015, https://filmandphilosophy.com/2015/01/29/the-importance-of-form-introduction-to-film-studies/.
27 See Marshall McLuhan, *Understanding Media: The Extensions of Man* (1964; repr., Cambridge: MIT Press, 1994); and Marshall McLuhan and Quentin Fiore, *The Medium Is the Massage: An Inventory of Effects* (New York: Random House, 1967; reissued, Berkeley, Calif.: Gingko, 2001).
28 Jeffrey Overstreet, "The Christian Message of David Fincher's Gone Girl . . . (Not Really)," *Patheos*, October 1, 2014, http://www.patheos.com/blogs/lookingcloser/2014/10/the-christian-message-of-david-finchers-gone-girl-not-really/.
29 See "How to Analyze a Movie: A Step-by-step Guide," *San Diego Film Festival*, http://sdfilmfest.com/how-to-analyze-a-movie-step-by-step-guide-to-reviewing-films-from-a-screeners-point-of-view/. See also Frame.
30 See chapter six by E. Darrell Holley, entitled "The Principles of the Christian Critical Tradition."
31 Overstreet.
32 Schaeffer, *Art and the Bible*, 44. Holley states similarly, "Technical excellence is very important, but it is not alone sufficient; a wrong presented beautifully becomes all the more wrong and wicked."
33 Holley deals with only Philippians 4:8. However, I have included verse 7 because it reflects the overall movement of Paul's broader point about how Christians should fill their minds.
34 Holley.
35 H. R. Rookmaaker, *Modern Art and the Death of a Culture* (Downers Grove, Ill.: Inter-Varsity Press, 1970; repr., Wheaton: Crossway, 1994). Jonathan Anderson and William A. Dyrness published a sort-of rebuttal, entitled *Modern Art and the Life of Culture*, but fail to engage the heart of Rookmaaker's argument. See Jonathan A. Anderson and William A. Dyrness, *Modern Art and the Life of a Culture: The Religious Impulses of Modernism*, Studies in Theology and the Arts (Downers Grove, Ill.: IVP Academic, 2016).
36 Francis A. Schaeffer, *How Should We Then Live? The Rise and Decline of Western Thought and Culture* (1976; repr., Wheaton: Crossway, 2005), 184.
37 Ibid., 187.
38 Roger Scruton, *Beauty: A Very Short Introduction* (2009; repr., Oxford: Oxford University Press, 2011), 82.
39 Stephen Hicks, "Why Art Became Ugly," *The Atlas Society*, September 1, 2004, https://www.atlassociety.org/post/why-art-became-ugly.
40 Ibid.
41 Paul Munson and Joshua Farris Drake, *Art and Music: A Student's Guide*, Reclaiming the Christian Intellectual Tradition, ed. David S. Dockery (Wheaton: Crossway, 2014), 21.
42 Ibid., 23. Munson and Drake analyze Mark 14:3–8 to substantiate this claim.
43 Frame.
44 Munson and Drake, 29.
45 Frame.
46 See F. Leroy Forlines, *The Quest for Truth: Answering Life's Inescapable Questions* (Nashville: Randall House, 2001), ix–xii.
47 Peterson's *The Wingfeather Saga* is an excellent four-volume series after the tradition of the writings of MacDonald, Tolkien, and Lewis.
48 Leroy Forlines, *Biblical Ethics: Ethics for Happier Living* (Nashville: Randall House, 1973), 198.
49 Basil the Great, "Address to Young Men on the Right Use of Greek Literature," in *Essays on the Study and Use of Poetry*, by Plutarch and Basil the Great, trans. Frederick Morgan Padelford, Yale Studies in English, vol. XV, ed. Albert S. Cook (New York: Henry Holt, 1902),

103. "[W]e must be conversant with poets, with historians, with orators, indeed with all men who may further our soul's salvation. Just as dyers prepare the cloth before they apply the dye, be it purple or any other color, so indeed must we also, if we would preserve indelible the idea of the true virtue, become first initiated in the pagan lore, then at length give special heed to the sacred and divine teachings, even as we first accustom ourselves to the sun's reflection in the water, and then become able to turn our eyes upon the very sun itself."
50 Forlines, *Biblical Ethics*, 93–94, 96, 200.
51 C. S. Lewis, *The Last Battle*, The Chronicles of Narnia (1956; repr, New York: HarperCollins, 1984), 168–69.
52 Forlines, *Biblical Ethics*, 47.
53 Ibid., 199.
54 See Carl F. H. Henry, *The Uneasy Conscience of Modern Fundamentalism* (1947; repr., Grand Rapids, Mich.: Eerdmans, 2003).
55 Russell D. Moore, "Retaking Mars Hill," *Touchstone: A Journal of Mere Christianity*, September 2007, http://www.touchstonemag.com/archives/article.php?id=20-07-020-f.
56 Forlines, *The Quest for Truth*, 247–48.
57 Ibid., *Biblical Ethics*, 47.
58 Moore.
59 Forlines, *The Quest for Truth*, 247–48.
60 Ibid., 247.
61 Frame.
62 Keller, 193, 197.
63 J. Matthew Pinson et al., *Sexuality, Gender, and the Church: A Christian Response in the New Cultural Landscape* (Nashville: Welch College Press, 2016), 3.
64 Augustine, 47. "[W]e should not avoid music because of the associated pagan superstitions if there is a possibility of gleaning from it something of value for understanding holy scripture. Nor, on the other hand, should we be captivated by the vanities of the theatre if we are discussing something to do with lyres or other instruments that may help us appreciate spiritual truths. We were not wrong to learn the alphabet just because they say that the god Mercury was its patron, nor should we avoid justice and virtue just because they dedicated temples to justice and virtue and preferred to honour these values not in their minds, but in the form of stones. A person who is a good and a true Christian should realize that truth belongs to his Lord, wherever it is found, gathering and acknowledging it even in pagan literature, but rejecting superstitious vanities and deploring and avoiding those who 'though they knew God did not glorify him as God or give thanks but became enfeebled in their own thoughts and plunged their senseless minds into darkness. Claiming to be wise they became fools, and exchanged the glory of the incorruptible God for the image of corruptible mortals and animals and reptiles.'"
65 Along these lines, Frame says, "Sometimes, one finds Christian themes and symbolism in films, even films which are not in themselves supportive of Christian values. Christians should be ready to be surprised when they attend films, and not only negatively."
66 Ibid.
67 Forlines, *Biblical Ethics*, 201.
68 Horner, 56.

Chapter Eight

1 These statistics are from a website from the University of Michigan Medical Center, which has several helpful facts about children and television: http://www.med.umich.edu/1libr/yourchild/tv.htm.
2 Rod Dreher, *Crunchy Cons: The New Conservative Counterculture and Its Return to Roots* (New York: Three Rivers, 2006), 33.

3 Examples include ancient pagan philosophers such as Plato and Aristotle, early Christian thinkers as diverse as Tertullian, Clement of Alexandria, and Augustine of Hippo, and other philosophers in the Christian tradition. See chapter three of this book for an excellent introduction to classical conservatism by Matthew Steven Bracey. See also Carson Holloway, *All Shook Up: Music, Passion, and Politics* (Dallas: Spence, 2008).
4 Kenneth A. Myers, *All God's Children and Blue Suede Shoes: Christians and Popular Culture* (Wheaton: Crossway, 2012); Marva J. Dawn, *Is It a Lost Cause? Having the Heart of God for the Church's Children* (Grand Rapids, Mich.: Eerdmans, 1997); T. David Gordon, *Why Johnny Can't Preach: The Media Have Shaped the Messengers* (Phillipsburg, N.J.: P&R, 2009); T. David Gordon, *Why Johnny Can't Sing Hymns: How Pop Culture Rewrote the Hymnal* (Phillipsburg, N.J.: P&R, 2010).
5 Myers, 180 (italics removed).
6 F. Leroy Forlines, *The Quest for Truth: Answering Life's Inescapable Questions* (Nashville: Randall House, 2001), 496. See also Leroy Forlines, *Biblical Ethics* (Nashville: Randall House, 1973).
7 See Myers, 34–36, 53.
8 Derek Kidner, *The Wisdom of Proverbs, Job & Ecclesiastes* (Downers Grove, Ill.: InterVarsity, 1985), 11.
9 Myers, 35.
10 Forlines, *The Quest for Truth*, 5; Forlines, *Biblical Ethics*, 52–67.
11 Myers, 98.
12 Ibid., 100. See Douglas Jones's discussion of the concept of nobility in Philippians 4:8 in his "Nobility: Living Like Royals," in *The Church and Pop Culture* (Moscow, Ida.: Canon, 2006), https://canonpress.com/products/the-church-and-pop-culture-cd.
13 Much country music in contemporary American culture has taken on the characteristics of pop-rock music with but a trace—a distant memory—of the traditional folk music of the American South.
14 Myers, 89.
15 Ibid., 120.
16 Dreher, 29–30.
17 Myers, 177.
18 John Seabrook, quoted in Michael Horton, *A Better Way: Rediscovering the Drama of God-Centered Worship* (Grand Rapids, Mich.: Baker, 2004), 189.
19 Wendell Berry, quoted in Marva J. Dawn, *A Royal "Waste" of Time: The Splendor of Worshiping God and Being Church for the World* (Grand Rapids, Mich.: Eerdmans, 1999), 80.
20 Richard Winter, *Still Bored in a Culture of Entertainment: Rediscovering Passion and Wonder* (Downers Grove, Ill.: InterVarsity, 2002), 48. See also Sam van Eman, *On Earth As It Is in Advertising? Moving from Commercial Hype to Gospel Hope* (Grand Rapids, Mich.: Baker, 2010).
21 See Quentin J. Schultze, *Habits of the High-Tech Heart: Living Virtuously in the Information Age* (Grand Rapids, Mich.: Baker Academic, 2002); and Nicholas Carr, *The Shallows: What the Internet Is Doing to Our Brains* (New York: W. W. Norton, 2010).
22 See, for example, David Murray, *Reset: Living in Grace-Paced Life in a Burnout Culture* (Wheaton: Crossway, 2017); and Cal Newport, *Digital Minimalism: Choosing a Focused Life in a Noisy World* (New York: Penguin, 2019).
23 See Neil Postman, *Technopoly: The Surrender of Culture to Technology* (New York: Vintage, 1993).
24 See Cal Newport, *Deep Work: Rules for Focused Success in a Distracted World* (New York: Grand Central, 2016).
25 "Screen Time and Children," *American Academy of Child and Adolescent Psychiatry*, https://www.aacap.org/AACAP/Families_and_Youth/Facts_for_Families/FFF-Guide/Children-And-Watching-TV-054.aspx.

26 Maggie Jackson, *Distracted: The Erosion of Attention and the Coming Dark Age* (Amherst, N.Y.: Prometheus, 2008); Mark Bauerlein, *The Dumbest Generation: How the Digital Age Stupefies Young Americans and Jeopardizes our Future* (New York: Penguin, 2009).
27 Gordon, *Why Johnny Can't Preach*, 61.
28 Matt Markins, "Broken Model," *CLEAR Living* (Spring 2008), 60–63.
29 Richard Stivers, quoted in Winter, 48.
30 C. S. Lewis, quoted in Myers, 65.
31 The word translated "steadfastness" in the ESV is variously translated as "patience," "perseverance," and "endurance."
32 True growth requires what Eugene Peterson (quoting, of all people, Friedrich Nietzsche) calls "a long obedience in the same direction." See Eugene H. Peterson, *A Long Obedience in the Same Direction: Discipleship in an Instant Society*, 2nd ed. (Downers Grove, Ill.: IVP, 2000)
33 Winter, 50.
34 C. S. Lewis, *An Experiment in Criticism* (Cambridge: Cambridge University Press, 1961), 19.
35 Myers, 91–94, 120, 129, 165.
36 Mercer Schuchardt, quoted in Dreher, 34.
37 See Andy Crouch, *Culture Making: Recovering Our Creative Calling* (Downers Grove, Ill.: InterVarsity, 2013).
38 Winter, 43.
39 Ibid., 34.
40 Ibid.
41 Albert Borgmann cites Mihaly Csikszentmihalyi and Eugene Rochberg-Halton's wide-ranging research on the meaning families give to the objects in their homes, discussed in their book *The Meaning of Things*. See Borgmann's book *Power Failure: Christianity and the Culture of Technology* (Grand Rapids, Mich.: Brazos, 2003).
42 Borgmann, 29.
43 Ibid.
44 Ibid., 29–31.
45 Dreher, 41–42. See Robert Putnam, *Bowling Alone: The Collapse and Revival of American Community* (New York: Simon and Schuster, 2001).
46 Winter, 34, 39–40.
47 Kristen Rogers, "US teens use screens more than seven hours a day on average—and that's not including school work," *CNN Health*, October 29, 2019, https://www.cnn.com/2019/10/29/health/common-sense-kids-media-use-report-wellness/index.html.
48 R. Albert Mohler, Jr., "A Generation Immersed in Media," *Albert Mohler*, December 4, 2008, https://albertmohler.com/2008/12/04/new-study-a-generation-immersed-in-media.
49 Wendell Berry, "The Work of Local Culture," in *What Are People For?* (San Francisco: North Point, 1990), 158–59.
50 Dawn, *Is It a Lost Cause?* 79.
51 See Christopher Lasch, *The Culture of Narcissism: American Life in an Age of Diminishing Expectations* (New York: W. W. Norton, 1991).
52 See Phillip T. Morgan's excellent chapter, "Tradition and History."
53 Michael S. Horton, "Better Homes and Gardens," in *The Church in Emerging Culture: Five Perspectives*, ed. Leonard Sweet (Grand Rapids, Mich.: Zondervan, 2003), 130.
54 Dreher, 26.
55 Michael Horton says that our vision of tradition should view the church as being like an old building that has stood the test of time for centuries and has been cared for and remodeled over generations, tying together past, present, and future. This building is "neither nostalgically stuck in the past," refusing to be tinkered with, "nor is it narrowly stuck in the present, given to innovations that pass into ridicule as quickly as they rose to

fame. Rather, it brings the past and the present together in conversation, as if to wave its hand to future generations to indwell it, care for it, repair it, and make their own contributions to its complexion. Scripture itself appeals to this analogy, speaking of a foundation laid once and for all by the prophets and apostles and a building that subsequently rises upon it to the end of the age" ("Better Homes and Gardens," 120–21). The modern, reinvented church is more like a "suburban strip mall, which replaced a dilapidated older structure deemed unworthy of upkeep, [but it is] destined itself to be replaced in a matter of years rather than centuries" (121).

56 Postman, *Technopoly*, 179. See also Neal Gabler, *Life: The Movie; How Entertainment Conquered Reality* (New York: Vintage, 2000).
57 See Diana West, *The Death of the Grown-up: How America's Arrested Development Is Bringing Down Western Civilization* (New York: St. Martin's, 2007). She argues that the generation gap that flowered with the 1960s counterculture had its origins in the creation of adolescent culture in the 1950s.
58 Jann Wenner, quoted in Myers, 137–38.
59 See John Makujina, *Measuring the Music: Another Look at the Contemporary Christian Music Debate* (Fort Worth, Tex.: Religious Affections, 2016).
60 Charles A. Reich, *The Greening of America* (New York: Random House, 1970), quoted in Myers, 139.
61 See Robert Pattison, *The Triumph of Vulgarity: Rock Music in the Mirror of Romanticism* (New York: Oxford University Press, 1987). Pattison celebrates this Romantic view of music, which, according to Carson Holloway, is consistent with the views of Romantic philosophers Jean-Jacques Rousseau and Friedrich Nietzsche, who left behind the classical Western philosophical view that music should calm the "animal passions" and promoted the Dionysian view that music should enliven the passions and quiet the rational impulse (see Holloway).
62 See Holloway. See also Roger Scruton, *Music as an Art* (London: Bloomsbury, 2019).
63 Calvin R. Stapert, *A New Song for an Old World: The Musical Thought of the Early Church*, Calvin Institute of Christian Worship Liturgical Studies, ed. John D. Witvliet (Grand Rapids, Mich.: Eerdmans, 2006).
64 "Dionysian" refers to the Greek God Dionysus, the god of wild pleasure and revelry.
65 See Neil Postman, *Amusing Ourselves to Death: Public Discourse in an Age of Show Business* (New York: Penguin, 1986).
66 Dreher, 33.
67 Dawn, *A Royal "Waste" of Time*, 73–74.
68 Myers, 163.
69 Ibid., 164.
70 See E. Darrell Holley, *The English Bible and English Primary Education in the Tudor and Stuart Periods*, Ph.D. diss., Florida State University, 1999.
71 Horton, *A Better Way*, 157.
72 Ibid., "Better Homes and Gardens," 119.
73 Ibid., 134.
74 Dawn, *A Royal "Waste" of Time*, 60.
75 Ibid., 60–62.
76 Ibid., 123.
77 Ibid.
78 Eric Brende, quoted in Dreher, 38.
79 Dreher, 230.
80 Dawn, *A Royal "Waste" of Time*, 85. See also Quentin J. Schultze, *Winning Your Kids Back from the Media* (Downers Grove, Ill.: InterVarsity, 1994); and Markins, 60–63.

Chapter Nine

1. John Calvin, *Institutes of the Christian Religion*, vol. 2, trans. Ford Lewis Battles, The Library of Christian Classics, ed. John T. McNeill (Philadelphia: Westminster Press), 1154.
2. Ronald H. Nash, *The Word of God and the Mind of Man* (Phillipsburg, N.J.: P&R, 1992), 66.
3. Vern Sheridan Poythress, *In the Beginning Was the Word: Language—A God-Centered Approach* (Wheaton: Crossway, 2009), 297.
4. The two most notable exponents of this idea have been Horace, the Roman literary critic of the first century B.C., and Sir Phillip Sidney, the English poet of the Renaissance.
5. William Faulkner, "Speech of Acceptance upon the award of the Nobel Prize for Literature," in *William Faulkner Reader* (New York: Random House, 1954), 3.
6. Edmund Burke, *Reflections on the Revolution in France* (New York: Oxford University Press, 1999), 77.
7. R.V. Young, *A Student's Guide to Literature*, The Preston A. Wells Jr. Guides to the Major Disciplines (Wilmington, Del.: ISI, 2000), 12–13.
8. The Christian approach to evaluating literature is more fully explained in chapter six of this book by E. Darrell Holley, entitled "The Principles of the Christian Critical Tradition."
9. Richard Weaver, *Ideas Have Consequences* (Chicago: University of Chicago Press, 2013), 135.
10. Malcolm Muggeridge, "The Great Liberal Death Wish," in *The Portable Conservative Reader*, ed. Russell Kirk (New York: Penguin, 1982), 602.
11. Ferdinand de Saussure, *Course in General Linguistics*, ed. Charles Bally, Albert Sechehaye, and Albert Riedlinger, trans. Roy Harris (Chicago: Open Court, 1986), 1.
12. Ibid., 114.
13. Francis A. Schaeffer, *He Is There and He Is Not Silent* (Carol Stream, Ill.: Tyndale House, 1972), in *The Francis A. Schaeffer Trilogy* (Wheaton: Crossway, 1990), 315.
14. Noah Webster, Introduction to *American Dictionary* (1828; repr., San Francisco: Foundation For American Christian Education, 1995), np.
15. Ibid.
16. *The New England Primer*, in *The Norton Anthology of American Literature*, ed. Nina Baym, vol. A, *Beginnings to 1820*, ed. Wayne Franklin, Philip F. Gura, and Arnold Krupat (New York: W. W. Norton, 2007), 355.
17. Thomas Sowell, Address to the American Enterprise Institute, printed in *The Washington Times*, Tuesday, 28 May 1991, C1, C3, quoted in Russell Kirk, *America's British Culture* (New Brunswick, N.J.: Transaction, 1993), 9.
18. Poythress, 17.
19. Ibid., 18.
20. Kirk, 26.
21. Webster, np.
22. Cicero, "De Officiis," in *The Great Tradition: Classic Readings on What It Means to Be an Educated Human Being*, ed. Richard M. Gamble (Wilmington, Del.: ISI, 2007), 84.
23. Ibid.
24. E. Darrell Holley, *Traditional English Grammar* (Nashville: Randall House, 2009), 16.
25. Mark Halpern, *Language and Human Nature* (Oakland, Calif.: Regent, 2006), 59.
26. Ibid., 117.
27. Holley, *Traditional English Grammar*, 14–15.
28. *American Heritage Dictionary*, 4th ed., s.v. "tree."
29. Proto-Indo-European, or "PIE" for short, is a parent language from which scholars have traced many of the world's languages, including English.
30. *American Heritage Dictionary*, 4th ed., s.v. "dog."
31. Stanley Fish, *Is There a Text in This Class? The Authority of Interpretive Communities* (Cambridge: Harvard University Press, 1980), 347.

32 E. D. Hirsh, *Validity in Interpretation* (New Haven: Yale University Press, 1967), 25–26.
33 Michel Foucault, "What Is an Author?" in *The Foucault Reader*, ed. Paul Rainbow (New York: Pantheon, 1984), 119.
34 Hirsch, 8.
35 Ibid., 26.

Chapter Ten

1 Some of the material in this chapter has appeared in other publications, including "Reclaiming a Holistic Approach to Christian Calling and Vocation," *The Helwys Society Forum*, November 8, 2010, https://www.helwyssocietyforum.com/reclaiming-a-holistic-approach-to-christian-calling-and-vocation/; "A 'Labor Day' Article," *The Helwys Society Forum*, September 2, 2013, https://www.helwyssocietyforum.com/a-labor-day-article/; and "In View of Vocation," *ONE Magazine* 17, no. 2 (February-March 2020): 8–10. Reprinted with permission.
2 Tom Nelson, *Work Matters: Connecting Sunday Worship to Monday Work* (Wheaton: Crossway, 2011), 83, 193–95.
3 Like the first third of this chapter, Timothy Keller organizes his discussion of vocation by the creation-Fall-redemption rubric. Similarly, James Hamilton bases his volume on work on the themes of creation, Fall, redemption, and restoration. See Timothy Keller with Katherine Leary Alsdorf, *Every Good Endeavor: Connecting Your Work to God's Work* (New York: Penguin, 2012); and James M. Hamilton, Jr., *Work and our Labor in the Lord*, Biblical Studies in Biblical Theology, ed. Dane C. Ortlund and Miles V. Van Pelt (Wheaton: Crossway, 2017).
4 Leroy Forlines, *Biblical Ethics: Ethics for Happier Living* (Nashville: Randall House, 1973), 58–59.
5 Albert Mohler, "Leisure and Labor—Two Gifts from God," *Albert Mohler*, September 4, 2006, http://www.albertmohler.com/2006/09/04/leisure-and-labor-two-gifts-from-god/?utm_source=Albert+Mohler&utm_campaign=548f2f9d5e-The_Briefing_2013&utm_medium=email&utm_term=0_b041ba0d12-548f2f9d5e-307593669.
6 Gene Edward Veith, Jr., *God at Work: Your Christian Vocation in All of Life*, Focal Point Series, ed. Gene Edward Veith, Jr. (2002; repr., Wheaton: Crossway, 2011), 52.
7 Carl F. H. Henry, quoted in John A. Bernbaum and Simon A. Steer, *Why Work? Careers and Employment in Biblical Perspective* (Grand Rapids, Mich.: Baker, 1986), 6–7. See also Andrew T. Walker, Introduction to *The Gospel and Work*, The Gospel for Life Series, ed. Russell Moore and Andrew T. Walker (Nashville: B&H, 2017), 2.
8 Kenneth J. Barnes, *Redeeming Capitalism* (Grand Rapids, Mich.: Eerdmans, 2018), 106; Augustine, *Sermons on Selected Lessons of the New Testament: Sermon 63*, ed. K. Knight (New Advent, 2009), para. 4, http://newadvent.org/fathers/160363.htm; Thomas Adams, quoted in Charles H. George and Katherine George, *The Protestant Mind of the English Reformers 1570–1640* (Princeton: Princeton University Press, 1961), 131–32.
9 Jim Mullins, "The Butcher, the Baker, and the Biotech Maker," *The Gospel Coalition*, October 29, 2014, https://www.thegospelcoalition.org/article/the-butcher-the-baker-and-the-biotech-maker/.
10 Ken Magnuson discusses this purpose of marriage as the "fruitfulness in labor" in *Invitation to Christian Ethics: Moral Reasoning and Contemporary Issues*, Invitation to Theological Studies Series (Grand Rapids, Mich.: Kregel Academic, 2020), 184–87. See also Christopher Ash, *Marriage: Sex in the Service of God* (Vancouver: Regent College, 2003), 119–22.
11 Forlines, *Biblical Ethics*, 53.
12 Keller, 113–28.
13 Bethany L. Jenkins, "What Are We For?" in *The Gospel and Work*, 9.
14 Keller, 75–150. Similarly, Sebastian Traeger and Greg Gilbert explore the idolatry and idleness of work in *The Gospel at Work: How Working for King Jesus Gives Purpose and Meaning to our Jobs* (Grand Rapids, Mich.: Zondervan, 2013), 23–42.

15 Doug Sherman and William Hendricks, *Your Work Matters to God* (1987; repr., Colorado Springs: Navpress, 1988), 97.
16 Keller, 95.
17 Greg Forster, "How Should the Christian Live?" in *The Gospel and Work*, 61.
18 Veith, 40.
19 Dallas Willard and Gary Black, Jr., *The Divine Conspiracy Continued: Fulfilling God's Kingdom on Earth* (New York: HarperOne, 2014), 294–95.
20 See Augustine, *The City of God against the Pagans*, ed. and trans. R. W. Dyson, Cambridge Texts in the History of Political Thought (1998; repr., Cambridge: Cambridge University Press, 2002).
21 The vocations discussed in this section are inspired by Veith, chs. 4–8.
22 Magnuson, 177–78, 182–87.
23 See Jonathan Leeman, *Political Church: The Local Assembly as Embassy of Christ's Rule*, Studies in Christian Doctrine and Scripture (Downers Grove, Ill.: IVP Academic, 2016), 162–71.
24 Nelson discusses implications for work from Jeremiah 31, explaining that we can convey God's "common grace" by being "good neighbors" and promoting "workplace justice" among our societal neighbors. See Nelson, *Work Matters*, 131, 133, 137.
25 Willard and Black, 273.
26 Dorothy L. Sayers, *Why Work?* (April 3, 1942), in *Letters to a Diminished Church: Passionate Arguments for the Relevance of Christian Doctrine* (Nashville: Thomas Nelson, 2004), 131.
27 Ken Riggs, "Redefining the Ministry," *Contact* (Jan. 1999), 9–10.
28 Nelson, *Work Matters*, 66.
29 Tom Nelson, "How Should the Church Engage?" in *The Gospel and Work*, 74. See also Tom Nelson, "Connecting Sunday to Monday," in *The Flourishing Pastor: Recovering the Lost Art of Shepherd Leadership* (Downers Grove, Ill.: InterVarsity Press, 2021), 168, 173.
30 Eugene Peterson, *The Wisdom of Each Other: A Conversation Between Spiritual Friends* (Grand Rapids, Mich.: Zondervan, 1998), 77.
31 C. S. Lewis, "Learning in War-Time," in *The Weight of Glory and Other Addresses* (New York: Macmillan, 1949), 46.
32 Joseph Hall, quoted in Charles Taylor, *Sources of the Self: The Making of the Modern Identity* (1989; repr., Cambridge: Cambridge University Press, 2006), 224 (spelling and grammar modernized).
33 William Perkins, quoted in Taylor, 224.
34 John Dod, quoted in Taylor, 223.
35 Wendell Berry, *Jayber Crow: The Life Story of Jayber Crow, Barber, of the Port William Membership, as Written by Himself* (New York: Counterpoint, 2000), 66.
36 Veith, 140.
37 Traeger and Gilbert, 91, 95.
38 Different translations render the nature of this relationship differently: master-slave (HCSB, NASB, NIV, NLT, NRSV), master-bondservant (ESV, NKJV), or master-servant (ASV, KJV). Some thinkers have resisted the application of these verses to employment relationships because of its association with slavery. It is beyond my purposes to sort through the details associated with this question. However, I believe the underlying principle stands: Christians should practice godly virtue in the context of their employment relationships.
39 Charles Kingsley, in *The Christian Advocate*, January 16, 1913: 80.
40 Dietrich Bonhoeffer, *Life Together: The Classic Exploration of Christian Community*, trans. John W. Doberstein (New York: Harper & Brothers, 1954), 88.
41 Forlines, *Biblical Ethics*, 59.
42 Sayers, 128.

43 F. Leroy Forlines, *The Quest for Truth: Answering Life's Inescapable Questions* (Nashville: Randall House, 2001), 55, 139.
44 Sayers, 128.
45 Ibid., 136–37.
46 Ibid., 137.
47 Ibid., 135–36.
48 Ibid., 132.
49 Ibid.
50 Ibid., 134.
51 Ibid., 132–33.
52 John Wesley, "The Use of Money," in *John Wesley*, ed. Albert C. Outler (1964; repr., New York: Oxford University Press, 1980), 241, 245, 247.
53 John Wesley, "Thoughts Upon Methodism," August 4, 1786, in *The Works of the Reverend John Wesley*, 7 vols. (New York: J. Emory and B. Waugh, 1831), 7:317.
54 Ibid., "The Use of Money," 241–43. Wesley justified the preference of church before community by appeal to Galatians 6:10: "So then, as we have opportunity, let us do good to everyone, and especially to those who are of the household of faith" (248).
55 Ibid., "Thoughts Upon Methodism," 7:317.
56 Forlines, *Biblical Ethics*, 178–79.
57 Ibid., 188–89.
58 Sayers, 125–26.
59 Martin Luther, "Psalm 147," trans. Edward Sittler, in *Luther's Works*, vol. 14, ed. Jaroslav Pelikan (St. Louis: Concordia, 1958), 114.
60 Keller, 20–21.
61 John Bolt, *Economic Shalom: A Reformed Primer on Faith, Work, and Human Flourishing*, The Oikonomia Series (Grand Rapids, Mich.: Christian's Library Press, 2013), 73.

Chapter Eleven

1 Craig Detweiler, *iGods: How Technology Shapes Our Spiritual and Social Lives* (Grand Rapids, Mich.: Brazos, 2013), 1.
2 W. Jackson Watts, "Is Technology Neutral?" *Helwys Society Forum*, October 10, 2011, http://www.helwyssocietyforum.com/is-technology-neutral/.
3 Detweiler, 23.
4 For discussion of sub-creation, see C. S. Lewis, "On Three Ways of Writing for Children" (1946), in *On Stories: And Other Essays on Literature* (Orlando, Fla.: Harcourt, 1982); and J. R. R. Tolkien, "On Fairy-Stories" (1947), in *Tree and Leaf* (New York: Harper Collins, 2001). See also George MacDonald, "The Fantastic Imagination" (1893), in *George MacDonald: The Complete Fairy Tales*, Penguin Classics (New York: Penguin, 1999).
5 Detweiler, 26.
6 Jacques Ellul, *The Presence of the Kingdom*, trans. Olive Wyon, 2nd ed. (Colorado Springs: Helmers & Howard, 1989), 55.
7 See Jeremy Begbie, *Music, Modernity, and God: Essays in Listening* (Oxford: Oxford University Press, 2013); Josef Pieper, *Only the Lover Sings: Art and Contemplation* (San Francisco: Ignatius Press, 1990); and Josef Pieper, *Leisure: The Basis of Culture,* trans. Gerald Malsbary (South Bend: St. Augustine's Press, 1998).
8 Andy Crouch, *Culture Making: Recovering Our Creative Calling* (Downers Grove, Ill.: IVP, 2008), 23.
9 Bill Gross, "The 7 Deadly Sins of Social Media," May 25, 2018, https://twitter.com/bill_gross/status/1000208707450368001?lang=en. See also Robinson Meyer, "The Seven Deadly Social Networks," *The Atlantic*, May 9, 2016, https://www.theatlantic.com/technology

/archive/2016/05/the-seven-deadly-social-networks/480897/. Tinder is especially susceptible to perversion and misuse.
10 See Siva Vaidhyanathan, *Antisocial Media: How Facebook Disconnects Us and Undermines Democracy* (New York: Oxford University Press, 2018).
11 Neil Postman, *Technopoly: The Surrender of Culture to Technology* (New York: Vintage, 1992), 21.
12 Ibid., 22.
13 Ibid., 23.
14 Ibid., 28.
15 Ibid.
16 Ibid., 35.
17 Ibid., 52.
18 Ibid.
19 Ibid., 48.
20 Ibid., 53–54.
21 Neil Postman, *Amusing Ourselves to Death: Public Discourse in the Age of Show Business* (New York: Penguin, 2005), xix.
22 Ibid., xix–xx.
23 Dietrich Bonhoeffer, *Ethics*, ed. Clifford J. Green, trans. Reinhard Kraus, Charles C. West, and Douglas W. Stott, Dietrich Bonhoeffer Works, vol. 6, ed. Wayne Whitson Floyd, Jr. (Minneapolis: Fortress, 2009), 116.
24 Jacques Ellul, *The Technological Society*, trans. John Wilkinson (New York: Vintage, 1964), 140.
25 Manuel Castells, *The Internet Galaxy: Reflections on the Internet, Business, and Society* (Oxford: Oxford University Press, 2003), 130–31, quoted in Andrew Zirschky, *Beyond the Screen: Youth Ministry for the Connected But Alone Generation* (Nashville: Abingdon, 2015), 53.
26 Zirschky, 65.
27 Ibid., 66–70.
28 Samuel Baker, "Who's Shaping Whom? Digital Disruption in the Spiritual Lives of Post-familial Emerging Adults," *Journal of Youth and Theology* 16 (2017): 118.
29 Zirschky, 53.
30 C. S. Lewis, "The Weight of Glory," in *The Weight of Glory and Other Addresses* (New York: HarperCollins, 2009), 26.
31 F. Leroy Forlines, *The Quest for Truth: Answering Life's Inescapable Questions* (Nashville: Randall House, 2001), 55, 139.
32 James K. A. Smith, *Desiring the Kingdom: Worship, Worldview and Cultural Formation*, Cultural Liturgies: Volume I (Grand Rapids, Mich.: Baker Academic, 2009), 26–32. Smith argues that people are not so much "thinking things" as much as they are "worshipping things." This perspective is helpful in showing that men and women are more than minds but fails, I believe, to emphasize the total personality of the human person, including his or her thoughts, emotions, wills, and desires. On anthropology, see also John F. Kilner, *Dignity and Destiny: Humanity in the Image of God* (Grand Rapids, Mich.: Eerdmans, 2015).
33 Leroy Forlines, "Conformity to the Personality of Christ: The Extent," in *Free Will Baptist Convention Sermons: 1935–2010* (Antioch, Tenn.: Executive Office of the National Association of Free Will Baptists, 2011), 137.
34 Carl F. H. Henry, *The Uneasy Conscience of Modern Fundamentalism* (Grand Rapids, Mich.: Eerdmans, 1947), 15.
35 F. Leroy Forlines, *Classical Arminianism: A Theology of Salvation*, ed. J. Matthew Pinson (Nashville: Randall House, 2011), 257.
36 Ibid., "The Pastor and His People," 6, unpublished notes.
37 Ibid., "Conformity to the Personality of Christ," 137.

38 See Sherry Turkle, *Reclaiming Conversation: The Power of Talk in a Digital Age* (New York: Penguin, 2016).
39 Michael W. Goheen and Craig G. Bartholomew, *Living at the Crossroads: An Introduction to Christian Worldview* (Grand Rapids, Mich.: Baker Academic, 2008), 115.
40 *Jurassic Park*, directed by Steven Spielberg (Universal, 1993).
41 Geoffrey W. Bromiley, "Eschatology: The Meaning of the End," in *God and Culture: Essays in Honor of Carl F. H. Henry*, ed. D. A. Carson and John D. Woodbridge (Grand Rapids, Mich.: Eerdmans, 1993), 67.
42 Ibid., 69.
43 Crouch, 170.
44 Ibid.
45 Ibid., 171.
46 Francis A. Schaeffer, *Back to Freedom and Dignity*, in *The Complete Works of Francis A. Schaeffer: A Christian Worldview*, vol. 1 (Westchester, Ill.: Crossway, 1982), 369.

Chapter Twelve

1 See Alvin Plantinga, *Where the Conflict Really Lies: Science, Religion, and Naturalism* (New York: Oxford University Press, 2011).
2 David Hutchings and James C. Ungureanu, *Of Popes and Unicorns* (Oxford: Oxford University Press, 2021), 1–22.
3 See Edward Grant, *The Foundations of Modern Science in the Middle Ages: Their Religious, Institutional and Intellectual Contexts* (Cambridge: Cambridge University Press, 1996); Stanley Jaki, *The Road of Science and the Ways to God* (Chicago: University of Chicago Press, 1978); and Rodney Stark, *For the Glory of God* (Princeton: Princeton University Press, 2004).
4 Most of the following historical information can be found in Andrew Ede and Lesley B. Cormack, *A History of Science in Society: From Philosophy to Utility*, 3rd ed. (Toronto: University of Toronto Press, 2017).
5 Lawrence M. Principe, "The Rise of Islam and Islamic Science," in *History of Science: Antiquity to 1700*, The Great Courses (Chantilly, Va.: The Teaching Company, 2002).
6 Galileo Galilei, *Dialogue Concerning the Two Chief World Systems: Ptolemaic and Copernican* (1632; repr., New York: Modern Library, 2001).
7 Maurice A. Finocchiaro, "Science, Religion, and Historiography of the Galileo Affair: On the Undesirability of Oversimplification," *Osiris* 16, Science in Theistic Contexts: Cognitive Dimensions (Chicago: University of Chicago Press, 2001): 114–32.
8 Steven L. Goldman, *Science Wars: What Scientists Know and How They Know It*, The Great Courses (Chantilly, Va.: The Teaching Company, 2013).
9 Thomas S. Kuhn, *The Structure of Scientific Revolutions*, 50th anniv. ed. (Chicago: University of Chicago Press, 2012).
10 Frederick Gregory, "Consolidating Newton's Achievement," *History of Science: 1700–1900*, The Great Courses (Chantilly, Va.: The Teaching Company, 2013).
11 See Alister McGrath, *Science and Religion: An Introduction* (Malden, Mass.: Blackwell, 1999).
12 Frederick Gregory, "Evolution French Style and a Victorian Sensation," *History of Science: 1700–1900*, The Great Courses (Chantilly, Va.: The Teaching Company, 2013).
13 Charles Lyell, *Principles of Geology*, Penguin Classics (1830; repr., London: Penguin, 1998).
14 Charles Darwin, *The Descent of Man*, Penguin Classics (1871; repr., London: Penguin, 2004); Charles Darwin, *On the Origin of Species: A Facsimile of the First Edition* (1859; repr., Cambridge: Harvard University Press, 2001).
15 See Richard Weikart, *From Darwin to Hitler: Evolutionary Ethics, Eugenics, and Racism in Germany* (New York: Palgrave Macmillan, 2006).
16 Goldman.

17 William Paley, *Natural Theology* (1802; repr., Oxford: Oxford University Press, 2008).
18 John C. Whitcomb, and Henry M. Morris, *The Genesis Flood* (Phillipsburg, N.J.: P&R, 1961).
19 *Reasons to Believe*, www.reasons.org.
20 *Biologos*, www.biologos.org.
21 Michael J. Behe, *Darwin's Black Box* (New York: Touchstone, 1996); Michael J. Behe, *The Edge of Evolution* (New York: Free, 2008); Philip Johnson, *Darwin on Trial* (Downers Grove, Ill.: InterVarsity Press, 1991); Stephen C. Meyer, *Darwin's Doubt* (New York: Harper One, 2014); Stephen C. Meyer, *Signature in the Cell* (New York: Harper Collins, 2009).
22 Katherine T. Phan, "Intelligent Design Professor Loses Appeal for Tenure," *Christian Post*, February 8, 2008, https://www.christianpost.com/news/intelligent-design-professor-loses-appeal-for-tenure.html; Michael Powell, "Editor Explains Reasons for 'Intelligent Design' Article," *Washington Post*, August 19, 2005, https://www.washingtonpost.com/wp-dyn/content/article/2005/08/18/AR2005081801680.html?noredirect=on,%20acc.
23 See J. P. Moreland, *Scientism and Secularism: Learning to Respond to a Dangerous Ideology* (Wheaton: Crossway, 2018).
24 Goldman.
25 Terry Mortenson and Thane H. Ury, *Coming to Grips with Genesis* (Green Forest, Ark.: Master, 2008).
26 Hugh Ross, *Navigating Genesis: A Scientist's Journey Through Genesis 1–11* (Covina, Calif.: RTB, 2014).
27 D. Russell Humphreys, "Nuclear Decay: Evidence for a Young World," *Institute for Creation Research*, October 1, 2002, https://www.icr.org/article/302/.
28 Jason Lisle, *Taking Back Astronomy* (Green Forest, Ark.: Master, 2006); Humphreys.
29 The information contained in this paragraph presents a general overview of the subject. Readers who want to read more on this topic may consult Timothy Clarey, *Carved in Stone: Geological Evidence of the Worldwide Flood* (Dallas: Institute for Creation Research, 2020); and John D. Morris, *The Young Earth* (Green Forest, Ark.: New Leaf, 2007).
30 Todd C. Wood, "An Evaluation of *Homo naledi* and 'Early' *Homo* from a Young-Age Creationist Perspective," *Journal of Creation Theology and Science Series B: Life Sciences* (2016): 6:14–30.
31 Stephen C. Meyer, *Return of the God Hypothesis: Three Scientific Discoveries that Reveal the Mind Behind the Universe* (New York: HarperOne, 2021).
32 Hugh Ross, "Anthropic Principle: A Precise Plan for Humanity," *Reasons to Believe*, January 1, 2002, https://reasons.org/explore/publications/facts-for-faith/anthropic-principle-a-precise-plan-for-humanity.
33 Charles B. Thaxton et al, *The Mystery of Life's Origin: The Continuing Controversy* (Seattle: Discovery Institute Press, 2020).
34 Michael J. Behe, *The Edge of Evolution: The Search for the Limits of Darwinism* (New York: Free, 2007); Stephen Buranyi, "Do We Need a New Theory of Evolution?" *The Guardian*, June 28, 2022, https://www.theguardian.com/science/2022/jun/28/do-we-need-a-new-theory-of-evolution.
35 Behe, *Darwin's Black Box*; Douglas Axe, *Undeniable: How Biology Confirms Our Intuition that Life Is Designed* (New York: HarperOne, 2017); Meyer, *Darwin's Doubt*.
36 Sarah Pruitt, "Scientists Find Soft Tissue in 75-million-year-old Dinosaur Bones," *History*, June 16, 2015, upd. August 26, 2018, https://www.history.com/news/scientists-find-soft-tissue-in-75-million-year-old-dinosaur-bones; Robert F. Service, "'I Don't Care What They Say about Me': Paleontologist Stares Down Critics in Her Hunt for Dinosaur Proteins," *Science*, September 13, 2017, https://www.science.org/content/article/i-don-t-care-what-they-say-about-me-paleontologist-stares-down-critics-her-hunt.

37 F. Leroy Forlines, *The Quest for Truth: Answering Life's Inescapable Questions* (Nashville: Randall House, 2001).
38 Hugh of St. Victor, *The Didascalicon of Hugh of Saint Victor: A Medieval Guide to the Arts* (1130s; repr., New York: Columbian University Press, 1991).

CHAPTER THIRTEEN
1 Plato, *The Republic*, trans. Benjamin Jowett (Mineola, N.Y.: Dover Thrift, 2000), 89.
2 Declaration of Independence (U. S. 1776).
3 Rod Dreher, *Crunchy Cons: The New Conservative Counterculture and Its Return to Roots* (New York: Crown Forum, 2006), 1.
4 Aristotle, *Politics* (Oxford: Oxford University Press, 1995), 8.
5 Abraham Kuyper, *Pro Rege: Living Under Christ the King*, vol. 2, ed. John Kok and Nelson D. Kloosterman, trans. Govert Buijs (Bellingham, Wash.: Lexham, 2017), 372.
6 Ibid.
7 Abraham Kuyper, *Our Program: A Christian Political Manifesto*, trans. and ed. Harry Van Dyke (Bellingham, Wash.: Lexham, 2015), 21.
8 See, for example, Abraham Kuyper, *Lectures on Calvinism* (1931; repr., Grand Rapids, Mich.: Eerdmans, 1987).
9 Ibid.
10 Ibid., 139.
11 Ibid., 142–43.
12 Ibid., 146.
13 See Dreher, *Crunchy Cons*; and Rod Dreher, *Live Not by Lies: A Manual for Christian Dissidents* (New York: Sentinel, 2020).
14 See E. F. Schumacher, *Small Is Beautiful: Economics As If People Mattered* (1973; repr., Point Roberts, Wash.: Hartley and Marks, 1999).
15 Plato, 223.
16 Edmund Burke, *Reflections on the Revolution in France*, in *The Portable Conservative Reader*, ed. Russell Kirk (New York: Penguin, 1982), 34.
17 Russell Kirk, *The Roots of American Order* (Wilmington, Del.: ISI, 2003), 6.
18 Mark David Hall, *Did America Have a Christian Founding?* (Nashville: Nelson, 2019), xxi–xxii.
19 Kirk, *Roots*, 29.
20 M. E. Bradford, *Original Intentions: On the Making and Ratification of the Constitution* (Athens, Ga.: University of Georgia, 1993), 17.
21 Nick Spencer, *Freedom and Order: History, Politics and the English Bible* (London: Hodder & Stoughton, 2011), 18–19.
22 Ibid., 29.
23 Ibid., 32.
24 Ibid., 53
25 "The Sentence of the High Court of Justice Upon the King" [1649], in *The Puritan Revolution: A Documentary History*, ed. Stuart E. Prall (London: Routledge & Kegan Paul, 1968), 192.
26 William Bradford, *Of Plymouth Plantation*, in *The Norton Anthology of American Literature: Beginnings to 1820*, ed. Robert S. Levine (New York: W. W. Norton, 2017), 149.
27 The term *British* applies to titles and events that take place after the Act of Union (1707), a law that formally unified England and Scotland.
28 Jonathan Mayhew, "A Discourse concerning Unlimited Submission and Non-Resistance to the Higher Powers: With some Reflections on the Resistance made to King Charles I. And on the Anniversary of his Death: In which the Mysterious Doctrine of that Prince's Saintship and Martyrdom is Unriddled," January 30, 1770, ed. Paul Royster, Electronic Texts in American Studies, Libraries at University of Nebraska-Lincoln,

https://digitalcommons.unl.edu/etas/44/?utm_source=digitalcommons.unl.edu%252Fetas%252F44&utm_medium=PDF&utm_campaign=PDFCoverPages.
29. Ibid.
30. Ibid., 21.
31. Stephen Langton, Paris, BnF lat. 14414. fol. 72ra, quoted in Spencer, 51.
32. United Nations Universal Declaration of Human Rights, article 24.
33. Russell Kirk, *The Conservative Mind: From Burke to Eliot*, 7th ed. (Washington, D.C.: Regnery, 1995), 48.
34. Ibid., 49.
35. Dreher, *Crunchy Cons*, 2.
36. Kuyper, *Our Program*, 142.

CHAPTER FOURTEEN

1. Mark A. Noll, *The Scandal of the Evangelical Mind* (Grand Rapids, Mich.: Eerdmans, 1994), 137.
2. For a critique of Noll's thesis, see Phillip T. Morgan, "Thomism to Augustinianism: Free Will Baptist Bible College and the Hybrid Christian Education Model" (presented at the National Association of Free Will Baptists Theological Symposium, Moore, Okla., October 23, 2018).
3. Herman E. Daly, "Sustainable Economic Development: Definitions, Principles, Policies," in *The Essential Agrarian Reader: The Future of Culture, Community, and the Land*, ed. Norman Wirzba (Berkeley, Calif.: Counterpoint, 2003), 63.
4. Harry C. Veryser, *It Didn't Have to Be This Way: Why Boom and Bust Is Unnecessary—and How the Austrian School of Economics Breaks the Cycle* (Wilmington, Del.: ISI, 2012), 148.
5. Greg Forster, *Economics: A Student's Guide*, Reclaiming the Christian Intellectual Tradition, ed. David S. Dockery (Wheaton: Crossway, 2019), 20–21.
6. Marco Rubio, "What Economics Is For," *First Things*, August 26, 2019, https://www.firstthings.com/web-exclusives/2019/08/what-economics-is-for.
7. M. L. Hollis, *The Dignity of Labor* (public address to the graduating class of Amory, Mississippi, High School, May 24, 1959), box G, envelope 17, National Association of Free Will Baptists Historical Collection, Welch College Library.
8. Martin Luther, *Luther's Works, Sermon on the Mount and the Magnificat*, ed. J. Pelikan, vol. 21 (St. Louis: Concordia, 1958), 237; see also Chad Brand, *Flourishing Faith: A Baptist Primer on Work, Economics, and Civic Stewardship*, The Oikonomia Series (Grand Rapids, Mich.: Christian's Library Press, 2012), 17.
9. Ibid., 4.
10. Annie Dillard, *Pilgrim at Tinker Creek* (New York: Harper Perennial Classics, 1999), 17.
11. Brand, 28–30.
12. Obviously, the Tenth Commandment applies to a wide range of situations beyond private property.
13. Wayne Grudem, *Politics According to the Bible: A Comprehensive Resource for Understanding Modern Political Issues in Light of Scripture* (Grand Rapids, Mich.: Zondervan, 2010), 262–63.
14. John Calvin, *Institutes of the Christian Religion*, trans. Henry Beveridge (Peabody, Mass.: Hendrickson, 2008), 259.
15. Brand, 30.
16. See J. R. R. Tolkien, "On Fairy-Stories" (1947), *Tree and Leaf* (New York: Harper Collins, 2001); and C. S. Lewis, "On Three Ways of Writing for Children" (1952), in *On Stories: And Other Essays on Literature* (Orlando, Fla.: Harcourt, 1982), 35–36.
17. Veryser, 37.
18. Roger Scruton, *Green Philosophy: How to Think Seriously about the Planet* (London: Atlantic, 2012), 178. For information on the medieval rise of capitalism, see Rodney Stark, *How

the West Won: The Neglected Story of the Triumph of Modernity (Wilmington, Del.: ISI, 2014), 131–35. For information on the distinct connection between England and Flanders in the rise of capitalism, see Morris Bishop, *The Middle Ages* (1968; repr., Boston: Houghton Mifflin, 1996), 45.
19 Ronald H. Nash, *Social Justice and the Christian Church* (Milford, Mich.: Mott Media, 1983), 81.
20 Ibid., 87.
21 Paul Heyne, *A Student's Guide to Economics*, The Preston A. Wells Jr. Guides to the Major Disciplines (Wilmington, Del.: ISI, 2000), 3–4.
22 Ibid., 4.
23 Veryser, 37–38.
24 Nash, 85–86.
25 Veryser, 3.
26 John Paul II, *Centesimus Annus*, in *Papal Economics: The Catholic Church on Democratic Capitalism* (Wilmington, Del.: ISI, 2013), 117.
27 Nash, 85.
28 Ibid.
29 Wendell Berry, *The Unsettling of America: Culture and Agriculture* (1977; repr., Berkeley, Calif.: Counterpoint, 2015), 154–55.
30 Frederick Copleston, *The History of Philosophy: Greece and Rome; From the Pre-Socratics to Plotinus*, vol. I (1946; repr., New York: Image, 1993), 225.
31 Adam Smith, *An Inquiry into the Nature and Causes of the Wealth of Nations*, vol. 1, Glasgow ed. (Indianapolis, Ind.: Liberty Fund, 1981), 15.
32 Smith, 15; Copleston, 225.
33 Veryser, 149.
34 Smith, 28.
35 Ibid., 22.
36 Stark, 325.
37 See Ronald Bailey and Marian L. Tupy, *Ten Global Trends Every Smart Person Should Know: And Many Others You Will Find Interesting* (Washington D.C.: Cato Institute, 2020).
38 Richard J. Hofstadter, *Social Darwinism in American Thought* (1944; repr., Boston: Beacon, 1992), 144.
39 Smith, 31, 37.
40 Daly, 65.
41 Ibid., 69.
42 Victor Claar discusses these dynamics in the context of fair-trade coffee. See Victor V. Claar, *Fair Trade? Its Prospects as a Poverty Solution*, ed. Anthony B. Bradley, Studies in Christian Social Ethics and Economics (Grand Rapids, Mich.: Acton Institute, 2010).
43 Smith, 65.
44 Ibid., 78n8.
45 Horace, *Odes*, book III, XVI, *Inclusam Danaen*, lines 39–40, in Horace, *The Complete Odes and Epodes*, trans. David West (New York: Oxford University Press, 1997), 95.
46 Nash, 87.
47 Heyne, 11.
48 Nash, 88.
49 Virgil, *Aeneid*, book III, lines 79–81, trans. Robert Fitzgerald (New York: Vintage Classics, 1983), 67.
50 Friedrich A. Hayek, *The Constitution of Liberty* (Chicago: The University of Chicago Press, 1960), 221.
51 Henry Hazlitt, *The Foundations of Morality*, 3rd ed. (Irvington-on-Hudson, N.Y.: Foundation for Economic Education, 2010), 326.

52 Nash, 83.
53 Veryser, 22–25.
54 Brand, 39.
55 Ibid., 40–42.
56 Smith, 26. The profit motive is also referenced positively in Scripture. In I Corinthians 9:24–25, Paul exhorts us to seek the prize of an incorruptible crown for having run the race of faith well. We were created to respond positively to incentives.
57 Ibid., 27.
58 For example, God assures Abraham that He will bless him for moving to a new land (Genesis 12:2), promises to give him all the land he can see in Canaan (13:14–15), and pledges He will reward Abraham richly for his faith (15:1). In Mark's Gospel, Jesus explains to His disciples that followers who have given up family or lands or wealth for the gospel will "receive a hundredfold now in this time . . . and in the age to come eternal life" (10:29–30).
59 Heyne, 24.
60 Nash, 57.
61 Ibid., 74.
62 Ibid., 75.
63 Brand, 73.
64 Nash, 59.
65 Friedrich A. Hayek, *Law, Legislation and Liberty: A New Statement of the Liberal Principles of Justice and Political Economy; Volume 2: The Mirage of Social Justice* (Chicago: The University of Chicago Press, 1976), 66.
66 Even Engels admitted the many benefits to personal liberty that accompanied economic freedom. See Frederick Engels, *Socialism: Utopian and Scientific*, trans. Edward Aveling (New York: Charles Scribner's Sons, 1892), 46–47.
67 For statistics regarding the increase in the standard of living, see Stark, 325.
68 Engels, 18–19, 23–24.
69 Hazlitt, 326.
70 William D. Dennison, *Karl Marx*, Great Thinkers (Phillipsburg, N.J.: P&R, 2017), 2.
71 Ibid., 88–98.
72 Karl Marx, *A Contribution to the Critique of Political Economy*, trans. N. I. Stone (Chicago: Charles H. Kerr and Company, 1904), 11; see also Engels, 45–46.
73 Karl Marx, *Critique of Hegel's 'Philosophy of Right'*, trans. Annette Jolin and Joseph O'Malley (Cambridge: Cambridge University Press, 1982), 131.
74 Engels, 41–42.
75 Dennison, 76–80.
76 Roger Scruton, *A Short History of Modern Philosophy: From Descartes to Wittgenstein*, 2nd ed. (New York: Routledge Classics, 2002), 231.
77 Engels, 43–44.
78 Dennison, 60–63; see also Engels, 8–9.
79 Mark Skousen, *The Big Three in Economics: Adam Smith, Karl Marx, and John Maynard Keynes* (Armonk, N.Y.: M. E. Sharpe, 2007), 88.
80 Dennison, 68–69.
81 Grudem, 262.
82 Stark, 339.
83 Jean-Louis Panne et al., *The Black Book of Communism: Crimes, Terror, Repression* (Cambridge: Harvard University Press, 1999), 4.
84 Ludwig von Mises, *Socialism: An Economic and Sociological Analysis*, trans. J. Kahane (Indianapolis, Ind.: Liberty Fund, 1981), 113.

85 Kerry Jackson, "Denmark Tells Bernie Sanders It's Had Enough of His 'Socialist' Slurs," *Investor's Business Daily*, November 9, 2015, https://www.investors.com/denmark-tells-bernie-sanders-to-stop-calling-it-socialist/; Michael Kelly-Gagnon, "Denmark: Not as Socialist (Nor as Successful) as You Think," *Huffington Post*, January 19, 2016, updated October 30, 2017, https://www.huffingtonpost.ca/michel-kellygagnon/denmark-not-socialist_b_9011652.html.

86 Suzanne Daley, "Danes Rethink a Welfare State Ample to a Fault," *New York Times*, April 20, 2013, https://www.nytimes.com/2013/04/21/world/europe/danes-rethink-a-welfare-state-ample-to-a-fault.html?_r=0.

87 Jesus Fernández-Villaverde and Lee E. Ohanian, "How Sweden Overcame Socialism," *Wall Street Journal*, January 9, 2019, https://www.wsj.com/articles/how-sweden-overcame-socialism-11547078767; Per Bylund, "How Government Cutbacks Ended Sweden's Great Depression," *Mises Institute Daily Articles*, December 25, 2013, https://mises.org/library/how-government-cutbacks-ended-swedens-great-depression.

88 Riitta Hjerppe, "An Economic History of Finland," *EH.net Encyclopedia*, ed. Robert Whaples, February 10, 2008, https://eh.net/encyclopedia/an-economic-history-of-finland/.

89 "2022 Index of Economic Freedom," *The Heritage Foundation*, 2022, https://www.heritage.org/index/ranking.

90 Hazlitt, 326.

91 Ivona Lacob, "Venezuela's Failed Socialist Experiment," *Forbes*, July 24, 2016, https://www.forbes.com/sites/ivonaiacob/2016/07/24/venezuelas-failed-socialist-experiment/#61f27f7141dd; Andres Malave, "How Socialism Failed Venezuela: Venezuela is Burning and We're Overlooking the Root Cause of Its Crisis," *U.S. News and World Report*, June 6, 2016, https://www.usnews.com/opinion/articles/2016-06-06/socialism-is-devastating-venezuela-and-americans-dont-seem-to-notice; Bret Stephens, "Yes, Venezuela Is a Socialist Catastrophe," *New York Times*, January 25, 2019, https://www.nytimes.com/2019/01/25/opinion/venezuela-maduro-socialism-government.html.

92 José Niño, "A History of Venezuelan Inflation," *Mises Wire*, January 7, 2018, https://mises.org/wire/history-venezuelan-inflation.

93 José Niño, "Venezuela Didn't Need High Oil Prices to Prosper Before Chavismo," *Mises Wire*, December 19, 2018, https://mises.org/wire/venezuela-didnt-need-high-oil-prices-prosper-chavismo.

94 David Montgomery, "AOC's Chief of Change: Saikat Chakrabarti Isn't Just Running Her Office. He's Guiding a Movement," *Washington Post*, July 10, 2019, https://www.washingtonpost.com/news/magazine/wp/2019/07/10/feature/how-saikat-chakrabarti-became-aocs-chief-of-change/?noredirect=on&utm_term=.5a2dd79b6206.

CHAPTER FIFTEEN

1 In this opening paragraph, we are appropriating an illustration that James K. A. Smith uses to demonstrate the liturgical habits of life. See James K. A. Smith, *Desiring the Kingdom: Worship, Worldview, and Cultural Formation*, Cultural Liturgies, Volume 1 (Grand Rapids, Mich.: Baker Academic, 2009).

2 See David G. McComb, *Sports in World History*, Themes in World History (New York: Routledge, 2004); and Nick J. Watson and Andrew Parker, eds., *Sports and Christianity: Historical and Contemporary Perspectives*, Routledge Research in Sport, Culture and Society (London: Routledge, 2015).

3 Jeremy R. Treat, "More Than a Game: A Theology of Sport," *Themelios* 40, no. 3 (December 2015): 393.

4 This phrase comes from the title of the following book: Andy Crouch, *Culture Making: Recovering Our Creative Calling* (Downers Grove, Ill.: IVP, 2008).

5 Treat, 393–94.
6 Leland Ryken, *Work and Leisure in Christian Perspective* (Eugene, Ore.: Wipf and Stock, 2002).
7 Paul Heintzman, *Leisure and Spirituality: Biblical, Historical, and Contemporary Perspectives*, Engaging Culture, ed. William A. Dyrness and Robert K. Johnston (Grand Rapids, Mich.: Baker Academic, 2015), 177.
8 Steve McMullin, "The Secularization of Sunday: Real or Perceived Competition for Churches," *Review of Religious Research* 55, no. 1. (March 2013): 44.
9 Carol Bragg, "Growth of Youth Sports," *ESPN The Magazine* (Summer 2014): 34.
10 Steven N. Waller, "Favourite Pew or Box Seat? Sabbath Beliefs as a Barrier to Sporting Event Attendance on Sunday: A Congregational Study," *The Journal of Religion and Popular Culture* 21, no. 2 (Summer 2009): 44–49.
11 Adam Shell, "Why Families Stretch their Budgets for High-priced Youth Sports," *USA Today*, September 7, 2017, https://www.usatoday.com/story/money/2017/09/05/why-families-stretch-their-budgets-high-priced-youth-sports/571945001/.
12 See Josef Pieper, *Leisure: The Basis of Culture* (San Francisco: Ignatius, 2009).
13 This phrase comes from the title of Neil Postman's *Amusing Ourselves to Death: Public Discourse in the Age of Show Business* (New York: Penguin, 2005).
14 David E. Prince, *In the Arena: The Promise of Sports for Christian Discipleship* (Nashville: B&H, 2016).
15 See Malcolm Gladwell, *Outliers: The Story of Success* (New York: Little Brown, 2008), 35–68.
16 See Edward E. Moody, *Surviving Culture: When Character and Your World Collide* (Nashville: Randall House, 2014).
17 David E. Prince, Tracey Bianchi, Michael Wright, and Leneita Fix, "When Church Gets Sidelined by Youth Sports," *Christianity Today*, May 21, 2018, https://www.christianitytoday.com/pastors/2018/may-web-exclusives/when-church-gets-sidelined-youth-sports.html.

CONCLUSION

1 Quoted in Oliver O'Donovan and Joan Lockwood O'Donovan, eds., *From Irenaeus to Grotius: A Sourcebook in Christian Political Thought* (Grand Rapids, Mich.: Eerdmans, 1999), 12–13.

Scripture Index

Genesis
1:1, 117, 221, 224, 232
1:2, 62, 72, 224
1:4, 221
1:5, 23
1:10, 63, 221
1:11–12, 225, 235
1:12, 63, 221
1:18, 63, 221
1:21, 63, 73, 221, 225, 235
1:24–25, 225, 235
1:25, 63, 221
1:26a, 167
1:26b, 65
1:26, 67
1:26–27, 18, 42, 114, 221, 232, 238
1:26–28, 65, 252, 254
1:26–29, 64
1:27, 205
1:28, 18, 114, 117, 177, 179–81, 199, 221, 228, 232, 235, 246, 271
1:31, 63, 114, 221
1–2, 61, 64, 66, 68, 224–25, 234, 236
1–11, 222–23
2, 66–69, 166, 177, 234
2,2–3, 273
2:5, 65, 114, 180
2:7, 67–68
2:7–8, 64
2:9, 66, 180, 223
2:15, 65–66, 179
2:15–17, 223
2:15–25, 64
2:16–17, 179, 272
2:17, 180
2:17a, 66
2:17b, 66
2:18, 35, 234

2:23–24, 222
2:24, 232, 234
2:25, 180
3, 64, 70, 114, 223, 237
3:1, 179
3:1–7, 180
3:2–3, 180
3:3b, 69
3:6, 180, 205
3:6b, 179
3:7a, 69, 180
3:7b, 180
3:12, 179
3:15, 69, 72
3:17, 70, 179
3:17–19, 252
3:18, 70
3:21, 180, 223
4:1–15, 237
4:9, 182
6:5, 72
7:11, 72
9, 66, 245, 247–48
9:1, 72
9:1–4, 72, 223
9:1–7, 254
9:6, 247
9:9, 66
9:12, 246
10:29–30, 316n58
12:2, 316n58
13:2, 253
13:14–15, 316n58
15:1, 316n58
25:29–34, 56
35:11–12, 73

Exodus
1:7, 73
3:21–22, 116
3:22, 13

12:35–36, 116
12:36, 13
13, 86
13:14, 86
20:3, 276
20:8–11, 74, 189, 273
20:11, 67, 223
20:12, 36, 149, 182
20:13, 247
20:15, 47, 254
20:17, 294n74
23:3, 254
23:6, 254
23:11, 254
23:12, 74
31:17, 223

Leviticus
4, 69
12, 69
13, 69
14, 69
16, 69
19:18, 67, 182
19:36, 254
25:4, 74
25:5–7, 74

Deuteronomy
4:9–10, 88
5, 86
5:12–15, 189, 273
5:15, 296
5:16, 36, 86
5:19, 47
5:21, 294n74
6:5, 67, 182, 282
6:7, 182
8:19–20, 88
28, 262

JOSHUA
10:12–14, 214

JUDGES
19, 108

2 SAMUEL
1:23, 109
2:7, 52
11, 108

1 KINGS
15:3, 87
21, 47

2 KINGS
15:3, 87
16:3, 88

1 CHRONICLES
29:26–28, 253

2 CHRONICLES
1:11–12, 253

JOB
42:10, 253

PSALMS
1:1–6, 43
8:3, 229
8:4, 229, 287n1
8:5, 229, 238
8:6–8, 229, 246
8:9, 229
14:3, 44
19:1, 222
24:1, 253
33:4–11, 222
115:16, 65
139:13, 178
139:23–24, 279
150:2b, 157

PROVERBS
1:2a, 39
1:5a, 96
1:7, 39
1:7b, 96
1:8, 39
6:6–11, 41
8, 62
15:16, 254
15:19, 253
16:11, 254
17:1, 254
19:15, 254
19:17, 52
22:2, 52
22:9, 52
27:17, 134
28:27, 52
31, 260

ECCLESIASTES
9:10, 283
12:1, 281

ISAIAH
1:12–17, 193
1:18, 222
9:6, 26
11:6, 223
42:5–7, 182
52:11, 8
54:9, 223
65–66, 117

JEREMIAH
1:5, 178
17:5–8, 43
17:9, 44, 70
29:5–6, 119
29:7, 119, 184, 232, 250
31, 308n24
32:17, 222

DANIEL
1:8–13, 279
1:14–16, 279
2:44, 26
3:8–18, 279
3:17–18, 279
3:19–30, 279

MATTHEW
2:6, 26
4:1–11, 180
4:18–22, 187
5:13, 11
5:13–16, 181
5:14–16, 1, 278
5:16, 15, 194
5:21–30, 86
5:23–24, 185
5:28, 109
6:24, 282
6:33, 276, 282
7:24–27, 183
7:24–28, 126
8:20, 255
9:9, 187
13:24–30, 119, 181
13:36–43, 181
15:1–9, 87
18:11, 117, 180
18:15–20, 185
19:21, 187
22:35–40, 205
24:36, 89, 95
25:14–30, 254
25:26, 253
25:31–46, 181
26:52, 187
28:18, 232
28:18–20, 117

MARK
5:18–19, 187
6:3, 253
6:31, 273
7:1–13, 87
8:35, 26
8:36, 279
12:17, 236
12:29–31, 183
12:31, 262
12:41–44, 254
13:32, 89
14:3–8, 301n42

LUKE
1:1–4, 89
3:12–13, 187
3:14, 187
6:39–45, 43

7:1–10, 187
9:23, 26
21:1–4, 52

JOHN
1:1, 119
1:1–3, 159
1:1–5, 222
1:14, 119
1:14b, 162
8:34, 249
8:36, 249
9, 186
9:5, 186
10:36, 14
12:31, 8
14:30, 8
15:19, 10, 132
15:19b, 7
16:7–11, 186
17, 2
17:6, 7
17:11, 11, 119
17:13, 10
17:14–16, 132
17:14–19, 7
17:15, 1, 11
17:15b, 1
17:17, 1, 14
17:18, 1, 14, 95
17:19, 14
20:21, 186

ACTS
2:44, 48
17, 10
17:22–34, 132
17:24–28, 222
17:28, 119

ROMANS
1:18–20, 36
1:18–21, 222
1:20, 229
1:20–25, 88
1:23, 282
1:27, 8
2:14–16, 36

4:4, 8
5:12, 44
6:16–19, 249
7, 133
7:14–25, 133
8:19–22, 70
8:20–22, 223, 253
12:1–2, 8
12:2, 152, 194
12:3–13, 194
12:10, 185
12:14–21, 194
12:15, 185
12:16, 185
13, 244
13:2, 244
13:2–3, 254
16:16, 185

1 CORINTHIANS
6:18–20, 115
6:19–20, 283
9:3–10, 253
9:19, 249
10:23, 138
10:31, 1, 134, 280
12, 181
12:12–31, 42
14:15, 104
15, 117–18
15:14–17, 89
15:20, 74
15:22, 44, 69
15:31, 26
15:33, 119
15:58, 118

2 CORINTHIANS
2:11, 120
4, 87
4:17, 87
5:10, 43
5:20, 181
6:14, 277
6:17, 8, 132
10:4–5, 96
10:5, 1, 99, 133, 138, 284
13:11, 185

GALATIANS
1:4, 2, 8, 152, 277
2:20, 26
3:26–28, 42
4:4, 89, 117
5:22–23, 133, 281
6:7–8, 281
6:10, 189, 309n54

EPHESIANS
1:3–10, 89
1:4, 72
1:10, 118, 133, 206, 230
1:19b–20, 180
2, 185
2:4, 180
2:8–9, 180
2:10, 205
4:1, 190
4:2–3, 190
4:17–32, 190
4:18, 252
4:28, 178, 190
5:1–21, 190
5:9, 133
5:15–19, 282
5:19, 104
5–6, 183
6:2, 86
6:5–8, 191
6:5–9, 190
6:12, 251

PHILIPPIANS
2:5, 283
3:20, 286
4:5, 282
4:7–8, 122, 124, 126
4:8, 2, 76, 100, 140, 199, 278, 283, 301n33, 303n12
4:8–9, 168
4:10–14, 52

COLOSSIANS
1:15, 74
1:15–17, 222
1:16, 74, 222
1:18, 75

1:19–20, 74
1:21, 95
3:2, 139, 145
3:9–10, 206
3:17, 191
3:23, 253, 280
3:23–24, 181, 191
3–4, 183

1 Thessalonians
5:15, 185
5:25, 185

2 Thessalonians
2:15, 87

1 Timothy
2:9, 109
3:1, 186
4:8, 254, 278
5:17, 185
6:6–12, 281
6:10, 193

2 Timothy
1:3, 86
1:13, 87

2:2, 87
2:11, 11
2:22, 281
3:1–7, 281

Titus
1:12, 117, 119
2, 183

Hebrews
2:14, 69
4:9, 75
6:5, 8
10:25, 185, 189, 275
11:3, 221–23
11:37–38, 255
12:1, 150

James
1:4, 145
1:9–11, 52
1:17, 111, 115, 254
1:22, 285
1:27, 8
2:1–13, 42
4:4, 8

1 Peter
1:10–21, 152
2:9, 16, 182
2:11, 8, 232

2 Peter
1:3, 278
2:9, 131
3:9, 182

1 John
1:1–3, 89
2:17, 8
3:13, 9
4:4, 8
5:19, 8

Jude
1:3, 149

Revelation
11:15, 26
21:4, 223
21:5, 1, 73, 284
21–22, 117
22:2, 223

Name Index

Abraham, 69, 73, 253, 316n58
Adam, 61, 66, 69, 72, 74, 114, 162, 166, 169, 179–80, 199, 208, 223, 225, 237, 246, 252–53, 256, 272, 282
Adams, John, 41
Adams, Thomas, 178
Alcuin of York, 241
Alfred the Great, 95, 241
Aquinas, Thomas, 21, 47, 261
Aratus, 119
Archimedes, 211
Aristotle, 43, 151, 211, 213, 217, 234, 239, 250, 261–62, 303n3
Ascham, Roger, 104
Ashford, Bruce, 1, 54
Augustine of Canterbury, 241, 249
Augustine of Hippo, 13, 43–44, 66, 90, 95, 106, 108, 116–17, 119–20, 127, 132, 178, 181, 202, 261, 302n64, 303n3
Austen, Jane, 141

Babbitt, Irving, 95
Bach, Johann Sebastian, 104, 107, 127, 189
Bacon, Francis, 214–15
Baker, Samuel, 203
Barna, George, 12
Bartholomew, Craig, 22, 206
Basil the Great, 127, 302n49
Bathsheba, 108
Behe, Michael, 218, 227
Berry, Wendell, 127, 143, 148, 188
Bezalel, 253
Black, Gary, Jr., 181, 185
Bloch, Marc, 88
Bloom, Allan, 104
Bolt, John, 50, 195
Bonhoeffer, Dietrich, 190, 202
Borgmann, Albert, 147–48, 304n41
Boswell, Matt, 127
Bracey, Matthew Steven, xiii, xv, 1, 33, 88, 113, 177, 296n20
Bradford, M. E., 240
Brahe, Tycho, 212, 214
Brand, Chad, 48, 254

Brende, Eric, 156
Bromiley, Geoffrey, 207
Bruegel, Pieter the Elder, 122, 127
Burke, Edmund, xiii, xv, 33, 35–36, 38–39, 41, 47, 49, 57–58, 82, 161, 238–39, 290n2, 290n5–6, 292n35

Cage, John, 30, 104
Cairns, Earl E., 89
Carey, William, 12, 15–16
Carnell, E. J., 26–27, 29, 290n46
Carson, D. A., 23
Cathy, Samuel Truett, 189
Calvin, John, 48, 100, 116–17, 127, 159, 254, 261, 263
Chakrabarti, Saikat, 269
Chamberlain, Wilt, 51–52
Chambers, Robert, 216
Charles I, King, 242–44
Chaucer, Geoffrey, 168
Chesterton, G. K., 36
Cicero, 103, 169, 250
Clark, Gordon, 89–90
Clement of Alexandria, 9, 303n3
Collins, Francis, 218
Copernicus, Nicolaus, 212–13
Crouch, Andy, 14, 114, 147, 199, 208, 317n4
Cuvier, Georges, 216

Daly, Herman, 251, 259
Daniel, 11, 279
Darwin, Charles, 24–25, 30, 63, 68, 215–20, 228, 258, 276
Darwin, Erasmus, 216
David, 43, 69, 108–09, 229, 253, 279
Dawkins, Richard, 220
Dawn, Marva, 135, 137, 149, 152–54, 157
Dennett, Daniel, 220
Dennison, William, 92, 264
Derrida, Jacques, 164–65, 173
Descartes, René, 22–24
Detweiler, Craig, 197–98
Dewey, John, 288n1
Dillard, Annie, 253

323

Dod, John, 188
Donne, John, 127
Dostoyevsky, Fyodor, 46, 50
Drake, Joshua Farris, 124, 301n42
Dreher, Rod, xiii, 33, 38, 58, 142, 150, 152, 156, 233, 237, 290n3, 291n8

Eliot, T. S., 17, 36, 105, 127, 161
Elisha, 253
Ellul, Jacques, 149, 198, 202
Engels, Friedrich, 263–65, 316n66
Epimenides, 119
Esau, 56
Ethelred, 241
Eve, 61, 66, 69, 72, 166, 179–80, 208, 223, 225, 237, 252–53, 272, 282

Faulkner, William, 161
Fish, Stanley, 173
Ford, Harrison, 128
Forlines, F. Leroy, xiii, 26, 28–29, 67–68, 73, 87, 127, 129–31, 133, 137, 178–79, 191, 193–94, 205–06, 228, 287n10
Forster, Greg, 31, 180, 251
Foucault, Michel, 173
Fourier, Charles, 264
Frame, John, 120, 125–26, 131–32, 302n65
Freud, Sigmund, 24–26

Galilei, Galileo, 211–14, 216–17, 219, 227
George III, 245
Getty, Keith, 127
Getty, Kristyn, 127
Giacometti, 104
Gibbon, Edward, 161
Gideon, 253
Gilbert, Greg, 308n14
Gladwell, Malcolm, 278, 280
Godet, Frédéric, 14
Goethe, 96
Godkin, Edwin Lawrence, 46
Goheen, Michael, 22, 206
Golding, William, 44
Gordon, T. David, 137, 144
Gramsci, Antonio, 93
Grant, Edward, 211
Green, Bradley, 84, 89, 94
Grudem, Wayne, 266

Hadad-yisʻi, 65
Hall, Joseph, 188

Hall, Mark David, 240
Hayek, Friedrich, 41, 263
Hazlitt, Henry, 261
Hegel, Georg Wilhelm Friedrich, 92, 97–100, 105, 265
Heintzman, Paul, 273
Helwys, Thomas, 189
Henley, William Ernest, 35
Henry, Carl F. H., 48, 130, 178, 205, 293n50
Henry, Matthew, 7
Herbert, George, 127
Herder, Johann Gottfried, 17
Heyne, Paul, 262
Hirsch, E. D., 173–75
Holley, Darrell, xiii, xvii, 2, 28, 97, 114, 121–22
Homer, 161
Hopkins, Gerard Manley, 127
Horace, 84, 260, 306n4
Horner, Grant, 120, 133
Horton, Michael, 153–54, 304n55
Hugh of St. Vincent, 230
Humboldt, Wilhelm von, 17
Humphreys, Russell, 226
Huxley, Aldous, 161, 201–02

Jacob, 56, 73, 108, 253
Jackson, Maggie, 144
Jaki, Stanley, 211
James, 187, 253
James, brother of Jesus, 8, 285
Jenkins, Bethany, 180
Jeremiah, 43, 119, 184, 232
Jesus, 1–2, 7–12, 14–16, 18, 25, 43, 67, 69, 75, 86–87, 89–90, 95, 116–18, 124–25, 133, 151, 153–55, 159–60, 180–82, 184–88, 191–92, 197–99, 205–06, 222, 230, 253–55, 262, 273, 276, 279–80, 282–83, 285, 316n58
Job, 253
John, 8, 10, 16, 89, 118, 120, 159, 162, 167, 186–87, 253
John Paul II, 256
Johnson, Philip, 218
Joseph of Arimathea, 253

Kant, Immanuel, 23–24
Kauflin, Bob, 127
Keller, Tim, 115–117, 120, 132, 180, 307n3
Kepler, Johannes, 212, 214
Kidner, Derek, 138
Kierkegaard, Søren, 19

NAME INDEX

King John, 242
Kingsley, Charles, 190
Kipling, Rudyard, 37
Kirk, Russell, 33, 35, 37–39, 41–42, 44, 46, 48–50, 53, 55–59, 82, 87, 167, 239–40, 245, 247–48, 290n3–4, 290n7, 291n24, 293n61
Kuhn, Thomas, 214
Kuyper, Abraham, xiii, 1, 12, 41–42, 234–37, 239

Lamarck, Jean-Baptiste, 216
Langton, Stephen, 242, 244
Lasch, Christopher, 149
Leo XIII, 41
Levin, Yuval, 30
Lewis, C. S., xiii, 1, 36, 41–42, 57, 96, 100–01, 141–42, 145–46, 188–89, 301n47
Linnaeus, Carl, 216
Lippmann, Walter, 43
Lisle, Jason, 226
Lloyd-Jones, Martyn, 189
Locke, John, 35, 44, 264, 293n63
Lot, 108
Luke, 89, 187
Luther, Martin, 88, 194, 253
Lyell, Charles, 216

Macaulay, Thomas Babington, 103–04
MacDonald, George, 127, 301n47
Markins, Matt, 144
Marx, Karl, 24, 26, 92–94, 165, 173, 245, 255, 263–67, 269, 289n27
Matthew, 187
Mayhew, Jonathan, 244–45
McGrath, Alister, 19, 23, 28
McLuhan, Marshall, 121
Melville, Herman, 71
Menander, 119
Meyer, Stephen, 218, 227
Mill, John Stuart, 35
Milton, John, 72, 117, 161, 168
Mohler, Albert, 178
Moore, Russell, 17, 131, 287n3, 295n104
More, Thomas, 104
More, Paul Elmer, 45
Morgan, Phillip, xiii, xviii, 2, 28, 81, 251, 298n59, 304n52, 314n2
Morris, Henry, 218, 312n29, 315n18
Moses, 25, 69, 73–74, 86, 116
Muggeridge, Malcolm, 162–63

Mullins, Jim, 178
Munson, Paul, 124–25, 301n42
Myers, Ken, xiii, 17, 137, 139–40, 146, 151, 153–54, 287n1, 300n3

Nagel, Thomas, 41
Nash, Ronald, 42, 45, 159, 255, 261–63
Nelson, Tom, 177, 187, 308n24
Newton, Isaac, 214–17, 219, 228
Niebuhr, H. Richard, 1, 16, 288n19, 300n3
Nietzsche, Friedrich, 24–26, 151, 165, 304n32, 305n61
Nero, 11
Noah, 66, 69, 72–73, 223, 246, 253–54
Noll, Mark, 251, 314n2
Novak, Michael, 41, 50, 53
Nozick, Robert, 51

Ocasio-Cortez, Alexandria, 269
O'Connor, Flannery, 127, 189
Oden, Thomas, 28, 135
Orwell, George, 201–02
Overstreet, Jeffrey, 121–22
Owen, Robert, 264

Paley, William, 217
Pappalardo, Chris, 54
Pattison, Robert, 151, 305n61
Paul, 8–9, 16, 42–44, 70, 74, 86–89, 99–102, 104–05, 107–10, 116–20, 122, 124, 132–33, 139, 154–55, 168, 175, 178, 180–81, 185, 190–91, 194, 229, 244, 253, 278, 281, 301n33, 316n56
Pelagius, 44, 293n63
Pelikan, Jaroslav, 36, 84
Penney, J. C., 189
Perkins, William, 188
Peter, 8, 182, 187, 232, 253
Peterson, Andrew, 127, 301n47
Peterson, Eugene, 187, 304n32
Picasso, Pablo, 106, 122–23
Pinson, Matthew, xiii, xviii–xix, 2, 91, 114, 128, 132, 135, 288n14, 298n59
Plantinga, Alvin, 189
Plato, 42, 64, 151, 161, 211, 231–32, 239, 249–50, 257, 303n3
Postman, Neil, 143, 150, 152, 200–02, 318n13
Poythress, Vern, 160, 167
Protagoras, 23
Proust, Marcel, 98
Ptolemy, 211, 213

Putnam, Robert, 148
Pythagoras, 21

Randolph, John, of Roanoke, 40
Ranke, Leopold Van, 92
Ransom, John Crowe, 35
Raper, Barry, 156
Rea, Robert, 88
Reich, Charles, 151
Rembrandt, 106, 127
Ricardo, David, 265
Richards, Jay, 50, 294n80
Riggs, Ken, 186
Robinson, David, 188
Rookmaaker, Hans, 23, 100–01, 108, 123, 299n14, 301n25
Ross, Allen P., 70
Ross, Hugh, 218
Rousseau, Jean-Jacques, 40, 43–44, 151, 293n63, 305n61
Rozenzweig, Roy, 81
Ryle, J. C., 10–11

Saint Simon, Claude de, 264
Sanders, Bernie, 269
Saussure, Ferdinand de, 163–65
Sayers, Dorothy, 101–02, 186, 189, 191–94
Schaeffer, Francis, xiii, xv, 27–28, 30, 64, 66–68, 75–76, 89, 99, 104, 106, 122–23, 164, 208, 288n4, 288n7, 289n35, 290n46
Schuchardt, Mercer, 147
Schultze, Quentin, 157
Schumacher, E. F., 237
Scruton, Roger, 33, 36, 41, 49, 123, 297n37
Seabrook, John, 143
Shakespeare, William, 102, 104, 106, 161, 167–68, 171–72, 250
Sidney, Sir Philip, 98, 306n4
Sire, James, 20
Smith, Adam, 256–59, 261, 316n56
Smith, James K. A., 317n1
Socrates, 231, 238
Solomon, 39, 175, 254
Solzhenitsyn, Alexandr, 102
Sophocles, 83, 239
Sowell, Thomas, 40–41, 43, 49–50, 167, 292n38, 293n56, 293n69, 294n80
Spencer, Herbert, 24
Spencer, Nick, 241
Stalin, Joseph, 267
Stapert, Calvin, 151

Stark, Rodney, 9, 211, 258, 266, 315n18, 316n67
Stephen, James Fitzjames, 45
Stewart, Jimmy, 128
Stivers, Richard, 144

Tacitus, 103
Talbot, Chris, xiii, xv, 2–3, 19, 91, 197, 285
Taylor, Charles, 28, 30
Thelen, David, 81
Tocqueville, Alexis de, 49
Tolkien, J. R. R., 56, 114, 141–42, 198, 301n47, 309n4
Traeger, Sebastian, 308n14
Travers, P. L., 142
Treat, Jeremy, 271–72
Trotsky, Leon, 97, 99
Tse-tung, Mao, 267
Turnbough, Jeff, 14

Vance, J. D., 45
Veith, Gene Edward, Jr., 21, 178, 181, 189, 308n21
Veryser, Harry, 252
Virgil, 84, 240, 250, 259
Voltaire, 215

Wallace, Alfred Russell, 216
Washington, George, 85
Watts, Jackson, 198
Weaver, Richard, 27–29, 94, 162
Webster, Noah, 166, 169
Wellhausen, Julius, 24–26, 30
Wells, David, 28, 30–31
Wenner, Jann, 150
Wesley, Charles, 12, 15–16
Wesley, John, 16, 193–194, 309n54
Whitcomb, John, 218
Wihtred of Kent, 241
Wilberforce, William, 189
Willard, Dallas, 181, 185
William of Ockham, 21
Williams, Charles, 102
Winter, Richard, 143, 147
Wood, Todd, 226
Wolters, Albert, 117
Wolterstoff, Nicholas, 36
Wright, Christopher J. H., 73, 117
Wright, N. T., 118

Young, R. V., 161

Zirschky, Andrew, 203

Subject and Title Index

60 Minutes, 197
1960s, 28, 51, 150–51, 214, 305n57
1970s, 147, 150–51, 267, 269
2001: A Space Odyssey, 197
a priori, 29, 210, 219–21, 293
Achilles, 161
aesthetics, 23, 33, 76, 104
Anglican Church, 216
America, 36, 92, 147, 151, 167–68, 240, 243, 245, 249, 268–69, 274
American Dictionary, 166, 169
American
    founders, 55, 94, 240–41
    freedom, 233, 248
    law, 232, 240–41, 245, 248
Amish, 11, 135
Amusing Ourselves to Death, 152, 318n13
anarchy, 55, 57
ancestors, 36, 38, 57, 83, 86, 90, 103, 149, 239, 245
angels, 64
Anglo-Saxons, 103, 241
animal cruelty, 75
anthropology, 44, 58, 202, 204–05, 310n32
Apple, 147, 197
Arabia, 103
Archbishop of Canterbury, 242
Aristotelian, 21, 43, 217
ark, the, 216
art(s), the, xvii–xviii, 1–2, 9, 18, 54, 62, 65, 76, 97, 101, 104, 106, 108, 110–11, 113–22, 125–130, 132–33, 136–37, 144, 178, 198, 211, 271, 277, 285, 288n14
Art and the Bible, 106
Artificial intelligence, 197
atheism, 46, 50, 217, 221, 264
Athens, 231, 239, 249
Augustinian, 21, 92, 314n2
autonomy, 23, 25, 56, 201

beauty, 59, 68, 71, 75–76, 101, 107, 109–11, 114–16, 118, 120, 123–26, 132, 142, 145, 154–55, 161, 163, 170, 249

biblical
    criticism, 27
    exegesis, 119
    interpretation, 138, 225
Big Brother, 201
Big Business, 44, 59, 237
Big Government, 44, 59, 237
Big Tech, 44, 184, 237
BioLogos Foundation, 218
bourgeoisie, 266
Bowling Alone, 148
Brave New World, 201
Brothers Karamazov, The, 46
Burger King, 140, 154–55
Burma, 49

Cambodia, 49, 294n80
Cambridge, 216
capitalism, 165, 174, 255, 264–65, 315n18
central government, centralized government, 53–54, 236–37, 249
charity, 48, 50, 53, 170, 193
China, 49, 83, 267, 294n80
Christian Critical Tradition, 2, 97, 99, 110, 114, 122–24, 126, 128, 133, 288n14, 298n1, 301n30, 306n8
Chronicles of Narnia, The, 129, 141
City of God, The, 43, 90, 95, 119, 181
City of Man, 119, 181
civilization, 12, 16, 25, 35, 37–39, 44, 57, 81, 95, 103, 110, 151, 167, 239, 255
class
    structure, 265–66
    warfare, 93
Clubhouse, 156–57
collectivism, 53, 55–56
colonialism, 256
common good, 34, 207, 231–33, 237–39, 245–46, 250
common grace, 11, 86, 114–15, 120, 126–27, 180, 232, 248, 272, 277, 284, 308n24
common law, 240–43, 245
communio sanctorum, 149

327

communism, communist, 49, 83, 92–93, 216, 263–67, 294n80
Concerto for Two Violins in D Minor, 104
Congress, 54, 58, 242, 245, 292n35
"Consciousness III", 151
conservation, 57, 75, 103, 233, 239
conservatism, 33–44, 46–48, 53–59, 81, 83, 207, 236, 246, 290n2–3, 291n8, 292n35, 303n3
Constitution, U.S., 54, 56, 58, 171, 231, 240, 245, 250, 292n35
consumer culture, 206–07
consumerism, 91, 137, 142–43, 146, 155, 204, 207, 273
contra mundum, 8, 16, 135
Contribution to the Critique of Political Economy, A, 265
Council of Trent, 212–213
Cours de linguistique Générale (Course in General Linguistics), 163
creation care, 2, 75, 77, 184
creation mandate, 64–65, 72–73, 75, 77, 114, 117, 177–78, 181–85, 191, 199, 246, 248, 272, 274, 278, 280, 284
Creation Regained, 117
creationism
    old earth, 218–19, 223–27
    young earth, 218–19, 223–27, 312n29
Creator, 26, 40, 63, 66–68, 76, 97, 99, 114, 116, 179–80, 182, 198–199, 222, 234, 271, 273, 276, 280–82
critical theory, 165, 173–74
Crunchy Cons, 58, 237, 290n3, 291n8
Cuba, 83, 267
Cubism, 122–23
cultural
    engagement, 2, 7, 15–16, 135
    exegesis, 119–20
    mandate, 65, 68, 71, 75, 114, 117, 126
    memory, 37, 85–86
    renewal, culture-renewing, 12–13, 61, 77, 133
    restoration, 74, 77, 117, 208, 286
culture-making, 77, 114, 157, 272, 317n4
"culture of narcissism", 149
custom, 36–40, 57, 82, 91, 119–120, 155, 233, 239, 285, 291n24, 300n3

Darwinism, 63, 217–19, 276
Decalogue, 67, 74
Declaratory Act, 244

Descent of Man, The, 216
deconstruction, deconstructionism, Deconstructionist, 123–24, 164–65, 168, 173
Defense of Poesy, 98
Deism, 215, 217
Denmark, 267–69
depravity, 24–25, 77, 114, 205, 229, 242
Dialogue Concerning the Two Chief World Systems, 212
Did America Have a Christian Founding?, 240
Didascalicon, 230
digital age, 197
Dirty Jobs, 188
discourse community, 164–65
Distracted, 144
Documentary Hypothesis, 25
dominion, 18, 65, 74–75, 144, 177–79, 199, 228–29, 254, 271
"Doxology", 274
dualism, 64, 136

early church, 8–9, 16, 43, 151, 178, 202
economic freedom, 255, 257–58, 263, 316n66
economic values, 254, 266
economics, 1, 18, 38, 46, 59, 62, 65, 77, 178, 237, 251–52, 255, 257–58, 263–66, 269, 272, 285
Eden, 66, 68, 70, 72, 117, 166, 169, 177, 179, 223
egalitarianism, 40, 43, 264
Egypt, 13, 73, 86, 116, 252, 255, 296n26
elections, 184
Emma, 141
empiricism, 22–23, 29
England, 12, 15, 41, 103, 214, 216, 240–44, 249, 263, 314n27, 315n18
English
    Bible, 167, 241
    Bill of Rights, 243, 245
    law, 240–41, 243–44, 248–49
    Parliament, 241–43
Englishmen, 241
Enlightenment, 22–24, 26, 40, 91–92, 172, 215, 239, 264
entertainment, 2, 9, 12, 18, 62, 76, 113, 122, 125–27, 129–130, 133, 136–137, 139, 147–48, 150, 156, 202, 273, 276, 288n14
environmentalism, 61, 77
epistemology, 23, 27, 90, 162
Epistle to Diognetus, 285

SUBJECT AND TITLE INDEX

equality, 41–43, 49, 101, 261, 264
eschatology, 206–07, 265, 287n3
eschaton, 206–07
ESPN, 275
eternal contract, 238
ethnicity, 42, 51
eugenics, 27, 41, 216, 218
evolution, 24, 37, 63, 68, 216–19, 221, 225–27
excellence, 16, 46, 50, 76, 101, 105–06, 110, 121–122, 131, 139, 170, 179, 190–93, 195, 199, 253, 255, 277–78, 280, 283, 301n32
executive branch, 55–56

Fall, the, 3, 61, 68–69, 72, 76, 114, 126, 177, 179–80, 222–24, 237–38, 246, 252–53, 265, 272, 282
faith and reason, 21
family, xv, 13, 18, 20, 45, 50, 58–59, 81–84, 86–87, 91, 96, 108, 121, 134, 139, 142–45, 148, 153, 156–57, 182–84, 189–90, 193, 195, 203, 206, 232–37, 246–47, 249–50, 257, 264, 266, 275–76, 316n58
federal government, 54–56, 248–49, 257
federalism, 54
feudalism, 265
fideism, 220–21, 228
fixity of species, 217
Flood, the, 66, 72–73, 223, 254
flood narratives, 223
Focus on the Family, 156–57
folk culture, 113, 128–29, 136–37, 140, 142, 144, 146–47
football, 177, 271
Forbes, 197
form, xiii, 13, 24, 28–30, 37, 46, 48, 103–07, 110, 113, 120–29, 131–33, 136, 140–42, 146, 150–53, 155, 157, 161, 171, 199–201, 203–04, 207, 210, 224, 231, 236, 239, 256–57, 259–64, 276, 288n14, 290n2, 302n64
fossil record, 216, 225–27
fossils, 216, 225–27
four basic relationships, 67, 77, 138, 179, 287n10
France, 242, 258
free market, 3, 50–52, 55, 59, 255–56, 258–60, 262, 266–67
free society, 46, 50–52
freedom
    of labor, 256–57
    of thought, 256
    political, 248–49, 256–57

French Revolution, 12, 83, 91, 236, 238
fruitfulness, 183, 189, 307n10
fundamentalism, 131
fundamentalists, 131, 218, 220, 228
Fusion magazine, xv, 17

Garden of Eden, 66, 117, 166, 177, 179, 223
gender, xv, 51, 93–94, 124, 224, 249
Generation Z, 149
Genesis Flood, The, 218
Genesis Record, The, 218
geologic column, 226
Germany, 264, 268
gods, the, 43, 45, 71, 123, 211, 276, 279
Great Commission, 117, 119, 132
Greening of America, The, 151
Greek, 13, 21–23, 64, 67, 83, 101, 103–05, 159, 163, 172, 211, 231, 233, 257, 286, 305n64
Green New Deal, 269
guilt, 25, 45, 69, 108, 131, 187, 189, 193, 204, 251–52, 269, 278

habeas corpus, 42, 243, 245
Hamlet, 102
Hanson Robotics, 197
hedonism, 277
heliocentrism, 201, 212–14
hell, 49, 69
heritage, 37, 81, 84, 86–87, 96, 155, 157, 167, 297n34
high culture, 113–14, 128–29, 136, 140–42, 165
historical
    ignorance, 84
    knowledge, 84, 89
    narrative, 85, 92
historico-grammatico hermeneutic, 172–74
Hollywood, 142
hospitality, 48, 145, 286
House of Burgesses, 243
human
    dignity, 42, 246–47
    flourishing, 34, 47–49, 51, 53–54, 56, 58, 75, 194–95, 231, 233, 235, 237, 250, 269, 286
Human Genome Project, 218
humanism (classical), 22
humanities, xviii, 1, 93, 163, 211, 220

idealism, 100, 264
idolatry, 88, 116, 120, 144, 153, 189, 271–72, 274, 278–80, 283–84, 308n14

Iliad, 161–62
image
  bearing, 272
  of God, 18, 65–68, 75–76, 99, 109, 114, 164, 230, 238, 310n32
  renewal, 76
imagination, xv, 152, 161, 215, 268
Imago Dei, 65, 74, 167, 170
immediacy, 144–46
imperfectability, 44, 46, 49, 55
incarnational, 89, 131
identity politics, 93–94
India, 12, 15, 103–04
individualism, 22–23, 30, 35, 39, 55–56, 148–49, 202–04, 207
  networked, 203–04
Industrial Revolution, 203, 206, 263
industrialization, 149, 228, 263–64
industry, 18, 47, 193, 268–69
inequality, 41–42
inerrancy, 25–26
inescapable questions of life, 127
inheritance, 36, 51, 137, 139, 149–50, 167–68, 239
injustice, 21, 34, 38–40, 42–44, 49, 51–52, 58, 93, 121, 231, 235, 293n68
innovation, 2, 18, 26, 46, 50, 57–58, 197–99, 201, 204, 206–08, 304n55
iPods, 156
Institute for Creation Research, 218, 226
Institutes of Justinian, 43
Institutes of the Christian Religion, 116
intelligent design, 216, 218–20, 227
integrationism, 221, 228
intemperance, 282
intergenerational faithfulness, 139, 150
interpretation, 13, 85, 90, 95, 102, 138, 166, 169–73, 175, 201, 207, 212–14, 217, 219, 221–27, 283, 291n15
interventionism, 256
"It Is Well with My Soul", 125
It's a Wonderful Life, 128
Ivory Coast, 49

Jayber Crow, 188,
Jerusalem, 208, 239–40, 245
joint-stock companies, 255
Judah, 87–88
Judeo-Christian religion, 20, 89, 97, 211
Judicial branch, 55

Jungle Books, The, 37
Jurassic Park, 207
justice
  commercial, 261–62
  distributive, 262–63
  remedial, 262
  universal, 262

kingdom, 7–11, 13–16, 18, 68, 70, 74–75, 77, 87, 135–37, 139, 152, 155, 157, 177, 181, 183, 187, 207, 230, 241, 254, 265–66, 268, 273, 276, 282, 285
kintsugi, 124
knowledge, 19, 21–22, 25, 29, 33, 39–40, 45, 49, 66, 84, 89–90, 92–95, 98, 115, 141, 144, 160, 162, 166, 172, 179, 210, 215, 220, 228–30, 237–39, 246, 256, 262, 272, 280, 285, 292n38, 293n63
kultur, 17

labor, 2, 18, 46–48, 50, 62, 74, 118, 177–78, 181, 185, 191, 194, 246–47, 251–59, 261–62, 265–66, 272, 285, 307n10
language, 20, 23, 39, 68, 72–73, 77, 103, 105, 110, 114, 119, 122, 133, 139, 141, 143, 147, 153, 155, 159–60, 162–75, 194, 214, 240, 285, 300n3, 306n29
Last Battle, The, 130
Last Supper, 106
law, 17, 35–37, 41–43, 56, 83, 103, 131, 138, 168, 170–72, 178, 188, 210–11, 215, 227, 231–32, 238, 240–50, 253, 255, 260–62, 265, 278, 281, 286, 290n7, 291n15, 292n35, 313n27
laziness, 251, 253–54
left-wing, 34
leftists, 77, 261–62
legalism, legalist(s)
  short-list, 131, 137–38
  long-list, 131, 133, 137, 276
legislative branch, 55
leisure, 1, 48, 54, 77, 147, 247, 273–74, 276–77, 280, 292n38
Les Misérables, 121
liberal arts, the, 104
liberalism, 27, 30, 33–34, 39–41, 44–45, 47–48, 55–56
liberal(ism), classical, 34
liberty
  individual, 252, 255–56, 261, 263, 269
light of the world, 186, 278

Lincoln-Douglas debates, 152
literature, 2, 14, 18, 62, 76–77, 97, 100, 102–03, 105–06, 109–10, 114, 116, 121, 132, 138, 159–63, 165–69, 173–75, 188, 233, 239–40, 272, 285, 289n26, 302n64, 306n8
Live Not By Lies, 237
local
    community, 53–54, 235
    government, 54–55, 236–37
    history, 96
Lockean, 35
logos, 116, 119, 159–65, 169, 171
London, 239–40
Lord of the Flies, 44
Lord of the Rings, The, 56, 129, 141

Magna Carta, 242–44
Mars Hill Audio, 17
market(s), 3, 45, 49–52, 55, 59, 141–43, 150, 184, 252, 254–69
Marxism, 24, 93, 173, 263, 265–66, 269
Mary Poppins, 142
"masks of God", 194
mass murder, 93, 267, 269
material rights, 49
material world, 64, 77, 89, 265
materialism, 92, 146, 265
Matrix, The, 197
Mayflower Compact, 243
means of grace, 9, 15, 130
memory, 37, 85–86, 94, 274, 303n13
metanarrative, 19–20, 29, 89–90, 92, 94, 96, 265
millennials, 149
mission, 7, 10, 12, 14–16, 118, 132, 177, 181, 187, 249
missionary, missionaries, 28, 119, 187, 241, 249
Moby Dick, 71, 296n20
moderation, 139, 282
modern art, 106, 123–24
modernism, 2, 20–31, 70, 123–124, 162
modernity, 21–22, 123, 136, 143, 149
modesty, 139, 274
monasticism, 11
money, 51–52, 103, 123, 155, 187, 193–94, 251, 256, 260–61, 263, 275–76, 279, 282
monopoly, 257
movies, 113, 120–22, 125–28, 132–33, 141, 192, 197, 272

music
    bluegrass, 140
    classical, 127, 140, 151
    folk-gospel, 124, 140, 303n13
    hip-hop, 124–25, 140
    rock, 17, 124–25, 140, 150–51, 303n13

National Institutes of Health, 218
natural
    distinction, 41, 43–44
    law, 35, 291n7
    rights, 49, 247
    selection, 24, 216
Natural Theology: Or, Evidences of the Existence and Attributes of the Deity, 217
nature's laws, 211
Nazism, 216, 218
neighbor, 18, 67, 118, 145, 148, 155, 169, 171, 173, 175, 182–85, 189, 191–92, 262, 294n74, 308n24
neighbor-love, 183–85
neighbor-harm, 184
Neo-Marxism, 93
Netflix, 135, 152
network, 203–04, 251
new creation, 74–75, 77, 118–19, 198, 222
new earth, 75, 117, 208, 223
New England Primer, The, 166
new heavens, 75, 117, 208, 223
New Song for an Old World: The Musical Thought of the Early Church, A, 151
New York, 142, 148, 239
NFL, 276
Nicomachean Ethics, 43
Nineteen Eighty-Four, 201
"noble savage", 44
nobility, 2, 56, 139, 303n12
nominalism, 21
non-church job, 181, 185–86
North Korea, 49, 267
noumenal world, 23
Nuda scriptura, 88

oikonomia, 67
oikophobia, 36
Old Testament, xviii, 67, 69, 72, 87, 138, 153, 211
oligarchy, 44, 55, 231
On the Origin of Species, 24, 216
"one another" passages, 185, 281

ontology, ontological, 42, 51, 162, 291n15
oppressed, oppression, oppressors, 29, 40, 92–94, 165, 173, 201, 244, 289n27, 298n49
order, 15, 35–39, 41–44, 46–47, 56–57, 62–65, 67–70, 73–77, 81, 83, 97, 115, 117, 139–141, 146, 160, 165, 168, 170, 179–80, 184, 198–99, 222, 228–29, 231, 233, 235–41, 245–50, 252, 256, 265, 271–74, 278, 281–82, 290n5–7, 291n24
ordinary means of grace, 9, 15, 130
Outliers, 278

Paradise Lost, 72, 104, 117
Paradise Regained, 117
Parliament, 103, 241–45
patriotism, 142
Pentateuch, 25
permanent things, 36, 59, 161, 168
Petition of Right, 243, 245
Pharisees, 75, 87
phenomenal world, 23
phenomenological language, 214
philology, 92, 163
Philosophy of Fine Art, 97
Platonism, 64
plundering of the Egyptians, 13
poetry, 76, 104, 113, 127, 136, 302n49
politics, xix, 1, 14, 18, 24, 26, 33–35, 38, 58–59, 62, 77, 93–94, 137, 178, 183–84, 200, 232–34, 241–42, 246–47, 250, 269, 272, 277, 285, 290n4–5, 291n24
Politics by Aristotle, 234
Politics of Prudence, The, 33, 290n4, 291n24
pollution, 75, 138
popular culture, pop culture, 2, 13–14, 17–18, 59, 76, 90–91, 95, 106, 113–15, 122, 128–29, 131, 135–47, 149–50, 154–57, 197, 276, 285, 287n1, 288n14
postmodernism, 2, 20–21, 26–31, 124, 163–64
poststructuralists, 164
post-word world, 162–63, 171–172, 175
poverty, 3, 12, 45, 48–52, 77, 184, 193, 218, 251, 254–55, 259, 265, 269
prejudice(s), 38–39
premodernism, 2, 20, 22, 29
prescription, 38–39, 49, 57, 236
presuppositions, 20–21, 28, 82, 92–93, 201–02, 211

pride, 30, 37, 40, 161, 193, 199, 263, 277
private property, 47–48, 50, 173, 253, 256, 266, 269, 314n12
progress, 26–27, 34, 38, 40, 57–58, 93, 198–99, 201, 204, 207, 239
progressive, progressivism, 16, 34–35, 37, 39–41, 43–45, 48, 51, 53–57, 64, 84, 87, 93, 195, 216, 218, 250, 266–67
proletariat, 93, 266
proto-*euangelion,* 72
Providence, 39–40, 189
prudence, 3, 33–34, 39, 53, 55–56, 58, 82, 94, 115–16, 123, 129, 183–84, 236, 239, 260, 263, 282, 290n4, 291n24
prudishness, 108
psychoanalysis, 25
public life, 2, 18, 77, 233, 235, 237–39, 245, 248
Puritans, 7, 98, 188, 242, 244

Quartering Act, 244
Quest for Truth, The, 228, 287n10

racism, 38, 93, 216
Raiders of the Lost Ark, 128
rationalism, 21–23, 250
rationality, 22, 38, 98, 100, 104, 139, 151–52
reader-response, 172–74
reconciliation, 74, 98, 185
recreation, 3, 18, 62, 118, 271–85
Redeemer, 11, 160, 182, 273
redemption, 11, 13–14, 17, 31, 61, 64, 69–70, 77, 87, 89, 113, 117, 119, 121, 124, 126, 132, 160–61, 205, 222, 238, 249, 265, 307n3
Reflections on the Revolution in France, 238
Reformation, 88, 153, 212–13, 242
Reformers, 88, 153, 194, 254
relativism, 14, 125, 129, 141, 217
religion, 8, 24, 26–27, 31, 33, 35–36, 38–39, 46, 88–90, 92, 94, 97–98, 116, 162, 183, 186, 193, 200, 209, 211–13, 216, 233, 263–66, 282, 284, 289n27, 291n8, 292n35
renewal, 12–13, 61, 64, 69–70, 72–74, 76–77, 107, 117, 250, 288n25
Republic, The, 231
rest, 63, 67, 73–75, 189–90, 223, 247–48, 273
restraint, 27, 54–56, 58–59, 247
resurrection, 70, 74–75, 77, 89, 117–18
revelation, 22–23, 35, 57, 77, 110, 159, 221, 235, 263, 265

revolutionaries, 150, 291n24
right-wing, 34, 131
righteousness, 101, 107–09, 129–30, 133, 182, 190, 193, 204, 249, 276, 281–82
rightness, 107–08
ritual impurity, 69
Rolling Stone, 150
Roman culture, 211, 276–77
Roman Catholic Church, 11, 212, 219
romanticism, 151, 305n61
Rome, 90, 95, 239
Roots of American Order, The, 239
running, 276
Russia, 49, 83, 97, 102–03, 264, 267–68, 294n80

Sabbath, 67, 74–75, 189, 296n26
sacred and secular, 187
salt and light, 11–12, 95, 181
satire, 106, 122
Scandal of the Evangelical Mind, The, 251
science and religion, 212–13, 216
scientism, 219–21, 228
secular culture, 135, 137, 147, 279
secularism, 186
senses, the, 21, 23, 210
seriousness, 101, 105–06, 109, 125
Sermon on the Mount, 11, 15, 86
seven deadly sins, 199
sexual, sexuality, 93–94, 108–09, 115, 126, 133, 150–52, 249, 282
    perversion, 94, 216
    revolution, 28, 249
shame, 69, 180
Sixties, the, 150
Slaughtered Ox, The, 106
slavery, 84, 86, 202, 238, 249, 265, 298n26, 308n38
slow food movement, 145
smart phone, 157, 198, 208
social
    justice, 43, 51, 77, 262–63
    media, 94, 199, 250
    order, 41, 43–44, 70, 228, 256, 291n6, 292n24
socialism, 3, 45–46, 48–50, 55, 93, 252, 256, 263–65, 267–68, 293n68, 294n80, 316n66
socioeconomic status, 42, 52
sola Scriptura, 88
Sophia, 197

South Park, 131
Soviet Union, 93, 267–68
spheres of sovereignty, 235–36, 247
sports, 1, 3, 18, 62, 65, 178, 271–85
Spotify, 139, 147
Stamp Act, 244
state government, 54
stewardship, 47, 61, 68, 75–76, 183–84, 199, 208, 228, 239, 252–54
stories, 20, 33, 37, 63, 95, 128–29, 148, 161, 168, 222–23
structuralists, 164
style, 17, 105–06, 121–22, 125, 128, 136, 138, 146, 150, 154–55, 157
"sub-creators", 114, 117, 198, 254
submission, 76, 139, 141, 201, 243–44
Sugar Act, 244
Sumer, 255
Sunday, 12, 177, 181, 187, 274–76
"Sunday-to-Monday gap," 177, 187
supernaturalism, 25, 27
superstructures, 265
Surprised by Hope, 118

tabula rasa, 19, 44
"Take Me Out to the Ball Game", 274
technocracy, 200–01
Technopoly, 143, 200
technopoly, 150, 201
technology, 1–2, 14, 18, 54, 62, 65, 76–77, 142–44, 152, 154, 156, 178, 197–202, 206–08
television, 113, 121, 125, 128, 135–36, 138–39, 142, 146, 148, 152–53, 157, 188, 198, 250, 302n1
telos, 18, 66, 74, 230, 234
Tempest, The, 106
Ten Commandments, 86, 241
    Fourth Commandment, 74
    Fifth Commandment, 86
    Eighth Commandment, 47, 253
    Tenth Commandment, 253, 294n74, 314n12
Tenth Amendment, 54
Tonight Show, The, 197
tool-using culture, 200
total depravity, 24, 114, 205, 229
total personality, 191, 205, 310n32
Tower of Babel, 46, 168, 222
tradition, 2, 22, 33–34, 36–41, 43, 56, 58, 59, 62, 77, 81–82, 84–88, 90–91, 94–97, 99,

110, 114, 116, 122–24, 126, 128, 133, 142, 145, 149–52, 155, 238, 165, 168, 170, 200, 212, 232–33, 237, 239, 242, 245–49, 259, 271, 276, 288n14, 294n80, 298n1, 300n17, 301n30, 301n47, 304n52, 304n55, 306n8
    Christian, 14, 47, 98, 108, 137–38, 157, 166, 178, 261, 303n3
    Greco-Roman, 43
    Hebrew-Christian, 2, 36, 39, 43–44, 116, 225
    Reformed, 21, 195
transcendence, 29, 39, 56, 58, 139, 145, 229
transcendent moral order, 35–37, 39, 290n7
transformation, 12–16, 18, 71, 77, 135, 137, 161, 194–95
Trinity, 167–68, 274
Triumph of Vulgarity, The, 151, 305n61
tyranny, 38, 55, 70–71, 236, 238, 242–43

Übermensch, 25
uniformitarianism, 28–29
uniformity, 40, 83
United Nations, 247
United States, 28, 49, 54–55, 58, 183, 201, 217–18, 232, 240, 242, 245, 248, 259, 263, 267–68
Universal Declaration of Human Rights, 247–48
Ur, 252
utilitarianism, 40, 177, 191, 290n7
Utopia, 24, 26–27, 44, 92–93, 264–66, 269, 293n61

value
    instrumental, 278, 280
    intrinsic, 64, 191, 278, 280
variety, 40–44, 203
Venezuela, 267–69
verbal culture, 167, 169, 171
viceregency, 228, 252, 254
video games, 156–57
Vikings, 95
Virginia, 243
virtue, 14, 18, 38–41, 53–54, 82, 96, 100, 115, 125, 127, 129, 133, 138–40, 142, 146, 152, 154, 163, 167–68, 190, 195, 232, 238–39, 245–46, 248–49, 262, 267, 281, 283, 292n35, 302n49, 302n64, 308n38
vocation, 1–2, 18, 54, 65, 68, 105, 177–79, 181–92, 194–95, 251, 253, 263, 272, 278, 280, 307n1, 307n3, 308n21

voting, 184, 250

Wall-E, 197
Wall Street Journal, 197
War for Independence, 240–41
wealth, 3, 24, 49–52, 54, 59, 72, 77, 84, 193, 233, 251, 253–56, 258–59, 261–64, 266, 268–69, 316n58
    disparity, 51–52
Wealth of Nations, The, 256
Welch College, xiii, xv, xvii–xix, 7, 156, 289n26, 298n59
West(ern), the, 81, 90, 93, 103, 110, 123, 162, 165, 217, 232, 255, 258, 267
    culture, 19–20, 22, 28, 33, 90, 211
    tradition, 91, 239
What Are People For?, 148
"When Church Gets Sidelined by Youth Sports", 280
Wii, 156
"will to power", 165
wisdom, xiv, 14, 33–34, 36, 38–40, 53, 56, 58–59, 62, 82, 84–85, 95–96, 98, 107, 115, 120, 126, 132–33, 136, 138, 141, 145, 149, 152, 157, 168, 238, 252, 260, 269, 279, 282
withdrawal, 115, 126, 130–31, 184, 272, 276
witness, 11, 30, 89, 113, 115, 119–20, 126, 131–32, 135, 137, 150, 192, 194, 233, 245, 278, 280
The Wizard of Oz, 121
Word of God, 74, 153, 188
World War I, 93
World War II, 150
worldliness, 125
worldview, xiii–xiv, 1–2, 9–10, 12, 16, 18–22, 24, 27–29, 31, 33, 41, 63, 71, 77, 85, 90–91, 106, 109, 113, 120, 123–127, 133, 174, 197, 199, 210, 228, 232, 263, 265, 269, 273, 285, 317n1
worship, 9, 75, 85, 104, 137, 139, 153–57, 166, 190, 222, 229, 255, 271, 273–77, 279, 282, 310n32, 317n1

youth, 149–50, 275–76, 279–81
YouTube, 135, 152–53

zeitgeist, 20
zivilisation, 17